Business Cycle Dynamics

Models and Tools

Tönu Puu
Iryna Sushko
Editors

Business Cycle Dynamics

Models and Tools

With 153 Figures
and 7 Tables

Springer

Professor Dr. Tönu Puu
CERUM, Umeå University
SE-90187 Umeå
Sweden
E-mail: tonu.puu@econ.umu.se

Dr. Iryna Sushko
Institute of Mathematics
National Academy of Sciences of Ukraine
3, Tereshchenkivska st.
01601 Kiev
Ukraine
E-mail: sushko@imath.kiev.ua

Cataloging-in-Publication Data

ISBN 978-3-642-06879-9 e-ISBN 978-3-540-32168-2

Springer is a part of Springer Science+Business Media
springeronline.com

Softcover reprint of the hardcover 1st edition 2006

Cover design: Erich Kirchner

Preface

The present volume can be seen as a rejoinder to the present editors' "*Oligopoly Dynamics - Tools and Models*", Springer-Verlag 2002. There is no doubt that, besides dynamic oligopoly theory, business cycle theory has been the fastest growing field within modern nonlinear economic dynamics.

The contributions are centred around the models of multiplier-accelerator type, emerging from Paul Samuelson's seminal work of 1939, as later developed into nonlinear formats by Hicks and Goodwin around 1950.

These nonlinear models left many open ends, because the tools then available (or at least then known to economists) did not permit any more systematic analysis. The situation is now very different due to the huge accumulation of new methods in nonlinear dynamics. The present focus on these causal or recursive models also implies a deviation from current main stream real business cycle theory, based on "rational expectations", i.e., self fulfilling forecasts held by the economic agents. In view of modern dynamics, in particular the possibility of mathematical chaos, the latter paradigm simply becomes untenable.

Again this volume, like the aforementioned volume, is collaborative work, bringing together some of the environments where nonlinear economic studies are carried out, i.e., the Universities of Bielefeld (Germany), Cartagena (Spain), Siena (Italy), Udine (Italy), Urbino (Italy), and the Institute of Mathematics, National Academy of Sciences of Ukraine, and the authors are a mixture of economists and mathematicians in approximately equal proportions.

Also, again, the collaboration took place within the precincts of *CERUM*, the *Centre for Regional Science* at Umeå University (Sweden), where a conference was held 10-11 June 2005. The book is produced according to a pre-organized plan fixed by the editors, and the authors were all particularly selected and invited. The final organisation of the book and the contents of the chapters were discussed during the conference.

The editors are indebted to several individuals and organisations for help and support. Thanks first go to *CERUM*, and its director, *Prof. Lars Westin*, who, besides taking the financial responsibility for the conference, acted as moderator during the entire conference, and to the conference secretary, *Ms. Susanne Sjöberg*, who organised everything practical in the best imaginable way.

The conference became financially possible due to generous grants from *The Bank of Sweden Tercentenary Foundation*, the *Gösta Skoglund Foundation*, and joint support from the *Umeå City Council* and *Umeå University Board*. In addition thanks are due to the *University of Bielefeld* and the *University of Urbino*, where some preparatory work was done. Further several of the authors are grateful for support of their own work from different sponsors, but acknowledgement of such will be given in the individual contributions.

Umeå and Kiev, 30 November 2005

Tönu Puu | Iryna Sushko

Contents

Aims and Scope

Tönu Puu

1 Introduction

The aim of the present volume is very simple: It is just to revive the type of business cycle modelling once current in economics in the wake of the seminal work by Samuelson (1939), Hicks (1950), Goodwin (1949) and others. Their common feature was that they all resulted in causal dynamical models, with sometimes surprisingly complex outcomes in view of the simplicity of the structure of most of the models, whether cast as differential equations in continuous time, or as discrete time difference equations (maps as we would nowadays say), using a fixed delay structure.

Nonlinearity was part of most of the models, and was, of course, responsible for the resulting complexity. It goes without saying that the mathematical tools available to economists those days did not allow for any systematic interpretation of the more complex results, so the analysis stayed at the level of numerical calculation of a few exemplifying orbits. Further, the computational means (slide rules and mechanical calculators for which even division was a true challenge) those days were far from our laptops today, so it would have been impossible to distinguish between transients and asymptotic orbits.

Some systematic methods were in fact developing under the heading of perturbation methods, in electrical and mechanical engineering for very similar models, cf. Duffing (1918) and van der Pol (1927). See Stoker (1950) and Hayashi (1964) for contemporary state of the art accounts. But, these seem not to have been known to economists, at least they were never used.

Today the prospects for dealing with these types of models are radically changed, but economists at large seem no longer to be interested in them. The focus has shifted to business cycle models based on the "rational expectations" paradigm.

2 Rational Expectations and Intertemporal Equilibrium

This seems to have first been introduced by Muth (1960), and later elaborated by Lucas (1976), Sargent (1984), and others. The work is strongly connected to econometric modelling of more or less sophistication, but, stripped to its bare bones, the message is simple: The agents in the models are as good as the economists constructing then, and hence know the models and their outcomes. As a result they are able to make, on average, correct, self-fulfilling forecasts of the future.

It would be impossible to understand this paradigm without its reference to general equilibrium economics, because a dynamical process with this self-fulfilling characteristic is the same as an equilibrium state in a static intertemporal equilibrium model.

Throughout the history of economics the equilibrium and the dynamic approaches were competitors. Most of the time the equilibrium outlook was the dominant. One could either explain the facts in terms of a causally recursive model or in terms of an equilibrium balance of forces, where there was no internal tendency to move the system out of equilibrium. Obviously the latter outlook is the less demanding, because one does not need to discuss what happens when the system is out of equilibrium.

This difference of outlooks obviously has a relation to the epistemological distinction between causal and teleological (or functional) explanation. In the first, things occur for certain reasons, in the latter to certain ends. As a matter of fact the Marshallian theory for partial market equilibrium was once criticised on the grounds that price could not be determined at once by supply and demand. See Schumpeter (1954). Economics is not alone among the sciences to have used teleological explanations. In physics conservative mechanical systems, such as the Lagrangean or the Hamiltonian, can be represented as minimization of "action", and in biology it is very common to explain the function of organs in terms of the service they perform for the organism.

The most grandiose equilibrium theory in economics ever conceived was of course the Walrasian general equilibrium theory for an arbitrary number of interdependent markets. See Walras (1874-1877). The original work considers not only the existence, in terms of equal numbers of equations and variables, but also the stability of such an equilibrium (in terms of "tâtonnement" processes).

However, both lines of thought needed further elaboration. A system of independent equations containing the same number of independent variables does not necessarily have a solution, as the equations can be incompatible. The first rigorous attempt was made by Wald (1936), later further elaborated by Arrow and Debreu (1954) and Debreu (1959). Not only the existence, but also the uniqueness of the solution was considered, and such constraints on production technology and consumer preferences were specified as to guarantee existence and uniqueness. Though the achievement is intellectually most impressive, it must be said that it is also totally void of information content in this general form.

The stability issue was meanwhile dealt with by Hicks (1939), who reached halfway, but gave a partly erroneous result, and finally solved by Samuelson (1947), who specified such conditions for the system that would guarantee local linear stability of the equilibrium.

All this is relevant for us because general equilibrium theorists were not content with the *temporary* existence and uniqueness of general equilibrium for an arbitrary system of markets. They also introduced "future" markets and prices for goods traded in the future. In this way the evolution existed already in the intertemporal equilibrium point - provided, of course, that every agent had perfect foresight of the future. In this way the rational expectations hypothesis is a natural outgrowth of general equilibrium theory.

So, given its dominance in contemporary mainstream economics, combined with the fact that Keynesian macroeconomics has been completely dismantled, it is natural that business cycle theory is put in the framework of rational expectations under the special heading of real business cycle theory.

3 Determinism and Predictability

However, it is a pity that the beautiful causal business cycle models, with their simple logical structure and complex way of working, have been scrapped. This is particularly true because today's knowledge of complex dynamical systems allows for numerical and analytical treatment of most issues left as open ends in the days the models of, loosely speaking, multiplier-accelerator type were proposed.

There is an additional reason why a revival of these classical recursive models is important: There is an inherent contradiction in the very idea of rational expectations. Suppose we accept the proposition that the average agents are no less knowledgeable than the economists who model their behaviour. This is probably something the general public, who constantly sees the multiplicity of professional forecasts, that only seem to share the feature that they all go wrong, would agree to.

Assuming there exists a unique true model for the economy, and that it is known to all the agents, is still a heroic assumption to make. Everyone, except addicted fans of rational expectations modelling, would agree to this, so there is no need to elaborate further. Supposing, however, that the assumptions *are true*, the agents would still need to make *forecasts* in order to choose a proper action.

But, the main message of modern systems theory is that determinism in principle and the possibility of forecasting are very different issues. Mathematical chaos makes prediction *impossible*. So, even if the all the agents know the true model, they will still all make *different* forecasts - *none* of which becomes true - and there is no reason to believe that any kind of average of these different expectations equals the actual realization of the process resulting from the actions chosen - it may itself be chaotic, and hence unpredictable.

This objection, however, does not affect the causal models, which hence not only provide an until now underexplored wealth of economic theory, but represent a type of models that do not become self-contradictory once we recognize the fact that determinism does not guarantee predictability.

Outline of the Book

The outline of the book is as follows. Given we need some relevant mathematical tools for the global analysis of such dynamical systems that result from models of the business cycle, a field in fast development, the exposition starts with two purely mathematical-methodological chapters The focus is on maps, not differential equations. Most of the contributions are phrased in a discrete time setting, quite like the case of most classical models, there is only one exception to this (Chapter 10), and there no use is made of other than classical methods. Chapter 1 deals with smooth maps, Chapter 2 with piecewise linear maps.

After these, Chapter 3 recalls the basics of Keyenesian macroeconomics, and stresses its importance for Samuelson's multiplier-accelerator model, in view of its stress on non-monetary issues and on the demand side of the economy. It also gives a historical background to the multiplier and the principle of acceleration.

Chapters 4 and 5 then develop the Samuelson model to a nonautonomous format where the coefficients in the recurrence equations are not constant but may change during the process.

The multiplier-accelerator model, of which the Hicksian version is the best known, came in two different variations. Both stress the fact that a linear accelerator, or termed otherwise, investment function, is unlikely to hold, both due to substantial considerations, and to the fact that it leads to oscillations that either explode, or that are completely damped out with time.

Hence some nonlinearity is needed that limits its action upwards and downwards, what Hicks called the floor (when income decreases so fast that more capital could be dispensed with than what disappears through natural depreciation), and what he called the ceiling (when income grows so fast that available resources put a limit to further expansion).

The Goodwin tradition, which arose independently of the Hicksian, incorporates both limits in the investment function. The pure Hicksian tradition only incorporates the floor in the investment function, and puts the ceiling as a constraint on total expenditures, by the way the only non-Keynesian element through which the supply side has some influence on the process.

Chapters 6 and 7 are in the Hicksian tradition, the first giving a full analysis of the original floor-ceiling model as Hicks left it, the second dealing with a slight variation where the floor is tied to the stock of capital.

The rest of the book deals with the Goodwin tradition, introducing various nonlinear investment functions, such as polynomial (Chapter 11), or piecewise linear (Chapter 12). Chapter 8 illustrates some of the important issues from Chapter 1, such as coexistent attractors and their bifurcations, and Chapter 9 is a variation where the formation of expectations is introduced as a basic element. Chapter 10, gives a fresh historical account of the emergence of Goodwin's original model, and is consequently formulated in terms of differential equations.

References

Arrow, K.J. and Debreu, G., 1954, "Existence of an equilibrium for a competitive economy.", *Econometrica* 22:265-290.

Debreu, G., 1959, *The Theory of Value*. Wiley, New York.

Duffing, G., 1918, *Erzwungene Schwingungen bei veränderlicher Eigenfrequenz*. Wieweg, Braunschweig.

Duesenberry, J., 1950, "Hicks on the trade cycle". *The Quarterly Journal of Economics* 64:464-76

Frisch, R., 1933, "Propagation problems and impulse problems in dynamic economics". *Economic Essays in Honour of Gustav Cassel*. Allen & Unwin, London.

Goodwin, R.M., 1949, "The business cycle as a self-sustaining oscillation" *Econometrica* 17:184-185.

Goodwin, R.M., 1950, "The nonlinear accelerator and the persistence of business cycles". *Econometrica* 19:1-17

von Haberler, G., 1937, *Prosperity and Depression*. Harvard University Press, Cambridge Mass.

Hansen, A.H., 1951, *Business Cycles and National Income, Norton*, New York.

Hayashi, C., 1964, *Nonlinear Oscillations in Physical Systems* (Princeton University Press, Princeton, N.J.)

Hicks, J.R., 1939, *Value and Capital*. Clarendon Press, Oxford.

Hicks, J.R., 1950, A *Contribution to the Theory of the Trade Cycle*. Oxford University Press, Oxford.

Lucas, R.E., 1976, Econometric policy evaluation: a critique". Brunner, K. and Melzer (Eds.), *The Phillips Curve and the Labor Market*, North-Holland, Amsterdam.

Muth, J.F., 1960), "Optimal properties of exponentially weighted forecasts", *Journal of the American Statistical Association* 55:200-306.

Phillips, A.W., 1954, "Stabilisation policy in a closed economy", *The Economic Journal* 64:290-323

van der Pol, 1926, "On relaxation oscillations", *Philosophical Magazine* 2:978-992.

Samuelson, P.A., 1939, "Interactions between the multiplier analysis and the principle of acceleration", *Review of Economics and Statistics* 21:75-8.

Samuelson, P. A., 1947, *Foundations of Economic Analysis*, Harvard University Press, Cambridge, Mass.

Schumpeter, J.A., 1954, *History of Economic Analysis*. Macmillan, London.

Sargent, T.J., 1984, Autoregressions, expectations, and advice, *American Economic Review* 74:408-415.

Stoker, J. J., 1950, *Nonlinear Vibrations in Mechanical and Electrical Systems* (Wiley, New York)

Wald, A., 1936, "Über einige Gleichungssysteme der mathematishen Ökonomie", *Zeitschrift für Nationaökonomie* 7:637-670.

Walras, L., 1874-1877, Elements d'économie politique pure. Corbaz, Lausanne.

1 Some Methods for the Global Analysis of Closed Invariant Curves in Two-Dimensional Maps

Anna Agliari, Gian-Italo Bischi and Laura Gardini

1.1 Introduction

It is well known that models of nonlinear oscillators applied to the study of the business cycle can be formulated both as continuous or discrete time dynamic models (see e.g. [23], [33], [34]). However, economic time is often discontinuous (discrete) because decisions in economics cannot be continuously revised. For this reason discrete-time dynamical systems, represented by difference equations or, more properly, by the iterated application of maps, are often a more suitable tool for modelling dynamic economic processes. So, it is useful to study the peculiarities of discrete dynamical systems and their possible applications to the study of self sustained oscillations. This is the main goal of this chapter, where we describe, on the light of some recent results about local and global properties of iterated maps of the plane, some particular routes to the creation/destruction of closed invariant curves, along which self sustained oscillations occur.

In fact, even if in the fifties and sixties the methods for the study of iterated maps were less developed than those for ordinary differential equations, the situation is now rapidly changing because many results have been obtained about discrete dynamical systems (see e.g. [25], [26], [24], [16], [42],[28], [29]). Indeed, the dynamic properties and bifurcations of one dimensional iterated maps are now quite well known, as well as their implications about periodic and chaotic behaviors of their trajectories (see e.g.[15], [40],[41]). Even for two-dimensional maps more and more results can be found in the literature, starting from the pioneering works [25] and [26], (see also [32], [35], [36], [1]). The qualitative methods for the study of discrete dynamical systems are in many aspects similar to those employed in continuous time systems, but important differences are worth to be emphasized. For example, a version of the Andronov-Hopf bifurcation theorem also exists for discrete dynamical systems, known as Neimark-Sacker bifurcation theorem, and it is quite similar to the one in continuous time, with the expected difference that while in the continuous-time case an equilibrium point undergoes an Hopf bifurcation when a pair of eigenvalues cross the line of vanishing real part, in the discrete-time case the Neimark-Sacker bifurcation occurs when a pair of eigenvalues cross the unitary circle of the complex plane. However, remarkable differences can be evidenced, both concerning the kind of motion along the closed invariant curve created at the bifurcation (it is no longer a unique trajectory but the closure of infinitely many distinct trajectories, either periodic or quasiperiodic) and the fate of such invariant curve as the parameters move far from their bifurcation values.

In this chapter, some global bifurcations that cause the creation and destruction of invariant closed curves via global bifurcations are also considered, related with the occurrence of saddle-node or saddle-focus heteroclinic or homoclinic connections and tangles. Some exemplary global bifurcations are shown through numerical explorations and qualitative geometrical explanations.

Indeed, several aspects in the study of the global dynamical properties of two-dimensional discrete dynamical systems are still obscure, and their study often require an interplay between analytical, geometric, numerical and graphical methods. Moreover, the differences between continuous and discrete dynamical systems become particularly evident when the latter are obtained by the iteration of noninvertible maps. A map is invertible if it maps distinct points into distinct points, whereas whenever distinct points which are mapped into the same point exist, then we say it is a noninvertible map. Hence, the geometric action of a noninvertible map can be expressed by saying that it "folds and pleats" the phase space, so that distinct points can be mapped into the same point (see e.g. [36], [3] for recent studies of the properties of noninvertible maps, [13], [12] and the monograph [39] for recent applications in economics). This introduces some peculiar dynamic properties when a business cycle model is represented by a discrete dynamical system obtained by the iteration of a noninvertible map.

1.2 Basic Definitions and Properties of Two-Dimensional Discrete Dynamical Systems

In this section we give some basic definitions and properties concerning two-dimensional discrete dynamical systems[1], represented by the iterated application of a map of the plane

$$x' = T(x), \qquad T : S \to S, \quad S \subseteq \mathbb{R}^2 \tag{1}$$

At any iteration it transforms a point $x \in S$ into a unique point $x' \in S$ called *rank-1 (forward) image* of x. A point x such that $T(x) = x'$ is a *rank-1 preimage* of x'.

If $x \neq y$ implies $T(x) \neq T(y)$ for each x, y in S, then T is an *invertible map* in S, because the inverse mapping $x = T^{-1}(x')$ is uniquely defined; otherwise T is said to be a *noninvertible map*, because points x exist that have several rank-1 preimages, i.e. the inverse relation $x = T^{-1}(x')$ is multivalued. So, noninvertible means "many-to-one", that is distinct points $x \neq y$ may have the same image, $T(x) = T(y) = x'$.

Geometrically, the action of a noninvertible map can be expressed by saying that it "folds and pleats" the space S, so that distinct points are mapped into the same point. This is equivalently stated by saying that several inverses are defined in some points of S, and these inverses "unfold" S.

For a noninvertible map, S can be subdivided into regions Z_k, $k \geq 0$, whose points have k distinct rank-1 preimages. Generally, for a continuous map, as the point x' varies in $\mathbb{R}^2$, pairs of preimages appear or disappear as it crosses the boundaries separating different regions. Hence, such boundaries are characterized by the presence of at least two coincident (merging) preimages. This leads us to the definition of the *critical curves*, one of the distinguishing features of noninvertible maps (see [25] and [36]):

Definition. The *critical curve* LC of a continuous map T is defined as the locus of points having at least two coincident *rank-1* preimages, located on a set LC_{-1}, called *set of merging preimages*.

Portions of LC separate regions Z_k of the phase space characterized by a different number of $rank-1$ preimages, for example Z_k and Z_{k+2} (this is the standard occurrence for continuous maps). The critical set LC is the generalization of the notion of local extrema (minimum or maximum value)

[1] The reader is addressed to [24], [32], [37], [36] for a more complete treatment.

of a one-dimensional map[2] and the set LC_{-1} is the generalization of local extremum point of a one-dimensional map (i.e. $T(LC_{-1}) = LC$)).

Starting from an initial condition $x_0 \in S$, the (forward) iteration by T uniquely defines a *trajectory*

$$\tau(x_0) = \{x_n = T^n(x_0),\ n = 0, 1, 2, ...\}$$

where T^0 is the identity function and $T^n = T \circ T^{n-1}$. The set of points that form a trajectory is also called *orbit*, however many authors consider these two terms as equivalent.

The simplest orbits are *fixed points*, that is a singleton $\{p^*\}$ such that $T(p^*) = p^*$, so that $T^n(p^*) = p^*$ for all n, and *cycles of period* k, that is a set of k ($k > 1$) distinct periodic points $\{p_1^*, p_2^*, ..., p_k^*\}$ such that $T(p_i^*) = p_{i+1}^*$ for $i = 1, 2, ..., k-1$ and $T(p_k^*) = p_1^*$. Observe that the periodic points of a cycle of period k are fixed points of the map T^k, and a fixed point is a $k-$cycle with $k = 1$.
We recall that a set $E \subset \mathbb{R}^n$ is *invariant* for the map T if it is mapped onto itself, $T(E) = E$. This means that if $x \in E$ then $T(x) \in E$, i.e. E is *trapping,* and each point of E is the forward image of at least one point of E. The simplest examples of invariant sets are the fixed points and the cycles of the map. More generally, the attracting (repelling) sets and the attractors (repellors) of a map are invariant sets.

An *attracting set* A is a closed invariant set such that a neighborhood U of A exists which is strictly mapped into itself and whose trajectories (i.e. the trajectories starting from any point of U) converge to A. A closed invariant set which is not attracting is called a *repelling set* if however close to A there are points whose trajectories goes away from A. An *attractor* (*repellor*) is an attracting (repelling) set containing a dense orbit. An attracting set may contain one or several attractors, coexisting with sets of repelling points, whereas an attractor is an undecomposable set. In the case of a cycle *attractor* (*repellor*) is synonymous of asymptotically stable (unstable). In particular unstable nodes and foci are also called *expanding*.

As the definition suggests, there exist points which converge to an attracting set (or to an attractor) A: The trapping set made up by all such points constitutes *the basin of attraction* of A and it can be obtained considering the union of the preimages of any rank of the neighborhood U (defined above):

$$B(A) = \bigcup_{n=0}^{\infty} T^{-n}(U) \tag{2}$$

[2]This terminology, and notation, originates from the notion of critical point as it is used in the classical works of Julia and Fatou.

where $T^{-1}(x)$ represents the set of all the rank-1 preimages of x and $T^{-n}(x)$ represents the set of all the rank-n preimages of x (i.e., the points mapped into x after n applications of T).

In other words, the basin of an attracting set A is the set of all the points that generate trajectories ultimately belonging to A or to the neighborhood U defined above.

As we are interested in the asymptotic behavior of the trajectories, we also introduce the ω*−limit set* of a point x: A point $q \in \omega(x)$ if there exists an increasing sequence $n_1 < n_2 < ... < n_k ...$ such that the points $T^{n_k}(x)$ tend to q as k goes to infinity (clearly such a point q belongs to the limit set of the trajectory $\tau(x)$). The set $\omega(x)$ is invariant and gives an idea of the long run behavior of the trajectory from x.

The same definition can be associated with the backward iterations of T, so obtaining the α*−limit set* of x: A point $q \in \alpha(x)$ if there exists an increasing sequence $n_1 < n_2 < ... < n_k ...$ such that the points $T_{j_k}^{-n_k}(x)$, for a suitable sequences of inverses j_k in case of a noninvertible map, tend to q as k goes to infinity (clearly such a point q belongs to the limit set of $\bigcup_{n \geq 0} T^{-n}(x)$).

In the particular case of a fixed point p^* of T we define the stable and unstable sets of p^* as

$$W^{st}(p^*) = \left\{ x : \lim_{n \to +\infty} T^n(x) = p^* \right\}$$

$$W^{un}(p^*) = \left\{ x : \lim_{n \to +\infty} T_{j_n}^{-n}(x) = p^* \right\}$$

respectively, where $T_{j_n}^{-n}$ means for a suitable sequence of inverses. This means that the stable set of p^* is the set of points x having p^* as ω-limit set and the unstable set of p^* is given by the points having p^* in their α-limit set.

If p^* is an asymptotically stable fixed point, then its stable set coincides with its basin of attraction, $B(p^*)$, and its unstable set is not empty if the map is noninvertible in p^*. If p^* is an expanding fixed point, then its unstable set is a whole area and its stable set is not empty if the map is noninvertible in p^*.

Other important sets in the study of the global properties of a map T are the stable and unstable sets of an hyperbolic[3] saddle fixed point p^*. Indeed,

[3]A fixed point p^* is said hyperbolic if the jacobian matrix evaluated at p^* has no eigenvalues of unit modulus.

if the map T admits several disjoint attracting sets, the stable sets of some saddles (fixed points or cycles) often play the role of separatrices between basins of attraction.

If p^* is a hyperbolic saddle and T is smooth in a neighborhood U of p^* in which T has a local inverse denoted as T_1^{-1}, the *Stable Manifold Theorem* states the existence of the local stable and unstable sets (defined in such a neighborhood U of p^*) as

$$W_{loc}^S(p^*) = \{x \in U : x_n = T^n(x) \to p^* \text{ and } x_n \in U\}$$

$$W_{loc}^U(p^*) = \left\{x \in U : x_{-n} = T_1^{-n}(x) \to p^* \text{ and } x_{-n} \in U\right\}.$$

The set $W_{loc}^S(p^*)$ (resp. $W_{loc}^U(p^*)$) is a one-dimensional curve as smooth as T, passing through p^* and tangent at p^* to the stable (resp. unstable) eigenspace. Then the global stable and unstable sets are made up, respectively, by all the preimages of any rank and the (forward) images of the points of the local sets, that is:

$$W^S(p^*) = \bigcup_{n\geq 0} T^{-n}\left(W_{loc}^S(p^*)\right) \tag{3}$$

$$W^U(p^*) = \bigcup_{n\geq 0} T\left(W_{loc}^U(p^*)\right). \tag{4}$$

where T^{-n} denotes all the existing preimages of rank-n.

If the map is invertible, the stable and unstable sets of a saddle p^* are invariant manifolds of T. If the map is noninvertible, the stable set of p^* is backward invariant, but it may be strictly mapped into itself (since some of its points may have no preimages), and it may be not connected. The unstable set of p^* is an invariant set, but it may be not backward invariant and (contrarily to what occurs in invertible maps) self intersections are allowed (several examples will be shown in this book).

It is worth to observe that analogous concepts are also given for continuous flows, but the main difference here is that the stable and unstable sets are not trajectories, but union of different trajectories (indeed infinitely many distinct trajectories). A qualitative representation of the local stable and unstable sets, W_{loc}^S and W_{loc}^U, of a saddle fixed point p^* is given in Fig.1, where E^S and E^U are the eigenspaces.

In the following, we shall consider the stable (resp. unstable) set of a saddle as given by the union of two branches merging in p^* denoted by ω_1 and ω_2 (resp α_1 and α_2) because all the points in these branches have p^* as *ω−limit set* (resp. in their *α−limit set).*

$$W^S(p^*) = \omega_1 \cup \omega_2 \ , \ W^U(p^*) = \alpha_1 \cup \alpha_2$$

The concepts of stable and unstable sets can be easily extended to a cycle of period k, say $\mathcal{C} = \{p_1^*, p_2^*, ..., p_k^*\}$, simply considering the union of the stable (unstable) sets of the points of the cycle considered as k fixed points of the map T^k. For example

$$W^{st}(\mathcal{C}) = \bigcup_{i=1}^{k} W^{st}(p_i^*) \quad , \quad W^{st}(p_i^*) = \left\{ x : \lim_{n \to +\infty} T^{kn}(x) = p_i^* \right\}$$

and analogously for the unstable set. In particular, for a k-cycle saddle we

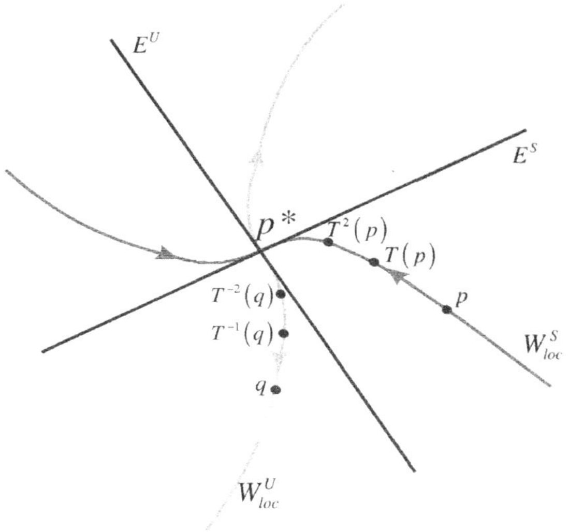

Figure 1: *The local stable and unstable sets of the saddle* p^*.

obtain the stable and unstable sets from (3) and (4) with the map T^k instead of T, that is

$$W^S(\mathcal{C}) = \bigcup_{i=1}^{k} W^S(p_i^*) = \bigcup_{i=1}^{k} (\omega_{1,i} \cup \omega_{2,i})$$
$$W^U(\mathcal{C}) = \bigcup_{i=1}^{k} W^U(p_i^*) = \bigcup_{i=1}^{k} (\alpha_{1,i} \cup \alpha_{2,i})$$

The importance of the stable and unstable sets is related to the fact that they are global concepts, that is, they are not defined only in a neighborhood of the fixed point (or cycle). Thus, being interested in the global properties of the map T, we may study its invariant sets, through a continuous dialogue between analytic, geometric and numerical methods, and focus our attention on the basins of attraction of its attractors and on the stable and unstable sets of some of its saddle points or cycles.

If the map is nonlinear, the stable and unstable sets may intersect, i.e. it may exist a point q such that $q \in W^{st}(p^*) \cap W^{un}(p^*)$, or

$$q \in W^S(p^*) \cap W^U(p^*) .$$

Such a point q is a *homoclinic point* and it can be proved that if a homoclinic point exists then infinitely many homoclinic points must also exist, accumulating in a neighborhood of p^*. Intuitively, this can be understood observing that the forward orbit of q and a suitable backward sequence is also made up of homoclinic points, and converge to p^*. The union of the forward orbit and a suitable backward orbit of a homoclinic point q is called a *homoclinic orbit of p^**, or *orbit homoclinic to p^**:

$$\tau(q) = \{..., q_{-n}, ..., q_{-2}, q_{-1}, q, q_1, q_2, ..., q_n, ...\}$$

where $q_n = T^n(q)$ and $T^n(q) \to p^*$ while $q_{-n} = T_{j_n}^{-n}(q)$ and $T_{j_n}^{-n}(q) \to p^*$ is a suitable backward orbit. More generally, an *orbit homoclinic to a cycle* approaches the cycle asymptotically both through forward and backward iterations, so that it always belong to the intersection of the stable and unstable sets of the cycle.

The appearance of homoclinic orbits of a saddle point p^* corresponds to a *homoclinic bifurcation* and implies a very complex configuration of W^S and W^U, called *homoclinic tangle*, due to their winding in proximity of p^*. The existence of an homoclinic tangle is often related to a sequence of bifurcations occurring in a suitable parameter range, and qualitatively shown in Fig.2: First, a homoclinic tangency between one branch, say ω_1, of the stable set of the saddle and one branch of the unstable one, say α_1, followed by a transversal crossing between ω_1 and α_1, that gives rise to a homoclinic tangle, and by a second homoclinic tangency of the same stable and unstable branches, occurring at opposite side with respect to the previous one, which closes the sequence. It is worth to recall that in the parameter range in which the manifolds intersect transversely, an invariant set exists such that the restriction of the map to this invariant set is *chaotic,* that is, the restriction is topologically conjugated with the shift map, as stated in the Smale-Birkhoff Theorem (see for example in [24], [35], [42], [9], [32]). Thus we say that the map possesses a *chaotic repellor*, made up of infinitely many (countable) repelling cycles and uncountable aperiodic trajectories. In the case shown in Fig.2 such a chaotic repellor certainly exists after the first homoclinic tangency and disappears after the second one.

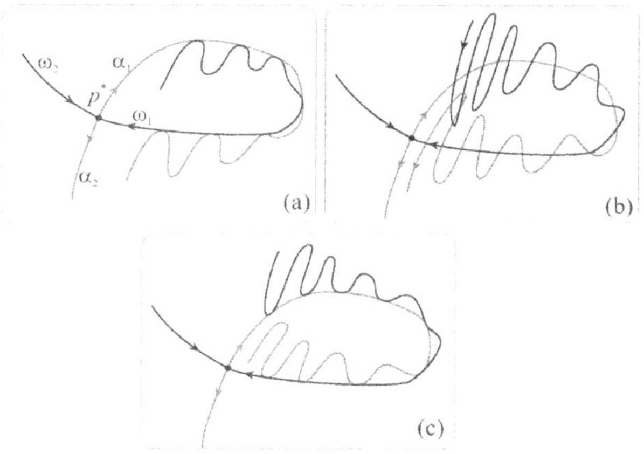

Figure 2: *Homoclinic tangle involving the branches α_1 of the unstable set and ω_1 of the stable one.*

Before and after the homoclinic tangle (i.e. before the first and after the last homoclinic tangencies), the dynamic behavior of the two branches involved in the bifurcation must differ: The invariant set towards which α_1 tends to (or equivalently the ω-limit set of the points of α_1) and the invariant set from which ω_1 comes from (or equivalently the α-limit set of the points of ω_1) before and after the two tangencies are different. Also at the bifurcation value, as in Fig.2a, are different from those of Fig.2c. Thus we can detect the occurrence of such a sequence of bifurcations looking at the asymptotic behavior of W^S and W^U.

We observe that if the saddle is a cycle $C = \{p_1^*, p_2^*, ..., p_k^*\}$, we may have homoclinic orbits of p_i^*, $i = 1, ..., k$, belonging to the stable and unstable sets of the periodic point p_i^* (considered as fixed points of the map T^k): In such a case we say that there exists points homoclinic to C. But it may also occur that the unstable set $W^U(p_i^*)$ transversely intersects $W^S(p_{i+1}^*)$, $i = 1, ..., k$

and $p_{k+1}^* = p_1^*$: In such a case we have *heteroclinic points* and *heteroclinic tangle* denotes the corresponding configuration of W^S and W^U sets. An example of heteroclinic tangle associated with a saddle cycle of period 4 is qualitatively shown in Fig.3: It involves the internal branches $\alpha_{1,i}$ and $\omega_{1,i}$ which, after a first tangency, transversely intersect each other and then have a second tangency.

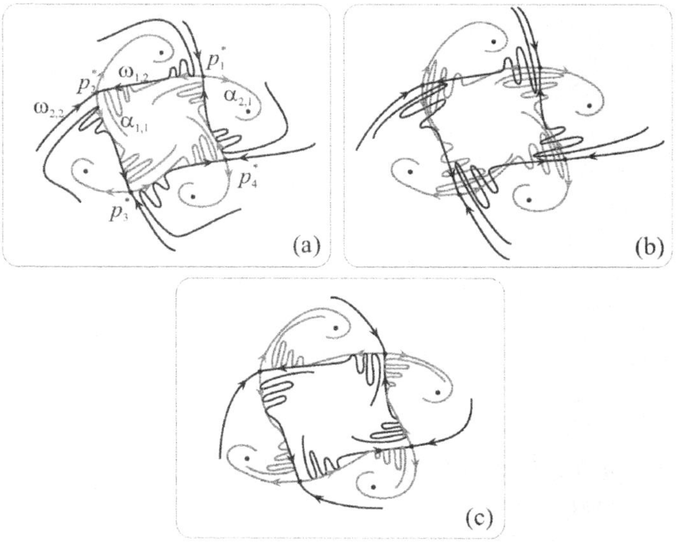

Figure 3: *Heteroclinic tangle associated with a saddle cycle of period 4 (or 4 saddle points of the map T^4).*

Let us also remark that, as in the case of a homoclinic tangle, also in a heteroclinic tangle the asymptotic behavior of the involved branches, before and after the two tangencies, changes. Dynamically, heteroclinic tangles are as important as homoclinic ones since it is possible to prove that also in such cases an invariant set exists on which the restriction of the map is *chaotic*. This homoclinic bifurcation is also called a *cyclical heteroclinic connection* in the sense of Birkhoff (see [10]), who first showed that the same properties occur when the stable and unstable manifolds of a saddle fixed point intersect transversely, or when there are two saddle fixed points, say s_i^* and s_j^*, such that $W^S(s_i^*) \cap W^U(s_j^*) \neq \emptyset$, thus giving cyclical heteroclinic points that form an heteroclinic connection (see also [19]). In such a case, the transverse intersections of $W^U(\mathcal{C})$ and $W^S(\mathcal{C})$ for the saddle cycle $\mathcal{C} = \{p_1^*, p_2^*, ..., p_k^*\}$, called *homoclinic points of non simple type* in [10] gives the same properties as the homoclinic points of a saddle fixed point (called *homoclinic points of simple type* in [10]). Thus the occurrence of a transverse homoclinic orbit of a saddle cycle is enough to prove the existence of chaotic dynamics, because it is possible to prove that in the neighborhood of any homoclinic orbit there are infinitely many repelling cycles and an invariant "scrambled set" on which the restriction of the map is chaotic in the sense of Li and Yorke (see for example in [20], [21], [42]).

It is worth to notice that if the map T is noninvertible and p^* is an expanding fixed point of T (i.e., a fixed point such that the Jacobian matrix evaluated at p^* has all the eigenvalues greater than 1 in modulus) then the *stable set of* p^* is given by the preimages of any rank of p^*, if they exist (as defined at the beginning of this section). The existence of a stable set for repelling points is a distinguishing feature of noninvertible maps, because such a set is empty in invertible maps. In fact, for a noninvertible map the only preimage of a fixed point p^* is p^*, as $T(p^*) = p^*$, whereas preimages $p_{-1}^* \neq p^*$ may exist if T is noninvertible, i.e. several rank-1 preimages exist. This implies that for noninvertible maps *homoclinic bifurcations* may also occur for expanding fixed points (repelling nodes and foci), whereas for invertible maps they can only occur for saddles. Another difference between invertible and noninvertible maps is associated with *non connected basins* of attraction, which are only possible for noninvertible maps, whereas they are always simply connected in invertible maps.

1.3 Closed Invariant Curves

The main interest in this chapter is to show some local and global bifurcations related to closed invariant curves in two-dimensional maps, as the dynamics related to such curves is what can be interpreted (in applied models) as cyclical behavior. As we shall see (in later sections and in several examples in later chapters), the appearance/disappearance of closed curves may be related to some global bifurcation. However, the most known mechanism leading to such curves is the Neimark-Sacker bifurcation.

Let us simply recall the properties of a focus fixed point $p^* = (x^*, y^*)$ of a smooth map T, for which the Jacobian matrix DT in p^* has complex-conjugate eigenvalues, assuming that the stability of the fixed point is investigated as a function of one parameter μ. As long as the eigenvalues are in modulus less than one, say for $\mu < \mu_0$, the focus is stable and locally (in a small neighborhood of p^*) the trajectories belong to spirals and tend to the fixed point. When the eigenvalues are in modulus greater than one, say for $\mu > \mu_0$, the focus is unstable (repelling) and locally the trajectories still belong to spirals, however they have a different asymptotic behavior. The crossing of the complex eigenvalue trough the unitary circle, at $\mu = \mu_0$, corresponds to a *Neimark-Sacker bifurcation*. The analytical conditions at which it occurs, and the so called "resonant cases", now belong to standard dynamical results, which can be found in many textbooks, see for example [28], [29], [24], [32], [42]. Let us here briefly recall the main features, which are useful in the study of applied models. A Neimark-Sacker bifurcation is related with closed invariant curves, existing in a small neighborhood of the stable fixed point when the bifurcation is subcritical, or of the unstable fixed point when it is supercritical. The critical case occurs when locally the map behaves as a linear map, that is, the dynamic behavior at the bifurcation value is that of a center, and locally infinitely many closed invariant curves exist (instead of only one, as it occurs before or after the bifurcation value in the subcritical or supercritical case, respectively). Fig.4a qualitatively shows a bifurcation diagram in the subcritical case: A repelling closed invariant curve

(a)

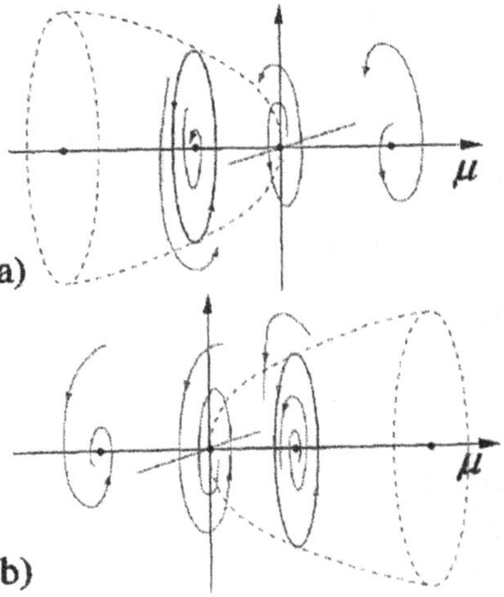

(b)

Figure 4: *Qualitative diagram of the Neimark-Sacker bifurcation:* (a) *subcritical case,* (b) *supercritical case.*

Γ exists surrounding the stable fixed point, for $\mu < \mu_0$. As μ increases the repelling closed curve decreases in size and shrinks merging with the fixed point at $\mu = \mu_0$, leaving a repelling focus. It is worth noting that in such a case the closed repelling curve is generally the boundary of the basin of attraction of the stable fixed point. After the bifurcation the fixed point is unstable and the ω-limit set of a point close to it depends on the nonlinearity of the map (it may converge to another attracting set or diverge).

Fig.4b qualitatively shows a bifurcation diagram in the supercritical case: At $\mu = \mu_0$ the fixed point becomes an unstable focus and for $\mu > \mu_0$ an attracting closed invariant curve Γ exists, surrounding the unstable fixed point. Thus the ω-limit set of points close to it is such closed invariant curve.

For μ in a neighborhood of μ_0 the closed invariant curve Γ (stable or unstable) is homeomorphic to a circle, and the restriction of the map to Γ is conjugated with a rotation on the circle. Thus the dynamics on Γ are either periodic or quasiperiodic, depending on the rotation number. Roughly speaking, the rotation number represents the average number of turns of a trajectory around the fixed point. When the rotation number is rational, say m/n, it means that a pair of periodic orbits of period n exists on Γ, and to get the whole periodic orbit a trajectory makes m turns around the fixed point. The dynamics occurring in such a case on Γ are qualitatively shown in Fig.5a in case of a supercritical bifurcation (Γ is attracting): The closed curve is made up by the unstable set of the saddle cycle, and Γ is also called a saddle-(stable) node connection. Instead, Fig.5b shows the subcritical case (Γ is repelling): The closed curve is made up by the stable set of the saddle cycle, and Γ is also called a saddle-(unstable) node connection. When the rotation number is irrational, the trajectories of T on the closed curve Γ are all quasiperiodic. That is, each point on Γ gives rise to a trajectory on the invariant curve which never comes on the same point, and the closure of the trajectory is exactly Γ.

Investigating the bifurcation of a fixed point of T as a function of two parameters, it is quite common to derive the so called *stability triangle*, whose boundaries represent the stability loss due to different properties of the eigenvalues. That is, one side represents a flip-bifurcation (one eigenvalue equal to -1), another side a fold or pitchfork-bifurcation (one eigenvalue equal to +1), and a third side the Neimark-Sacker bifurcation (complex eigenvalues in modulus equal to +1). In the supercritical case, such a portion of bifurcation curves is the starting point of so called "periodicity tongues", or *Arnol'd tongues,* associated with different rational rotation numbers m/n. A peculiar property of such tongues is associated with the summation rule [27]: Between any two tongues with rotation numbers m_1/n_1 and m_2/n_2 there is also a tongue associated with the rotation number $m'/n' = (m_1 + m_2)/(n_1 + n_2)$.

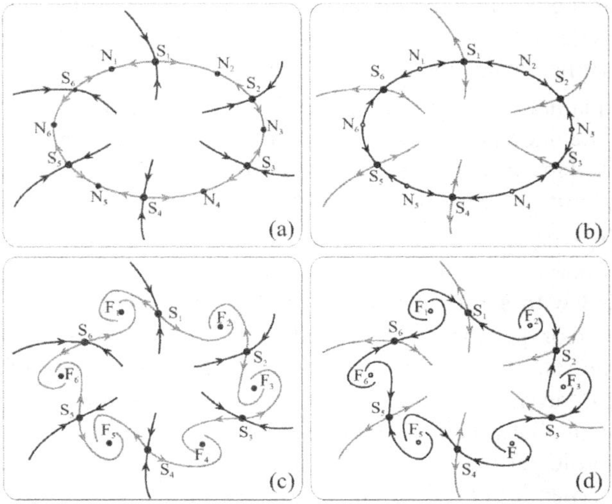

Figure 5: *Dynamics on a closed invariant curve* Γ: (a) *saddle-(stable) node connection,* (b) *saddle-(unstable) node connection,* (c) *saddle-(stable) focus connection,* (d) *saddle-(unstable) focus connection.*

It is clear that properties and bifurcations similar to those described above for a fixed point can occur also for a $k-$cycle of any period $k > 1$, simply considering the k periodic points as fixed points of the map T^k. In such a case the closed invariant curves Γ_k of the map T^k belong to a $k-$cyclical set for the map T. Several examples of bifurcation diagrams and invariant closed curves Γ (cyclical or not), with rational rotation numbers and saddle-connections or with quasiperiodic trajectories, will be shown in later chapters, associated with several business cycles models.

The dynamic evolution of Γ clearly depends on the nonlinearity of the map. Several examples will be given, both in piecewise linear maps (see the next chapter and Chapter 12) and in smooth maps (Chapters 8, 9, 11), together with a survey of possible mechanisms leading to the destruction of a closed curve. We only note here that the destruction may occur in two different ways: Either because the invariant closed curve Γ becomes no longer homeomorphic to a circle, or because the restriction of the map on Γ becomes no longer conjugate with a rigid rotation or an invertible map of the circle. The first case naturally occurs when the cycle node (stable or unstable) on Γ becomes a focus: Fig.5c-d qualitatively represent this case, together with a saddle-focus connection, which may be stable (Fig.5c) or unstable (Fig.5d).

We finally remark that when a pair of parameters are let to vary in a parameter plane outside the stability triangle, from the region close to a supercritical pitchfork (or flip) bifurcation curve towards the region where a supercritical Neimark-Sacker bifurcation occurs, then global bifurcations associated with (attracting and repelling) closed invariant curves must necessarily occur. Some of the mechanisms explaining such global bifurcations are described in the next sections.

1.4 Effects of Critical Curves on Invariant Closed Curves

In this section we consider the transformations of an invariant closed curve, born from a focus fixed point of a noninvertible map of the plane via a supercritical Neimark-Sacker bifurcation, as some parameter is gradually moved away from its bifurcation value. As stated in the previous section, just after the bifurcation an attracting invariant closed curve, say Γ, exists around the unstable focus. It is smooth and homeomorphic to a circle, with radius proportional to the square root of the distance from the bifurcation set in the parameter space (see e.g. [24], p.305).

The dynamics of the iterated map restricted to Γ is conjugate to a map of the circle, and may be characterized by an irrational or a rational rotation number. In the former case, the motion along Γ is non periodic (also called quasiperiodic) and the iterated points are densely distributed along the whole invariant curve, whereas in the latter case, if the rational rotation number has the form m/n, the motion is n-periodic, i.e., an attracting cycle of period n exists embedded into Γ, and the n periodic points are cyclically visited every m turnings around the unstable focus. The latter situation is observed when the parameters are chosen inside a m/n Arnold tongue. The whole curve Γ is covered by the iterated points only in the case of irrational rotation number, otherwise only the periodic points are visited by the asymptotic dynamics, so that it is difficult to see Γ numerically, when the period n is small, even if the closed invariant curve exists (given by the saddle-node connection).

However, the Neimark-Sacker bifurcation theorem only gives local results in the parameter space, in the sense that it says nothing about the changes in the shape, or even the existence, of the invariant curve, as the parameters move away from the bifurcation values. Indeed, the closed invariant curve may suddenly disappear, or drastically change its shape, or evolve into an annular chaotic attractor (a chaotic ring). In the case of a noninvertible map of the plane, important modifications of the shape and global properties of Γ occur due to the folding action of the critical curves.

In order to illustrate this point, let us consider an exemplary case, obtained by using the quadratic map $T:(x,y)\to(x',y')$ defined by

$$T:\left\{\begin{array}{l} x'=y \\ y'=y-\lambda x+x^2 \end{array}\right. \tag{5}$$

where λ is a real parameter (see [36] for a more detailed study of this map). Given x' and y', if we solve the algebraic system with respect to the unknowns x and y we obtain

$$T_1^{-1}:\left\{\begin{array}{l} x=\frac{\lambda}{2}-\sqrt{\frac{\lambda^2}{4}+y'-x'} \\ y=x' \end{array}\right. ;T_2^{-1}:\left\{\begin{array}{l} x=\frac{\lambda}{2}+\sqrt{\frac{\lambda^2}{4}+y'-x'} \\ y=x' \end{array}\right. \tag{6}$$

So, a point (x',y') has two distinct rank-1 preimages if $y'>(x'-\lambda^2/4)$, and no preimages if the reverse inequality holds. This means that the map (5) is a Z_0-Z_2 noninvertible map, where Z_0 (region whose points have no preimages) is the half plane $Z_0=\left\{(x,y)\,|\,y<x-\lambda^2/4\right\}$ and Z_2 (region whose points have two distinct rank-1 preimages) is the half plane $Z_2=\left\{(x,y)\,|\,y>x-\lambda^2/4\right\}$. The line $y=x-\lambda^2/4$, which separates these two regions, is the critical curve LC, i.e. the locus of points having two merging rank-1 preimages, located on the line $x_1=\lambda/2$, that represents LC_{-1}. Any point $(x,y)\in Z_2$ has the two rank-1 preimages symmetrically located at opposite sides with respect to LC_{-1}: $T_1^{-1}(x,y)\in R_1$ and $T_2^{-1}(x,y)\in R_2$, where R_1 is the region defined by $x<\lambda/2$ and R_2 is defined by $x>\lambda/2$. We notice that, being (5) a continuously differentiable map, the line LC_{-1} belongs to the set of points at which the Jacobian determinant vanishes, i.e. $LC_{-1}\subseteq J_0$, where $J_0=\{(x,y)\,|\det DT(x,y)=2x-\lambda=0\}$, and the critical curve LC is the image by T of LC_{-1}, i.e. $LC=T(LC_{-1})=T(\{x=\lambda/2\})=\left\{(x,y)\,|y=x-\lambda^2/4\right\}$.

The folding action related to the presence of the critical lines can be expressed by saying that the image of any region U separated by LC_{-1} into two portions, say $U_1 \in R_1$ and $U_2 \in R_2$, is folded along LC, in the sense that $T(U_1) \cap T(U_2)$ is a nonempty set included in Z_2. This means that two points $p \in U_1$ and $q \in U_2$, located at opposite sides with respect to LC_{-1}, are mapped in the same side with respect to LC, in the region Z_2. This can be equivalently expressed by stressing the "unfolding" action of T^{-1}, obtained by the application of the two distinct inverses in Z_2 which merge along LC. Indeed, if we consider a region $V \subset Z_2$, then the set of its rank-1 preimages $T_1^{-1}(V)$ and $T_2^{-1}(V)$ is made up of two regions $T_1^{-1}(V) \in R_1$ and $T_2^{-1}(V) \in R_2$, that are disjoint if $V \cap LC = \emptyset$ whereas they merge along LC_{-1} if $V \cap LC \neq \emptyset$.

The map (5) has two fixed points, $O = (0,0)$ and $P = (\lambda, \lambda)$. It is easy to see that O is stable for $0 < \lambda < 1$, and as λ is increased through the bifurcation value $\lambda = 1$ a supercritical Neimark-Sacker bifurcation occurs at which a stable invariant closed curve arises around the unstable focus O, as shown in Fig.6a, obtained for $\lambda = 1.02$. In the situation shown in Fig.6a the other fixed point, P, is a saddle, whose stable set constitutes the boundary that separates the basin of attraction of the closed invariant curve Γ (the white region) from the basin of diverging trajectories, also called basin of infinity (the grey region). Notice that in Fig.6a the invariant curve Γ appears to be smooth and of approximately circular shape, so that the quasi-periodic motion along it is very similar to purely trigonometric oscillations. It can also be noticed that Γ is entirely included in the region R_1, i.e. it has no intersections with LC_{-1}. It is important to remark that just after its creation Γ cannot be too close to LC_{-1}, because at the Neimark-Sacker bifurcation the eigenvalues are complex conjugate and belong to the unit circle of the complex plane, whereas along LC_{-1} one eigenvalue must necessarily be zero being $\det(DT) = 0$ along LC_{-1}. Therefore, intersections between Γ and LC_{-1} are only possible when the parameters are sufficiently far from the Neimark-Sacker bifurcation values.

We now describe the changes of the stable invariant closed curve Γ as the parameter λ is increased. Indeed, as far as the attracting invariant closed curve Γ does not intersect LC_{-1} it can be thought of as entirely contained in one sheet of the Riemann foliation. This means that a neighborhood $U(\Gamma)$ of Γ exists such that not only $T(U) \subset U$ (since Γ is attracting) but a unique inverse exists, say T_1^{-1}, such that $T_1^{-1} : T(U) \to U$. This implies that the curve Γ, as well as the area of the phase plane enclosed by Γ, say $a(\Gamma)$, is both forward invariant (under T) and backward invariant (under T_1^{-1}).

The situation changes when Γ grows up until it has a contact with the set of merging preimages LC_{-1}, and then intersects it, as shown in Fig.6b, obtained for $\lambda = 1.3$. We now describe the consequences of the contact between Γ and LC_{-1}.

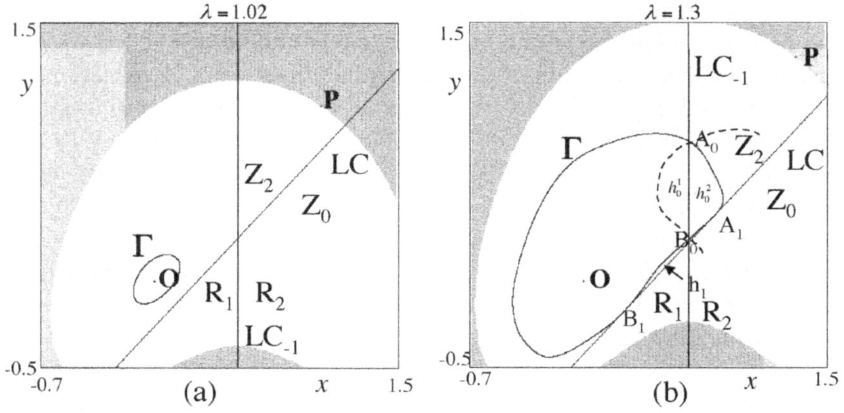

Figure 6: (a) *Just after the supercritical Neimark-Sacker bifurcation of the fixed point O a smooth attracting closed curve* Γ *appears.* (b) *Far away from the bifurcation value, the area inside* Γ *is no longer invariant.*

Let A_0 and B_0 be the two points of intersection between Γ and LC_{-1}, and let R_1 and R_2 the two regions, separated by LC_{-1}, giving the ranges of the two inverses T_1^{-1} and T_2^{-1}, respectively. Then the points $A_1 = T(A_0)$ and $B_1 = T(B_0)$, which must belong both to Γ and to $LC = T(LC_{-1})$, are points of tangential contact between Γ and LC. In fact, the arc $A_0B_0 = \Gamma \cap R_2$ must be mapped by T in the arc $A_1B_1 = T(A_0B_0)$, entirely included in the region Z_2, on one side of LC (i.e. on the side of region Z_2). If we look at the area $a(\Gamma)$, bounded by the invariant curve, it is easy to see that such an area is no longer invariant under application of T. In fact, $T_1^{-1}(A_1B_1)$ gives an arc inside $a(\Gamma)$ but not belonging to the invariant curve, while $A_0B_0 = \Gamma \cap R_2$ is given by $T_2^{-1}(A_1B_1)$. It means that the region h_1, located between the arc A_1B_1 of Γ and LC, is "unfolded" by the action of the two inverses T_1^{-1} and T_2^{-1} in two distinct preimages, located in the regions R_1 and R_2 respectively, represented in Fig.6b by the two portions $h_0^1 = T_1^{-1}(h_1)$ and $h_0^2 = T_2^{-1}(h_1)$ of $a(\Gamma)$ bounded by the two arcs A_0B_0 inside and along Γ respectively. In other words, the two portions h_0^1 and h_0^2 of $a(\Gamma)$ are both "folded" by T along LC *outside* the area $a(\Gamma)$ (as both cover the area h_1 which is outside Γ). This implies that the area $a(\Gamma)$, bounded by Γ, is no longer forward invariant (since some points inside Γ are mapped outside it, and are exactly the points belonging to h_0^1 and h_0^2).

This phenomenon of forward invariance of a closed curve, together with noninvariance of the area inside it, is specific to noninvertible discrete maps, that is, it cannot be observed neither in two-dimensional invertible maps nor in two-dimensional continuous dynamical systems. The property of noninvariance of $a(\Gamma)$ and the creation of convolutions of Γ are two aspects of the same mechanism, related to the fact that curves crossing LC_{-1} are folded along LC and are confined into the region with an higher number of preimages.

Another consequence of the intersection between Γ and LC_{-1} is that for a periodic cycle not belonging to Γ, it may happen that some of the periodic points are inside and the others are outside the invariant curve Γ. In the case of the map (5) this may be observed for example when $\lambda = 1.4014$, because a stable cycle of period 7 coexists with the stable invariant curve Γ (see Fig.7, where the seven periodic points of the stable cycle are labelled as $C_1, ..., C_7$). As it can be seen in the figure, the periodic point C_1, inside Γ in the region h_0^2, is mapped in the point $C_2 \in h_1$, i.e. outside $a(\Gamma)$.

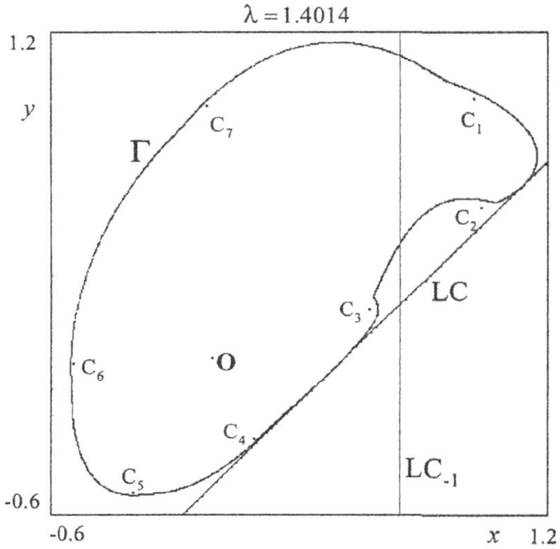

Figure 7: *The periodic point C_1, inside Γ in the region h_0^2, is mapped in the point $C_2 \in h_1$, i.e. outside $a(\Gamma)$.*

As the parameter λ is further increased, the convolutions become more and more pronounced and another phenomenon peculiar of noninvertible maps can be seen, that is the appearance of knots, or loops, or self intersections of the unstable set of the saddle belonging to the closed invariant curve, and such a dynamic situation is soon followed by homoclinic situations (intersections between the stable and unstable sets of the saddle) leading to a chaotic attractor, also called "weakly chaotic ring" in [36] for their particular shape. An example is given in Fig.8a obtained with $\lambda = 1.505$. As emphasized in the enlargement shown in Fig.8b, the attractor is no longer a closed invariant curve, as it includes loops and self-intersections. The mechanisms through which such loops and chaotic rings are created, and the related loss of invariance of Γ have been recently studied by many authors (see e.g. [36], [17] or [18] and references therein), and still have some open problems.

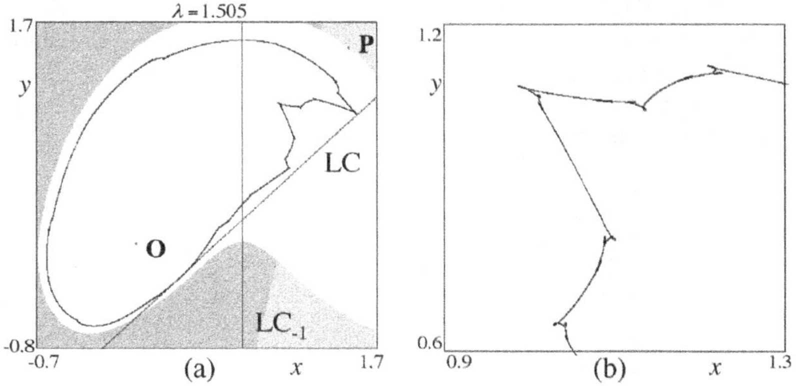

Figure 8: (a) *A "weakly chaotic ring" caused by some homoclinic bifurcation.* (b) *The enlargement shows the loops and the self-intersections of the attractors.*

As the parameter λ is further increased, so that it is more and more far from the Neimark-Sacker bifurcation value, a fully developed chaotic ring is created, like the one shown in Fig.9, obtained for $\lambda = 1.54$, on which the dynamics are characterized by chaotic time series that exhibit some particular time patterns, as shown in Fig.9b. It is worth to notice that in Fig.9a the attractor is very close to the boundary of the basin of diverging trajectories (gray points in the figure). This suggests that a further increase of λ will lead to a contact between the attractor and the boundary of its basin, and this represents a global bifurcation that marks the destruction of the attractor (more properly, it becomes a chaotic repellor after the contact). Such bifurcation is known as final bifurcation, or boundary crisis, and here corresponds to the first homoclinic bifurcation of the saddle fixed point P on the basin boundary. Indeed, its unstable set tends to the attractor while its stable set belongs to the frontier of the basin, thus a contact of the attracting set with the basin boundary also implies a contact between the stable and unstable sets of P. Of course, this contact between an invariant attracting set and its basin boundary may occur at the beginning of the story, i.e. soon after the creation of the closed invariant curve Γ. In other words, even if the Neimark-Sacker bifurcation theorem marks the appearance of Γ, it gives no indications about its survival as the parameters are moved away from their bifurcation values.

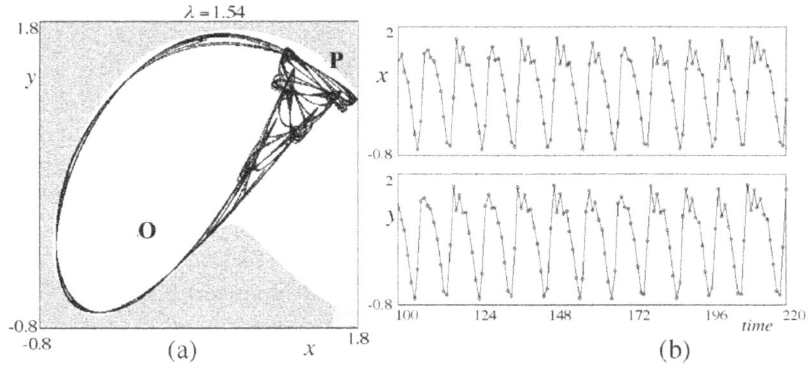

Figure 9: (a) *The fully developed chaotic ring.* (b) *The corresponding chaotic time series.*

To sum up, just after a supercritical Neimark-Sacker bifurcation, the long run dynamics of a discrete dynamical system is characterized by endogenous oscillations that may be quasiperiodic or periodic, converging towards a smooth and attracting closed curve Γ. Then, when the parameters move along a path away from the Neimark-Sacker bifurcation value, the closed invariant curve grows up, i.e. oscillations of increasing amplitude characterize the asymptotic dynamics. Such enlargement of Γ may lead to its disappearance or to some changes of its shape, due to the nonlinearities of the map. If the map is noninvertible, the intersections between Γ and LC_{-1} gives rise to convoluted shapes of the invariant curve, until it is replaced by an annular chaotic attractor.

As usual, sets of parameters are met at which stable cycles are created via a saddle-node bifurcation. The periodic points of these stable cycles may belong to Γ, or may be inside $a(\Gamma)$, or outside $a(\Gamma)$ or, if Γ intersects LC_{-1}, some of the periodic points may be inside and other outside $a(\Gamma)$. Furthermore, several coexisting attractors may be simultaneously present, such as coexisting attracting cycles or quasiperiodic or chaotic attractors together with attracting cycles.

An important property of noninvertible maps is that in any case, segments of the critical curves LC, together with a suitable number of their images $LC_i = T^i(LC)$, may be used to bound a trapping region where all the attracting sets are included. Such trapping sets, also called absorbing areas in [36], act like a bounded vessel inside which the asymptotic dynamics of the bounded trajectories are ultimately confined (see also [3], [12], [39]).

1.5 Invariant Closed Curves and Saddle Connections

In this section we present some global bifurcations involving invariant closed curves, which may be related to the appearance/disappearance of endogenous fluctuations, to qualitative changes in their amplitude and to complex structure in their basins of attraction. These bifurcations are related to the dynamic behavior of the stable and unstable sets of same saddle cycle, so they can be observed both with invertible and noninvertible maps. In the following we restrict our attention to (at least locally) invertible maps.

Before proceeding, it is worth to recall that the bifurcations related to invariant curves are well known in continuous dynamical systems, but in discrete models are still an open problem (see [32]): Here we give some qualitative results obtained by computer assisted proofs, with the awareness that further investigations need for a more complete understanding.

As already stated above, from a local point of view, in a nonlinear discrete map endogenous fluctuations naturally appear when a fixed point is destabilized through a supercritical Neimark-Sacker bifurcation: A stable focus becomes unstable and an attracting closed curve appears around it, becoming wider and wider when the parameters move away from the bifurcation value. Generally this local bifurcation has no global effect, in the sense that after the bifurcation the trajectories of points close to the unstable focus reach the attracting closed curve. However, some recent papers (see, among others, the endogenous business cycle models studied in [38] and in [31] or the cobweb model with predictor selection proposed in [14]) have stressed the importance of homoclinic tangencies and homoclinic tangles of saddles in the transition from local regular to global irregular fluctuations, due to increasing complexity of the attractors. Moreover, if the map T exhibits some multistability phenomena, then the invariant closed curve may interact with other attractors and interesting dynamic phenomena may occur, often associated with homoclinic or heteroclinic tangles.

Different, but still interesting, problems arise when the Neimark-Sacker bifurcation is of subcritical type, that is, when a repelling closed curve coexists with a stable focus, and generally such a repelling closed curve gives the boundary of the basin of attraction of the stable focus. Indeed, a subcritical bifurcation may be seen as a catastrophe phenomenon, in the sense that after its occurrence no attractors exist in the phase space or, if an attractor exists, it is quite far from the bifurcating fixed point. Instead, in the case of a supercritical Neimark-Sacker bifurcation, the phase portrait is completely different: The attracting closed curve which appears after the bifurcation is very small and close to the fixed point.

The dynamical behavior of a subcritical Neimark-Sacker bifurcation is very importand in the economic literature (as well as in other applied models). In fact, the existence of a repelling closed curve which bounds the basin of attraction of the stable fixed point implies that small shocks of the system have no effects on its dynamical behavior, while large enough shocks may lead to another attractor. This requires the coexistence of the fixed point with a different attracting set, and may cause *hysteresis* phenomena. Indeed, in such a case, if a parameter is varied so that a stable focus becomes unstable via a subcritical Neimark-Sacker bifurcation, i.e. a repelling curve shrinks and at the bifurcation merges with the fixed point, leaving a repelling focus, then the trajectories that start close to the fixed point reach the second attractor. In this case, a simple restoration of the previous value of the bifurcation parameter does not permit to move again the state of the system to the stable equilibrium, since the phase point is out of its basin. An example of this situation is the so called "*crater bifurcation*" scenario (see [30]): Two invariant closed curves, one repelling and one attracting, appear surrounding the fixed point when it is still stable. As the parameters move, the attracting closed curve moves away from the fixed point whereas the repelling one, which play the role of separatrix between the basins of attraction, shrinks merging with the fixed point in a subcritical Neimark-Sacker bifurcation. After such a bifurcation, the trajectories, previously converging to the fixed point, are converging to the attracting closed curve (which is quite far from the fixed point). The phase portrait so obtained (unstable focus and attracting closed curve) may suggest that a supercritical Neimark-Sacker bifurcation has occurred, but looking at the amplitude of the fluctuations we obtain the correct understanding of the bifurcation sequence giving rise to it.

When a Neimark-Sacker bifurcation of subcritical type occurs, it is also interesting to study the mechanism which gives rise to the appearance of the repelling closed curve, or to the two closed curves in the case of a crater bifurcation. Such occurrence may be related to the appearance of a pair of cycles (a saddle cycle and a repelling one) on the boundary of the basin of attraction of the fixed point. The heteroclinic connection of these cycles, formed by the stable set of the saddle cycle which comes from the periodic repelling points, constitutes a repelling closed curve. An example of this situation is given in [8]. Sometimes, for example when a crater bifurcation occurs, more complex situations are possible: We shall see that, as in the supercritical case, homoclinic tangencies and homoclinic tangles of saddles play an important role in the mechanism associated with the appearance/disappearance of closed invariant curves.

In continuous dynamical systems one of the mechanism associated with the appearance and disappearance of closed invariant curves involves a *saddle connection*: A branch of the stable set of a saddle point (or cycle) merges with a branch of the unstable one (of the same saddle or a different one), giving rise to an invariant closed curve.

When the involved saddle is a fixed point, the saddle connection can be due to the merging of one branch of the stable set and one of the unstable set, as in Fig.10a: We shall call such a situation *homoclinic loop*. Otherwise, if both the branches of the stable and unstable sets are involved in the saddle connection we obtain an eight-shaped structure that we shall call *double homoclinic loop* (see Fig.10b).

Homoclinic loops and double homoclinic loops can also involve a saddle cycle of period k, being related to the map T^k, but in this case we can also obtain an *heteroclinic loop*: Indeed, the map T^k exhibits k saddles points and a branch of the stable set of a saddle may merge with a branch of another periodic point of the saddle cycle. Stated in other words, if S_i, $i = 1, ..., k$, are the periodic points of the saddle cycle and $\alpha_{1,i} \cup \alpha_{2,i}$ ($\omega_{1,i} \cup \omega_{2,i}$) are the unstable (stable) sets of S_i, then a heteroclinic loop is given by the merging, for example, of the unstable branch $\alpha_{1,i}$ of S_i with the stable branch $\omega_{1,j}$ of a different periodic point S_j. Then each periodic point of the saddle cycle is connected with another one, and an invariant closed curve is so created that connects the periodic points of the saddle cycle. In Fig.10c an heteroclinic loop is shown, related to a pair of saddles (or a saddle cycle of period 2).

All these loops correspond to structurally unstable situations and cause a qualitative change in the dynamic behavior of the dynamical system. Since they cannot be predicted by a local investigation, i.e., a study of the linear approximation of the map, we classify them as global bifurcations. Indeed, we study this kind of bifurcation looking at the asymptotic behavior of the stable and unstable sets of the saddle: If a bifurcation associated with a loop has occurred, before and after the bifurcation the involved branch of the unstable set converges to different attracting sets, and the points of the involved stable branch have a different α-limit set, as well.

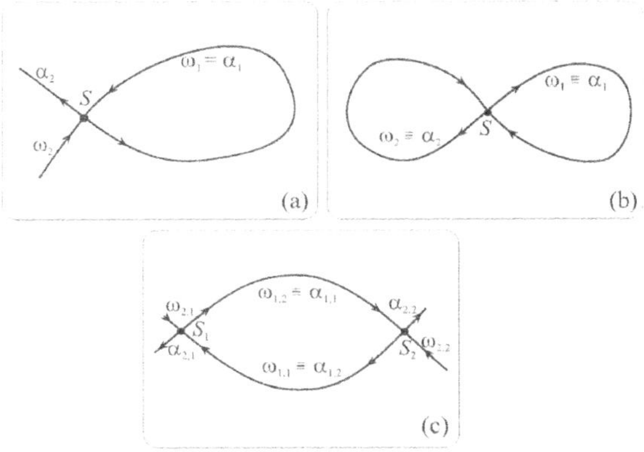

Figure 10: *Saddle connections*: (a) *homoclinic loop,* (b) *double homoclinic loop,* (c) *heteroclinic loop.*

Although homoclinic and heteroclinic loops may also occur in discrete dynamical systems, in this case they are frequently replaced by homoclinic tangles, as described in Section 1.2. That is, a tangency between the unstable branch $W_1^U(S) = \cup\alpha_{1,i}$ with the stable one $W_1^S(S) = \cup\omega_{1,i}$ occurs, followed by transverse crossings of the two manifolds, followed by another tangency of the same manifolds, but on opposite sides.

In the following we shall qualitatively describe some global bifurcations that involve closed invariant curves and may occur in the business cycle models. We first consider global bifurcations causing the appearance/disappearance of closed invariant curves, then the case in which at least a closed invariant curve coexists with some cycle and we shall see as these interact. All the global bifurcations here presented involve homoclinic connections of the periodic points of a saddle cycle.

1.6 Appearance of an Invariant Closed Curve (Homoclinic Loop)

In this section we show a mechanism which may cause the appearance of an invariant closed curve (or cyclical closed invariant curves), already known in the literature, see e.g. [35], [32], [2].

In the simplest starting situation, an attracting set A coexists with a saddle point S^* and a repelling fixed point P^*: A qualitative draft of the global bifurcation is given in Fig.11, where we assume that the attracting set A is a focus fixed point as well as P^*. Initially (see Fig.11a), the unstable set of the saddle converges to the attracting set A, and a branch of it, say α_1, turns around the repelling focus P^*. The α-limit set of the points of the branch ω_1 of the stable set of the saddle is the fixed point P^* and ω_2 comes from the boundary of the basin of attraction of A. After the bifurcation (Fig.11c), we have a bistability situation: The attracting set A coexists with an attracting closed curve Γ_s surrounding the repelling focus. The basins of attraction of A and Γ_s are separated by the stable set of the saddle point S^*. The attracting closed curve Γ_s is the ω-limit set of the points of the unstable branch α_1 and the stable branch ω_1 no longer exits from P^*, coming from the boundary of the set of the feasible trajectories (or the basin boundary of a different attracting set). The changes in the asymptotic behavior of the two branches suggest that the appearance of the curve Γ_s is due to a global bifurcation involving ω_1 and α_1. Indeed, we can conjecture that at the bifurcation the stable branch ω_1 and the unstable branch α_1 merge, giving rise to a *homoclinic loop*, as shown in Fig.11b, whose effect is to create a closed invariant curve. Obviously, this is a schematic representation of the mechanism involved, since we expect that, as usual with discrete maps, the single bifurcation value of the homoclinic loop is replaced by an interval of values associated with an homoclinic tangle between the two branches α_1 and ω_1, as shown in Fig.2: A tangency, followed by transverse crossing, that gives homoclinic points to the saddle S^*, followed by a second tangency between the same manifolds at which the transverse homoclinic points to S^* disappear.

The same mechanism may also give rise to a repelling closed curve Γ_u, but in such a case we start from the coexistence of at least two attractors, say an attracting set A, an attracting fixed point P^* and a saddle S^*, as in Fig.12a, where the attracting set A is a fixed point. The stable set of the saddle separates the basins of attraction of A and P^*. The branch ω_1 of $W^S(S^*)$ turns around P^*. The branch α_1 of the unstable set $W^U(S^*)$ tends to P^* whereas the ω-limit set of the points of the branch α_2 is the attracting set A. After the homoclinic loop, or homoclinic tangle, of the two branches

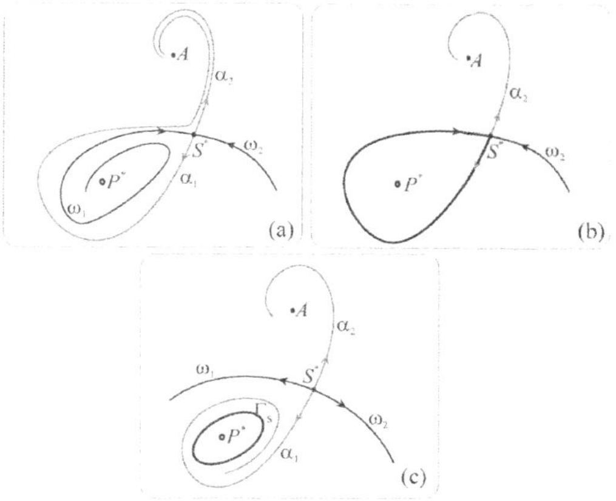

Figure 11: *Qualitative representation of a mechanism leading to the appearance of an attracting closed curve.*

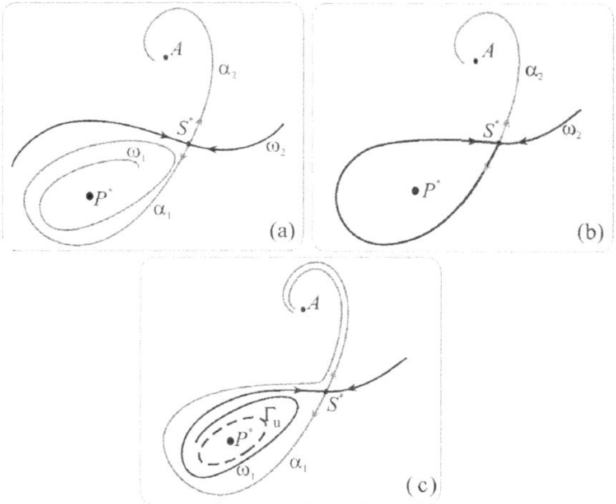

Figure 12: *Qualitative representation of a mechanism leading to a repelling closed curve.*

α_1 and ω_1, shown in Fig.12b, a repelling closed curve Γ_u appears, bounding the basin of attraction of P^* (see Fig.12c). Such a curve is the α-limit set of the points of the branch ω_1 of the set $W^S(S^*)$ and A is the ω-limit set of the points of the whole unstable set $W^U(S^*)$.

It is worth to observe that in the two cases considered above, the appearance of a closed invariant curve is due to a mechanism associated with a homoclinic loop, or tangle, and if the fixed points surrounded by the homoclinic loop is repelling (resp. attracting) then the closed curve which appears is attracting (resp. repelling). The case associated with the attracting fixed point P^* is also interesting because it may explain the appearance of the repelling closed curve involved in the Neimark-Sacker bifurcation of subcritical type.

Clearly the bifurcations described above may involve saddles and attracting or repelling cycles of period k ($k > 1$) instead of fixed points: In such a case the mechanisms previously described occur for the map T^k and lead to k cyclical invariant closed curves, repelling or attracting, for the map T.

1.7 Appearance of Two Invariant Closed Curves (Heteroclinic Loop)

In this section we describe the mechanism that may be associated with the appearance/disappearance of two disjoint invariant closed curves, one attracting and one repelling. This mechanism has been investigated also in [7] and [2], where it was associated with a Neimark-Sacker bifurcation of subcritical type.

It is know that when the map T depends on two parameters, two invariant curves can coexist if a bifurcation of codimension 2 occurs, called *Chenciner bifurcation* or *generalized Hopf bifurcation*; see [32] for mathematical details, and [22] for an application in economics. When such a bifurcation occurs, in the parameter space a curve exists crossing which an attracting closed curve, Γ_s, and a repelling one, Γ_u, appear very close one to each other. The way in which they appear suggests a "saddle-node" bifurcation for closed invariant curves, but it is well known that such a bifurcation, although usual in continuous flows, is an exceptional case in discrete time. Here we shall present a sequence of global bifurcations which give rise to Γ_s and Γ_u and involves two cycles, one of which is a saddle. We shall qualitatively describe this sequence when a saddle cycle and a focus cycle exist, since this is the case effectively observed in our study, and we shall conclude with a conjecture about the situation in which the focus cycle is replaced by a node cycle.

As in the previous section, we start from a situation, shown in Fig.13a, in which only an attracting set A exists (a stable focus in Fig.13a). Moreover, we assume that a pair of cycles of period k, a saddle S and a repelling focus C, exist: The emergence of these two cycles can be due to a standard saddle-node bifurcation, and then the node cycle turns into a focus. The stable

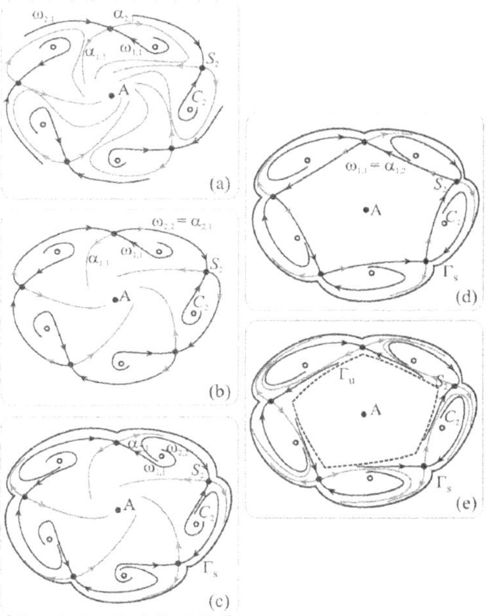

Figure 13: *Qualitative representation of a sequence of global bifurcations leading to the appearance of two closed invariant curves, one attracting and one repelling.*

set $W^S(S)$ of the saddle cycle is such that the outer branch $\omega_2 = \bigcup_{i=1}^{k} \omega_{2,i}$ comes from outside (the boundary of the set of feasible trajectories or from the basin boundary of coexisting attracting sets) whereas the α-limit set of the points of the inner one $\omega_1 = \bigcup_{i=1}^{k} \omega_{1,i}$ is the repelling focus C. The unstable set $W^U(S) = \bigcup_{i=1}^{k} (\alpha_{1,i} \cup \alpha_{2,i})$ reaches the attracting set A: Stated in other words, A is the ω-limit set of the points of the two branches $\alpha_{1,i}$ and $\alpha_{2,i}$, $i = 1, ..., k$. As the parameters are moved, the branches $\omega_2 = \bigcup_{i=1}^{k} \omega_{2,i}$ and $\alpha_2 = \bigcup_{i=1}^{k} \alpha_{2,i}$ are closer and closer and at the bifurcation they merge giving rise to a *heteroclinic loop* (see Fig.13b). More precisely, each stable branch $\omega_{2,i}$ of a periodic point of the saddle merges with the unstable branch $\alpha_{2,j}$ of a different periodic point of the same saddle cycle, giving rise to a closed connection among the periodic points of S. However, as already remarked, this transition may occur via a homoclinic tangle of $W_2^U(S)$ and $W_2^S(S)$, which includes a tangency between the two manifolds, followed by transverse crossings, and a tangency again of $W_2^U(S)$ and $W_2^S(S)$, as qualitatively shown in Fig.3.

After the bifurcation, originated by this structurally unstable situation, an attracting closed curve Γ_s exists as well as a saddle-focus connection made up by the stable set $W^S(S)$, surrounded by Γ_s (see Fig.13c). That a global bifurcation really occurred is proved by the changes in the asymptotic behaviors of the to branches involved in the heteroclinic loop, as it can be seen in the qualitative picture: After the bifurcation the stable set of the saddle constitutes a closed invariant curve (a repelling saddle-focus connection), which did not exist before the bifurcation, while the involved unstable branch of the saddle tends to A before the bifurcations and tends to the attracting closed curve Γ_s after. Thus *two invariant curves* exists after the bifurcation: An attracting one Γ_s and an unstable saddle-focus connection, and a multistability situation between the attracting set A and the closed curve Γ_s is created. Moreover, note that the unstable saddle-focus connection made up by the stable set of S, and connecting the periodic points of S and C, bounds the basin of attraction of A, and separates the two basins of attraction of A and Γ_s.

Such a bifurcation of the outer branches is often followed by a similar bifurcation of the inner ones. In fact, also the inner branches ω_1 of the stable set and α_1 of the unstable one approach each other (as some parameters are changed). At a new bifurcation, each stable branch $\omega_{1,i}$ of a periodic point of S merges with the unstable branch $\alpha_{1,j}$ of a different periodic point of the same saddle cycle, giving rise to a closed connection between the periodic points of S and the periodic points of the cycle C, shown in Fig.13d. The effect of this second *heteroclinic loop,* or more often homoclinic tangle, are shown in Fig.13e: A repelling closed curve Γ_u appears, replacing the saddle-focus connection (and replacing it in the role of separatrix between the basins of attraction of A and Γ_s). Once more, the occurrence of this global bifurcation can be checked observing the behavior of the branches α_1 and ω_1 involved in it.

Summarizing, we have seen that the coexistence of two closed invariant curves, one attracting and one repelling, in discrete maps can be achieved by a double mechanism: Starting from a repelling cycle and a saddle cycle, a first saddle connection (or tangle) causes the appearance of the attracting one associated with an (unstable) heteroclinic connection saddle - repelling cycle that plays the role of separatrix of basins, which is then replaced by the second closed curve, repelling, whose appearance is associated with a second saddle connection (or tangle).

The same mechanism can be observed starting with an attracting $k-$cycle (born together with a saddle), instead of a repelling one, i.e., a situation of bistability due to the coexistence of the attracting set A and a $k-$cycle C. In such a case the sequence of bifurcations takes place in a "reversed" way: First the appearance of a repelling closed curve Γ_u associated with a saddle-attracting cycle connection and then the appearance of an attracting closed curve, replacing the heteroclinic connection. We use the qualitative figure 14 to illustrate such a sequence. At the beginning, the attracting set A (a stable focus in Fig.14a) coexists with an attracting focus cycle C of period k, born as node cycle via saddle-node bifurcation together with a saddle cycle S of the same period. The stable set $W^S(S) = \bigcup_{i=1}^{k} (\omega_{1,i} \cup \omega_{2,i})$ of the saddle cycle separates the basins of attraction of the two attracting sets, A and the cycle C. The unstable set $W^U(S) = \bigcup_{i=1}^{k} (\alpha_{1,i} \cup \alpha_{2,i})$ reaches the attracting sets: More precisely, the outer branches $\alpha_{2,i}$ converge to the cycle C, whereas A is the ω-limit set of the points of the inner branches $\alpha_{1,i}$. Differently from the case previously analyzed, as some parameters are changed first the inner branches $\omega_1 = \bigcup_{i=1}^{k} \omega_{1,i}$ and $\alpha_1 = \bigcup_{i=1}^{k} \alpha_{1,i}$ approach each other, merging at the bifurcation so giving rise to a *heteroclinic loop*, (see Fig.14b), or heteroclinic tangle. This bifurcation gives rise to a repelling closed curve Γ_u (see Fig.14c) which is the α-limit set of the points of the branches $\omega_{1,i}$ of the stable set of the saddle S. Also the asymptotic behavior of the branches $\alpha_{1,i}$ is changed: Indeed with the branches $\alpha_{2,i}$ they give rise to a heteroclinic connection, reaching the periodic points of the attracting cycle C. The effect of this global bifurcation is a change in the basin of attraction of A: After the bifurcation it is bounded by the closed repelling curve Γ_u, so that it has been significantly reduced. Moreover another invariant closed curve exists, made up by the unstable set of the saddle S, which connects the points of the two $k-$cycles.

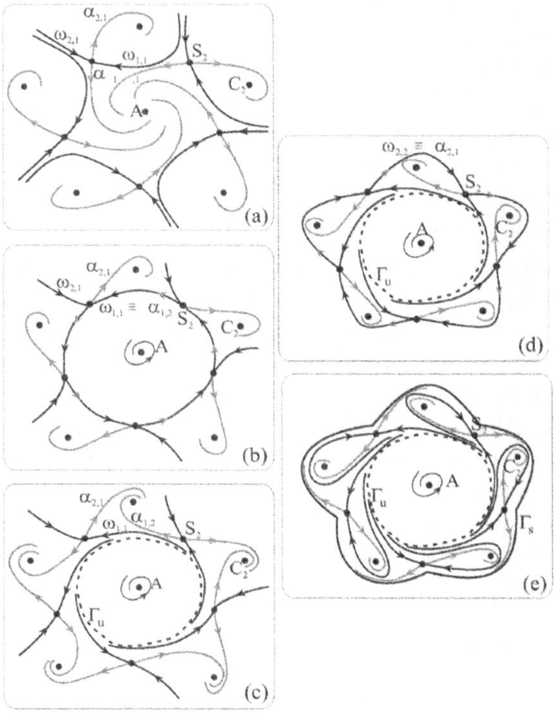

Figure 14: *Qualitative representation of a sequence of global bifurcations leading to the appearance of two repelling closed curves, one repelling and one attracting.*

Stronger effects on the dynamics are obtained after a second heteroclinic loop, made up by the merging of the outer branches, shown in Fig.14d. Indeed, after such a global bifurcation we obtain the coexistence of three attracting sets: The focus cycle C, the set A and an attracting closed curve Γ_s, whose appearance is associated with the heteroclinic loop, or tangle (see Fig.14e).

The repelling closed curve Γ_u bounds the basin of attraction of A; those of Γ_s and C are separated by the stable set of the saddle cycle S. The branches of the unstable set have as ω-limit set the closed curve Γ_s on one side, and the attracting cycle C on the other side.

We remark again that if the cycle involved in the global bifurcation together with the saddle is repelling (attracting) then the closed curve appearing after the first step is attracting (repelling), together with a repelling (attracting) saddle-connection. The second step involves the saddle-connection, after which two invariant closed curves still exist: We simply observe a change in their topological structure.

The global bifurcations arising when cycles and invariant closed curves coexist will be the topic of the next sections. Before that, let us observe that if the repelling (or attracting) focus, considered in our examples, is replaced by a repelling (or attracting) node, then the same sequence of bifurcations can occur and the two curves appear more close to each other. In Fig.15 a

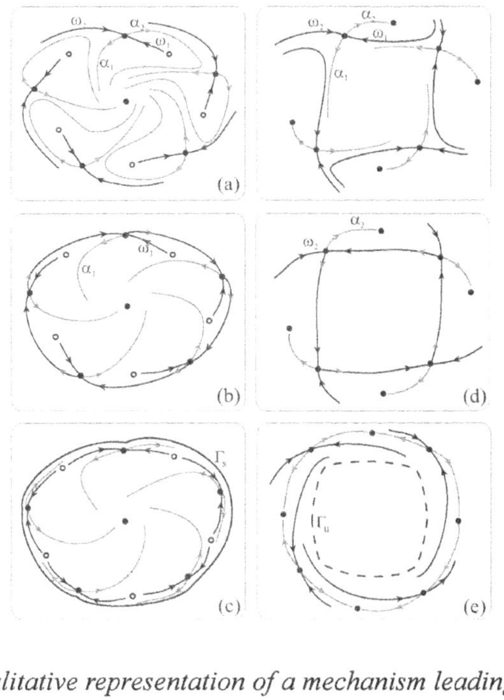

Figure 15: *Qualitative representation of a mechanism leading to two invariant closed curves associated either with a repelling node cycle* (a,b,c) *or an attracting node cycle* (d,e,f).

qualitative draft is given: Fig.15a-b-c refer to the repelling cycle whereas Fig.15d-e-f to the attracting one.

Moreover, if the node cycle is of very high period, then the saddle-node connection appearing at the first step looks like an invariant closed curve: In this case, the phase space recall in its shape that associated with a "saddle-node" bifurcation of invariant closed curves. It is for this reason that we propose this mechanism as a generic sequence of global bifurcations giving rise to two coexisting closed curves. More theoretical studies need to confirm such a conjecture.

1.8 Coexistence of Curves and Cycles and Their Interactions (Heteroclinic Loop)

In this section we show a mechanism that causes the transition from an attracting closed invariant curve, say Γ_a, with a pair of cycles of period k outside it, a saddle S and an attracting one, C, inside a wider attracting closed invariant curve, say Γ_b. This transition takes place via the occurrence of two heteroclinic loops of the saddle S, first with the merging of the unstable branches $W_1^U(S) = \cup\alpha_{1,i}$ and the stable ones $W_1^S(S) = \cup\omega_{1,i}$ and then via the merging of the unstable branches $W_2^U(S) = \cup\alpha_{2,i}$ and the stable ones $W_2^S(S) = \cup\omega_{2,i}$.

Similar bifurcation sequences have been observed in [4] and [5], associated with a two-dimensional map having a fixed point which may lose stability via a supercritical Neimark-Sacker bifurcation and a supercritical pitchfork or flip bifurcation. Examples in economic dynamic modelling can be found, for instance, among Kaldorian discrete-time models (see [11], [6]). Further examples are given in several chapters of this book.

Let us consider the situation described in Fig.16. In Fig.16a we have an attracting closed invariant curve Γ_a (which may also follow from the situation described in Fig.11-13), and a pair of cycles that have been created via a saddle-node bifurcation outside Γ_a. Such external cycles do not form an heteroclinic connection, whereas the stable set of the saddle S bounds the basin of attraction of the related attracting fixed points C_i of the map T^k. The unstable branches $\alpha_{1,i}$ of S_i tend to the attracting curve Γ_a, while the unstable branches $\alpha_{2,i}$ of S_i tend to the attracting cycle.

At the bifurcation (Fig.16b) we may have that the closed invariant curve Γ_a merges with the unstable branches $W_1^U(S) = \cup\alpha_{1,i}$ and with the stable ones $W_1^S(S) = \cup\omega_{1,i}$ as well, in a *heteroclinic loop*, or tangle, of the saddle S, causing the disappearance of the attracting closed invariant curve Γ_a, and leaving another closed invariant curve, see Fig.16c, which is now the heteroclinic connection involving the saddle S and the related attracting cycle C. After the bifurcation of the heteroclinic loop a closed curve still exists, but differently from Γ_a it includes the two cycles on it (Fig.16c).

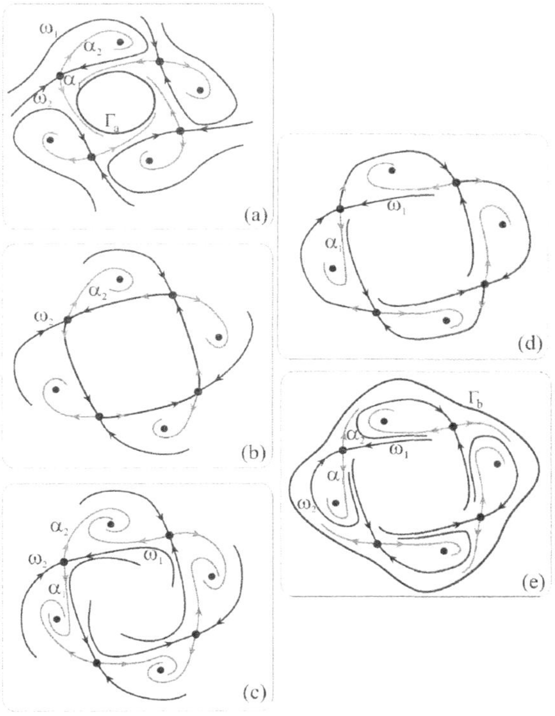

Figure 16: *Qualitative representation of a mechanism causing the transition from an attracting closed invariant curve into a wider one.*

Starting from this situation, a second heteroclinic loop (or tangle) may be formed. The heteroclinic connection turns into a heteroclinic loop in which the unstable branches $W_2^U(S) = \cup\alpha_{2,i}$ merge with the stable ones $W_2^S(S) = \cup\omega_{2,i}$ (see Fig.16d). After the bifurcation a new closed attracting curve exists, say Γ_b, and the two cycles are both inside Γ_b (Fig.16e). The stable set of the saddle S separates the basins of attraction of the k attracting fixed points C_i of the map T^k. The unstable branches $\cup\alpha_{1,i}$ tend to the attracting cycle while the unstable branches $\cup\alpha_{2,i}$ tend to Γ_b.

As mentioned before, in the case of discrete dynamical systems, the dynamic behaviors more frequently observed is such that the heteroclinic loop of Figs.16b-d are replaced by homoclinic tangles. That is, a tangency occurs between the two manifolds involved in the bifurcation, followed by transverse intersections and a tangency again on the opposite side, after which all the homoclinic points of the saddle S, existing during the tangle, are destroyed (several examples are shown in [4] and [5]).

It is worth noticing that all the unstable periodic points associated with the first homoclinic tangle, due to $W_1^U(S) \cap W_1^S(S) \neq \emptyset$, are in the region interior to the set of periodic points of the saddle S, whereas in the strange repellor associated with the second homoclinic tangle, in which $W_2^U(S) \cap W_2^S(S) \neq \emptyset$, all the unstable cycles are "outside" the saddle cycle S. The existence of a strange repellor has noticeable consequences with regard to the trajectories starting on the area occupied by it, since they are characterized by a long chaotic transient.

Notice also that before the first heteroclinic loop (tangle) of Fig.16 we have two distinct attracting sets: Γ_a and the stable $k-$cycle outside it; after the second one of Fig.16, we have again two distinct attractors: Γ_b, which is wider than Γ_a, and the $k-$cycle inside it, while between the two heteroclinic loops only one attractor may survive, that is the k-cycle.

It is plain that this process may be repeated many times. In fact, by a saddle-node bifurcation a new pair of cycles may appear outside Γ_b, so that we are again in the situation of Fig.16a, and the sequence of bifurcations described in Fig.16 may repeat.

We finally remark that the sequence of bifurcations here described, that cause the transition of a pair of cycles from outside to inside a closed invariant curve, may occur through different mechanisms when the map is noninvertible. In fact, in noninvertible maps the invariant curve may intersect the critical set LC_{-1}, and when this occurs the periodic points of a cycle may be part inside and part outside the closed invariant curve (see [36], [17]).

1.9 From an Invariant Closed Curve to Two Closed Curves (Double Homoclinic Loop)

The last case we consider in this chapter is an example of double homoclinic loop that involves a repelling closed curve Γ_u and a saddle point S. Two attracting sets, A_i, $i = 1, 2$, are also coexisting, or cyclical ones. The repelling closed invariant curve Γ_u surrounds the two attracting sets A_i and the saddle S. The stable set of S, $W^S(S)$, formed by the union of the preimages of any rank of the local stable set, turns around infinitely many times approaching the repelling curve Γ_u, as qualitatively shown in Fig.17a. $W^S(S)$ constitutes the boundary that separates the basins of A_1 and A_2. As the parameters are varied along the bifurcation path, the repelling closed invariant curve Γ_u shrinks in the proximity of the saddle S, and consequently the stable and unstable sets of the saddle approach each other, until Γ_u disappears or, more precisely, *becomes a chaotic repellor at the homoclinic tangency* (see Fig.17b) at which the unstable set of S, $W^U(S)$, has a contact with the stable one.

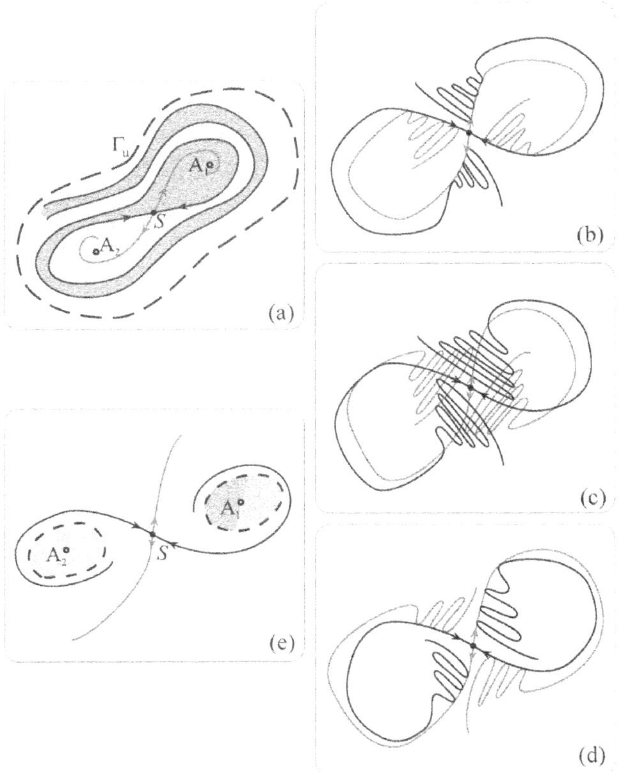

Figure 17: *Qualitative representation of a mechanism causing the transition from an invariant closed curve to two closed curves.*

This homoclinic tangency is followed by a transverse intersections of the two manifolds, $W^U(S)$ and $W^S(S)$, and a dynamic scenario like the one shown in Fig.17c is obtained, which is followed by another homoclinic

tangency (see Fig.17d) leading to the disappearance of all the homoclinic orbits of S and of the chaotic repellor. After this second tangency, $W^U(S)$ is completely outside of the stable set, so that the stable and unstable sets are again disjoint, $W^U(S) \cap W^S(S) = \emptyset$, and the preimages of the local stable manifolds reach *two disjoint closed invariant curves which have been created around the two attracting sets* A_i, see Fig.17e.
If the map is symmetric with respect to the saddle S then the homoclinic tangencies of the manifolds occur at the same time (an example of business cycle model leading to such a bifurcation can be found in Chapter 8). In the case of a map without symmetry properties, we still may have a transition from the situation of Fig.17(a) to that of Fig.17(e), but the two homoclinic loops may occur separately, that is, first the manifolds $W_1^U(S)$ and $W_1^S(S)$ are involved and then $W_2^U(S)$ and $W_2^S(S)$, or vice-versa (an example of business cycle model leading to such a bifurcation can be seen in Chapter 11).

References

[1] Abraham, R., and Ueda, Y., (Eds.), 2000, *The Chaos Avant Garde. Memories of the early days of chaos theory*, World Scientific.

[2] Agliari, A., 2005, "Homoclinic connections and subcritical Neimark bifurcations in a duopoly model with adaptively adjusted productions", *Chaos Solitons & Fractals* (to appear).

[3] Agliari, A., Bischi, G.I., and Gardini, L., 2002, "Some methods for the Global Analysis of Dynamic Games represented by Noninvertible Maps", Chapter 3 in *Oligopoly and Complex Dynamics: Tools & Models*, T. Puu and I. Sushko (eds.), Springer Verlag.

[4] Agliari, A., Bischi, G.I., Dieci, R., and Gardini, L., 2005, "Global Bifurcations of Closed Invariant Curves in Two-Dimensional maps: A computer assisted study", *International Journal of Bifurcation and Chaos* 15(4), pp. 1285-1328.

[5] Agliari, A., Bischi, G.I., Dieci, R., and Gardini, L., 2005, "Homoclinic tangles associated with closed invariant curves in families of 2D maps", (Grazer Math. Ber. *submitted*).

[6] Agliari, A., Dieci, R., and Gardini, L., 2005, "Homoclinic tangle in Kaldor's like business cycle models", *Journal of Economic Behavior and Organization* (to appear).

[7] Agliari, A., Gardini, L., and Puu, T., 2005, "Some global bifurcations related to the appearance of closed invariant curves", *Mathematics and Computers in Simulation* , vol.68/3, pp. 201-219.

[8] Agliari, A., Gardini, L., and Puu, T., 2006, "Global bifurcation in duopoly when the fixed point is destabilized via a subcritical Neimark bifurcation", *International Game Theory Review*, vol.8 n.1, in press.

[9] Bai-Lin, H., 1989, *Elementary Symbolic Dynamics*, World Scientific, Singapore.

[10] Birkhoff, G.D., and Smith, P., 1928, "Structure analysis of surface transformations", *Journal de Mathematique* S9(7), pp. 345-379.

[11] Bischi, G.I., Dieci, R., Rodano, G., and Saltari, E., 2001, "Multiple attractors and global bifurcations in a Kaldor-type business cycle model", *Journal of Evolutionary Economics* 11, pp. 527-554.

[12] Bischi, G.I, and Kopel, M., 2001, "Equilibrium Selection in a Nonlinear Duopoly Game with Adaptive Expectations", *Journal of Economic Behavior and Organization*, vol. 46/1, pp. 73-100.

[13] Bischi, G.I., Gardini, L., and Kopel, M., 2000, "Analysis of Global Bifurcations in a Market Share Attraction Model", *Journal of Economic Dynamics and Control*, 24, pp. 855-879.

[14] Brock, W.A., and Hommes, C.H., 1997, "A Rational Route to Randomness", *Econometrica* 65, pp. 1059-1095.

[15] de Melo, W., and van Strien, S., 1991, *One-Dimensional Dynamics*, Springer-Verlag, Berlin Heidelberg New York.

[16] Devaney, R.L., 1987, *An Introduction to Chaotic Dynamical Systems*, The Benjamin/Cummings Publishing Co., Menlo Park, California.

[17] Frouzakis, C.E., Gardini, L., Kevrekidis, I.G., Millerioux, G., and Mira, C., 1997, "On some properties of invariant sets of two-dimensional noninvertible maps", *International Journal of Bifurcation and Chaos*, 7(6), pp. 1167-1194.

[18] Feudel, U., Safonova, M.A., Kurths, J., and Anishchenko, V.S., 1996, "On the destruction of three-dimensional tori", *International Journal of Bifurcation and Chaos*, 6, pp. 1319-1332.

[19] Gardini, L., 1994, "Homoclinic bifurcations in n-dimensional endomorphisms, due to expanding periodic points", *Nonlinear Analysis*, 23(8), pp. 1039-1089.

[20] Gavrilov, N.K., and Shilnikov, L.P., 1972a, "On three dimensional dynamical systems close to systems with structurally unstable homoclinic curve I", *Mat. USSR Sbornik,* 17, pp. 467-485.

[21] Gavrilov, N.K., and Shilnikov, L.P., 1972b, "On three dimensional dynamical systems close to systems with structurally unstable homoclinic curve II", *Mat. USSR Sbornik,*19, pp. 139-156.

[22] Gaunersdorfer, A., Hommes, C.H., and Wagener, F.O.O., 2003, "Bifurcation Routes to Volatility Clustering under Evolutionary Learning ", CeNDEF Working paper 03-10 University of Amsterdam.

[23] Gabisch, G., and Lorenz, H.W., 1989, *Business Cycle Theory*, 2nd ed. Springer-Verlag, Berlin Heidelberg New York.

[24] Guckenheimer, J., and Holmes, P., 1983, *Nonlinear Oscillations, Dynamical Systems, and Bifurcations of Vector Fields*, Springer-Verlag (New York).

[25] Gumonwski, I., and Mira, C., 1980, *Dynamique Chaotique. Transition ordre-desordre*, Cepadues:Toulouse.

[26] Gumowski I., and Mira C., 1980, *Recurrences and discrete dynamic systems*, Lecture notes in Mathematics, Springer.

[27] Herman, M., 1979, "Sur la conjugaison différentiable de difféomorphismes du cercle à des rotations", Publ. Math.I.H.E.S. 49, pp. 5-233.

[28] Iooss, G., 1979, *Bifurcation of Maps and Applications*, North-Holland Publishing Company, Amsterdam.

[29] Iooss, G., and Joseph, D.D., 1980, *Elementary Stability and Bifurcation Theory*, Springer-Verlag (New York).

[30] Kind, C., 1999, "Remarks on the economic interpretation of Hopf bifurcations", *Economic Letters* 62, pp. 147-154.

[31] Kozlovski, O., Pintus, P., van Strien, S., and de Vilder, R., 2004, "Business-Cycle Models and the Dangers of Linearizing", *Journal of Optimization Theory and Applications*, forthcoming.

[32] Kuznetsov, Y.A., 2003, *Elements of Applied Bifurcation Theory*, Springer-Verlag (New York).

[33] Medio, A., 1979, *Teoria Nonlineare del Ciclo Economico*, Il Mulino, Bologna.

[34] Medio, A., 1998, "Nonlinear dynamics and chaos part I: A geometrical approach" *Macroeconomic Dynamics*, 2, pp. 505–532.

[35] Mira, C., 1987, *Chaotic Dynamics. From the one-dimensional endomorphism to the two-dimensional noninvertible maps*, World Scientific, Singapore.

[36] Mira, C., Gardini, L., Barugola, A., and Cathala, J.C., 1996, *Chaotic Dynamics in Two-Dimensional Noninvertible Maps*, World Scientific, Singapore.

[37] Palis, J., and Takens, F., 1994, *Hyperbolicity and Sensitive Chaotic Dynamics at Homoclinic Bifurcations*, Cambridge University Press, Cambridge.

[38] Pintus, P., Sands, D., and de Vilder, R., 2000, "On the transition from local regular to global irregular fluctuations", *Journal of Economic Dynamics & Control* 24, pp. 247-272.

[39] Puu, T., 2000, *Attractors, Bifurcations and Chaos*, Springer-Verlag, Berlin Heidelberg New York.

[40] Sharkovsky, A.N. , Kolyada, S.F., Sivak, A.G. and Fedorenko, V.V., 1997, *Dynamics of One-Dimensional Maps*, Kluer Academic Publishers, London.

[41] Thunberg, H., 2001, "Periodicity versus chaos in one-dimensional dynamics", *SIAM Review*, 43(1), pp. 3-30.

[42] Wiggins, S., 1988, *Global Bifurcations and Chaos, Analytical Methods*, Springer Verlag, New York.

2 Center Bifurcation for a Two-Dimensional Piecewise Linear Map

Iryna Sushko and Laura Gardini

2.1 Introduction

It is already well known that the main bifurcation scenario which can be realized considering a business cycle model in dynamic context, is related to a fixed point losing stability with a pair of complex-conjugate eigenvalues. In the case in which such a model is discrete and defined by some smooth nonlinear functions, the Neimark-Sacker bifurcation theorem can be used, described in the previous chapter. While for piecewise linear, or piecewise smooth, functions which are also quite often used for business cycle modeling, the bifurcation theory is much less developed. The purpose of this chapter is to describe a so-called *center bifurcation* occurring in a family of two-dimensional piecewise linear maps whose dynamic properties are, to our knowledge, not well known. Namely, we shall see that in some similarity to the Neimark-Sacker bifurcation occurring for smooth maps, for piecewise linear maps the bifurcation of stability loss of a fixed point with a pair of complex-conjugate eigenvalues on the unit circle can also result in the appearance of a closed invariant attracting curve homeomorphic to a circle. However, differently from what occurs in the smooth case, the closed invariant curve is not a smooth, but a piecewise linear set, appearing not in a neighborhood of the fixed point, as it may be very far from it. In fact, we shall see that the position of the closed invariant curve depends on the distance of the fixed point from the boundary of the region in which the linear map is defined (i.e., from what we shall call critical line LC_{-1}).

We shall describe the global dynamics of a piecewise linear map at the moment of the center bifurcation and after it, comparing the cases in which the map is invertible and noninvertible. For this study we consider a family of two-dimensional piecewise linear maps $F : \mathbb{R}^2 \to \mathbb{R}^2$ given by

$$F : (x, y) \mapsto \begin{cases} F_1(x, y), (x, y) \in R_1; \\ F_2(x, y), (x, y) \in R_2; \end{cases} \tag{1}$$

where

$$\begin{aligned} F_1 &: \begin{pmatrix} x \\ y \end{pmatrix} \mapsto \begin{pmatrix} (c+a)x - ay \\ x \end{pmatrix}, \\ R_1 &= \{(x, y) : y \le x + d/a\}; \end{aligned}$$

$$\begin{aligned} F_2 &: \begin{pmatrix} x \\ y \end{pmatrix} \mapsto \begin{pmatrix} cx - d + b(x + d/a - y) \\ x \end{pmatrix}, \\ R_2 &= \{(x, y) : y > x + d/a\}. \end{aligned}$$

For convenience, as it will be explained below, we shall assume that the real parameters a, b, c and d satisfy the following conditions:

$$a > 0, \ -(c+1)/2 < b < 1, \ 0 < c < 1, \ d > 0. \tag{2}$$

Our choice of the map F is due to the fact that for $b = 0$ it is a piecewise linear Hicksian multiplier-accelerator model with a lower constraint d, called 'floor', introduced in Chapter 3 and described also in Chapter 6 (the case in which an upper constraint, called 'ceiling', is not involved in asymptotic dynamics). As we shall see, in such a case we have a particular kind of noninvertibility in which a whole half-plane R_2 is mapped into one straight line, so that the map is of so-called $(Z_0 - Z_\infty - Z_1)$ type. While for $b \neq 0$ the map F can be either invertible (for $b > 0$), or noninvertible (for $b < 0$) of $(Z_0 - Z_2)$ type, so that we can compare the results of the center bifurcation in these cases.

The map F is given by two linear maps F_1 and F_2 defined, respectively, below and above the straight line

$$LC_{-1} = \{(x, y) : y = x + d/a\}.$$

The image of this line by F is called *critical line LC or LC_0*:

$$LC_0 = F(LC_{-1}) = \{(x, y) : y = (x + d)/c\},$$

and its image $LC_i = F^i(LC_0)$, $i = 1, ...$, which is a curve made up by a finite number of linear segments, is also called *critical line* (of higher rank).

Although this notation is more properly used when the map is noninvertible, we keep it in any case. As stated above, invertibility is controlled by the parameter b. For $b > 0$ a point on the right of LC has a unique rank-1 preimage by F_1^{-1} (giving a point in R_1), while a point on the left of LC has a unique rank-1 preimage by F_2^{-1} (giving a point in R_2). Instead, for $b < 0$ a point on the left of LC has no rank-1 preimage, while a point on the right of LC has two distinct rank-1 preimages: One preimage by F_1^{-1} (giving a point in R_1), and the other by F_2^{-1} (giving a point in R_2).

The map F has a unique fixed point $(x^*, y^*) = (0, 0)$ which is the fixed point of the map F_1, while the fixed point of the map F_2 belongs to the main diagonal of the phase plane, which is in R_1, so that it is not a fixed point of F. Using eigenvalues $\lambda_{1,2}$ of the Jacobian matrix of the map F_1, given by

$$\lambda_{1,2} = (a + c \pm \sqrt{(a + c)^2 - 4a})/2, \tag{3}$$

we get that for the parameter range given in (2) the fixed point (x^*, y^*) is attracting for $a < 1$ and repelling for $a > 1$, being a node for $(c + a)^2 > 4a$ and a focus for $(c + a)^2 < 4a$.

Thus, in the range (2) the fixed point loses stability at $a = 1$ with a pair of complex-conjugate eigenvalues crossing the unit circle, so that a *center bifurcation* occurs, which is the main interest of the present chapter. It is clear that in a piecewise linear map the local bifurcation of a fixed point depends only on a corresponding linear map (here F_1), while the global behavior in the phase space depends on the interaction between the other linear maps (which may give rise to any kind of dynamics). In our case, in the region R_2 the map F_2 is defined, so that although the map F has no fixed points in that region, the eigenvalues of F_2, say $\mu_{1,2}$, are important in the global behavior of F. We have

$$\mu_{1,2} = (b + c \pm \sqrt{(b + c)^2 - 4b})/2,$$

so that for $0 < c < 1$ the fixed point of the linear map F_2 is:

- a repelling node for $(c + b)^2 > 4b$ and $b > 1$;
- an attracting node for $(c + b)^2 > 4b$ and $-(c + 1)/2 < b < 1$;
- a flip saddle for $b < -(c + 1)/2$;
- a focus for $(c + b)^2 < 4b$, attracting for $0 < b < 1$ and repelling for $b > 1$.

Here we are interested in the study of the dynamics after the center bifurcation of (x^*, y^*), when the fixed point is an unstable focus and the dynamics are bounded. To this purpose we restrict our analysis to the range of b for which the fixed point of the map F_2 is stable, that is $-(c+1)/2 < b < 1$. Indeed, when the fixed point of the map F_2 is unstable we may have divergent trajectories: If, for example, $b > 1$, then for $a > 1$ (when the fixed point of F is unstable), we have only divergent dynamics, because the two linear maps are both expanding, so that any combination of the two maps is also expanding and no stable cycle can exist. Also for $b < -(c+1)/2$, when the fixed point of the map F_2 is a flip saddle (i.e., with one negative eigenvalue), we may have both bounded and unbounded trajectories. This explains our choice of the parameter range given in (2).

It is clear that when the fixed point (x^*, y^*) of F is stable then it is *globally stable* (because for the range (2) the two linear maps are both contracting, so that any combination of the two maps is also contracting and a repelling cycle cannot exist). While when the fixed point (x^*, y^*) of F is unstable ($a > 1$) we can have bounded dynamics only as long as it is a focus, i.e. for $(c+a)^2 < 4a$ (because when it is a repelling node then all the trajectories are divergent, except for the fixed point).

As remarked above, at $a = 1$ the fixed point (x^*, y^*) undergoes the center bifurcaiton, and the dynamic behavior occurring at this particular bifurcation value is described in the next section. We shall see that independently on the sign of b (invertible or non invertible map) and independently on the type of eigenvalues of the linear map F_2, the map F admits an invariant region, whose size depends on the distance of the fixed point from the critical lines. We shall also comment the global behavior of F (i.e. the dynamics of points outside the invariant region). Then, in the next sections, we shall describe the global behavior of F after the center bifurcation, showing that only the boundary of the region remains invariant, being an attracting closed curve $\mathcal{C}$, and the dynamics of F on $\mathcal{C}$ are either periodic, or quasiperiodic, depending on parameters.

2.2 Dynamics at the Bifurcation Value ($a = 1$)

In this section we first describe the phase portrait of the map F exactly at the bifurcation value $a = 1$. In such a case the fixed point (x^*, y^*) is locally a center: The map F_1 is defined by a rotation matrix (whose determinant equals 1), and it is characterized by a rotation number which may be rational, say m/n, or irrational, say ρ. It is clear that locally, in some neighborhood the fixed point, the behavior of F is that of the linear map F_1, thus we have a region filled with invariant ellipses, each point of which is either periodic of period n (in case of a rational rotation number m/n) or quasiperiodic (in case of an irrational rotation number ρ). Now the problem we are faced on is to answer the following questions: How big is this region? What is its boundary? What occurs to points outside it? We answer distinguishing the two different cases on the kind of rotation number (rational or irrational).

The invariant region we are looking for clearly is completely included in the region R_1 (i.e., the region of definition for F_1), and it is given by the set of points of R_1 whose trajectories entirely belong to R_1. Thus it must include all the ellipses (invariant for F_1) which are completely included in R_1, so that such a region must necessarily include a region bounded by an invariant ellipse which is tangent to the straight line LC_{-1}. So we can immediately answer to some of the previous questions in the case of an irrational rotation number.

If F_1 is defined by a rotation matrix with an irrational rotation number ρ, which holds for $a = 1$, and

$$c = c_\rho \stackrel{def}{=} 2\cos(2\pi\rho) - 1, \tag{4}$$

then any point from some neighborhood of the fixed point is quasiperiodic, and all the points of the same quasiperiodic orbit are dense on the invariant ellipse to which they belong. (Note that for $c > 0$ we have $\rho < 1/6$). In such a case an invariant region Q exists in the phase space, bounded by an invariant ellipse $\mathcal{E}$ of the map F_1, tangent to LC_{-1}, and, thus, also tangent to LC_i, $i = 0, 1, ...$ We can state the following

Proposition 1. *Let $a = 1$, $c = c_\rho$ given in (4). Then in the phase space of the map F there exists an invariant region Q, bounded by an invariant ellipse $\mathcal{E}$ of the map F_1 tangent to LC_{-1}. Any initial point $(x_0, y_0) \in Q$ belongs to a quasiperiodic orbit dense in the corresponding invariant ellipse of F_1.*

Fig.1 shows the invariant region Q of the map F at $a = 1$, $c = 0.4$, $d = 10$. (Indeed, because of numerical precision, we cannot show a true quasiperiodic case, but only its approximation by a periodic case of some high period).

It is clear that such a region also exists (i.e., the region Q defined above) and is invariant, when the map F_1 is defined by a rotation matrix with a rational rotation number, but in such a case Q is not the largest invariant area. In fact, there are also other points outside the tangent ellipse $\mathcal{E}$ which

are periodic with an orbit completely included in the region R_1. For the sake of clarity we shall show this via an example.
So let F_1 be defined by a rotation matrix with a rational rotation number, which holds for $a = 1$, and

$$c = c_{m/n} \stackrel{def}{=} 2\cos(2\pi m/n) - 1, \tag{5}$$

obtained from $\mathrm{Re}\,\lambda_{1,2} = \cos(2\pi m/n)$, then any point in some neighborhood of the fixed point is periodic with rotation number m/n and all the points of the same periodic orbit are located on an invariant ellipse[1].

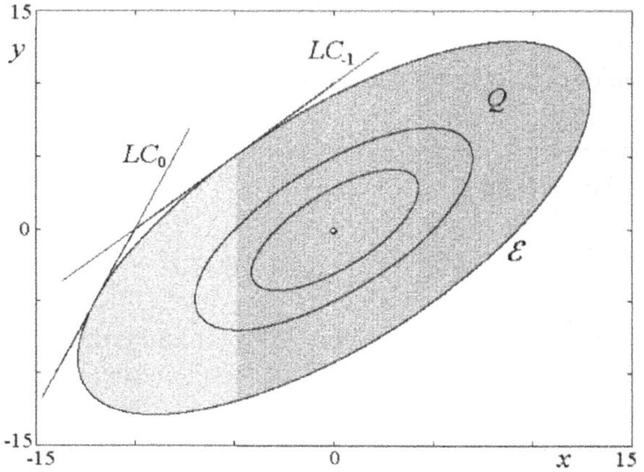

Figure 1: *The invariant region Q of the map F at $a = 1$, $c = 0.4$, $d = 10$. F_1 is associated with an irrational rotation number.*

For short we call *m/n-cycle* a periodic orbit of period n with the rotation number m/n. We can construct the invariant region, say P, existing for $a = 1$ in the phase space by using as an example the case $m/n = 2/13$ (see Fig.2). As noticed above, the region P must include all the invariant ellipses of the map F_1 which are entirely located in the region R_1. That is, P includes a region bounded by an invariant ellipse, say $\mathcal{E}_1$, tangent to LC_{-1}. However there are other periodic orbits belonging to R_1 : Note that there exists a segment $S_1 \subset LC_{-1}$, which we call *generating segment*, such that its end points belong to the same m/n-cycle $p = \{p_1, ..., p_n\}$ located on an invariant ellipse of F_1 which crosses LC_{-1}, denoted $\mathcal{E}_2$ (note that $\mathcal{E}_2$ is

[1]Note that for $c > 0$ we have $m/n < 1/6$.

not invariant for the map F). In our example $S_1 = [p_1, p_7] \subset LC_{-1}$, and $p = \{p_1, ..., p_{13}\}$ is the corresponding 2/13-cycle. Obviously, the generating segment S_1 and its images by F_1, that is the segments $S_{i+1} = F_1(S_i)$, $S_{i+1} \subset LC_{i-1} = F_1(LC_{i-2})$, $i = 1, ..., 12$, form an invariant polygon P with 13 edges completely included in the region R_1, inscribed in $\mathcal{E}_2$ and whose boundary is tangent to $\mathcal{E}_1$.

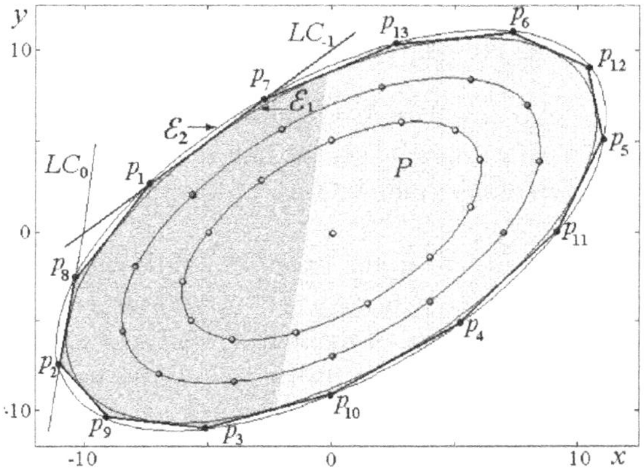

Figure 2: *The invariant polygon* P *of the map* F *at* $a = 1$, $c = 2\cos(2\pi m/n) - 1$, $d = 10$ *and* $m/n = 2/13$, *so that* F_1 *is defined by a rotation matrix with the rotation number* $2/13$.

Such a polygon P can be constructed for any rotation number m/n. Summarizing we can state the following

Proposition 2. *Let* $a = 1$, $c = c_{m/n}$ *given in (5). Then in the phase space of the map* F *there exists an invariant polygon* P *with* n *edges whose boundary is made up by a 'generating segment'* $S_1 \subset LC_{-1}$ *and its* $n-1$ *images* $S_{i+1} = F_1(S_i) \subset LC_{i-1}$, $i = 1, ..., n-1$. *Any initial point* $(x_0, y_0) \in P$ *is periodic with rotation number* m/n.

To end our description of the dynamics at the bifurcation value $a = 1$, we have to clarify the behavior of a trajectory with an initial point (x_0, y_0) which does not belong to the invariant region (either P or Q). It is easy to see that there are the following possibilities:

- If $b = 0$ then the eigenvalues of the Jacobian matrix of F_2 are $\mu_1 = c$, $\mu_2 = 0$, so that any initial point $(x_0, y_0) \in R_2$ is mapped by F_2 in one step into a point of the straight line LC_0. Then in the case of a rational rotation number it is mapped in a finite number of steps exactly to the boundary of the invariant region P, and ultimately it will be periodic, while in case of an irrational rotation number the generic trajectory tends to the boundary of the invariant region Q.

- For $0 < b < 1$ the fixed point of the map F_2 is an attracting node, the map F is invertible and, thus, the trajectory of any point $(x_0, y_0) \in R_2$ is attracted to the boundary of the invariant region.
- If $-(c+1)/2 < b < 0$ then F_2 is a noninvertible map with an attracting fixed point in R_1. It can be shown that $(x_0, y_0) \in R_2$ is mapped in a finite number of steps to the interior of the invariant region.

We already remarked that in the case $b > 1$ the fixed point of the map F_2 is either a repelling focus (for $(c+b)^2 < 4b$), or a repelling node (for $(c+b)^2 > 4b$), and a trajectory of the map F with initial point (x_0, y_0) not belonging to the invariant region is divergent. While for $b < -(c+1)/2$, the fixed point of F_2 is a flip saddle, and in such a case there may be initial points having divergent trajectories as well as points mapped to the interior of the invariant region. However, as already noticed above, the following consideration is restricted to the range $-(c+1)/2 < b < 1$, so that the fixed point of F_2 is attracting.

The dynamics of the map F at the bifurcation value considered in this section give the name to the *center bifurcation*, and we notice again that the magnitude of the invariant area (P or Q) depends on the distance of the fixed point from the critical line. But we are mainly interested in the description of what occurs 'after', for $a > 1$: We shall see that an invariant region survives after the bifurcation, that is for $a = 1+\varepsilon$ for some sufficiently small $\varepsilon > 0$. However, among all the infinitely many invariant curves existing at the bifurcation only one survives, modified, after the bifurcation: The one which is farthest from the fixed point and gives the boundary of the invariant region. That is, the boundary of the 'old' invariant region is transformed into an attracting closed invariant curve on which the dynamics of F is reduced to a rotation with rational or irrational rotation number.

2.3 Noninvertibility of $(Z_0 - Z_\infty - Z_1)$ Type $(a > 1, b = 0)$

In order to investigate what occurs after the center bifurcation, for $a > 1$, we consider first the map F given in (1) at $b = 0$. It was already mentioned that in such a case any initial point $(x_0, y_0) \in R_2$ is mapped by F_2 in one step into a point of the critical line LC_0. All consequent iterations by F_2 give points on this straight line approaching the attracting fixed point of F_2 (which belongs to R_1), until the trajectory enters R_1 where the map F_1 is applied. Then the trajectory begins to rotate in the couterclockwise direction, moving away from the unstable focus (x^*, y^*), and in a finite number of iterations it enters the region R_2 where the map F_2 is applied again. Thus, for an orbit the map F_2 plays the role of a return mechanism to the region R_1, and the dynamics are bounded, as longs as the fixed point of F is a focus. Moreover, due to the zero eigenvalue of the map F_2, the dynamics of F are reduced to a one-dimensional subset C of the phase space which is obtained iterating a suitable segment of LC_{-1}. It is easy to see that after a finite number of iterations of LC_{-1} we necessarily get a closed area whose boundary is a closed invariant curve. An example is shown in Fig.3: The closed invariant curve C is obtained by 7 iterations of the segment $[a_0, b_0]$ of $LC_{-1} : C = \cup_{i=1}^{7} F^i([a_0, b_0]))$.

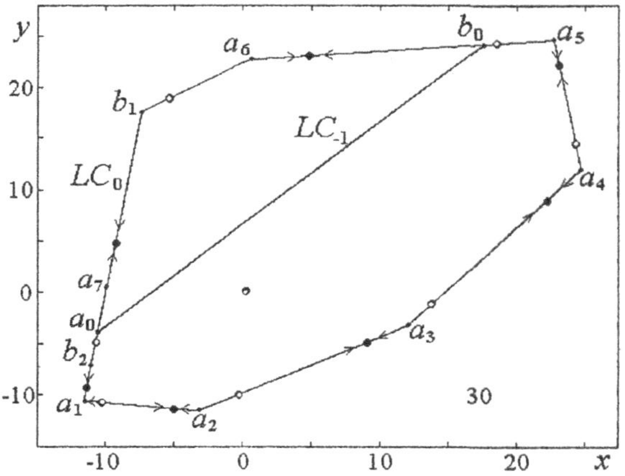

Figure 3: *The attracting closed invariant curve C of the map F at* $a = 1.5$, $b = 0$, $c = 0.15$, $d = 10$. *Points of the attracting and saddle cycles of period 7 are shown by black and white circles, respectively.*

It is clear that any point with initial condition in R_1, except for the fixed point, has a trajectory which spirals away from the fixed point and enters the region R_2 in a finite number of steps, then application of F_2 gives a point of LC_0, which in a finite number of iterations is mapped into a point of the segment $[a_1, b_1]$ of LC_0. This proves that the closed curve C is globally attracting for F, except for the fixed point.

We are now interested in the dynamics of F on C. First note that the map F is orientation preserving on C: It can be easily shown that for any three ordered points $u, v, w \in C$, their images by F are ordered in the same way on C. It follows that we cannot have any folding which means that the restriction of F on C is invertible and, thus, chaotic dynamics are impossible (indeed, it becomes possible in the case $c < 0$ when there are segments of C which are folded, but we don't consider this case here). Therefore, we conclude that the dynamics of F on C are either periodic, or quasiperiodic. If F has an attracting cycle of period n, it has also a saddle cycle of the same period. Fig.3 shows an attracting cycle (node) and a saddle cycle of period 7, and we remark the double meaning of the closed invariant curve: It is the saddle-connection made up of the closure of the unstable set of the saddle (approaching the points of the node), and also the union of a finite number of critical segments. However, in a certain sense the phase portrait of the map F at $a > 1$ is similar to that of a smooth map after the Neimark-Sacker bifurcation: Namely, there exists a closed invariant attracting curve C on which the map F is reduced to a rotation with rational or irrational rotation number. In contrast to the smooth case, for the map F such a curve is not smooth, but piecewise linear, and it appears not in the neighborhood of the fixed point, but far enough from it: Its location depends on the position of the critical line LC_0.

The considerations given above can be summarized as follows:

Proposition 3. *Let $a > 1, b = 0, (c+a)^2 < 4a$. Then in the phase space of the map F there exists a globally attracting invariant closed curve C which is a broken line made up by a finite number of images of a segment belonging to LC_{-1}. The dynamics of F on C are either periodic, or quasiperiodic.*

Fig.4 shows a two-dimensional bifurcation diagram in the (a, c) - parameter plane in which the regions corresponding to different attracting cycles of period $n \leq 32$ are shown by different gray tonalities. If the (a, c) - parameter point belongs to an n-periodicity region, then the map F has an attracting and saddle cycles of period n, located on an attracting closed invariant curve, as stated in proposition 3.

Let us give some comments on the structure of the bifurcation diagram shown in Fig.4. Similar bifurcation diagrams for piecewise linear and piecewise smooth dynamical systems were described in Gallegati *et al.*, 2003,

Hao Bai-Lin, 1998, Sushko *et al.*, 2003, Zhusubaliyev and Mosekilde, 2003. We can note that locally, near the bifurcation line $a = 1$, the periodicity regions look like the Arnol'd tongues described for smooth maps when the Neimark-Sacker bifurcation occurs (although the dynamics are different in the phase space).

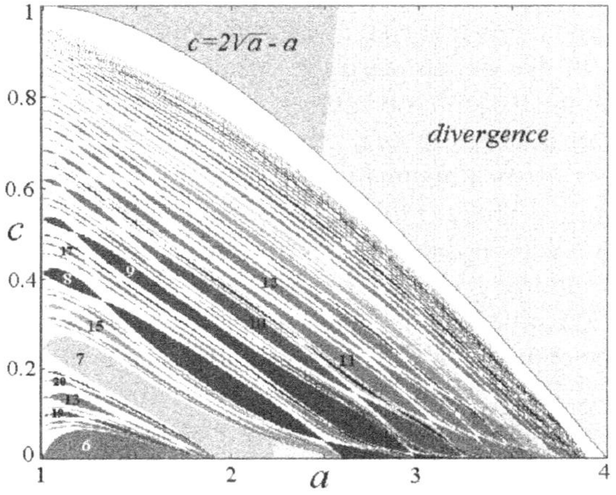

Figure 4: *Two-dimensional bifurcation diagram of the map* F *in the* (a, c)*-parameter plane at* $b = 0$, $d = 10$. *Regions corresponding to attracting cycles of different periods* $n \leq 32$ *are shown by various gray tonalities.*

It is worth to note that the summation rule which holds for the rotation numbers in the general case with smooth maps, also holds in the piecewise linear case. That is, if m_1/n_1 and m_2/n_2 are two rotation numbers associated with the parameter c_1 and c_2, respectively, at $a = 1$, then also the rotation number $(m_1 + m_2)/(n_1 + n_2)$ exists in between. The white region in Fig.4 is related either to attracting cycles of higher period $n > 32$, or to quasiperiodic trajectories. Indeed, similar to the smooth case, the parameter values corresponding to quasiperiodic trajectories form curves located between the two nearest periodicity regions and issuing from the bifurcation line $a = 1$ at points corresponding to irrational rotation numbers. The so-called 'sausage' structure of the periodicity regions with several subregions is typical for piecewise smooth and piecewise linear systems (see, e.g., Hao Bai-Lin, 1998, Sushko *et al.*, 2003, Zhusubaliyev and Mosekilde, 2003). In fact, different subregions of the same periodicity region of the map F are related to different compositions of the maps F_1 and F_2 which are applied to get the corresponding cycle (attracting or saddle).

The difference between two-dimensional bifurcation diagrams for a piecewise linear and a smooth map in the case of a center bifurcation or Neimark-Sacker bifurcation, respectively, consists not only in the qualitative shape of the periodicity regions (the 'sausage' structure mentioned above), but also in the kind of bifurcations associated with the boundaries of these regions. It is known that in the smooth case the Arnol'd tongues are bounded by curves corresponding to saddle-node bifurcation and either period-doubling, or Neimark-Sacker bifurcation occurring for the related cycle. While for piecewise linear maps such boundaries are related to *border-collision bifurcations* (see Nusse and Yorke, 1992). In the next section we describe the special case associated with the bifurcation value $a = 1$, while here we describe those associated with the boundaries of the regions for $a > 1$. The border-collision bifurcation, related to the boundary of a periodicity region, involves the merging of the corresponding attracting and saddle cycles, similar to the smooth saddle-node bifurcation, but it is not related to one eigenvalue which become in modulus equal to 1. Instead, it is related to a collision of points of these cycles with the critical line LC_{-1}, i.e. the border separating the regions of different definitions of the map. The waist points of the 'sausage' structure correspond to particular border-collision bifurcations.

The effects of a border-collision bifurcation can be better seen from the dynamics occurring in the phase space (and some times they cannot be understood from a bifurcation diagram). For example, let us add some observations related to the number of the segments of critical lines which form an attracting invariant closed curve $\mathcal{C}$ at $a > 1$, which also may change when a periodic point crosses though LC_{-1}. If we take the (a, c)-parameter point inside the leftmost subregion of a periodicity region shown in Fig.4, related to an attracting m/n-cycle, then the invariant attracting closed curve $\mathcal{C}$ is made up by exactly n segments of the critical lines LC_i, $i = 0, 1, ..., n-1$. It can be shown that in such a case 2 points of the corresponding attracting cycle belong to the region R_2 and $n-2$ points are in R_1. Fig.5 presents an example in the case $m/n = 2/13$, when the curve $\mathcal{C}$ is made up by 13 segments of critical lines. While if the (a, c)-parameter point moves to the next subregions, the number of periodic points in R_2 first increases, and the number of segments of $\mathcal{C}$ decreases (see Fig.6 which shows an example of $\mathcal{C}$ made up by 7 segments in case $m/n = 5/36$), but then, if the (a, c)-point continues to move to the right inside the periodicity region, some periodic points enter R_1 again, so that the numbers of segments of $\mathcal{C}$ increases again.

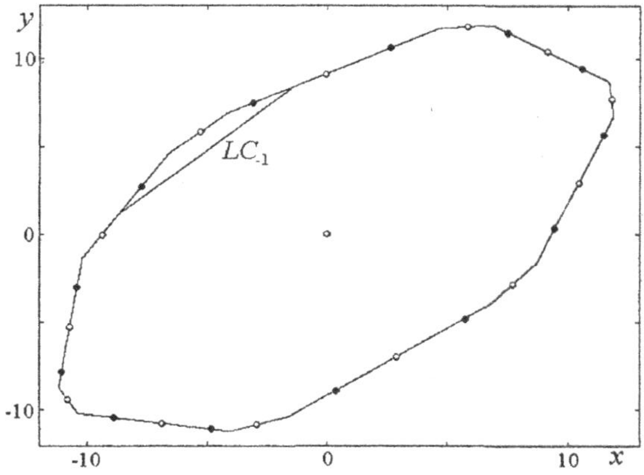

Figure 5: *The attracting closed invariant curve C of the map F made up by* 13 *segments, in the case* $m/n = 2/13$, *at* $a = 1.015$, $c = 0.13613$, $d = 10, b = 0$. *Points of the attracting and saddle cycles are shown by black and white circles, respectively.*

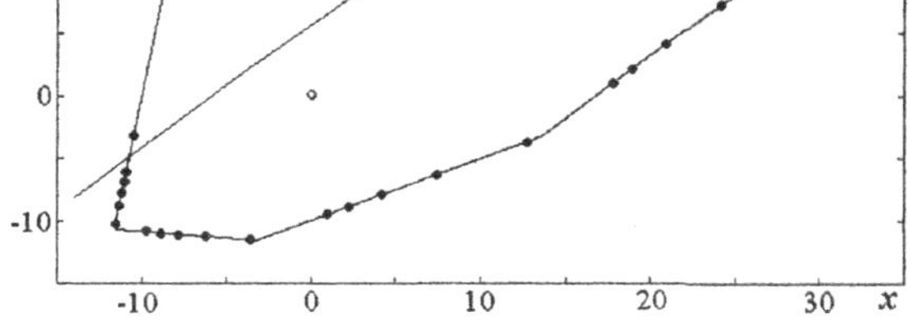

Figure 6: *The attracting closed invariant curve C made up by* 7 *segments, in the case* $m/n = 5/36$, *at* $a = 1.68$, $c = 0.15$, $d = 10$, $b = 0$.

2.4 Border Collision Bifurcations

In the previous section we have presented the bifurcation diagram in the case $b = 0$ (Fig.4) and in the next two sections we shall consider those related with $b \neq 0$. We shall see that when the parameter a belongs to a neighborhood of $a = 1$, i.e., for $a = 1 + \varepsilon$ for some sufficiently small $\varepsilon > 0$, the structure of the periodicity regions is similar for all the range $-(c+1)/2 < b < 1$, and we have a qualitatively similar behavior. That is, the effect of a center bifurcation is the appearance of an attracting closed invariant curve $\mathcal{C}$ which is a broken line made up by a finite number of segments when $b = 0$, or by infinitely many segments when $b \neq 0$. Here we describe the effect of the special kind of border collision bifurcation related to a center bifurcation. In Section 2.2 we have described the dynamics at the bifurcation value $a = 1$, which holds for any value of b. Starting from $a = 1$ let us increase a little bit the value of a, entering a periodicity tongue.

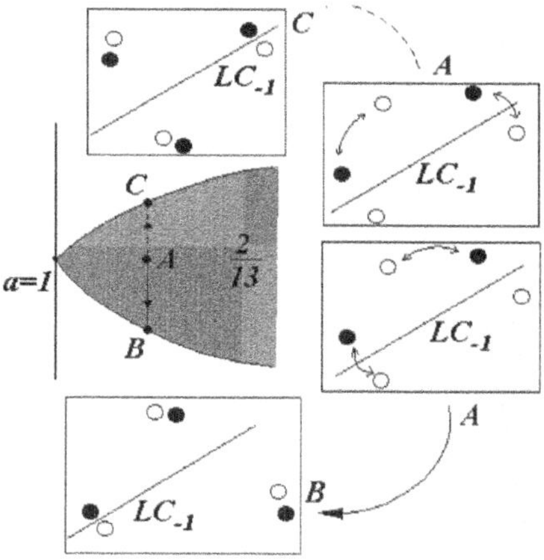

Figure 7: *Qualitative figure of the border-collision bifurcations with few points of the saddles and the attracting nodes shown by white and black circles, respectively.*

To fix the ideas let us consider the case $m/n = 2/13$ used also in Section 2.3. Then the position of the periodic points of the node and the saddle of period 13 at a point $A = (a, c)$ of the tongue shown in Fig.7 is qualitatively the same as the one shown in Fig.5 (also the qualitative shape of the closed curve C is similar, even if the segments constituting C become infinitely many when $b \neq 0$). Thus, among the infinitely many periodic points existing at the bifurcation value on a segment of LC_{-1}, only two cycles survive, a saddle and a node, having points which are not close to each other. As already remarked in the previous section, only 2 points of the corresponding attracting cycle belong to the region R_2 and $n-2$ points are in R_1, and only 1 point of the corresponding saddle cycle belongs to the region R_2, as it is qualitatively shown in Fig.7 for the parameter point A. Then the effects of the border collisions occurring at the boundaries of the tongue can be easily shown moving the parameter point from A to B and from A to C. As the point A moves towards B, then the points of the saddle cycle moves toward those of the node giving the merging of only one pair of points, as shown in the qualitative picture, which is exactly what occurs in a standard border-collision bifurcation. Thus, periodic points merge and disappear (even if no eigenvalue is equal to 1) when two of them merge on LC_{-1}. A similar behavior, but with the merging of a different pair of periodic points on LC_{-1}, occurs when we move the parameter point from A to C.

2.5 Center Bifurcation for $b > 0$: Invertible Case

In this section we describe the center bifurcation which occurs for the fixed point of the map F given in (1) when the map is invertible, that is for $b > 0$. As already mentioned in the previous sections we assume $a > 1$, $0 < c < 1$ and $(c+a)^2 < 4a$, so that the fixed point of F is an unstable focus. The fixed point of the map F_2, belonging to R_1, is unstable for $b > 1$ (focus for $(c+b)^2 < 4b$ or node for $(c+b)^2 > 4b$) and in these cases all the trajectories of the map F (except for the fixed point) are diverging. Thus, we consider the range $0 < b < 1$.

Let $a = 1+\varepsilon$, $\varepsilon > 0$. The dynamics of F in such a case can be described as follows: A trajectory with an initial point in some neighborhood of the unstable focus (x^*, y^*) rotates under the map F_1 in the couterclockwise direction, moving away from (x^*, y^*), and in a finite number of iterations it necessarily enters the region R_2 where the map F_2 is applied. Then the trajectory under the map F_2 moves back to the region R_1 (given that F_2 has the attracting fixed point in R_1).

For some sufficiently small $\varepsilon > 0$ the dynamics of F are bounded. To see this first note that for b close to 0 the above statement is obvious. For the values of b close to 1, note that at $a = 1$, $b = 1$ we have $F_1 = F_2$, so that if $b \to 1_-$ and $a \to 1_+$ then the distance between the fixed points of F_1 and F_2 tends to 0, so that choosing ε small enough we get a bounded invariant region. In other words, we can say that the invariant region (Q or P, as described in propositions 1 and 2), existing in the phase space for $a = 1$, exists also after the center bifurcation, but now an inner point of this region, being no longer periodic or quasiperiodic, is attracted from the boundary, as well as an initial point outside the invariant region. Note that due to the invertibility of F a trajectory cannot jump from inside the invariant region to outside and vice versa. For a sufficiently small ε the boundary is an attracting closed invariant curve $\mathcal{C}$, to which the dynamics of F are reduced. It can be shown that for the parameter range considered, the restriction of F to $\mathcal{C}$ is invertible, so, as in the previous case ($b = 0$), the trajectory on $\mathcal{C}$ is regular.

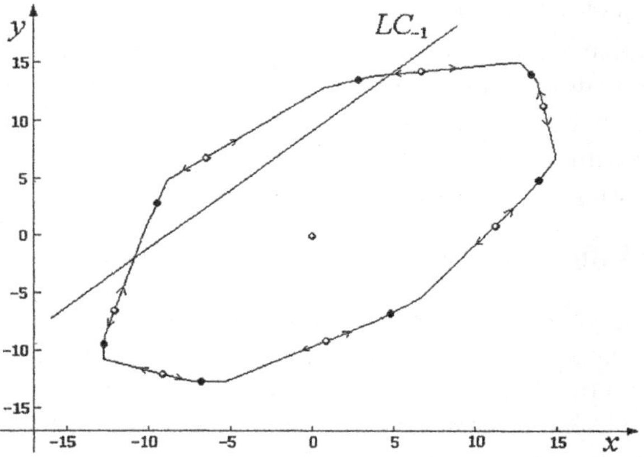

Figure 8: *The attracting closed invariant curve* C *at* $a = 1.1$, $b = 0.1$, $c = 0.25$, $d = 10$. *Points of the attracting and saddle cycles of period* 7 *are shown by black and white circles, respectively.*

Fig.8 presents an example of attracting closed invariant curve $\mathcal{C}$ on which the map F is reduced to a rotation with the rotation number $1/7$. That is, there exist an attracting and a saddle cycle of period 7, so that the curve $\mathcal{C}$ is formed by the closure of the unstable set of the saddle 7-cycle, approaching the points of the attracting 7-cycle (i.e. a saddle-connection). Differently from the case $b = 0$ in which the curve is made up by a finite number of segments (belonging to the images of LC_{-1}), now it can be shown that there are infinitely many corner points on $\mathcal{C}$, so that it consists of infinitely many linear segments approaching the periodic points of the attracting node.

A typical two-dimensional bifurcation diagram of the map F in the (a, c)-parameter plane for a fixed values of b is shown in Fig.9 where $b = 0.1$. We notice that as long as the fixed point of the map F_2 is an attracting node, that is for $c > c^* = 2\sqrt{b} - b$, which at $b = 0.1$ becomes $c > c^* \approx 0.5325$, the (a, c)-bifurcation diagram looks similar to that of the case $b = 0$ (see Fig.4), and we conjecture that complex dynamics can not occur. While for $c < c^*$ the periodicity regions are stopped on the right by the gray region denoting divergence to infinity, and, as we shall see below, chaotic dynamics may occur, as well as multistability.

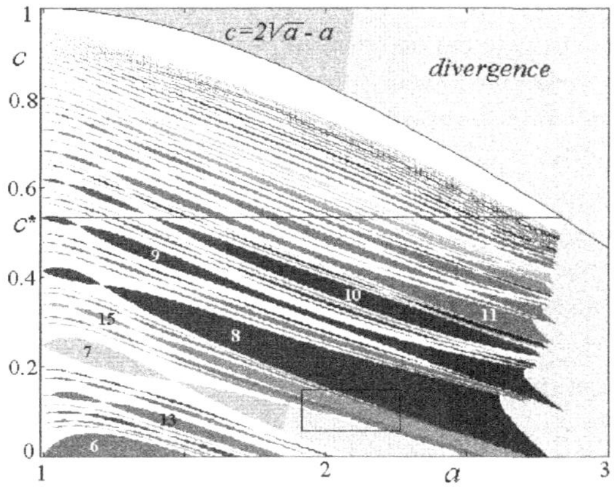

Figure 9: *Two-dimensional bifurcation diagram of the map* F *in the* (a, c)-*parameter plane at* $b = 0.1$, $d = 10$. *Regions corresponding to attracting cycles of different periods* $n \leq 32$ *are shown by various gray tonalities.*

It is worth to notice that the periodicity tongues shown in the two - dimensional bifurcation diagram correspond to attracting cycles, but they are not necessarily related to closed invariant curves, made up by the saddle-connection. Indeed, we know that for values of a close to 1 the closed invariant curve $\mathcal{C}$ exists but increasing a it may be destroyed. Thus let us first give here the possible mechanisms leading to the destruction of a closed invariant curve $\mathcal{C}$ which, in a certain sense, are similar to those occurring in the smooth case (to compare, see Aronson *et al.*, 1982):

- A border-collision bifurcation occurring when a point of the attracting cycle and a point of the saddle cycle collide and merge on LC_{-1} and, as a result, these cycles disappear (Nusse, Yorke, 1992, Banerjee *et al.*, 2000). This bifurcation often occurs on the boundary of a periodicity tongue, as already described in the previous section.

- The attracting n-cycle existing on C may lose stability via flip bifurcation. The result of the flip bifurcation in the piecewise linear case (see Maistrenko *et al.*, 1998) in general is the appearance of a $2n$-cycle of chaotic attractors (i.e., cyclic chaotic attractors made up of $2n$ disjoint pieces), which becomes a one-piece chaotic attractor via a sequence of pairwise merging of the pieces.

- The attracting n-cycle (node) existing on C may become a focus. Indeed, in such a case we can say that a closed invariant curve still exists but is no longer homeomorphic to a circle. Thus this bifurcation denotes a qualitative change of the structure of the invariant curve, but not its disappearance. However, we list it here, as some other authors do, denoting the change of saddle-node connection into saddle-focus one. The saddle-focus connection may be destroyed by a center bifurcation of the n-focus, giving rise to n cyclical closed invariant curves. That is, the closed curve may be destroyed by a center bifurcation occurring in the map F^n.

- The saddle n-cycle may undergo a homoclinic bifurcation. That is, the closed invariant curve is destroyed and replaced by a homoclinic tangle with infinitely many points homoclinic to the saddle (so that also a chaotic repellor exists, made up of infinitely many repelling cycles). As we shall see in the example given below, such a homoclinic tangle may occur inside a periodicity tongue.

In the bifurcation diagram shown in Fig.9 it can also be seen that near the line $a = 1$ the bifurcation structure is similar to the case $b = 0$, but for larger values of a the dynamics become more complicated: As the numerical simulation shows, the periodicity regions can be overlapped, so that the map F can have two coexisting attracting cycles, as well as an attracting cycle coexisting with a chaotic attractor. To give an example, let us enlarge a part of the bifurcation diagram where we have bistability (see Fig.10 with an enlargement of the window indicated in Fig.9, where one of the bistability regions is dashed).

To see which kind of bifurcation occurs when the (a, c)-parameter point crosses the bistability region, let us fix $a = 2.07$, $b = 0.1$ and increase the value of c (the corresponding parameter path is indicated by the straight line with an arrow in Fig.10). The phase portrait of the map F at $c = 0.07$, and its

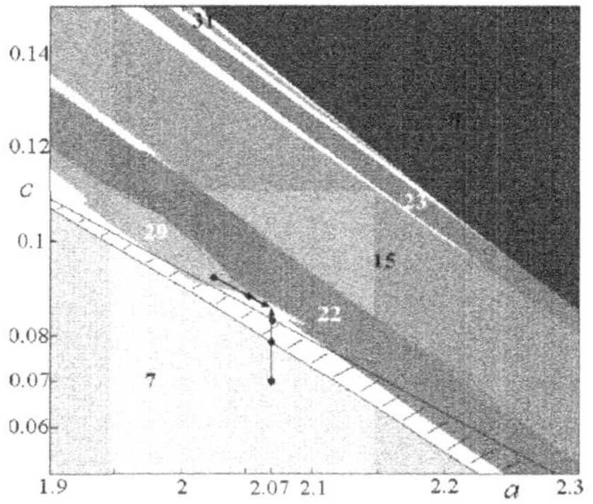

Figure 10: *The enlarged window of Fig.9; A dashed region corresponds to an attracting 7-cycle coexisting with another attractor (regular or chaotic).*

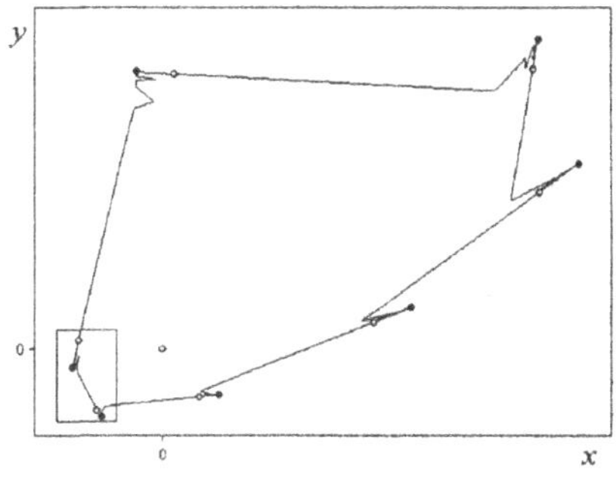

Figure 11: *An attracting closed invariant curve C at $a = 2.07$, $b = 0.1$, $c = 0.07$, $d = 10$. Points of the attracting and saddle cycles of period 7 are shown by black and white circles, respectively.*

enlarged part are shown in Figs.11 and 12(a): An attracting closed invariant curve is formed by the unstable set of the saddle 7-cycle, approaching the points of the attracting 7-cycle, which is the only attractor of the map F.

Fig.12(a) shows also some branches of the unstable set of the saddle, so that it can be seen that stable and unstable sets have no intersection.

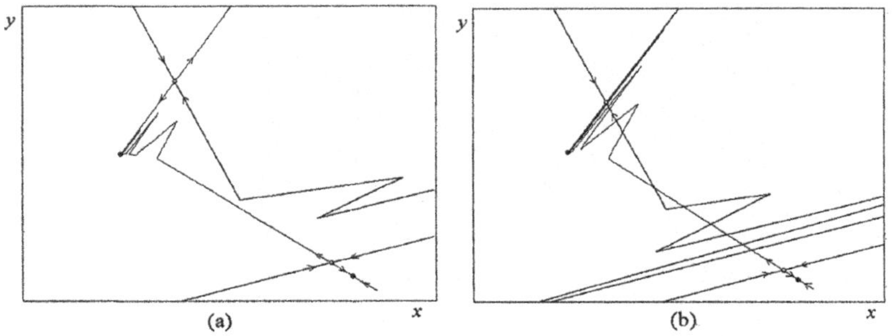

Figure 12: *The enlarged window of the phase portrait of F shown in Fig.11 at* $a = 2.07$, $b = 0.1$, $d = 10$ *and (a)* $c = 0.07$ *(before the intersection of the stable and unstable sets of the 7-saddle) (b)* $c = 0.074$ *in (after the homoclinic bifurcation of the saddle).*

Increasing the value of c, at $c \approx 0.0715$ the first homoclinic bifurcation (or homoclinic contact, the analogue of a homoclinic tangency in smooth maps) occurs for the saddle cycle. After the tangency, the attractor of the map F is still the 7-cycle node, but the closed invariant curve no longer exists: It has been destroyed by the homoclinic tangency and it has been replaced by the homoclinic tangle, with a chaotic repellor. Fig.12(b) presents the enlarged part of the phase space of the map F at $c = 0.074$ during the homoclinic tangle. In order to remark the role of the chaotic repellor and the complex structure of the stable set of the saddle, we show the basins of attraction of the 7 fixed points for the map F^7. For the parameter values used in Fig.12(a), when the unstable set of the saddle gives rise to the closed invariant curve, the stable set of the saddle has a simple structure, and separates the basins (the 7 invariant regions) in a simple way, as shown in Fig.13(a). While for the parameter values used in Fig.12(b), when the unstable set of the saddle intersects the stable one and the closed invariant curve no longer exists, the stable set of the saddle has a complex structure, and separates the basin in a complex way, as shown in Fig.13(b). It is worth to note that the map here is invertible, so that the 7 basins, although with complex structure, must be simply connected (in the next section we shall see instead disconnected basins in the noninvertible case).

On further increasing of the parameter, at $c \approx 0.0777$ the last homoclinic bifurcation (or homoclinic tangency) occurs for the saddle 7-cycle (the related phase portrait is shown in Fig.14(a)). This value of c approximately corre-

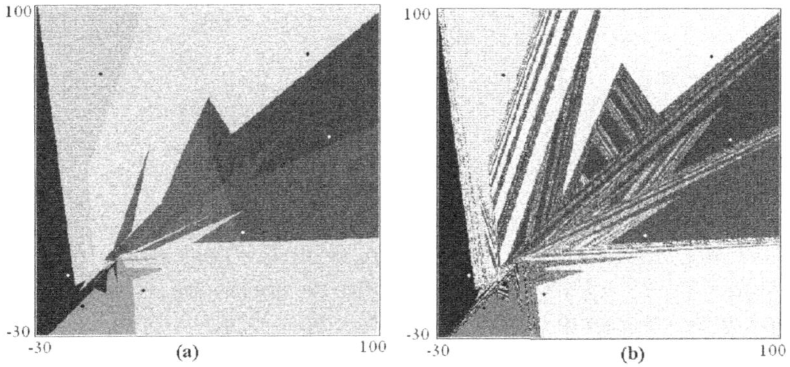

Figure 13: *Baisns of attraction of the 7 fixed points of the map F^7 (i.e. the 7-cycle of F) at $a = 2.07$, $b = 0.1$, $d = 10$ and $c = 0.07$ in (a); $c = 0.074$ in (b).*

sponds to the crossing of the lower boundary of the bistability region, so that after this bifurcation the map F has the attracting 7-cycle coexisting with a chaotic attractor: Fig.14(b) presents an enlarged part of the phase portrait of F at $c = 0.0778$, where the basins of two attractors are shown by different gray tonalities. The whole phase portrait is shown in Fig.15(a). Note that after the last homoclinic tangency the unstable set of the saddle is not related to a closed invariant curve: One branch tends to the 7-cycle and the other branch tends to the chaotic attractor. While the stable set of the 7-saddle gives the boundary of the two basins of attraction.If we continue to increase the value of c then at $c \approx 0.082595$ a 'saddle-node' border-collision bifurcation occurs when the attracting cycle and the saddle merge and disappear (see Fig.15(b)). This value of c is related to the crossing the upper boundary of the bistability region, so that after the bifurcation the chaotic attractor is the unique attractor of F. We can get the same attractor as a result of a sequence of other bifurcations if the (a, c)-parameter point moves starting from a point inside the 29-periodicity region, for example, $a = 2.025$, $c = 0.0925$. These values corresponds to the attracting and saddle 29-cycles of the map F. If, for example, the parameters change as shown by the thick line with an arrow

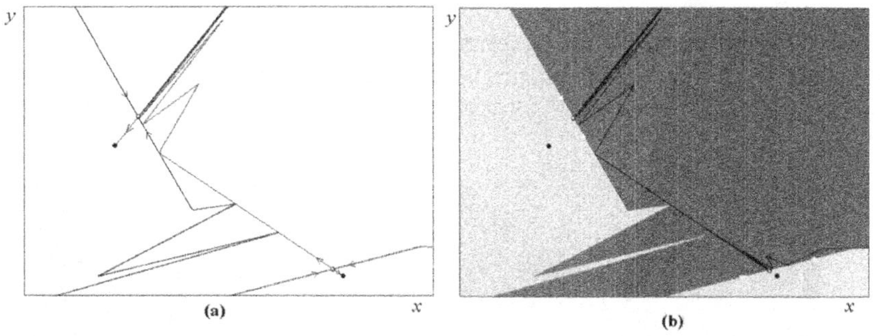

Figure 14: *The enlarged part of the phase portrait of the map* F *at* $a = 2.07$, $b = 0.1$, $d = 10$, *and (a)* $c = 0.0777$ *(near the last homoclinic bifurcation of the saddle 7-cycle); (b)* $c = 0.0778$ *(after the homoclinic bifurcation; The basins of the coexisting attracting 7-cycle and chaotic attractor are shown in different gray tonalities).*

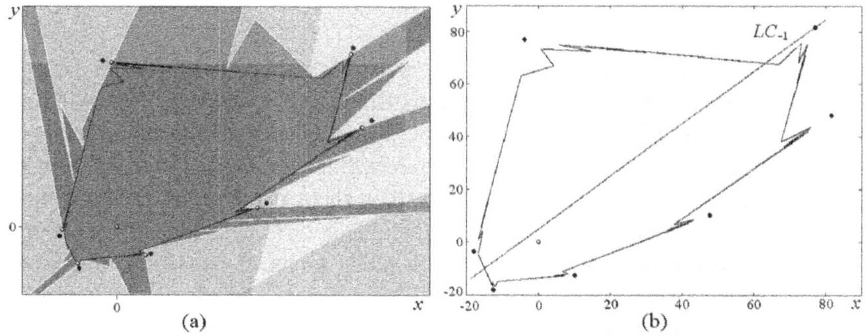

Figure 15: *In (a) phase portrait of the map* F *at* $a = 2.07$, $b = 0.1$, $c = 0.0778$, $d = 10$ *with basins of attraction of coexisting attracting 7-cycle and chaotic attractor. In (b) two attractors of the map* F *at* $a = 2.07$, $b = 0.1$, $c = 0.082595$, $d = 10$, *near the 'saddle-node' border-collision bifurcation when the attracting and saddle 7-cycles merge and disappear due to the collision with* LC_{-1}.

in Fig.10, then at $a \approx 2.05$, $c \approx 0.0872$, the attracting 29-cycle undergoes a flip bifurcation (i.e. the invariant closed curve is destroyed via a flip bifurcation) resulting in a 2×29-cyclic chaotic attractor. Then, after the pairwise merging of the cyclical pieces of the chaotic attractor, the map F has a 29-cyclic chaotic attractor (for example, at $a = 2.056$, $c = 0.0859$), which after further merging of pieces becomes a one-piece chaotic attractor, an example is shown in Fig.15(b).

2.6 Center Bifurcation for $b < 0$: Noninvertible Case

In this last section we describe the center bifurcation occurring in the map F given in (1) when it is noninvertible, for $-(c+1)/2 < b < 0$. We recall that we assume $a > 1$, $0 < c < 1$ and $(c+a)^2 < 4a$, so that the fixed point of F is an unstable focus, while in the given range for b the fixed point of the map F_2, belonging to R_1, is a stable node (with one positive and one negative eigenvalue).

For values of the parameter a in a right neighborhood of 1 the dynamics are qualitatively similar to those occurring in the invertible case, as already remarked in section 2.2 of this chapter. Let us only emphasize the main difference, due to the fact that no point of the phase plane can be mapped in the so called region Z_0, above the critical line LC (as those points are without preimages). For the parameter values taken inside a periodicity tongue the map F still has a pair of cycles, a saddle and a node, and the unstable set of the saddle gives rise to a saddle-node connection, which is a closed invariant curve $\mathcal{C}$ made up by infinitely many linear pieces (with corner points). But the area bounded by such a closed curve *is not invariant.* This is due to the fact that arcs which cross the critical curve LC_{-1} are *folded* on the critical line LC creating corner points, whose forward images give again corner points. An example is shown in Fig.16, for parameter values inside a periodicity tongue with rotation number $1/7$. In that figure, the arrows indicate the points of intersection between the invariant curve $\mathcal{C}$ and LC_{-1} and two more arrows indicate their images on LC. The non invariance of the area bounded by $\mathcal{C}$ is immediately clear from that figure: All the points between the line LC_{-1} and the invariant curve $\mathcal{C}$ are mapped outside the area bounded by the curve, between the curve and the critical line LC. That points from outside can be mapped inside the area bounded by $\mathcal{C}$ is immediately evident: All the points on the right of LC, belonging to Z_2, have two distinct rank-1 preimages, one on the right and one on the left of LC_{-1}.

Another important difference between the invertible and noninvertible case is related with the unstable set of the saddle cycles: Self intersection may occur, while it is impossible in invertible maps. This is one more mechanism which causes the destruction of the closed invariant curve C which for noninvertible maps is to be added to the list already given in the previous section. Summarizing in short we can list such mechanisms as follows:

- border-collision bifurcation (which may occur at the boundary of a periodicity tongue);
- flip bifurcation of the attracting cycle on C;
- transition of the node existing on C into a focus (followed by a center bifurcation);
- the saddle may undergo a homoclinic bifurcation (transverse intersections between stable and unstable sets of the saddle);
- the unstable set of the saddle may develop selfintersections, giving infinitely many loops on the invariant curve.

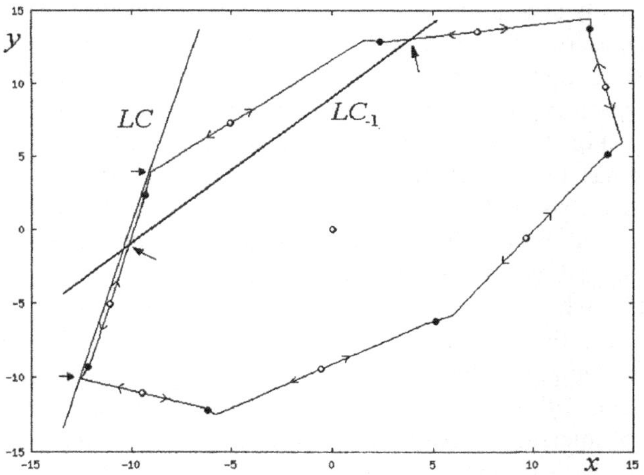

Figure 16: *The attracting closed invariant curve C at $a = 1.1$, $b = -0.05$, $c = 0.25$, $d = 10$.*

Let us illustrate the last kinds of bifurcations by an example, taking the parameter values in the periodicity tongue associated with the rotation number $1/6$, shown in the bottom-left of the (a, c) parameter plane of Fig.17.

Let us fix $a = 1.1$, $b = -0.4$ and increase the value of c (the corresponding parameter path is indicated by the straight line with an arrow in Fig.17).

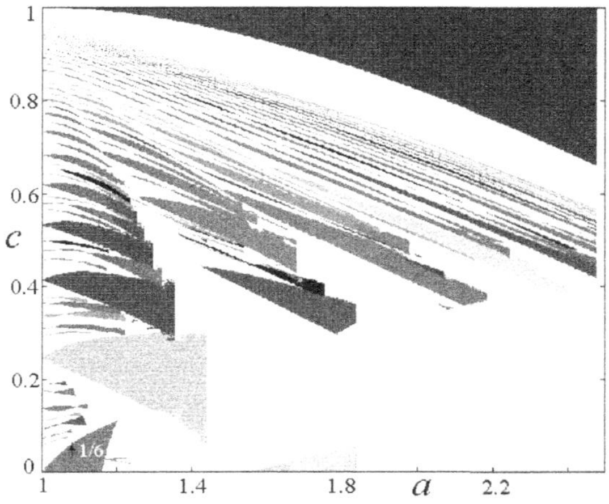

Figure 17: *Bifurcation diagram in the* (a, c) *parameter plane at* $b = -0.4$ *and* $d = 10$.

The phase portrait of the map F at $c = 0.05$ has a unique attractor: a stable node of period 6, and in Fig.18 (a) we present the basins of attraction of the 6 fixed points for the map F^6 (black points in the figure). The stable set of the saddle cycle (white points in the figure) gives the basin boundary. While the unstable set of the saddle is an invariant set which is no longer homeomorphic to a circle, as self intersections already exist. This is shown by an enlarged part of the phase space in Fig.18 (b).

In Fig.18 (a) one more peculiarity of noninvertible maps can be seen: The basins are not simply connected. However the disjoint portion of the basin shown there is entirely included in the region Z_0 so that it has no other preimages. While increasing the value of c, at $c = 0.06$ that portion of the basin intersects the critical curve LC thus giving a portion in the region Z_2 and this small portion has infinitely many preimages, clearly visible in Fig.19 (a). The related unstable set of the saddle is still with self intersections, as shown in the enlargement of the phase space in Fig.19 (b), but is it also possible to see that it is now close to the stable set of the same saddle (basin boundary in Fig.19 (a)), and this denotes that a homoclinic bifurcation is going to occur.

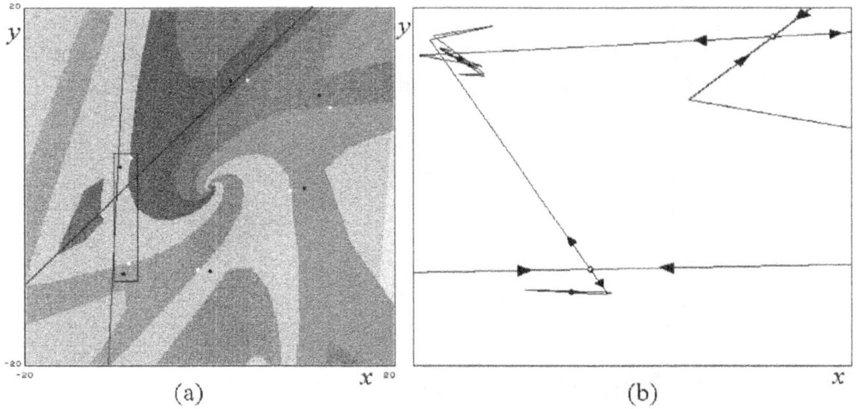

Figure 18: *(a) Basins of attraction of the* 6 *fixed points of the map* F^6 *at* $a = 1.1$, $b = -0.4$, $c = 0.05$; *(b) The enlarged part of (a) with some branches of the stable and unstable sets of the saddle* 6*-cycle.*

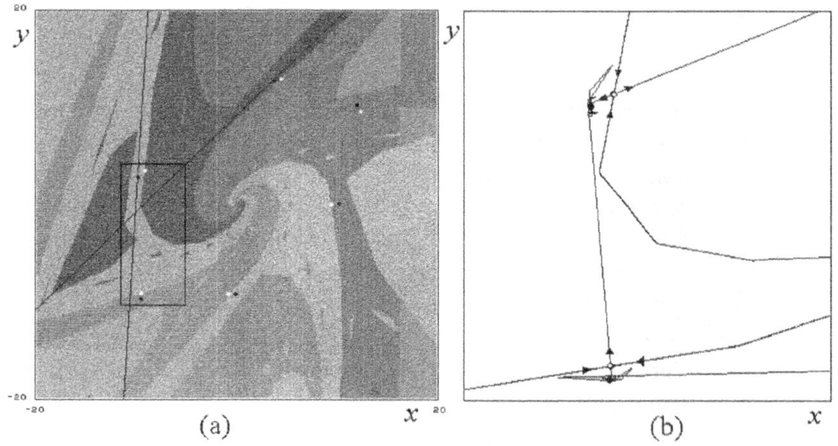

Figure 19: *(a) Basins of attraction of the* 6 *fixed points of the map* F^6 *at* $a = 1.1$, $b = -0.4$, $c = 0.06$; *(b) The enlarged part of (a) with some branches of the stable and unstable sets of the saddle* 6*-cycle, near a homoclinic bifurcation.*

In fact, Fig.20 (a) ($c = 0.0615$) shows the homoclinic tangency and Fig.20 (b) ($c = 0.064$) shows the homoclinic transverse intersections between the stable and unstable sets. It is clear that a strange repellor also exists in such a regime, with the homoclinic tangle of the saddle cycle, and this can be seen in the complex structure of the basins, with many disconnected component in a fractal structure, as shown in Fig.21.

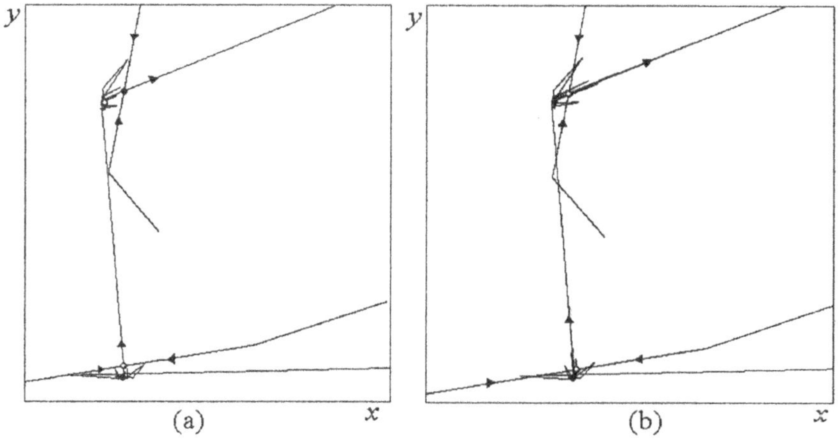

Figure 20: *The enlarged part of the phase space with some branches of the stable and unstable sets of the saddle* 6*-cycle at* $a = 1.1$, $b = -0.4$, $c = 0.0615$ *(a) and* $c = 0.064$ *(b).*

It is worth noticing one more property of the noninvertible maps, which is the existence of absorbing areas inside which all the asymptotic dynamics occur. Consider for example the case shown at $c = 0.064$, for which a strange repellor exists: We can say that all the unstable cycles constituting the strange repellor must belong to the annular absorbing area shown in Fig.22 (a). This area can easily be constructed by taking the images of the critical curves. In fact, an invariant area has necessarily the boundary given by the images of the segment of LC_{-1} belonging to the area itself, which is called *generating segment*[2] (see, e.g., Mira *et. al.*, 1996). In our case, by taking 6 images of that segment we get the external boundary of a simply

[2]Given a noninvertible map F and an invariant area A (i.e., such that $F(A) = A$), the generating arc is defined by $A \cap LC_{-1}$.

connected invariant area, which includes also the unstable fixed point. But as it is an unstable focus, we can also construct an annular absorbing area by taking more images of the same segment. In fact, with 6 more iterations we get the inner boundary of an area of annular shape shown in Fig.22 (a). It is clear that any point of the phase space belonging the hole around the unstable focus is such that its trajectory enters the annular area and never escapes. This means that all the limit set of the trajectories belongs to that annular area, in particular all the cycles of F, except for the focus fixed point.

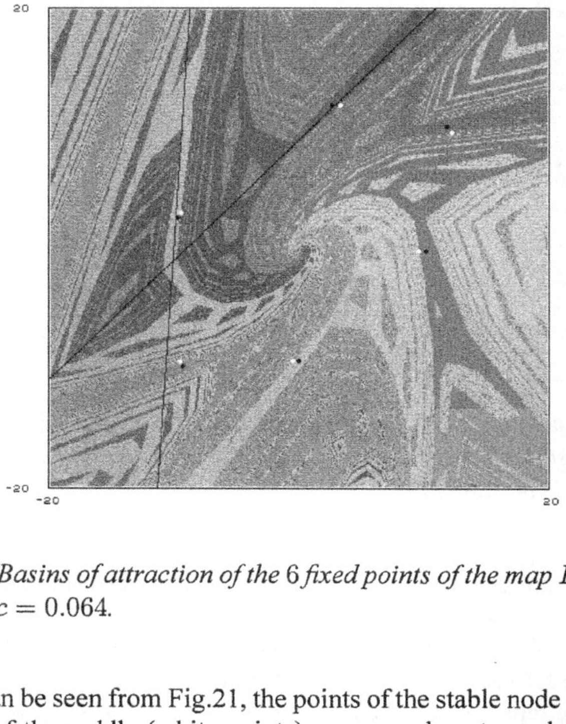

Figure 21: *Basins of attraction of the* 6 *fixed points of the map* F^6 *at* $a = 1.1$, $b = -0.4$, $c = 0.064$.

As it can be seen from Fig.21, the points of the stable node (black points) and those of the saddle (white points) are very close to each other, and on further increase of c the parameter point reaches the boundary of the periodicity tongue, where a saddle-node merging occurs via a border-collision bifurcation. After such bifurcation the pair of 6-cycles disappear and the map F is left with a chaotic attractor: That is, the chaotic repellor existing in the annular area shown in Fig.22 (b), is transformed into a chaotic attractor with knots and self intersection.

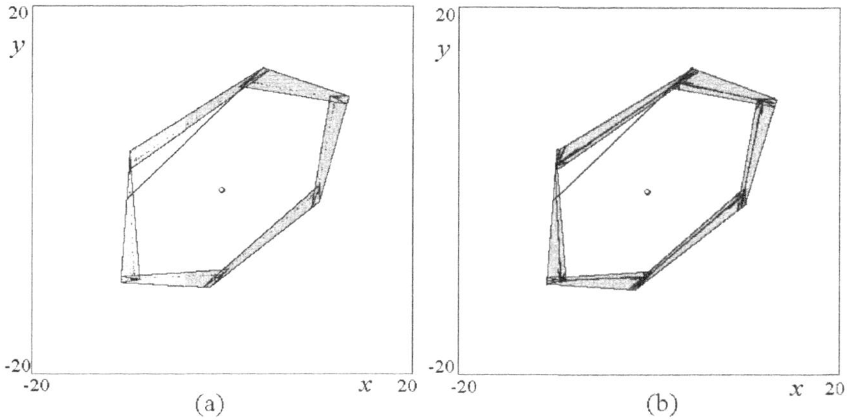

Figure 22: *The annular absorbing area of the map* F *at* $a = 1.1$, $b = -0.4$, $c = 0.064$ *(a) and* $c = 0.071$ *(b).*

References

Afraimovich, V.S., Shil'nikov, L.P., 1983, "Invariant two-dimensional tori, their destruction and stochasticity", *Gorkii University*, Gorkii, Russia, pp. 3-26.

Aronson, D.G., Chory, M.A., Hall, G.R., McGehee, R.P., 1982, "Bifurcations from an invariant circle for two-parameter families of maps of the plane: A computer-assisted study", *Commun. Math. Phys.* 83, pp. 303-354.

Banerjee, S., Ranjan, P., Grebogi, C., 2000, "Bifurcations in Two-Dimensional Piecewise Smooth Maps - Theory and Applications in Switching Circuits", *IEEE Trans. Circuits Syst.-I: Fund. Theory Appl.* 47 No. 5, pp. 633-643.

Boyland, P.L., 1986, "Bifurcations of circle maps: Arnol'd tongues, bistability and rotation intervals", *Commun. Math. Phys.*, 106, pp. 353-381.

Guckenheimer, J., Holmes, P., 1983, *Nonlinear Oscillations, Dynamical Systems, and Bifurcations of Vector Fields*. Springer-Verlag.

Gumovski, I., Mira. C., 1980, *Recurrences and Discrete Dynamical Systems*. Springer-Verlag.

Hao Bai-Lin, 1989, *Elementary Symbolic Dynamics and Chaos in Dissipative Systems*. World Scientific, Singapore.

Hommes, C.H., 1991, *Chaotic dynamics in economic models*. Wolters-Noodhoff, Groningen.

Hommes, C.H., Nusse, H., 1991, "Period three to period two bifurcations for piecewise linear models", *Journal of Economics* 54(2), pp. 157-169.

Kuznetsov, Y., 1995, *Elements of applied bifurcation theory*. Springer-Verlag.

Maistrenko, Y., Sushko, I., Gardini, L., 1998, "About two mechanisms of reunion of chaotic attractors", *Chaos, Solitons & Fractals*, 9(8), pp. 1373-1390.

Mira, C., Gardini, L., Barugola, A., Cathala, J.C., 1996, *Chaotic dynamics in two-dimensional noninvertible maps*. Singapore, World Scientific.

Nusse, H.E., Yorke, J.A., 1992, "Border-collision bifurcations including "period two to period three" for piecewise smooth systems", *Physica D*, 57, pp. 39-57.

Sushko, I., Puu, T., Gardini, L., 2003, "The Hicksian floor-roof model for two regions linked by interregional trade", *Chaos Solitons & Fractals*, 18, pp. 593-612.

Zhusubaliyev, Z.T., Mosekilde, E., 2003, *Bifurcations and Chaos in Piecewise-Smooth Dynamical Systems*, Singapore, World Scientific.

3 Short History of the Multiplier-Accelerator Model

Tönu Puu

3.1 Introduction

Business cycle theory is as old as business cycles themselves. To find this out the reader may consult for instance Schumpeter (1954), the great source for all history of economic analysis, or the standard reference on business cycles, Haberler (1937). The variety of explanations is overwhelming, from the influence of sun spot activity, to mere accumulation of random variables.

Most theories used different explanations for upswing and downturn. The scenery changed thoroughly once Samuelson (1939) suggested one single model, analogous to the simple harmonic mechanical oscillator, though based on two substantial economic hypotheses: multiplier analysis, and the principle of acceleration. According to the first, consumers spend a fixed fraction of their incomes, so that any initial income change leads to a convergent geometric series of subsequent spending, which multiplies up the initial change by a factor reciprocal to the fraction saved. According to the second, capital is assumed to be needed in a fixed proportion to the output to be produced, so investments, by definition the change in capital stock, are proportionate to the change of output.

Keynesian macroeconomics provided an essential background to this model. Though Keynes (1936) produced no dynamical theory, just a theory for sustained unemployment, it was he who focused the dependence of consumption and savings on income. The classics had focused the rate of interest as equilibrating force for investments and savings. The main concern of Keynes was to minimize the role of interest: For one thing, interest rates would be inert downwards, due to speculation resulting in infinitely elastic liquidity preference, i.e. demand for cash reserves. For another, investments would be inelastic with respect to interest rates even if the latter had been less inert.

In this sense Samuelson drew the full consequences of Keynesian macroeconomics, as he skipped the monetary repercussions altogether.

Samuelson's model is Keynesian also in the sense that it only rests on facts of the *demand* side. Just recall that the Keynesian system as stated, for instance, by Hicks (1937), produces an overdetermined system of equations where the supply function for labour literally becomes redundant. Everything is thus determined through demand.

Further, according to the acceleration principle, investments just follow the expected increase of *demand*. It is to this end that capital accumulates so as to keep the right proportion to production.

Of course, Samuelson also made the theory dynamic. As mentioned, the combination of multiplier and accelerator produces a linear model, a simple harmonic oscillator, which can be explosive or damped (disregarding a structurally unstable boundary case). So, in order to have bounded, and yet sustained oscillations, two solutions were proposed: (i) Frisch (1933) suggested that damped linear oscillatory systems be kept going through exogenous shocks, just as the violin string through the rosin on the bow according to Lord Rayleigh's classical model of 1894. (ii) Hicks (1950) suggested bounds, floor and ceiling, to limit the motion of an otherwise explosive linear model.

Hicks further offered substantial explanations for these bounds: If investors follow the linear principle of acceleration, then, in periods of sharp income decrease, investments may become, not only negative, i.e. disinvestments, but may even exceed the disinvestment which occurs when no worn out capital is replaced at all. As this means active destruction of capital, which is not a feature of reality, it must be prevented through imposing a "floor" at the depreciation level.

Likewise, if income grows very fast, then other inputs than capital, labour or raw materials, may become limiting, and a "ceiling" must be imposed. It can be incorporated in the investment function along with the floor, which means that it is the investors who abstain from further expenditures once they realize that output cannot be increased due to limitations in the availability of other inputs, or it can be imposed as a limit to total expenditures, investment, plus consumption, plus anything else. This, by the way, is one and the only element in the Hicksian reformulation of Samuelson's model through which the supply side becomes active.

3.2 Keynesian Macroeconomics and the Business Cycle

To understand the background to business cycle modelling of multiplier-accelerator type, it is important to recognize the significance of Keynesian macroeconomics, emergent with the "*General Theory of Employment, Interest, and Money*" in 1936. Not only is it the first complete statement of a model of the economy in terms of macroeconomic variables, such as income, consumption, savings, and investment, but its main message is to negate the importance of the monetary factors: the rate of interest, the nominal wage rate, and the quantity of money.

We must however not forget that the Keynesian theory was completely static, and that, as we will see, it would be very difficult to interpret its relations in any dynamic sense. Nevertheless, it set the stage for Samuelson's business cycle machine of 1939, which actually drew the full consequences of Keynesian macroeconomics and ignored the monetary phenomena altogether, through just keeping the multiplier, and adding a different principle, the acceleration principle, for the determination of investment.

As a background to multiplier-accelerator modelling we will therefore recapitulate the Keynesian system, which tends to become forgotten by the economics profession of today. Despite his unusually high sophistication in mathematics, Keynes did not believe in the usefulness of mathematical modelling in economics, so he never wrote down a complete model, and, still worse, what he described verbally remained a bit ambiguous. However, most interpreters of the Keynesian system, such as Hicks in "*Mr. Keynes and the Classics*" 1937, or Klein in "*The Keynesian Revolution*" 1947, interpreted the model and its relations in the same way. The main difference lies in the *measurement units* for the variables. It is easiest to interpret savings, investment, and income as monetary variables. However, Keynes was very insistent on the proper interpretation of the variables to be in *real* terms, deflating them by the price level or even by the wage level. For this reason it would be wrong to just stick to the popular monetary model, as some of the main Keynesian results, in particular the failure of lowering wages as a means to attain full employment, do not show up in the monetary model. To this end we present both variants

The Hicksian interpretation of 1937 with its IS and LM curves has become the main frame whenever the Keynesian model is discussed. For a change, we will base the following exposition on a another graphical construction, due to Palander (1942), which is even more pedagogical, and more useful for detecting features of the Keynesian system that the IS-LM analysis does not show. Unfortunately, this most detailed and elegant exposition, has never been available for a wider readership because it was only published in Swedish.

3.3 The Model in Monetary Variables

Let S denote savings and Y denote income. The Keynesian savings function then reads:

$$S = S(Y) \tag{1}$$

This is an important deviation from classical economics where savings were assumed to depend primarily on the rate of interest, thus together with the investment function providing an equilibrium mechanism for the determination of the rate of interest. Keynes retains the classical form of the investment function:

$$I = I(r) \tag{2}$$

where I denotes investment and r denotes the rate of interest. The idea is that if all investments are ranked after their internal rate of yield, the "marginal efficiency of capital", and the cumulative sum of investment costs I for those that yield more than the current rate r of interest is computed, then one obtains I as a decreasing function of r.

Keynes stressed in particular that at low rates of interest, this sum of investments carried through becomes highly *inelastic* with respect to the rate of interest, as we see in the NW quadrant of Fig. 1. Keynes also stressed that other factors, in particular speculative behaviour, make the investment function shift drastically and erratically. In business cycle modelling the growth rate of income was made a mechanical determinant for investment, and the rate of interest was trashed altogether.

As for the savings function, it was assumed to start at zero income with zero slope, all income being used for consumption. With increasing income the slope was assumed to approach unity asymptotically, all further increments of income being saved once consumption was saturated. We can see this shape of the savings function in the NE quadrant of Fig. 1.

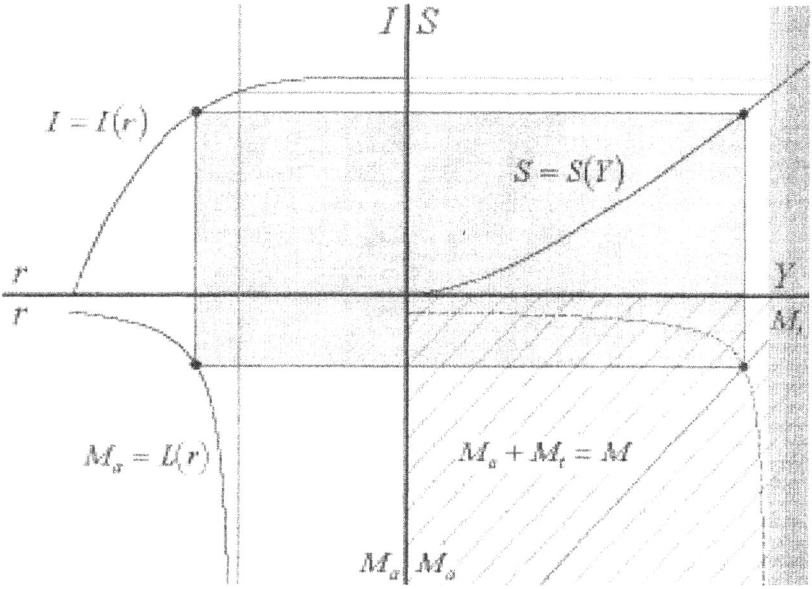

Fig. 1. *Palander's first diagram of the Keynes monetary system.*

It is interesting to note that Keynes gave evidence for the global shapes of the behavioural functions, and that they were all assumed to be *nonlinear*.

To the saving and investment functions we now add the equilibrium condition:

$$I = S \tag{3}$$

For this reason we are able to place the diagrams back to back in Fig. 1. Note that substituting (1)-(2) in (3) gives the implicit function $I(r) = S(Y)$ whose graph is the Hicksian IS-curve. As both (1) and (2) are monotonic, we could construct this curve through starting at any value of Y on the right, go up vertically to the savings function, then draw a horizontal line to the investment function on the left, and finally drop a vertical line to the r axis, quite as in the upper half of the rectangle in Fig. 1.

Likewise, we could expect the lower half of the diagram to represent the Hicksian LM-curve. This indeed is so. In the SE quadrant we see a family of grayshaded straight lines showing the partitions of given total quantities of money M in transactions money M_t and asset money M_a, also called speculation cash. The black line represents an actual, or given, fixed quantity of money:

$$M_t + M_a = M \tag{4}$$

The rest of the gray parallel lines represent options for monetary policy through the banking system.

How can we depict transactions money M_t and income Y on the same axis? The clue is in terms of an old equation from the quantity theory of money:

$$M_t = k \cdot Y \tag{5}$$

which Keynes retained. Money was simply assumed to circulate with a constant velocity, usually denoted V, to generate the expenditures creating income Y. In the quantity theory of money its total quantity *created* income in this mechanical way, as it also did later in the monetarism revival. What was new in the Keynesian theory was that only a part of total money, net of asset holding for cash, was used for transactions. The constant k in (5) is just the reciprocal of the circulation velocity, i.e., equal to $1/V$. Given the constant proportionality, we can hence use different scales above and below the axis, and display Y and M_t on the same.

Note that it is (5) that is the hardest piece to interpret in a causal sense. Is it income, generated by investment and consumption, that just absorbs part of the money supply for transactions, or is it the other way around? Does transaction money in some sense create income? It seems safest to see (5) as a pure equilibrium condition without any causal interpretation. Hicks in "*Mr. Keynes and the Classics*" implied a causality from income to transactions demand, which Allen (1956) used for putting up a dynamical system around the IS-LM diagram in terms of a cobweb, whereas the quantity theorists, classical and modern, no doubt saw causality the other way. Let us however again recall that the Keynesian theory is an *equilibrium* theory for unemployment with no obvious dynamisation possibilities at all.

The remaining piece on display in Fig. 1 is the demand for "speculation" cash or asset money, the liquidity preference function, which no doubt is one of the most ingenious pieces in the Keynesian model. According to Keynes, wealth owners share their total wealth between assets, represented by bonds and hoarded cash, waiting to be invested in bonds, once the circumstances for security price rises become more favourable.

Wealth owners have (differing) expectations about the normal level of the interest rate. The lower it actually is, the fewer of course expect it to decrease further and the more expect it to rise. Financial asset prices and interest rates tend to be related through reciprocity. The case is simplest for a perpetual bond yielding £1 each period. With the interest rate r, its current market value is simply the infinite geometric series of discounted yields, i.e. $\sum_{t=0}^{\infty} 1/(1-r)^t = 1/r$. The relation between bond price and interest is thus represented by the positive branch of a hyperbola. It means that the lower the interest rate, the higher are bond prices. Hence, if most wealth owners consider interest rates to be unusually low and hence bound to rise, they also expect bond prices to fall. To avoid losses, they keep more cash, waiting until the expected rise has actually taken place.

But this is not all! The lower interest rates are, the larger are the price changes, i.e., the expected losses, that go with a given rise in the rate of interest. Suppose the rate of interest rises from 1 percent to 10 percent in steps of 1 percent. The security price then decreases correspondingly from £100 to £10, but in decrements of £50, £16.67, £8.33, £5, £3.33, £2.38, £1.79, £1.39, and £1.11 respectively. No doubt, the losses are most dramatic when the rate of interest is low - *in the first step the asset owner loses half his fortune*, whereas the latest steps are rather negligible. Of course, the gains, should the direction of change be reversed, are equally immense, but, as we recall, nobody believes in further decrease when the interest rate is low already.

For these reasons, when the interest rate approaches a critically low value, all wealth owners prefer to hold cash in stead of bonds, and the demand for asset money becomes virtually infinite. As a consequence, asset money demand swallows all the available supply, without influencing the rate of interest notably. This splitting of cash effectively undoes the quantity theory of money, even though Keynes kept it in his system as an element, though applied to the transactions demand only.

The liquidity preference function:

$$M_a = L(r) \tag{6}$$

hence has a lower asymptote, indicated by the vertical line in the left part of Fig. 1. It is impossible in the Keynesian system to push the rate of interest below this critical value, and hence the investments above the corresponding value. Investments are limited from above due to this lower bound to the interest rate. Not enough, Keynes also said that investments become insensitive to the rate of interest when it is low. Hence, investments are limited for two different reasons, and the operation of the multiplier accordingly also limits the possible incomes that can be generated in the system. This is shown by the two shaded inaccessible regions on the right of the diagram.

The equilibrium point in Palander's diagram is obtained through letting a rectangle rest with each of its corners on the graphs of the savings function, the investment function, the line representing a fixed quantity of money, and the liquidity preference function. To find this rectangle, Palander used the strategy of a construction curve in the SE corner of the diagram. Draw just any number of rectangles with only three of the corners resting on the savings, investment, and liquidity preference curves, and let the fourth trace the dashed curve showing possible divisions between M_t and M_a. Then, fixing total money supply, one of the policy instruments available, we select one of the straight lines, and find the remaining corner of the equilibrium rectangle at the intersection of the corresponding line and the constructed dashed curve.

The advantage of this way of graphical display is that we easily see how the asymptote to the rate of interest translates to a corresponding asymptote to transactions cash, i.e., to income on the right hand side of the diagram. If we try increasing the supply of money further, we find that nothing but the quantity of asset money increases, and can hence verify the Keynesian dictum that monetary policy becomes inefficient when interest rates are low. Not so fiscal policy, because taxation could be analysed through translating the savings function horizontally, government expenditures through translating it vertically, but we do not want to enter the Keynesian model in that much detail.

Palander's four quadrant exposition is superior to the IS-LM, because it so clearly lets us see these facts about monetary policy. However, this is not all. Hicks stopped at the IS-LM diagram, but Palander supplied another four quadrant diagram, which we display in Fig. 2, and which lets us find out the facts of the labour market, which was Keynes's main interest.

As we established an equilibrium (monetary) income Y in Fig. 1, we can now realize that this monetary income is the product of the price level p, and the real income Q, deflated through price level, i.e.:

$$p \cdot Q = Y \tag{7}$$

If we now display this hyperbola in Q, p - space in the NE quadrant of Fig. 2, we can interpret (7) as a kind of aggregate demand function.

Having Q on the horizontal axis to the right, we can now also draw a graph of the aggregate production function:

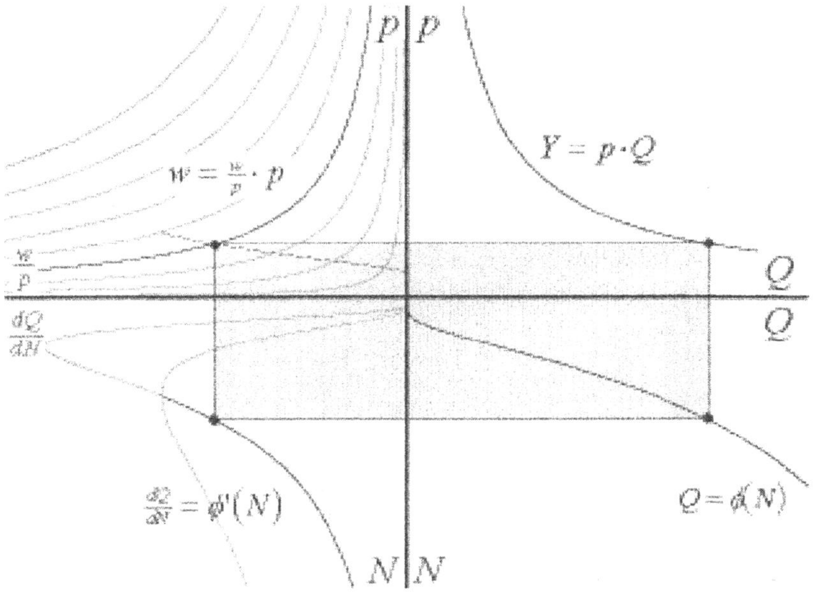

Fig. 2. *Palander's second diagram of the monetray Keynes system.*

$$Q = \phi(N) \tag{8}$$

in the SE quadrant, where N denotes labour force This is the traditional shape of a production function with first increasing and then decreasing returns.

To the left we display its derivative, i.e. the marginal productivity curve $\frac{dQ}{dN} = \phi'(N)$, which first increases, and then decreases, quite as it should in the classical increasing/decreasing returns case. Along with the marginal productivity curve we also display the average productivity curve $\frac{Q}{N} = \phi(N)/N$. It is shaded gray, as is the part of the marginal productivity curve that has not yet intersected the maximum of the average productivity curve. We want to interpret $\frac{dQ}{dN} = \phi'(N)$ as a demand function for labour, because at profit maximum marginal productivity should equal the real wage rate $\frac{w}{p}$. As we know from elementary production theory, only the portion of the marginal productivity curve, where marginal productivity does not exceed average productivity, results is positive profits, so only the section of the decreasing part coloured black is our labour demand curve. Along this curve:

$$\tfrac{w}{p} = \phi'(N) \tag{9}$$

holds.

As we display the labour force axis pointing down, the marginal productivity pointing left, we can also put the real wage rate on the same axis pointing left.

There is now only the NW quadrant left empty. On the axes we have real wages $\frac{w}{p}$ horizontally, and price p vertically. Suppose we fix the money wage rate w. Then we have the identity:

$$\tfrac{w}{p} \cdot p = w \tag{10}$$

which is a hyperbola in the NW quadrant. Observe that we are not going to count it among the equations of the Keynesian system, as it is just an identity. We could count it, but then we would have to add the real wage rate as a new variable.

We drew a whole family of hyperbolas, shaded gray, because the money wage rate is again a means of economic policy, now one controlled by trade unions and other labour market agents.

We can again use the strategy of fitting a rectangle with its corners resting on the four curves, but as an aid we can again leave the point in the NW quadrant out, let only three points rest on the other curves, and use the fourth corner to construct the dashed curve in Fig. 2. It shows possible relations between price level and the real wage rate. By choosing a hyperbola in the NW quadrant, i.e., selecting a money wage rate, we can find its intersection with the constructed curve, and so complete the equilibrium rectangle.

At this stage it is appropriate to note that, though we have a demand curve for labour, we have no supply curve! In the Keynesian system it is just *redundant*. We have 9 equations, (1)-(9), and 9 variables, Y, S, I, M_t, M_a, r, Q, N, and p. The wage rate w and the quantity of money M are fixed policy variables, and $k = 1/V$ is a constant determined by transaction practice.

Let us now check out an important argument due to Keynes. *Lowering money wages are of no help for obtaining full employment.* As a matter of fact this *cannot* be seen in the diagram. Given the dashed construction curve, we can lower real wages even down to zero by lowering money wages, and hence increase employment to any extent we wish. This has been the cause of some misunderstanding, as some authors claim that Keynesian theory still needs sticky wages. However, we should recall that we dealt with the model in monetary terms. With the variables defined in real terms we can indeed verify Keynes's dictum that even if money wages were not sticky, lowering them in unemployment might not result in sufficiently low real wage rates.

3.4 The Model in Real Variables

To see this, we have to change Palander's diagrammatic method just a little. Fig. 3 is very similar to Fig. 1, with the savings function, the investment function, the liquidity preference function, and the construction curve for the distribution of the stock of money between transactions cash and asset money. There is, however, one big difference: All variables are now *in real terms*. Real savings $s = S / p$ are a function of real income, $Y / p = Q$, so:

$$s = s(Q) \tag{11}$$

Likewise, it is now real investment, i.e., $i = I / p$, which is a function of the rate of interest r:

$$i = i(r) \tag{12}$$

Again we have the equilibrium equality between savings and investments:

$$s = i \tag{13}$$

Transaction money, *in real terms*, $m_t = M_t / p$, is proportional to real income:

$$m_t = k \cdot Q \tag{14}$$

and the demand for asset money, *again in real terms*, is:

$$m_a = l(r) \tag{15}$$

Equations (11), (12), and (15) just rephrase (1), (2), and (6) in real terms, whereas (13) and (14) can be obtained from (3) and (5) through division by p.

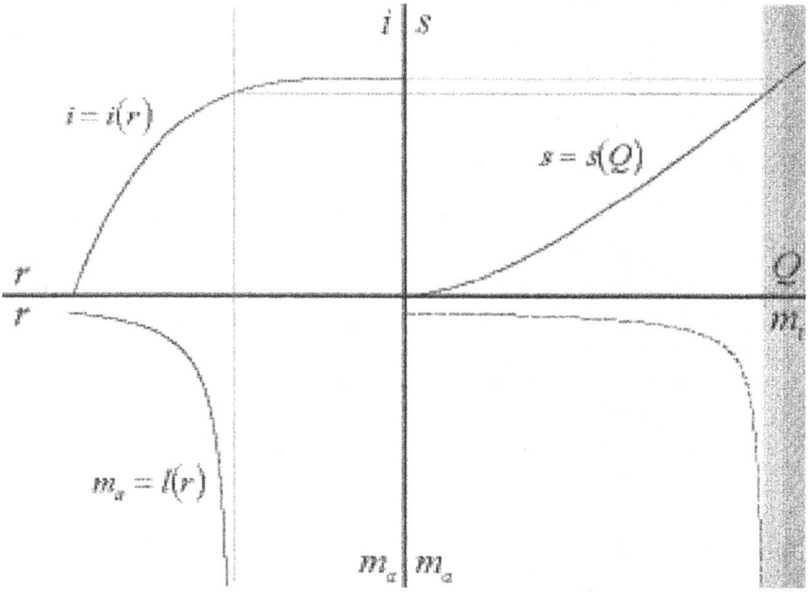

Fig. 3. *Palander inspired first diagram for the real Keynes model.*

Corresponding to the total nominal amount of money, we now also have a *real* amount of money $m = M / p$, which is the sum of (real) transactions demand and asset demand, i.e.,

$$m_t + m_a = m \tag{16}$$

This is again obtained from (4) through dividing by p. The big difference is that, unlike M, m is *not* a parameter for monetary policy, as it *depends on the price level* which must be determined endogenously in the model

Now suppose we erase everything in Fig. 3, except the constructed distribution curve for the different components of (real) money demand, and leave just it for Fig. 4. Further, suppose we take a point such as the black dot on this construction curve. This time we do not move horizontally from the dot to the axis, but follow the constant (real) money line diagonally to the vertical axis. The axis intercept obviously gives us the sum $m_t + m_a = m$ of transactions and asset demand for money in real terms, corresponding to the point chosen. So, reading off the intercept, we can indeed write m on the left side of the vertical axis.

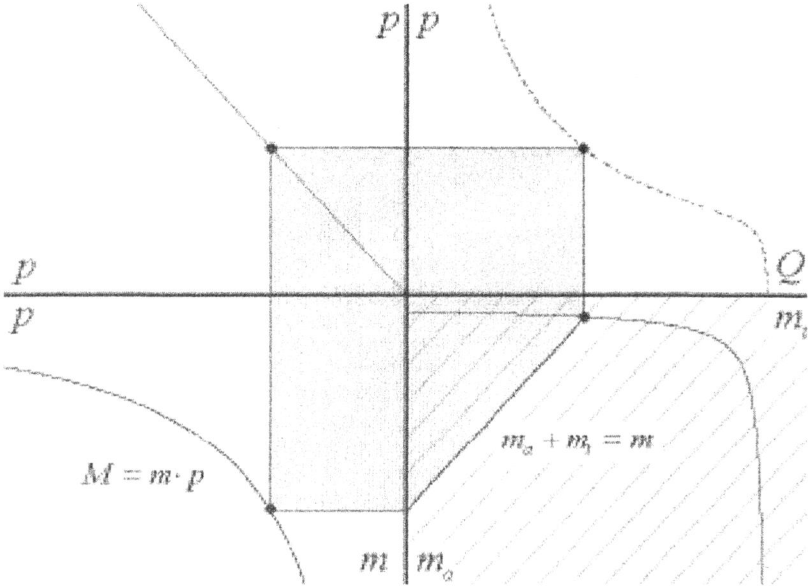

Fig. 4. *Demand function in the real Keynes model.*

What else do we have? From definition, $m = M / p$, so:

$$M = m \cdot p \tag{17}$$

Putting p on the left horizontal axis, we can display (17) as a hyperbola whenever M is fixed by the monetary authorities. For the rest we just put p on the remaining axes, and use a diagonal in the NW quadrant to shift vertical coordinates to horizontal and *vice versa*.

We can again use the rectangle construction, this time with one corner cut off, and, starting from any point on the curve in the SE quadrant, construct the dashed curve in the NE quadrant of Fig. 4. The axes there are Q and p respectively, so we again arrived at an aggregate demand curve. This time it is not a hyperbola as in Fig. 1. The shape is distinctly different, as it goes down to the Q axis at a certain value. Ultimately this is due to the shape of the liquidity preference function, which hence limits possible total output in the real version of the Keynesian model, but, as we saw, not so in the monetary version of it.

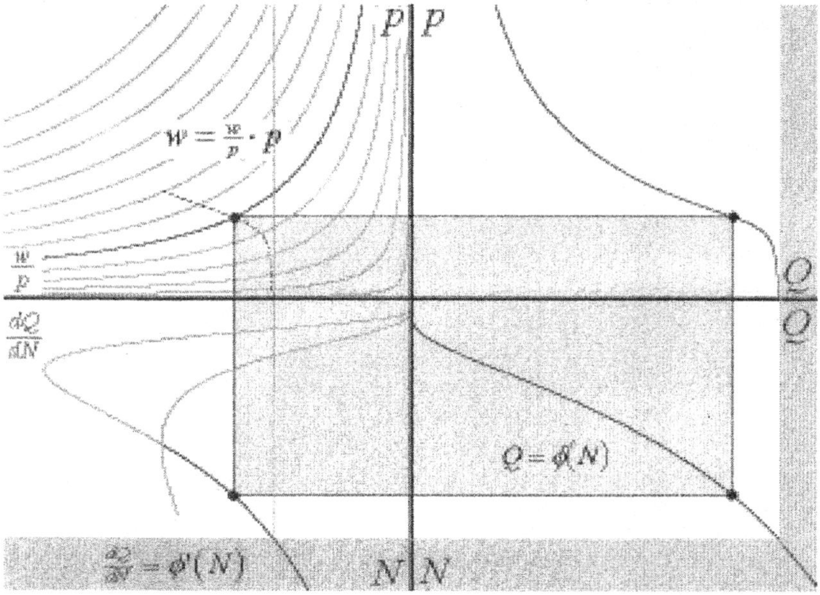

Fig. 5. *Wage rate and unemployment in the real Keynes model.*

In Fig. 5 we reproduce all the curves from Fig. 2, as most of the variables there are in real terms already. We just replace the hyperbola shaped demand function with the just derived demand function that goes down to the horizontal axis. As we will see this alters the conclusions about the effects of lowering money wages drastically, and fully justifies all Keynes's original assertions.

Again, we can use the method of rectangles with corners resting on the demand function, the production function, the labour demand function, and the given money wage hyperbola. However, as before, we use the three first to construct a dashed possibility curve in the NW quadrant, relating possible real wage rates to prices. The equilibrium is where this dashed curve intersects a hyperbola representing the given money wage.

What is new is that the shape of the demand function in the NE quadrant also results in a *minimum obtainable real wage rate*, shown by the vertical line in the left part of Fig. 5. No matter how much we lower the nominal wage, can we undercut this minimal real wage rate. As a result, the possible employment becomes limited, quite like production. This is shown by the shaded strips which represent the inaccessible areas.

3.5 Demounting Keynesianism

It did not last long before an active demounting of Keynesian macroeconomics started. The process could be attributed to different causes. First, the Korean War inflation in 1953 drastically changed the scenario from the Wall Street Crash of 1929 and the Great Depression which inspired Keynes. Second, Keynesian macroeconomics favoured active fiscal policy as means to achieve political goals, so those who did not want that much of political intervention preferred some different scientific paradigm. Third, there was a seemingly irresistible urge among economists to *unify* macroeconomics and Walrasian general equilibrium theory, which means *deriving* macroeconomics from microeconomics. See for instance Barro and Grossman (1976).

The last urge remained a great mystery for the present author, as economics always took physics as an example. Once statistical mechanics and thermodynamics arouse as a theory relating volumes, temperatures, and pressures, nobody tried to actually *derive* the relations from Newtonian principles of energy conservation in a closed container where billions of molecules collided.

But, this was exactly what all those economists who for decades were concerned with the "microfoundations of macroeconomics" tried. However, they did not retrieve the Keynesian macoreconomics, but something entirely different, a model where unemployment was again due to sticky wages, chosen unemployment for job search, and the like, quite as before Keynes.

There is nothing wrong in science to take a new start with new categories, such as income, investment, and the rest, as Keynes did, quite like the cited case of statistical mechanics. It is a destructive idea in science to try to find "the unified theory of everything".

The political issue is easier to understand, clearly the Chicago school with Milton Friedman as figurehead, which just revived the quantity theory of money, had a political mission.

Finally, there is the interesting case of Don Patinkin, who formulated a huge micro based theory in macroeconomic terms. See Patinkin (1956). The difference to Keynes was that he introduced a new variable, "real balances", i.e., the quotient of money supply to price level, as an argument in the behavioural equations. The argument goes as follows: Idle money balances are owned by somebody, so suppose that the price level is decreasing more and more. The owners of such balances then find themselves more and more wealthy, and, eventually, they start consuming their wealth. This obviously is in contradiction to Keynes's idea that, once consumption was saturated, people would even save all their income. Wealth was not even included as a determinant for consumption.

If one includes the argument *M/p*, along with others, in any consistent model, with any number of relations, and any number of variables, then a fixed value of this *M/p* is determined along with the other arguments, and hence the price level *p* becomes proportional to the quantity of money *M*, quite as in Friedman's world. One does not need such an elaborate model to arrive at this simple conclusion.

Fortunately, the dismounting of Keynesianism never affected the dynamical theories inspired by Keynes, because none of the new protagonists had anything in terms of dynamics to offer.

3.6 Statics and Dynamics of the Multiplier

Above we emphasized that the Keyenesian model is essentially static, a conclusion about which all contemporary commentators agree. The primary mission of the model was to show how *sustained involuntary* unemployment, such as experienced in real life, not due just to sticky prices or market imperfections, could be explained.

The truly original contribution was to construct a model in terms of new macroeconomic variables, which only gradually, under the influence of the Keynesian general theory itself, became operationalized through national accounting.

Another important feature was that most relations of the model were assumed nonlinear. These nonlinearities did not produce multiple equilibria, but, provided a supply function for labour was included, the system contained one equation too many, so it became overdetermined. However, the supply function for labour was treated as redundant, and equilibrium was determined through the remaining equations at unemployment.

Substantially, the influence of monetary issues was denied. As we have seen, (i) lowering nominal wages could not help to achieve full employment, (ii) the rate of interest tended to stick to a lower limit, any additional wealth created by monetary policy being caught in the "liquidity trap", and (iii) investments were but negligibly influenced by the rate of interest, even in case it had been more flexible. Keynes regarded investments as highly variable, though influenced by other factors than the rate of interest, so some different mechanism to explain changes of investment would be needed in a dynamical perspective. As we will see, this was provided by the principle of acceleration. For Keynes, investments were just a capricious and varying element, which triggered with it repercussions through subsequent spending by the consumers.

These repercussions are, already in Keynes's original theory, something that can also be interpreted dynamically. Not only was, for once, the direction of causality from income to consumption obviously nonambiguous, but it also had a distinctive dynamical interpretation.

Suppose we can approximate the savings function (1), i.e., $S = S(Y)$ by a straight line over some interval. The same then holds also for the consumption function $C = C(Y) = Y - S(Y)$. Due to linearity, as assumed, the slope $\frac{dC}{dY} = c$ is locally a constant, quite as the slope $\frac{dS}{dY} = s$. From $Y = C + S$ obviously $c + s = 1$.

Now, assume we have an initial increase in investment ΔI. This results in an initial income change $\Delta Y = \Delta I$. However, this initial income change results in additional subsequent consumption spending, first $c \cdot \Delta I$, then further $c^2 \cdot \Delta I$, and so forth, in an infinite but convergent geometric series, so the total increase of income amounts to:

$$\Delta Y = \sum_{i=0}^{i=\infty} c^i \cdot \Delta I = \frac{\Delta I}{1-c} = \frac{\Delta I}{s} \tag{18}$$

This idea is discussed already by Keynes. Convergence of the series is due to the fact that c and s are in the unit interval. Of course (18) can also be obtained directly through differentiating (1) and equating ΔI to ΔS, i.e., putting $\Delta I = \frac{dS}{dY} \cdot \Delta Y$, whence, given $\frac{dS}{dY} = s$, $\Delta Y = \Delta I / s$. The name multiplier is due to the fact that $s < 1$, and so $1/s > 1$, hence multiplying up the initial increase in investments through subsequent spending by consumers.

We have thus seen that the multiplier idea is there in Keynesian economics both in a dynamical and in an equilibrium sense right from the outset. Once we have a generation mechanism for investments we only need to add an explicit period structure to land at the idea of the dynamic multiplier.

It is not so easy to say who has first priority to the idea of the multiplier, neither who first formalized it in its static and dynamic form. Obviously, Keynes described it very clearly in 1936, though to some extent it seems to be a collective achievement, in which particular credit is due to Richard Kahn. See Kahn (1931), which, however does not give a complete account of his achievement. It should also be recalled that other multiplier mechanisms were explored, in particular the credit multiplier, which explained how the banking system could expand total credit when only a fraction of deposits were kept as bank reserve, an idea having roots back in the 19th Century.

3.7 The Principle of Acceleration

Quite as it is difficult to say where the idea of the multiplier originated, so is it difficult to trace the origin of the principle of acceleration. At least Aftalion (1909) seems to have had a clear idea of it, though he only described things in verbal terms. The idea is twofold: First, capital equipment is built up or decays in anticipation of changes in consumer demand, so investment has a *lead* in time as compared to consumption. Second, as investments are related to expected *changes* of consumption, they tend to amplify or "accelerate" the process, hence bringing in a feature of instability. When multiplier and accelerator are linked together in one single feed back process, it is, of course, no longer possible to say whether investment has a lead over consumption or rather lags behind. The accelerator idea arose in the "overproduction" school of business cycles. See von Haberler (1937).

As formalized by Samuelson (1939), the principle says that investment is proportional to the rate of change of consumption, i.e., $I = a \cdot \Delta C$, where the proportionality factor a is the "accelerator" coefficient. Hence it is the natural companion to the multiplier, which relates consumption to investment, whereas the accelerator does the reverse. It also supplies the missing determinant for investment once the monetary factors in truly Keynesian spirit are scrapped.

There are several ways to motivate the principle of acceleration. The simplest is maybe to assume a fixed proportion production technology as represented by a production function $Q = \min(\frac{K}{a}, \frac{L}{b})$, where K denotes capital, L denotes labour, and a, b are fixed coefficients. Given this type of production function, producers will need neither more nor less capital than $K = a \cdot Q$. Given the definition of net investment as change of capital stock, $I := \Delta K$, and focusing the aggregate production of consumers' goods, we have $C = Q$ in equilibrium. Hence $I = a \cdot \Delta Q = a \cdot \Delta C$, quite as stated above.

Later Hicks (1950) realized that there is no need to restrict the action of the accelerator to changes in consumption expenditures alone, it should act in equal measure on all components of income, consumption, public spending, and investment itself. Hence $I = a \cdot \Delta Y$, which we will use in the following, even though it yields a slightly inaccurate representation of Samuelson's original model. The difference in terms of model performance it marginal. As we will see below, Hicks also introduced other changes to the model, which, however, changed it radically.

3.8 Modelling in Continuous or in Discrete Time

Given the components, multiplier and accelerator, it remains to decide how to model the dynamical process, in discrete time, or in continuous time, i.e., to use difference equations or differential equations. Samuelson (1939) chose the latter, though the pieces could also be combined in continuous time, as Harrod (1950) preferred.

This set a tradition for some time. Growth theory was modelled through *first order* differ*ential* equations, business cycle theory through *second order* diffe*rence* equations. It is noteworthy that both models were *linear*. The combination of growth with continuous time, and cycles with discrete time must have been a pure coincidence.

Harrod interpreted the rate of change of income as a time derivative, i.e. $\Delta Y = \dot{Y} = \frac{d}{dt} Y$. Hence, investments became $I = a \cdot \dot{Y}$. In the linear format the savings function reads $S = s \cdot Y$, so, using the equilibrium condition $I = S$, one gets the simple first order differential equation:

$$\dot{Y} = \frac{s}{v} Y \tag{19}$$

with its obvious closed form solution:

$$Y = Y_0 \exp(\tfrac{s}{v} t) \tag{20}$$

To do Harrod justice it must be emphasized that he explicitly stated that the equilibrium growth path had to be considered *unstable*. There are several verbal discussions in the book demonstrating this. These also show that Harrod was groping for a higher order process which would model what happens if the actual route deviated from this unstable equilibrium path, though he failed to formulate it mathematically. That a second order process in continuous time is fully viable as a model was demonstrated a few years later by Goodwin (1951) and Phillips (1954).

Harrod cannot be blamed for interpreting all this as a growth theory, the flaw is due to his followers. As a growth theory it contains the absurdity that growth is favoured through a high rate of saving and a low accelerator, though second order models show the reverse. It was further known from Samuelson (1947), that no unstable equilibrium is ever of any interest.

3.9 Cycles in Continuous Time

To show how the Harrod model can be made second order, let us consider Phillips (1954), where an adaptive process was assumed, such that income just increased in proportion to the difference of investments and savings, i.e., $\dot{Y} \propto (I - S)$. A similar adaptive delay was assumed also in the adjustment of investments, i.e., $\dot{I} \propto (v\dot{Y} - I)$. We follow the very clear account of the model as given by Allen (1956).

In Phillips's equations adjustment speeds appeared, and, for generality, Phillips assumed different speeds for the two adaptive processes, as did Allen. The precedence of Samuelson and Hicks, who assumed *identical* unit lags in the discrete format for all kinds of adjustments, makes it a licit simplification to assume also equal adjustment speeds in continuous time. Then we only need to assume a suitable measurement unit for time to make the speeds unitary, and so dispense with the adjustment symbols altogether. We then have: $\dot{Y} = I - sY$ and $\dot{I} = v\dot{Y} - I$.

Next, just differentiate the first equation once more, and use the original equations to eliminate investment and its time derivative, thus obtaining the reduced form equation:

$$\ddot{Y} - (v - 1 - s)\dot{Y} + sY = 0 \tag{21}$$

This linear second order differential equation is capable of producing damped or explosive oscillations, depending on the sign of (v - 1 - s), quite as in the corresponding discrete time process as formulated by Samuleson, which we will discuss below.

We can immediately write the general solution in the oscillatory case:

$$Y = e^{\alpha t}\left(A\cos\omega t + B\sin\omega t\right) \tag{22}$$

where

$$\alpha = \tfrac{1}{2}(v-1-s) \tag{23}$$

$$\omega = \tfrac{1}{2}\sqrt{4s-(v-1-s)^2} \tag{24}$$

and A, B are two arbitrary constants to accommodate the initial conditions. Provided $(v-1-s)^2 > 4s$ holds, the second order model can also generate pure growth, at the rates $\tfrac{1}{2}\left((v-1-s)\pm\sqrt{(v-1-s)^2-4s}\right)$. Hence we see that, *in contrast to the first order Harrod case*, the growth rate is indeed *lowered* by the rate of saving, and *increased* by the accelerator.

We also see from (23) that the oscillatory process is either explosive or damped, depending on the sign of $\alpha = \tfrac{1}{2}(v-1-s)$. There is just one unlikely boundary case, the case of a centre, with $v = 1 + s$, where there is a bounded simple harmonic oscillation that goes on for ever. As for stability, it is neutrally stable, but different initial conditions can lead to an infinity of different oscillations with different phase and amplitude.

Goodwin (1951) used a similar model, but with a nonlinear investment function, and then just one attractive limit cycle replaced this family of orbits, at the same time as it, unlike this exceptional boundary case, was robust for wide ranges of parameter changes. There is no need to enter these matters in more detail, as we will meet them again in the context of second order models in discrete time, which became main frame, perhaps because many of the variables naturally are periodized concepts.

3.10 Samuelson's Business Cycle Model

As mentioned, Samuelson chose to model in discrete time, and he chose a second order process. There is a basic time period unit, and all variables are dated, either *flows*, such as income, investment, and savings, attributed to periods, or *stocks*, such as capital, attributed to moments of time. In this language $S_t = s \cdot Y_{t-1}$, or, which is the same, $C_t = (1-s) \cdot Y_{t-1} = c \cdot Y_{t-1}$. We encountered this idea already in the context of the dynamic multiplier. There is a time lag, incomes earned during a given time period are spent during the following. The need for capital is proportional to the volume of production (i.e., to real income), but it takes time to build up capital, so proportionality is to *expected* income, which, in terms of the simplest forecasting rule of all, just projects past income. Hence, capital stock needed is $K_t = a \cdot Y_{t-1}$, and, investment accordingly becomes $I_t = K_t - K_{t-1} = a \cdot (Y_{t-1} - Y_{t-2})$. In addition, we only need the income formation equation $Y_t = C_t + I_t$. Finally, substituting for C_t and I_t, we readily obtain the reduced form recurrence equation in the income variable alone:

$$Y_t = (a+c) \cdot Y_{t-1} - a \cdot Y_{t-2} \tag{25}$$

It is second order, as we see, and hence capable of generating growth or cycles. However, like Phillips's model, it is linear.

It is easily solved in closed form. There exists just one fixed point $Y_t = Y_{t-1} = Y_{t-2} = 0$, which is stable if, and only if, $a < 1$. Provided $(a+c)^2 > 4a$, the general solution is:

$$Y_t = A\lambda_1^t + B\lambda_2^t \tag{26}$$

where A, B are arbitrary coefficients so chosen as to accommodate the initial conditions, and where

$$\lambda_{1,2} = \frac{a+c}{2} \pm \frac{1}{2}\sqrt{(a+c)^2 - 4a} \tag{27}$$

As long as $(a+c)^2 > 4a$ holds, $\lambda_{1,2}$ are real numbers. With $a, c > 0$, they are both positive, and obviously we always have $\lambda_2 < \lambda_1$. Hence, the first solution term in (26) is bound to dominate with time. Asymptotically, $Y_t \to A\lambda_1^t$, with income growing at the constant rate λ_1 when $a > 1$.

When $(a+c)^2 < 4a$, then $\lambda_{1,2}$ become complex conjugates. If so, it is more convenient to write the general solution as:

$$Y_t = \rho^t \left(A \cos \omega t + B \sin \omega t \right) \tag{28}$$

where

$$\rho = \sqrt{a} \tag{29}$$

and

$$\omega = \arccos \frac{a+c}{2\sqrt{a}} \tag{30}$$

The arbitrary coefficients, A and B, are again chosen so as to fit given initial conditions.

We see that with complex conjugate roots, the solution is the product of a power function and a stationary trigonometric oscillation. This is the case of primary interest in connection with business cycle theory. Depending on whether $\rho<1$ or $\rho>1$, i.e., whether $a<1$ or $a>1$, the power function leads to damping or to explosion. Only in the unlikely boundary case when $\rho=a=1$ does the solution produce standing oscillations representing bounded persistent motion.

This, of course, is due to the linearity of the model, and it presents a problem and a challenge. If $\rho<1$, then the model is hardly dynamical at all, because it can only show how any initial motion is damped out and the system without exogenous shocks goes to eternal equilibrium. If, on the other hand, $\rho>1$, then the model explodes, and the amplitude of the swings goes to infinity, which means that income eventually oscillates between plus and minus infinity. Such exponential growth, which was the basis for economic growth theory for decades, is not a feature of reality, at least not globally, an interpretation which the "limits-to-growth" movement and the "Club of Rome" took as motive for a broad attack launched at the whole of linear dynamical economics. See Forrester (1961).

Of course, negative income makes things even more absurd. To make things straight, we have to insert a digression here about the negativity of income in the depression phases. The full Samuelson model also contains "autonomous expenditures", for consumption, investment, or government spending, whatever, qualified by the property that they do not depend on anything in the cycle.

Replace the income formation equation by $Y_t = A + C_t + I_t$, where A denotes these autonomous expenditures. Equation (25) then becomes $Y_t = A + (a + c) \cdot Y_{t-1} - a \cdot Y_{t-2}$.

If we substitute $Y_t = Y_{t-1} = Y_{t-2} = A/(1-c) = A/s$, we easily find that it is reduced to an identity. There is hence a constant solution, A/s. It represents an equilibrium income level, obtained through applying the multiplier $1/s$ to the autonomous expenditures A, which replaces the zero equilibrium for (25) as stated above. In mathematical terms this is a particular solution. If we now replace Y_t by $A/s + Y_t$, Y_{t-1} by $A/s + Y_{t-1}$, and Y_{t-2} by $A/s + Y_{t-2}$ in $Y_t = A + (a + c) \cdot Y_{t-1} - a \cdot Y_{t-2}$, then we find that all the terms containing the autonomous expenditures cancel, and that (25) is regained.

However, the variable is now, not income, but its deviation from equilibrium, and so negative values are no longer absurd *per se*. Of course, increasing amplitude oscillations eventually produce downward deviations from equilibrium so large that even income becomes negative, which, of course *is* absurd.

As a conclusion, neither $\rho < 1$, nor $\rho > 1$ is any good. There remains the case $\rho = 1$, which results in constant amplitude simple harmonic oscillations, but apart from the fact that the motion produced is much too regular to mimic any real business cycle, modern mathematics discards such specific cases, which at the slightest change transform the outcome of the model to something qualitatively different, as being *structurally unstable* or *nongeneric*, and they are forbidden in good scientific practice. See Arnol'd, who even advises to take friction in account in mathematical models of the pendulum, no matter what we know about its empirical existence, just because the frictionless pendulum produces a structurally unstable model.

For the case $\rho < 1$ we could use an argument on "impulse" and "propagation" supplied by Frisch in 1933, even before the Samuelson model. According to it a dynamical process with an inherent capability of producing regular damped oscillations, could be kept going through exogenous random shocks that put it in motion whenever it tends to come to rest. This idea was formally modelled by Lord Rayleigh in the context of the violin string, the tensioned string supplying the tendency to oscillation, and the rosin of the bow supplying the exogenous shocks.

Even more interesting was the treatment of the model by Hicks, who assumed $\rho > 1$, i.e., the explosive case, but made the model nonlinear through addition of his famous "floor" and "ceiling". This, however, is one of our main topics, so we deal with it below in a section of its own.

3.11 Quasiperiodicity in Samuelson's Model

First we have to finish up the discussion of Samuelson's model through emphasizing features which are seldom discussed at all.

The solution (28) is a product an exponential growth factor, increasing whenever $a > 1$, and a simple harmonic oscillation. Note that the frequency of oscillation, despite its regular look, as a rule is an *irrational* multiple of 2π, so the oscillatory motion is *quasiperiodic*, i.e., *not* periodic in terms of the basic predefined unit time period. Hence, the time series produced by the oscillatory factor *never* repeat. Only when it happens that

$$\frac{a+c}{2\sqrt{a}} = \cos\frac{2\pi m}{n} \tag{31}$$

where m and n are integers, does the oscillatory part of the solution become periodic.

In Fig. 6 we see that this happens on the set of parabola shaped curves. We drew the curves for the basic resonances (with $m = 1$), and $n = 5, \ldots 10$. Lower basic resonances do not fall within the admissible parameter range. As $n \to \infty$, $\lim_{n\to\infty} \cos 2\pi \frac{m}{n} = 1$, so the periodic oscillation curves accumulate towards the curve:

$$\frac{a+c}{2\sqrt{a}} = 1 \tag{32}$$

which is the same as $(a+c)^2 = 4a$, representing the borderline between real and complex roots.

Fig. 6 displays the box $(a,c) \in [0,4] \times [0,1]$, further a vertical line at $a = 1$, and the parabola (32), which touches the top of this box, and towards which the periodicity curves accumulate. As mentioned, they are shown for $m = 1$ and n from 5 up to 10, and are labelled accordingly. All features, *except the periodicity curves*, are well known from Samuelson's original article, though the picture looks slightly different due to the fact that, as we know, he applied the accelerator to consumption expenditures only.

Above the parabola (32), the zero fixed point for (25) is a node, below it a focus. To the left of the line $a = 1$ the fixed point is stable, to the right it is unstable.

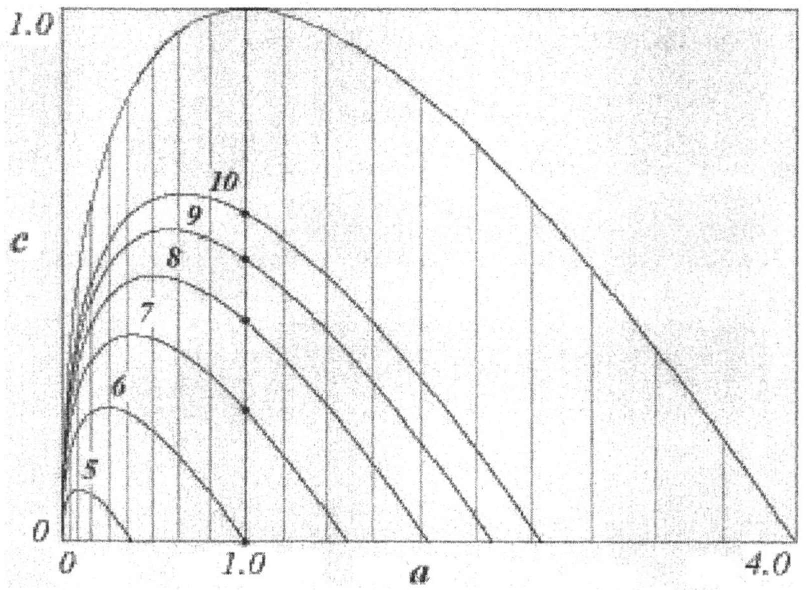

Fig. 6. *Periodic orbits in the oscillatory factor of the Samuelson model.*

New features are the set of periodicity parabolas (31). The meaning of the parabolas is that they are obtained for parameter combinations such that the oscillatory part of the solution (25) becomes periodic.

The significant fact is that they are all thin *curves*, with zero area measure. Once we, in the spirit of Hicks, make the model *nonlinear*, the curves swell to thick tongues (so called Arnol'd tongues), so periodicity becomes main frame and no longer a rare phenomenon.

We stopped the display at $n = 10$, because for higher n the stack of resonance curves accumulates and ultimately seems to fill the entire area, so that we can no longer see any distinct curves. This is, of course, deceptive, due to the finite resolution of the computer screen, which cannot display true 1-dimensional objects.

The same in fact happens over the entire area if we consider other resonances than the basic, i.e., those with $m > 1$. It is easiest to see this by studying the intersection points of the periodicity parabolas with the vertical line at $a = 1$, marked by black dots in Fig. 6.

Substituting $a = 1$ into (31), we obtain $\cos(2\pi m / n) = (1 + c)/2$, so, for any m and n, we can solve for the value of $c = 2 \cdot \cos(2\pi m / n) - 1$.

As we know, the picture displays the fundamental resonances, with $m = 1$ and $n = 5, \ldots 10$ in (31). But 1:6 is the same as 2:12, and 1:7 the same as 2:14, so we can find a 2:13, i.e., a 13-period resonance curve (not shown) between those labelled 6 and 7 in the picture.

Indeed we have $2\cos(2\pi/6)-1=0$, and $2\cos(2\pi/7)-1\approx 0.25$. Further $2\cos(4\pi/13)-1\approx 0.14$, so the 13-period resonance indeed fits between the 6-period and the 7-period ones according to (31). And so it continues: As 1:6 is the same as 4:24, and 2:13 the same as 4:26, we could again find a 4:25, i.e., a 25-period curve, with $2\cos(8\pi/25)-1\approx 0.07$ between those for periods 6 and 13, and so on, *ad infinitum*.

Considering all rational numbers m/n in (31), we need not choose any particularly high numbers m and n to see the entire screen area completely filled. (In reality both numerator and denominator range to infinity.) Again this is deceptive, due to the finite resolution of the screen. In reality, though the rational numbers are an infinite set, as are therefore the periodicity curves, they are still by far outnumbered by the irrationals. If we pick parameter values at random we *never* hit a rational point, i.e. any of the infinitely many periodic curves of Fig. 6. As mentioned, this turns out completely different for the nonlinear models to be introduced.

Fig. 6 also contains one additional feature, the grey vertical lines, which represent constant growth rates, spaced at 10% intervals, left of the line $a = 1$, *decrease* rates, ranging from -90% to -10%, right of the line $a = 1$, *increase* rates, ranging from +10% to +90%. Note that they represent *growth rates per period*, so in the right part of the diagram growth is enormous. Just consider the intersection point between the periodicity curve labelled 10 and the fifth gray line to the right of $a = 1$, where $a = 2.25$. For this parameter value we get $\rho = 1.5$ from (29). The growth over just one cycle is accordingly 1.5^{10} which approximates to 5666%, so, no matter how we define the period, the growth rates in the Samuelson model are always unrealistically huge.

By conclusion, we wanted to emphasize two features that have hardly ever been mentioned in connection with the Samuelson model: *The total absence of periodicity in the oscillations, and the absurdly huge growth rates.*

3.12 Hicksian Floor and Ceiling

As we already indicated, Hicks (1950) introduced nonlinearities in the model, thus at once removing some factual absurdities in the assumptions, and making the Samuelson model capable of producing *persistent but still bounded oscillations*.

According to the original principle of acceleration, investments are proportional to past change of income, so if income decreases, investments become negative, i.e., *dis*investments. This is not absurd in itself as long as we talk of *net* investment, as it just means that capital stock decreases. However, capital stock cannot decrease more than the maximal depreciation on capital in the absence of any renewal of worn out equipment. This provides a *lower bound* on disinvestment. If the principle of acceleration results in disinvestment that exceeds maximum depreciation, then it can only be realised through an *active destruction* of capital. As no such thing happens in reality, it is obvious that the bound must be effective. Limiting *net* investment to maximum depreciation is just the same as requiring *gross* investment to be *nonnegative*.

This is the Hicksian "floor", which requires replacing the principle of acceleration $I_t = a \cdot (Y_{t-1} - Y_{t-2})$, as stated above, by:

$$I_t = \max\{a(Y_{t-1} - Y_{t-2}), -I^f\} \tag{33}$$

where I^f denotes the absolute value of the floor disinvestment. It is clear that this makes the model nonlinear, and, in case of oscillatory motion, it is, as Duesenberry (1950) pointed out, sufficient to produce bounded motion on its own.

Hicks also introduced an upper bound. Given some fixed proportions production function, such as $Y = \min(\frac{K}{a}, \frac{L}{b})$, it is obvious that it can never be useful to increase capital stock above the value $\frac{a}{b} \cdot L$. Hence available labour force (or other limiting factors included in the production function) impose an upper bound, the "ceiling". As Hicks never wrote down the complete formal model with floor and ceiling, it remains a little ambiguous how the ceiling should be interpreted. The question is whether it is the investors who abstain from further investment when the ceiling is reached, something like:

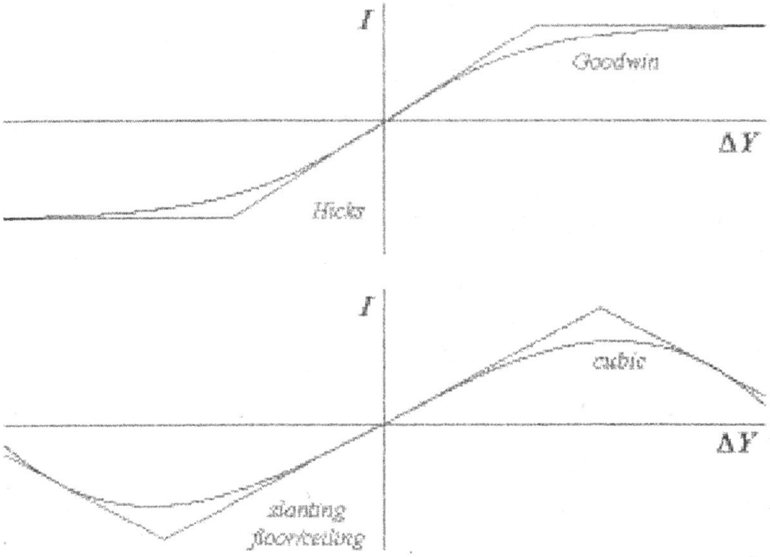

Fig. 7. *Various possible nonlinear investment functions under the principle of acceleration.*

$$I_t = \min\left\{I^c, \max\left\{a\left(Y_{t-1} - Y_{t-2}\right), -I^f\right\}\right\} \tag{34}$$

so that the ceiling as well is incorporated in the investment function, or whether one prefers not to specify who abstains from intended expenditures.

Though Hicks himself seems to have been in favour of the latter, many contributions interpreted it the other way, in particular the pioneering work by Goodwin (1951), though he preferred a *smooth* nonlinear investment function, such as a hyperbolic tangent or an arctangent, rather than a straight line cut off by lower and upper bounds. See Fig. 7 (top), where the investment function with vertical bounds, and a smooth alternative are shown.

As mentioned, Goodwin also preferred to model in continuous time. He was able to show the existence of a limit cycle in the model. However, more spectacular phenomena, such as chaos, could not occur, because they never do in second order differential equations.

Further, even in discrete time, a smooth shape with horizontal asymptotes is too mild for chaos, though its Taylor series with linear-cubic terms including backbending sections works, as shown by the present author in Puu (1989), further analysed in Puu and Sushko (2004). See Fig. 7 (bottom). The same holds true for a function with slanting bounds shown in the same picture.

There are good factual reasons for the backbending sections of the cubic and the corresponding piecewise linear function. As a rule, once a boom becomes overheated, or a slump too pronounced, the public sector usually enters the stage with contracyclical measures. This can be because of a deliberate wish to actively fight too violent swings in the cycle, but we get the same result if some responsible agencies just have long run budgets for infrastructure investments, and prefer to concentrate activities to periods when labour and materials are cheap and idle. Of course, the backbending pieces should never be allowed to get down to the horizontal axis, but small backbending segments are sufficient for chaotic outcomes.

As we said, Hicks never wrote down the complete formal model with floor and ceiling, though, from his verbal comments, one may conclude that he did not want to incorporate the ceiling along with the floor in the investment function, but rather to put it as a constraint on total spending, thus constraining income to:

$$Y_t = \min\{C_t + I_t, Y^c\} \tag{35}$$

where Y^c denotes maximum capacity production. Hicks did not quite make up his mind about what actually happens at the ceiling. He suggested inflation as the most likely event, which in the end fits expenditures in real terms to available resources, but at the same time he did not want to include prices or any other monetary variables.

A model, which, according to (33), incorporates the floor only in the investment function: $I_t = \max\{a(Y_{t-1} - Y_{t-2}), -I^f\}$, and uses the income formation equation (35): $Y_t = \min\{C_t + I_t, Y^c\}$, with consumption, as usual defined by $C_t = c \cdot Y_{t-1}$, was first fully analysed by Hommes (1991), though the formalization seems to have been due to Rau (1974). Quite as Hicks intended, such a model shows sustained oscillations of limited amplitude, and it actually makes periodicity main frame, as shown in Gallegati *et al.* (2003).

But, Hicks wanted more than this, he also wanted to incorporate growth along with cycles in the process, to be more precise, not in terms of growing *amplitude* of the swings, as in Samuelson's original model, but a *growth trend* around which bounded cyclic oscillations took place. However, he did not obtain this trend *within* the model, so he inserted it as an *exogenous* growth of the autonomous expenditures, assuming something like $A_t = A_0(1+g)^t$.

Of course, then (35) transforms to $Y_t = \min\{C_t + I_t + A_t, Y^c\}$. In his drawings Hicks, moreover, indicated that, in order to have a tractable model, both bounds as well must be growing at the same rate as the autonomous expenditures. Gandolfo (1985) used this combination of assumptions in an exercise, where the reader was challenged to prove a proposition, which, by the way, is not true. Given the three exogenously given and equal growth rates, the model can easily be transformed into the stationary case analysed by Hommes. It is this case which is analysed in Gallegati *et al.*

As we already stressed, Gandolfo's case is what best seems to conform to Hicks's drawings (in semilogarithmic scale, where exponential curves are transformed into straight lines).

There is a big problem with this setup. Of course, it is arbitrary to assume equal growth rates for autonomous expenditures, floor, and ceiling, but this is not the real problem. As Hicks related the floor to maximum depreciation on capital, it is obvious that, with accumulating capital, the floor level should be *receding, rather than growing.*

In some recent publications, Puu *et al.* (2005) and Sushko *et al.* (2004), a model was analysed where the floor was actually tied to the stock of capital, by putting (33) in the form:

$$I_t = \max\{a(Y_{t-1} - Y_{t-2}), -rK_{t-1}\} \tag{36}$$

Obviously, one has to include capital in the model, but this is no problem, because there already *exists* a capital formation theory inherent in the Hicksian model. Investments are defined $I_t = K_t - K_{t-1}$, so one can just put it the other way and write:

$$K_t = K_{t-1} + I_t \tag{37}$$

As there is a theory for investments (36), there is also one for capital formation in terms of the cumulative sum of past investments. One feature of this model is that, due to the growing capital stock, a growth trend in income is actually generated endogenously, without introducing any exogenous growth terms at all. Another is that limited amplitude growth rate cycles take place around this trend, and that the average growth rates over cycles are reduced by orders of magnitude from those of the original multiplier-accelerator model.

We could not leave Hicks's contributions without emphasizing that he also introduced distributed lag systems for multiplier and accelerator, thus raising the order of the recurrence equation. Numerical simulations at that time sometimes produced just irregularity, as nobody could yet put the tag "chaos" on it, but Hommes (1991) showed that just raising the order of the difference equation by one results in chaotic motion. The order can, of course, also be raised through coupling different open economies together through interregional trade, each modelled by a second order process. See Sushko *et al.* (2003).

3.13 The Hicksian Revolution

It is obvious that Hicks's book of 1950 had a tremendous influence on business cycle modelling. The same year saw Duesenberry's penetrating review, and the following year Goodwin's model as well as Baumol's and Hansen's books. Allen (1956) cannot be too highly recommended as a concise compendium of the state of the art after the "Hicksian revolution".

In 1950 an important conference on business cycles was held at Oxford. A delightful memorial of that is the following poem composed during the conference by Sir Dennis Robertson. It reflects both the non-mathematician's frustration at the mathematical language, which even Keynes avoided, but which was creeping into economics. Its main importance is that it accurately focused the main topic of the conference, as well as showing a full understanding of the fact that it was nonlinearity that was brought into dynamic economics. The poem was originally published in the proceedings of that conference, but republished in Robertson (1956):

As soon as I could safely toddle
My parents handed me a model.
My brisk and energetic pater
Provided the accelerator,
My mother, with her kindly gumption,
The function guiding my consumption;
And every week I had from her
A lovely new parameter,
With lots of little leads and lags
In pretty parabolic bags.

With optimistic expectations
I started on my explorations,

And swore to move without a swerve
Along my sinusoidal curve.
Alas! I knew how this would end;
I've mixed the cycle and the trend,
And fear that, growing daily skinnier,
I have at length become non-linear.
I wander glumly round the house
As though I were exogenous,
And hardly capable of feeling
The difference 'tween floor and ceiling.
I scarcely now, a pallid ghost,
Can tell ex ante from ex post;
My thoughts are sadly inelastic,
My acts incurably stochastic.

References

Aftalion, A, 1909, La réalité des surproductions générales, Révue d'Économie Politique 23:81-117, 201-29, 241-59.

Allen, R.G.D., 1956, *Mathematical Economics*. Macmillan, London.

Arnol'd, V.I., 1983, *Geometrical Methods in the Theory of Ordinary Differential Equations*, Springer, Berlin.

Barro, R.J. and Grossman, H.I., 1976, *Money, Employment, and Inflation*, Cambridge University Press, Cambridge.

Baumol, W.J., 1951, *Economic Dynamics*, Macmillan, London.

Duesenberry, J., 1950, "Hicks on the trade cycle". *The Quarterly Journal of Economics* 64:464-76

Forrester, J.W., 1961, *Industrial Dynamics*, MIT Press, Cambridge Mass.

Frisch, R., 1933, "Propagation problems and impulse problems in dynamic economics". *Economic Essays in Honour of Gustav Cassel*. Allen & Unwin, London.

Gallegati, M., Gardini, L., Puu, T., and Sushko, I., 2003, "Hicks's Trade Cycle Revisited: Cycles and Bifurcations", *Mathematics and Computers in Simulations*, 63:505-527

Gandolfo, G., 1985, *Economic Dynamics: Methods and Models*. North-Holland, Amsterdam.

Goodwin, R.M., 1951, "The nonlinear accelerator and the persistence of business cycles". *Econometrica* 19:1-17

von Haberler, G., 1937, *Prosperity and Depression*. Harvard University Press, Cambridge Mass.

Hansen, A.H., 1951, *Business Cycles and National Income, Norton*, New York.

Harrod, R.F., 1948, *Towards a Dynamic Economics*, Macmillan, London.

Hicks, J.R., 1937, "Mr. Keynes and the 'classics'". *Econometrica* 5:147-59.

Hicks, J.R., 1950, A *Contribution to the Theory of the Trade Cycle*. Oxford University Press, Oxford.

Hommes, C.H., 1991, *Chaotic Dynamics in Economic Models*. Wolters-Noodhoff, Groningen.

Kahn, R.F., 1931, "The relation of home investment to unemployment", *The Economic Journal* 41:173-98.

Keynes, J.M., 1936, *The General Theory of Employment, Interest, and Money*, Macmillan, London.

Klein, L., 1947, *The Keynesian Revolution, Macmillan*, New York.

Palander, T.F., 1942, "Keynes allmänna teori och dess tillämpning inom ränte-, multiplikator- och pristeorien", *Ekonomisk Tidskrift* 44:233-72

Patinkin, D., 1956, *Money, Interest, and Prices*, Row & Peterson, Evanstone, Ill.

Phillips, A.W., 1954, "Stabilisation policy in a closed economy", *The Economic Journal* 64:290-323

Puu, T., 1989, "Nonlinear economic dynamics", *Lecture Notes in Economics and Mathematical Systems* 336, (Springer-Verlag, Berlin)

Puu, T., Gardini, L. and Sushko, I., 2005, "A multiplier-accelerator model with floor determined by capital stock", *Journal of Economic Behavior and Organization*, 56:331-348

Puu, T. and Sushko, I., 2004, "A business cycle model with cubic nonlinearity", *Chaos, Solitons & Fractals* 19:597-612

Rau, N., 1974, *Trade Cycle: Theory and Evidence*. Macmillan, London.

Robertson, D.H., 1956, *Economic Commentaries*, Staples Press, London.

Sushko, I., Puu, T. and Gardini, L., 2003, "Business cycles in two regions linked by interregional trade: The Hicksian floor-roof model revisited", *Chaos, Solitons & Fractals* 18:593-612

Sushko, I., Gardini, L. and Puu, T., 2004, "Tongues of periodicity in a family of two-dimensional maps of real Möbius type", *Chaos, Solitons & Fractals*, 21:403-412

Samuelson, P.A., 1939, "Interactions between the multiplier analysis and the principle of acceleration", *Review of Economics and Statistics* 21:75-8.

Samuelson, P. A., 1947, *Foundations of Economic Analysis*, Harvard University Press, Cambridge, Mass.

Schumpeter, J.A., 1954, *History of Economic Analysis*. Macmillan, London.

Strutt, J.W.S., Lord Rayleigh, 1894, *The Theory of Sound*, Macmillan, London.

4 Multiplier-Accelerator Models with Random Perturbations

Volker Böhm *

4.1 Introduction

In his original contribution Samuelson (1939) for the first time presented one of the major structural reasons of possible cyclical behavior in macroeconomic models: the interaction of the multiplier and the accelerator principles which induces a *second order delay equation* of real aggregate output. While he realized that his model could not generate permanent cycles, it was Hicks (1950) in a subsequent extension introducing ceilings and floors showing that permanent "harmonic" fluctuations arise in a natural way under the Multiplier-Accelerator principle. These models have received wide interest within dynamical systems theory, since they supply a wide range of explanations of truly complex business cycle phenomena originating from a linear model with restrictions implying a minimal degree of non-linearity.

As an alternative to such restrictions, the introduction of random perturbations to linear delay systems has also served as an explanation of business cycle phenomena which has mainly been studied within linear time series analysis. The recent development of new techniques from the theory of stochastic dynamical systems allows an extension of results within the dynamic frame work for the Multiplier-Accelerator model. Most importantly, however, these techniques combined with the availability of efficient and fast numerical techniques allow a significantly more detailed insight into the range of qualitative features of the random Multiplier-Accelerator model.

*Acknowledgement: I am indebted to Thorsten Pampel, George Vachadze, and Jan Wenzelburger for useful discussions and criticism. This research was part of the project "Endogene stochastische Konjunkturtheorie" supported in part by the Deutsche Forschungsgemeinschaft under grant BO 635/9-3.

This chapter takes this new view of random dynamical systems theory to examine the classical Multiplier-Accelerator model when random perturbations are introduced to model parameters. The emphasis of the chapter is on the revelation of the dynamical richness of business cycle scenarios which may occur in such simple economic models.

4.2 Random Dynamical Systems

The traditional description of the dynamic evolution of stochastic economic models is carried out using the mathematical formalization of stochastic processes, i. e. as a family of random variables given a specified exogenous structure of stochastic properties. When the standard tools of stochastic processes are used, the actual evolution of the stochastic data, (the sample paths), is often suppressed in favor of results and characterizations of the evolution of the probabilistic features or the statistical properties of the model. In this case the experimental perspective of the characteristics of a specific sample path, i. e. the empirical observation becomes of secondary importance. In many economic applications, however, as well as from a dynamical systems point of view, it is often natural and desirable to analyze the generation of stochastic orbits directly. This can be done in many situations by modelling the stochastic environment of a dynamical economic system in an explicit fashion.

Consider for example a parameterized dynamical system $F : \mathbb{R}^m \times \mathbb{R}^n \to \mathbb{R}^n$, given by a family of mappings

$$F(\cdot, \xi) : \mathcal{X} \subset \mathbb{R}^n \to \mathcal{X}, \tag{1}$$

where $\xi \in \mathbb{R}^m$ is a vector of parameters which is subjected to random perturbations and x is the vector of endogenous variables. The evolution of x (the orbit) for a *given* value of the parameter $\xi \in \mathbb{R}^m$ is described in the usual way by

$$x_t = F_\xi^t(x_0) \qquad F_\xi \equiv F(\cdot, \xi), \tag{2}$$

i. e. the *dynamics* follow the rules and the description of a deterministic dynamical system once the value of a particular ξ is given. Now let ξ follow a given random path described by $\omega := (\ldots, \xi_{s-2}, \xi_{s-1}, \xi_s, \xi_{s+1}, \ldots)$. Then, the generation of the random path

$$x_{t+1} = F_{\xi_t}(x_t) = F(x_t, \xi_t) \qquad \text{for all} \quad t \tag{3}$$

means that the change of ξ implies choosing at each t a *different mapping*. If $F(\cdot, \xi)$, $\xi \in [\underline{\xi}, \overline{\xi}]$ is a family of contraction mappings with upper and lower bounds $[\underline{\xi}, \overline{\xi}]$, then for any random path ω the associated evolution of x will eventually be trapped in some compact interval $[\underline{x}, \underline{\underline{x}}]$. For a one dimensional system, for example, the dynamic evolution of $\{x_t\}$ can be visualized as in Figure 1 for any initial value x_0 and a given $\omega = (\ldots, \underline{\xi}, \overline{\xi}, \underline{\xi}, \overline{\xi}, \overline{\xi}, \underline{\xi}, \ldots)$.

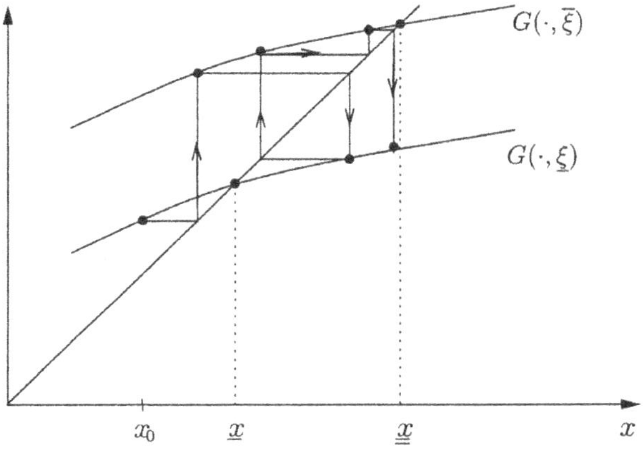

Figure 1: *A random orbit of x for ω.*

Formally a random dynamical system in the sense of Arnold (1998)[1] has two building blocks:

- a model describing a dynamical system perturbed by noise
- and a model of the noise.

1) The exogenous noise process is modelled as a so called *metric dynamical system* known from ergodic theory.

Let $\vartheta : \Omega \to \Omega$ be a measurable invertible mapping on a probability space $(\Omega, \mathcal{F}, \mathbb{P})$ which is measure preserving with respect to $\mathbb{P}$ and whose inverse ϑ^{-1} is again measurable. Assume that $\mathbb{P}$ is ergodic with respect to ϑ and let ϑ^t denote the t-th iterate of the map ϑ. The collection $(\Omega, \mathcal{F}, \mathbb{P}, \{\vartheta^t\}_{t \in \mathbb{Z}})$ is called an *ergodic metric dynamical system* (for details see Arnold (1998)).

[1] A synthesis of this view of dynamical systems with noise has been developed by many researchers among them Kesten (1973), Brandt (1986), Borovkov (1998), Lasota & Mackey (1994).

Any stationary ergodic process $\{\xi_t\}_{t\in\mathbb{N}}$, $\xi_t : \Omega \longrightarrow \mathbb{R}^m$ can be represented by an ergodic dynamical system. This implies that there exists a measurable map $\xi : \Omega \rightarrow \mathbb{R}^m$ such that for each fixed $\omega \in \Omega$, a sample path of the noise process is given by $\xi_t(\omega) = \xi(\vartheta^t\omega)$, $t \in \mathbb{Z}$. Such a process is often referred to as a *real noise process* .

2) The second ingredient is a parameterized family of invertible time-one maps of topological dynamical systems $F : X \times \mathbb{R}^m \longrightarrow X, X \subset \mathbb{R}^K$ inducing the *random difference equation* $F : X \times \Omega \longrightarrow X$,

$$x_{t+1} = F(x_t, \xi(\vartheta^t\omega)) \equiv F(\vartheta^t\omega)x_t. \tag{4}$$

For any x_0, the iteration of the map F under the perturbation ω induces a measurable map $\phi : \mathbb{Z} \times \Omega \times X \longrightarrow X$ defined by

$$\phi(t, \omega, x_0) := \begin{cases} (F(\vartheta^{t-1}\omega) \circ \ldots \circ F(\omega))x_0 & \text{if} \quad t > 0 \\ x_0 & \text{if} \quad t = 0 \\ (F(\vartheta^t\omega)^{-1} \circ \ldots \circ F(\vartheta^{-1}\omega)^{-1})x_0 & \text{if} \quad t < 0 \end{cases} \tag{5}$$

such that $x_t = \phi(t, \omega, x_0)$ is the state of the system at time t.

- For any $x_0 \in X$ and any $\omega \in \Omega$, the sequence $\gamma(x_0) := \{x_t\}_{t\in\mathbb{Z}}$ with $x_t = \phi(t, \omega)x_0$ is called an orbit of the random dynamical system ϕ.

- For any t and s one has:

$$\phi(t + s, \omega, x_0) = F(\vartheta^{t+s}\omega) \circ \ldots \circ F(\omega)x_0 \tag{6}$$

$$= \phi(t, \vartheta^t\omega, \phi(s, \omega, x_0)) \tag{7}$$

Many stochastic processes can be described as metric dynamical systems. As an example, consider the representation for a standard i. i. d. process. Let $\{\xi_t\}$ denote a family of independent and identically distributed random variables with values in $W \subset \mathbb{R}^m$, which have the common distribution (measure) λ. Then one has:

- $\Omega := W^{\mathbb{Z}} = \cdots\cdot W \times W \times W \times \cdots$

- $\mathcal{F} = \mathcal{B}(\Omega)$ Borel σ-algebra

- $\omega = (\ldots, \xi_{s-1}, \xi_s, \xi_{s+1}, \ldots)$ with $\omega(s) \equiv \xi_s$

- $\theta : \Omega \longrightarrow \Omega$ is the so called shift map with $\omega \mapsto \theta\omega$ and $\theta\omega(s) = \omega(s+1) \equiv \xi_{s+1}$
- $\xi : \Omega \longrightarrow \mathbb{R}^m$ is the evaluation map with $\xi(\omega) \equiv \omega(0)$
- $\xi_t = \xi(\theta^t \omega)$
- $\mathbb{P} = \lambda^{\mathbb{Z}}$

4.3 Random Fixed Points

The long run behavior of a random dynamical system is described by random attractors, the random analogue of an attractor of a deterministic dynamical system, the random fixed point being a special case[2].

Definition 4.1
Consider a random dynamical system ϕ induced by the continuous mapping $F : X \times \mathbb{R}^m \longrightarrow X$ with real noise process $\xi_t = \xi \circ \vartheta^t$, $\xi : \Omega \longrightarrow \mathbb{R}^m$ measurable, over the ergodic dynamical system $(\Omega, \mathcal{F}, \mathbb{P}, (\vartheta^t))$.

*A **random fixed point** of ϕ is a random variable $x_* : \Omega \longrightarrow X$ on $(\Omega, \mathcal{F}, \mathbb{P})$ such that almost surely*

$$x_*(\vartheta\omega) = \phi(1, \omega, x_*(\omega)) = F(x_*(\omega), \xi(\omega)) \quad \textit{for all} \quad \omega \in \Omega', \tag{8}$$

where $\Omega' \subset \Omega$ is a ϑ-invariant set of full measure, $\mathbb{P}(\Omega') = 1$.

Thus, a random fixed point is a stationary solution of the stochastic difference equation generated by the metric dynamical system. Some implications of the definition can be observed directly. If F is independent of the perturbation ω, then the Definition 4.1 coincides with the one of a deterministic fixed point. Definition 4.1 implies that $x_*(\vartheta^{t+1}\omega) = F(x_*(\vartheta^t\omega), \xi(\vartheta^t\omega))$ for all times t. Therefore, the orbit $\{x_*(\vartheta^t\omega)\}_{t\in\mathbb{N}}$, $\omega \in \Omega$ generated by x_* solves the random difference equation

$$x_{t+1} = F(x_t, \xi_t(\omega)).$$

Stationarity and ergodicity of ϑ implies that the stochastic process $\{x_*(\vartheta^t)\}_{t\in\mathbb{N}}$ is stationary and ergodic.

[2] Schmalfuß (1996, 1998), also Arnold (1998).

The random fixed point x_* induces an invariant distribution $x_*\mathbb{P}$ on $\mathbb{R}^K$ defined by

$$x_*\mathbb{P}(B) \quad := \quad \mathbb{P}\{\omega \in \Omega \,|\, x_*(\omega) \in B\}\,. \tag{9}$$

The invariance of the measure $\mathbb{P}$ under the shift ϑ implies the invariance of $x_*\mathbb{P}$, i. e. $(x_*\vartheta)\mathbb{P}(B) = x_*\mathbb{P}(B)$. If, in addition, $\mathbb{E}||x_*|| < \infty$, then

$$\lim_{T\to\infty} \frac{1}{T} \sum_{t=0}^{T} 1_B(x_*(\vartheta^t \omega)) = x_*\mathbb{P}(B) \tag{10}$$

for every $B \in \mathcal{B}(X)$. In other words, the empirical law of an orbit is well defined and it is equal to the distribution $x_*\mathbb{P}$ of x_*. Finally, if the perturbation corresponds to an i. i. d. process the orbit of the fixed point x_* will be an ergodic Markov equilibrium in the usual sense (cf. Duffie, Geanakoplos, Mas-Colell & McLennan 1994). The following definition of a stable random

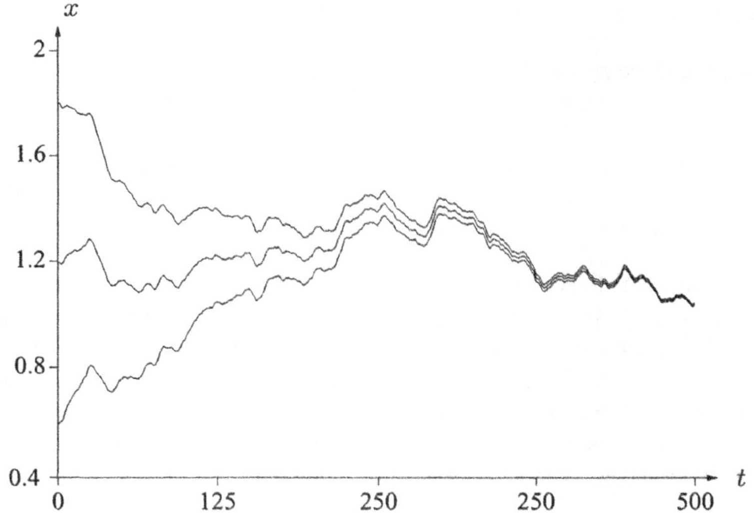

Figure 2: *Asymptotic convergence to a random fixed point.*

fixed point (due to Schmalfuß (1996, 1998)) includes the notion of stability given by Definition 7.4.6 in Arnold (1998).

Definition 4.2

A random fixed point x_* is called ***asymptotically stable*** *with respect to a norm $\|\cdot\|$, if there exists a random neighborhood $U(\omega) \subset X$, $\omega \in \Omega$ such that $\mathbb{P}$- a.s.*

$$\lim_{t\to\infty} \|\phi(t,\omega,x_0) - x_*(\vartheta^t\omega)\| = 0 \quad \textit{for all } x_0(\omega) \in U(\omega).$$

Figure 2 portrays the convergence property of a random fixed point for the one dimensional growth model for three random orbits associated with different initial conditions and the same noise path.

The following theorem, which is due to Arnold (1998)[3], will be the central result applied to the random Multiplier-Accelerator model supporting the numerical analysis and implying the dynamic and statistical properties to be exhibited. Consider *invertible* affine transformations on $\mathbb{R}^n$ defined by pairs (A, b) where A is an invertible $n \times n$ matrix and $b \in \mathbb{R}^n$. Let $\mathcal{A}$ denote the space of non singular $n \times n$ matrices and assume A, A^{-1}, and b to be bounded.

Theorem 4.1

Let $F_\xi : \mathbb{R}^n \to \mathbb{R}^n$ be an invertible affine random dynamical system with stationary noise process $\{\xi_t\}$ on the probability space $(\Omega, \mathcal{F}, \mathbb{P})$. Assume $\xi : \Omega \to (\mathcal{A}, \mathbb{R}^n)$ with $\xi(\omega) = (A(\omega), b(\omega))$, which implies the random difference equation

$$x_{t+1} = A(\vartheta^t\omega)x_t + b(\vartheta^t\omega) \tag{11}$$

and the random dynamical system[4]

$$\phi(t,x,\omega) := \begin{cases} \Phi(t,\omega)\left(x + \sum_{j=0}^{t-1} \Phi(j+1,\omega)^{-1} b(\vartheta^j\omega)\right), & t > 0 \\ x & t = 0 \\ \Phi(t,\omega)\left(x - \sum_{j=t}^{-1} \Phi(j+1,\omega)^{-1} b(\vartheta^j\omega)\right) & t < 0 \end{cases} \tag{12}$$

where

$$\Phi(t,\omega) := \begin{cases} A(\vartheta^{t-1}\omega)\cdots A(\omega), & t > 0 \\ I & t = 0 \\ A^{-1}(\vartheta^t\omega)\cdots A^{-1}(\vartheta^{-1}\omega) & t < 0. \end{cases} \tag{13}$$

---

[3]Theorem 5.6.5 and Corollary 5.6.6.

[4]See Chapter 5 in Arnold (1998).

1. *There exists a unique random fixed point* $x_* : \Omega \to \mathbb{R}^n$ *such that*

$$x_*(\vartheta^{t+1}\omega) = A(\vartheta^t\omega)x_*(\vartheta^t\omega) - b(\vartheta^t\omega) \qquad \mathbb{P} - a.s. \tag{14}$$

2. x_* *induces an invariant distribution* $x_*\mathbb{P} \equiv \mu_*$
3. *with unique support* $supp(\mu_*) = A_*$
4. *if* $A(\omega)$ *are contracting maps,* x_* *is globally attracting, i. e. for any* x_0

$$\lim_{t\to\infty} |\phi(t,\omega,x_0) - x_*(\vartheta^t\omega)| = 0 \qquad \mathbb{P} - a.s. \tag{15}$$

and has the explicit form

$$x_*(\omega) := \sum_{t=-\infty}^{-1} \Phi(t+1,\omega)^{-1}\, b(\vartheta^t\omega) \tag{16}$$

4.4 Random Multiplier Accelerator Models

Consider the standard Multiplier-Accelerator model (in the version of Hicks (1950)) defined by the three equations

$$\begin{aligned} C &= m^0 + mY_{-1} \qquad 0 < m < 1 \qquad m_0, v_0 \geq 0 & (17)\\ I &= v^0 + v(Y_{-1} - Y_{-2}) \qquad v > 0 & (18)\\ Y &= C + I & (19) \end{aligned}$$

implying the determination of aggregate real income in each period as

$$Y = (m_0 + v_0) + (m+v)Y_{-1} - vY_{-2}, \tag{20}$$

which is a linear delay equation of order two. Using the form

$$f(y_1, y_2) := (m_0 + v_0) + (m+v)y_2 - vy_1 \tag{21}$$

for the delay map f implies the associated two dimensional affine dynamical system $F : \mathbb{R}^2 \to \mathbb{R}^2$ defined by

$$\begin{aligned} F(y_1, y_2) &:= (y_2, f(y_1, y_2)) & (22)\\ &= (y_2, (m_0 + v_0) + (m+v)y_2 - vy_1) & (23)\\ &= \begin{pmatrix} 0 & 1 \\ -v & m+v \end{pmatrix} \begin{pmatrix} y_1 \\ y_2 \end{pmatrix} + \begin{pmatrix} 0 \\ m_0 + v_0 \end{pmatrix}. & (24) \end{aligned}$$

The function F has the unique fixed point (stationary state)

$$\bar{y} = \left(\frac{m_0 + v_0}{1 - m}, \frac{m_0 + v_0}{1 - m} \right). \tag{25}$$

The accelerator v has no influence on the steady state $\bar{y}$ while aggregate demand $m_0 + v_0$ does not influence the stability of the steady state. $\bar{y} >> 0$ requires $m < 1$. $\bar{y}$ is asymptotically stable if and only if $0 \leq m < 1$ and $0 \leq v < 1$. From the characteristic equation

$$\chi(\lambda) := \lambda^2 - (m + v)\lambda + v$$

one finds that the eigenvalues $\lambda_{1,2}$ are complex if and only if $m < 2\sqrt{v} - v$. Thus, for stability considerations (the projection into $\mathbb{R}^2$ of) the space of parameters can be partitioned into a complex and into a real region as depicted in Figure 3. Therefore, for $(m, v) \in [0, 1)^2$ the mapping F is a linear contraction with a unique steady state which is either a stable node or a stable focus. The above description shows that the Multiplier-Accelerator

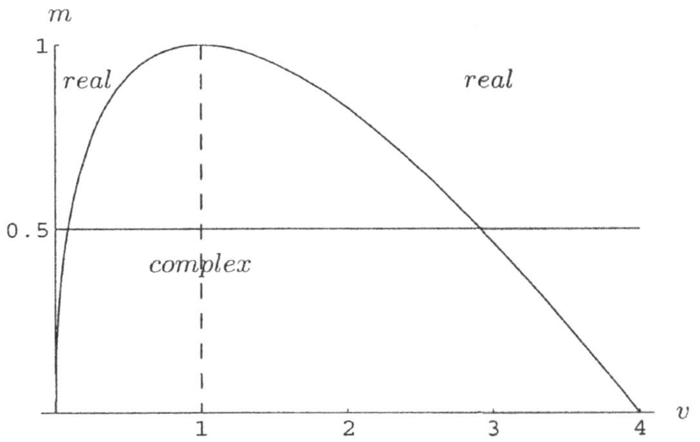

Figure 3: *Regions of eigenvalues in Multiplier-Accelerator Model.*

model consists of a family of affine parameterized maps $F_\mu : \mathbb{R}^2 \to \mathbb{R}^2$ with parameters $\mu \in \mathbb{R}^3_+$. Without restricting economic generality, one may assume $v_0 \equiv 0$ capturing all effects of aggregate demand in the parameter $0 \leq m_0$ and thus restrict the analysis to situations of nonnegative parameter values $\mu := (m_0, m, v) \in \mathbb{R}^3_+$, i. e. aggregate demand, the multiplier, and the accelerator. In most applications, economic reasoning suggests further that the multiplier m takes values only between zero and one and that the accelerator v is restricted to values between 0 and 4. Therefore, for the rest of the analysis define the set of possible parameter values as

$$M := \{(m_0, m, v) \in \mathbb{R}^3 \,|\, 0 \le m_0 \le \bar{m}_0, 0 \le m \le 1, 0 \le v \le 4\}. \quad (26)$$

As a consequence, the *Random Multiplier Accelerator Model* consists of the random family of affine maps $F_\mu : \mathbb{R}^2 \to \mathbb{R}^2$ with an associated (vector valued) stochastic process of parameters $\{\mu_t\}_{t=0}^{\infty}$ defined on the probability space $(\Omega, \mathcal{F}, \mathbb{P})$ which takes values in M, i. e. $\mu_t : \Omega \to M$. More specifically, let $\mu(\omega) \equiv (m_0(\omega), m(\omega), v(\omega))$, and define

$$A(\omega) := \begin{pmatrix} 0 & 1 \\ -v(\omega) & m(\omega) + v(\omega) \end{pmatrix} \quad \text{and} \quad b(\omega) := \begin{pmatrix} 0 \\ m_0(\omega) \end{pmatrix}.$$

which implies the random difference equation

$$x_{t+1} = A(\vartheta^t \omega) x_t + b(\vartheta^t \omega)$$

(as in equation (11)) and the random dynamical system as in equation (12). This formulation fits precisely into the mathematical framework presented in Section 4.2. As a consequence, one has the following result for the class of random multiplier accelerator models.

Proposition 4.1
Let the random multiplier accelerator model F_μ be given as in equation (24) and (26) and assume that the random perturbation is described by a stationary and ergodic process $\{\mu_t\}$ defined on a probability space $(\Omega, \mathcal{F}, \mathbb{P})$ with values in a compact set $\bar{M} := \{(m_0, m, v) \in \bar{M} \,|\, m < 1, v < 1\} \subset M$.

(i) There exists a unique random fixed point $y^* : \Omega \longrightarrow \mathbb{R}^2_+$, given by

$$y^*(\omega) := \sum_{t=-\infty}^{-1} \Phi(t+1, \omega)^{-1} b(\vartheta^t \omega), \quad (27)$$

with

$$\Phi(t, \omega) := \begin{cases} A(\vartheta^{t-1}\omega) \cdots A(\omega), & t > 0 \\ I & t = 0 \\ A^{-1}(\vartheta^t \omega) \cdots A^{-1}(\vartheta^{-1}\omega) & t < 0. \end{cases} \quad (28)$$

(ii) y^* is asymptotically stable and induces a unique (stationary) invariant distribution $y^*\mathbb{P}$ on $\mathbb{R}^2$ defined by

$$(y^*\mathbb{P})(B) \quad := \quad \mathbb{P}\{\omega \in \Omega \,|\, y^*(\omega) \in B\} \tag{29}$$

for every $B \in \mathcal{B}(\mathbb{R}^2)$.

(iii) Moreover,

$$\lim_{T\to\infty} \frac{1}{T} \sum_{t=0}^{T} 1_B(y^*(\vartheta^t\omega)) = y^*\mathbb{P}(B) = \mathbb{P}\{\omega \in \Omega | y^*(\omega) \in B\} \tag{30}$$

for every $B \in \mathcal{B}(\mathbb{R}^2)$.

Equation (30) states that the empirical law of an orbit is well defined and it is asymptotically equal to the distribution $y^*\mathbb{P}$ of y^*.

The result follows as a direct application of Theorem 4.1. The given noise process can be represented as a real noise process in the sense of Arnold (1998). The assumption that the multiplier m as well as the accelerator v are assumed to be strictly less than one imply that the family of mappings F_μ are contractions. Therefore, existence, uniqueness, and asymptotic stability of the random fixed point y^* follows from Theorem 4.1. While the result here is formulated for the simple two dimensional Multiplier-Accelerator model, the mathematical framework is much more general. It covers the whole class of affine random contraction mappings of finite dimension and not only delay systems. Such random models have unique globally attracting random fix points (stationary solutions). Most importantly, however, these properties hold for very general stationary and ergodic perturbations whether smooth or discrete, including in particular Markov processes and so called Markov switching models. Thus, from a time series perspective, Arnold's result sets a bench mark for the description of the invariance of affine economic models. Therefore, a large spectrum of qualitatively different sample profiles can be shown to appear, all consistent with a unique stationary and asymptotically stable solution. Observe that this was primarily obtained by the *dynamic* features of the construction chosen by the approach given in Arnold (1998).

The major purpose of the remainder of this section is to examine the *dynamic qualitative* properties of some specific random examples using numerical simulations. This will reveal insights into the nature of the recurrence of the stochastic multiplier accelerator model and into the role of the different parameters determining the invariant behavior. This can be done safely (with proper care of the numerical analysis) due to the ergodicity property given in condition (30). In this case, a statistical examination of the long run behavior of one generic sample path suffices to characterize the invariant statistical properties of the model.

¿From an economic point of view the three perturbations correspond to structurally different situations:

1. a perturbation of the additive parameter m_0 corresponding to random exogenous demand in consumption or investment;

2. a perturbation of the multiplicative parameters, $0 \leq m, v \leq 1$, corresponding to random propensities to consume or a random accelerator.

The numerical experiments will use i. i. d. processes only, in spite of the fact that general Markov processes fall under the assumptions of Proposition 4.1 as well. First, the analysis investigates the additive noise situation separately from each of the multiplicative effects. The additive noise will be chosen to be smooth, while the multiplicative and accelerator will be chosen from discrete sets. Mixing these two types reveal some specific and interesting features.

4.5 The Dynamics with Smooth Additive i. i. d. Noise

Consider the random equation (21) with an aggregate demand shock $\xi \geq 0$

$$f_\lambda(y_1, y_2, \xi) := m_0 + \xi + (m+v)y_2 - v y_1 \tag{31}$$

which is distributed uniformly on some compact interval

$$\xi \sim [0, 2\lambda], \qquad \lambda \geq 0, \tag{32}$$

implying a mean $\mathbb{E}\xi = \lambda$ and a variance $\mathbb{V}\xi = \lambda^2/3$. In time series analysis such systems are referred to as a second order autoregressive process, denoted AR(2). Equation (31) induces a parameterized two dimensional random dynamical system $F_\lambda : \mathbb{R}^2 \to \mathbb{R}^2$ given by

$$F_\lambda(y_1, y_2, \xi) \quad := \quad (y_2, f_\lambda(y_1, y_2, \xi)) \tag{33}$$

$$= \begin{pmatrix} 0 & 1 \\ -v & m+v \end{pmatrix} \begin{pmatrix} y_1 \\ y_2 \end{pmatrix} + \begin{pmatrix} 0 \\ m_0 + \xi \end{pmatrix} \tag{34}$$

with additive noise, a so called Vector Autoregressive System of order 1, denoted VAR(1) in time series analysis. The characteristics of the stationary distribution are known from the standard time series approach and can be calculated explicitly in this particular case.

Under the hypotheses of Proposition 4.1 the unique stationary solution can be characterized numerically by the limiting statistical behavior of any *single* sample path to be calculated from data. On the other hand, the true moments of the random fixed point y^* can also be calculated given the noise distribution $\xi \sim [0, 2\lambda]$ for any $\lambda \geq 0$.

The stationarity of y^* implies that the first moment $\mathbb{E}y^*$ must satisfy

$$\mathbb{E}y^* = \begin{pmatrix} 0 & 1 \\ -v & m+v \end{pmatrix} \mathbb{E}y^* + \begin{pmatrix} 0 \\ m_0 + \mathbb{E}\xi \end{pmatrix}.$$

Hence, y_1^* and y_2^* have the same mean given by

$$\mathbb{E}\begin{pmatrix} y_1^* \\ y_2^* \end{pmatrix} = \left(I - \begin{pmatrix} 0 & 1 \\ -v & m+v \end{pmatrix}\right)^{-1} \begin{pmatrix} 0 \\ m_0 + \mathbb{E}\xi \end{pmatrix} = \frac{m_0 + \lambda}{1-m}\begin{pmatrix} 1 \\ 1 \end{pmatrix}. \tag{35}$$

The covariance matrix $\mathbb{C}\mathrm{ov}(y_1^*, y_2^*)$ satisfies

$$\mathbb{C}\mathrm{ov}(y_1^*, y_2^*) = \begin{pmatrix} 0 & 1 \\ -v & m+v \end{pmatrix} \mathbb{C}\mathrm{ov}(y_1^*, y_2^*) \begin{pmatrix} 0 & 1 \\ -v & m+v \end{pmatrix}^T + \begin{pmatrix} 0 & 0 \\ 0 & \mathbb{V}\xi \end{pmatrix}.$$

As the solution one obtains

$$\mathbb{C}\mathrm{ov}(y_1^*, y_2^*) = \begin{pmatrix} v_{11} & v_{12} \\ v_{21} & v_{22} \end{pmatrix} \tag{36}$$

with

$$\mathbb{V}y^* = v_{11} = v_{22} = \frac{\lambda^2}{3(1-v)} \frac{1+v}{(1+v)^2 - (m+v)^2} \tag{37}$$

and

$$v_{12} = v_{21} = \frac{m+v}{1+v} v_{22} = \frac{\lambda^2}{3(1-v)} \frac{m+v}{(1+v)^2 - (m+v)^2}. \tag{38}$$

Therefore,

$$0 < v_{12} = v_{21} < v_{11} = v_{22}, \qquad \text{for all } \lambda > 0,\ 0 < m < 1.$$

Observe, that the first moment is independent of the accelerator and it depends on (m, λ) only. The multiplier and accelerator together induce a positive cross correlation on the time series. Both correlation coefficients increase as the accelerator increases. Notice in particular, that with a higher accelerator the attractor increases in size, including values of the state variable less than $m_0/(1-m)$ and larger than $(m_0 + 2\lambda)/(1-m)$. For small values of v, the attractor lies inside the cube defined by these two values. Since ξ has a uniform distribution, the attractor as well as the distribution must be symmetric but not uniform. Table 1 shows the list of theoretical and computed values.

To examine the qualitative properties of the (dynamic) invariant behavior, two different cases will be discussed first to examine the role of the accelerator. Choose $m = 0.75$ for the multiplier and consider two values $v = 0.1$ and $v = 0.8$ for the accelerator. $v = 0.1$ implies real eigenvalues such that the associated deterministic fixed point is a stable node implying monotonic convergence without rotation. In contrast, $v = 0.8$ implies complex eigenvalues and a corresponding stable focus in the deterministic case. Most importantly, however, for each pair $0 << (m, v) << 1$, the set valued mapping associating the support of the invariant distribution with each parameter pair (m, v) will have compact images which depend on λ alone and not on the particular noise chosen on $[0, 2\lambda]$. This implies that the attractor i. e. the support of the measure of the random fixed point will be a compact set which depends on the interval $[0, \lambda]$, the support of ξ, but is independent of the particular form of the distribution. In this case, one would expect that under additive noise the complex case exhibits a much stronger rotation of the random orbits in the state space than in the case with real eigenvalues.

Figure 4 provides time series characteristics for the case $v = 0.1$ (left column) and $v = 0.8$ (right column). All calculations are carried out for the same noise path. Panel (a) and (b) show the convergence to the random fixed point for five different initial values of y_1, while (e) and (f) show typical time windows of the corresponding long run development of the (one dimensional projection of the) random fixed point. Panel (c) and (d) show the first 50 iterates with connecting lines. Observe that, in spite of the fact that for $v = 0.1$ the deterministic fixed points are stable foci, the orbits show a low rotation phenomenon, caused by the stochastic displacement of the mappings. For $v = 0.8$, however, a strong rotation property appears induced by the complex eigenvalues of the matrix.

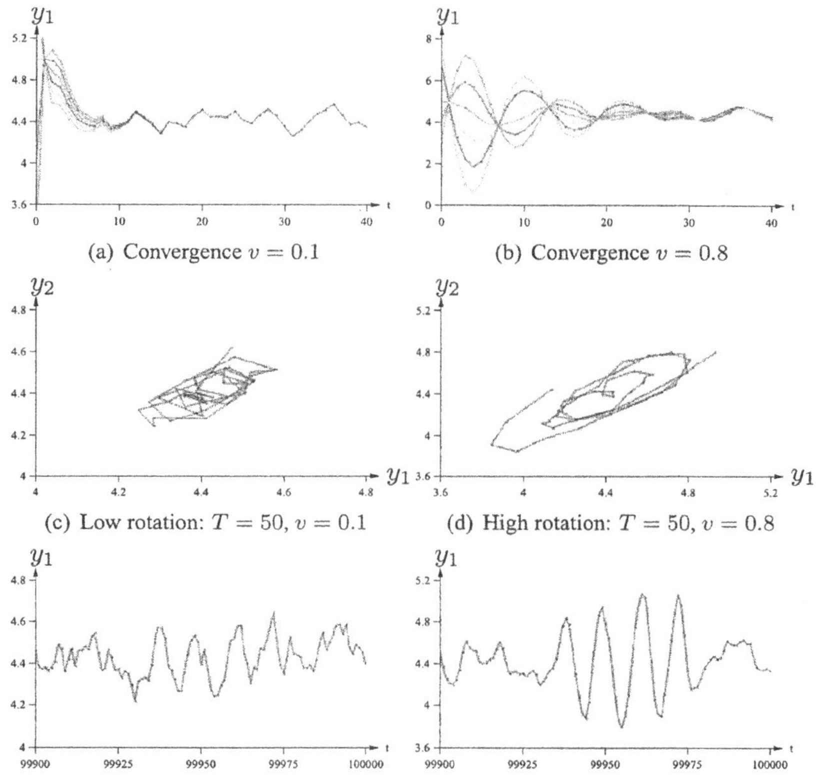

(a) Convergence $v = 0.1$ (b) Convergence $v = 0.8$

(c) Low rotation: $T = 50$, $v = 0.1$ (d) High rotation: $T = 50$, $v = 0.8$

(e) $T = 10^5$, $v = 0.1$ (f) $T = 10^5$, $v = 0.8$

Figure 4: *Transients and the role of the accelerator* v *;* $m = 0.75$, $\lambda = 0.1$.

The difference in the cyclical behavior becomes even more apparent when the long run of the random fixed point is examined. Panels (a) - (d) of Figure 5 show the two attractors with corresponding relative frequencies (densities). The grey shading of the profile of the invariant distribution indicate equidistant levels of frequencies.

The attractor under low rotation is almost a parallelogram while under high rotation it has an elliptical form. Observe that both are perfectly symmetric with respect to the diagonal which implies that their respective marginal distributions must be identical. Since the noise is strictly additive, the mean is the same while the variance is higher in the case with $v = 0.8$ (see panels (e) and (f)). Table 1 provides numerical results of some of the

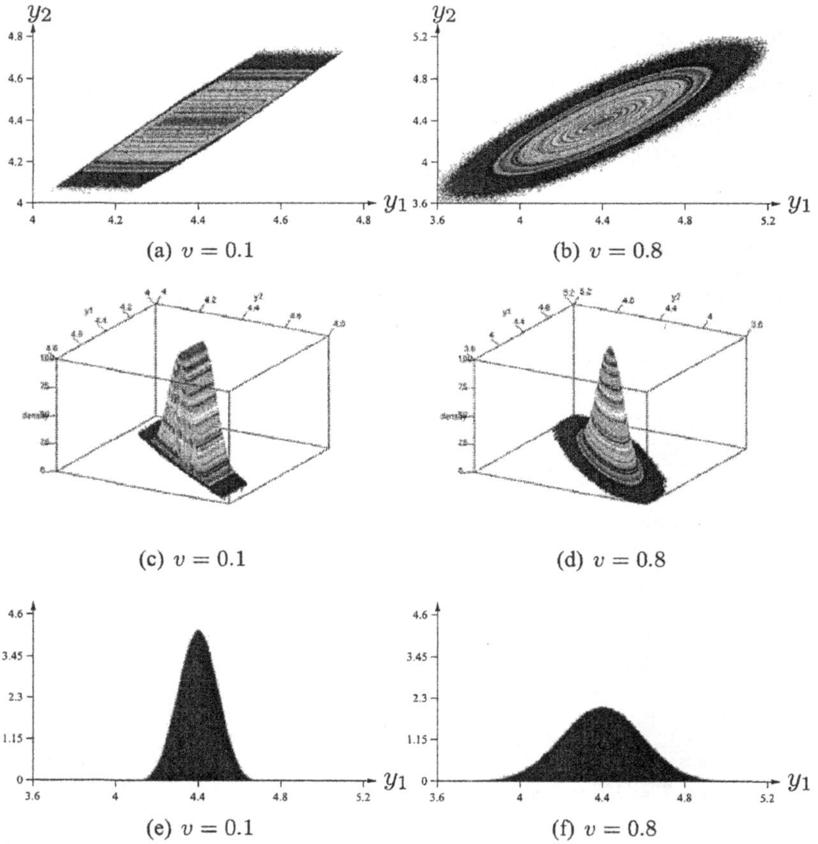

Figure 5: *The role of the accelerator* v ; $T = 10^7$, $m = 0.75$, $\lambda = 0.1$.

standard statistics for the two cases, confirming the symmetry (low skewness), and the high variance for the situation with $v = 0.8$.

To complete the description of the statistical features, Figure 6 provides data on autocorrelation for a large sample, which confirms the typical characteristics of the autocorrelation functions of an AR(2) for both the high rotation and the low rotation case (see for example Hamilton 1994).

The bifurcation diagram Figure 7 shows the change to the elliptic shape of the support of the invariant distribution and the increasing variance as the accelerator increases.

statistic	$v = 0.1$		$v = 0.8$	
	theoretical	estimate	theoretical	estimate
mean	4.4	4.39986	4.4	4.39985
variance	0.008357	0.00837783	0.0358	0.0360081
stand. dev.	0.09141662	0.0915305	0.189208879	0.189758
skewness	0	0.00297042	0	-0.00375951

Table 1: *Statistics:* $m_0 = 1$, $m = 0.75$; $\lambda = 0.1$.

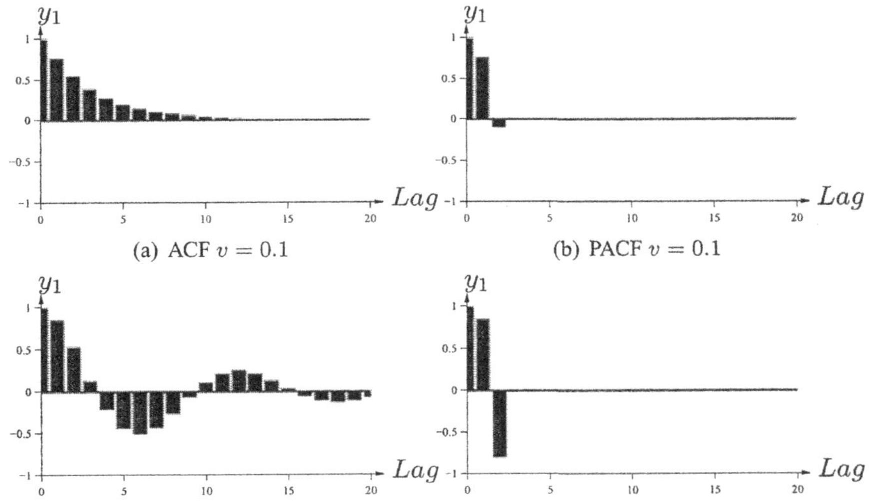

(a) ACF $v = 0.1$

(b) PACF $v = 0.1$

(c) ACF $v = 0.8$

(d) PACF $v = 0.8$

Figure 6: *The role of v on correlation;* $m = 0.75$, $\lambda = 0.1$.

4.6 The Samuelson Model with Mixed Additive Noise

Consider now the situation with mixed discrete/continuous additive noise

$$\begin{aligned} f(y_1, y_2) &:= (m_0 + v_0) + \xi + (m + v)y_2 - vy_1 \\ \xi &\sim [0, 2\lambda], \quad \text{uniformly} \quad \lambda \geq 0 \\ m_0 &\sim \{0, 1\}, \text{ discrete with equal probability} \end{aligned} \tag{39}$$

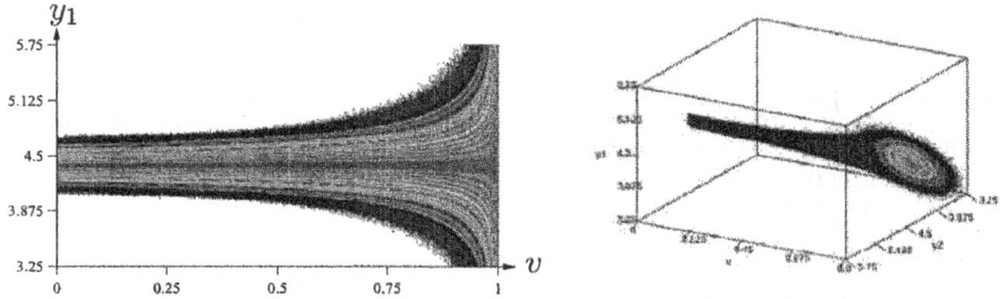

(a) $\lambda = 0.1, m = 0.75$ (b) $\lambda = 0.1, m = 0.75$

Figure 7: *Bifurcation of the accelerator* $v \in [0, 1]$*;* $m = 0.75$, $\lambda = 0.1$.

describing a discrete switch of aggregate demand plus a small continuous noise, both of which follow an i. i. d. process. According to Proposition 4.1, there exists a unique random fixed point (stationary solution) which is asymptotically stable.

With finite discrete noise only ($\lambda = 0$) the system becomes a so called *Iterated Function System*[5](IFS) which often possesses complex or 'fractal' attractors made up of uncountably many disjoint compact sets of Lebesgue measure zero (Cantor sets). Such attractors are caused by gaps of the images of the finite list of mappings on invariant sets of the state space, i. e. subsets which are left with probability one in finite time. As a consequence the corresponding invariant measures will typically be 'fractal' and without densities. The experiment here is designed to reveal the effect of discrete noise on the attractor and examine the role of additional small smooth noise, to determine to what extent "smoothing by noise" appears.

For the situation described by the system (39), the numerical analysis reveals the following property: there exists $0 << (m, v) << 1$, a pair of values $(m_0^1 < m_0^2)$, and a small level of noise $\lambda > 0$ such that the attractor consists of 2^k self similar disconnected subsets of $\mathbb{R}^2$, for some $k > 1$ (see Figure 8). The invariant measure has 2^k modes and has the same shape on each subset. Thus, the associated random fixed point (stationary solution) moves in a random fashion between the disjoint subsets and not in any specific harmonic or periodic way. The autocorrelation functions are not distinguishable from those of the smooth noise only (Figure 6). For example, panel (c) and (d) of Figure 8 show a 16 piece attractor and the associated histogram with 16 modes for $\lambda = 0.025$. As the continuous noise increases the attractor as well as the measure becomes more smooth with only four

[5]See Barnsley (1988) or Lasota & Mackey (1994).

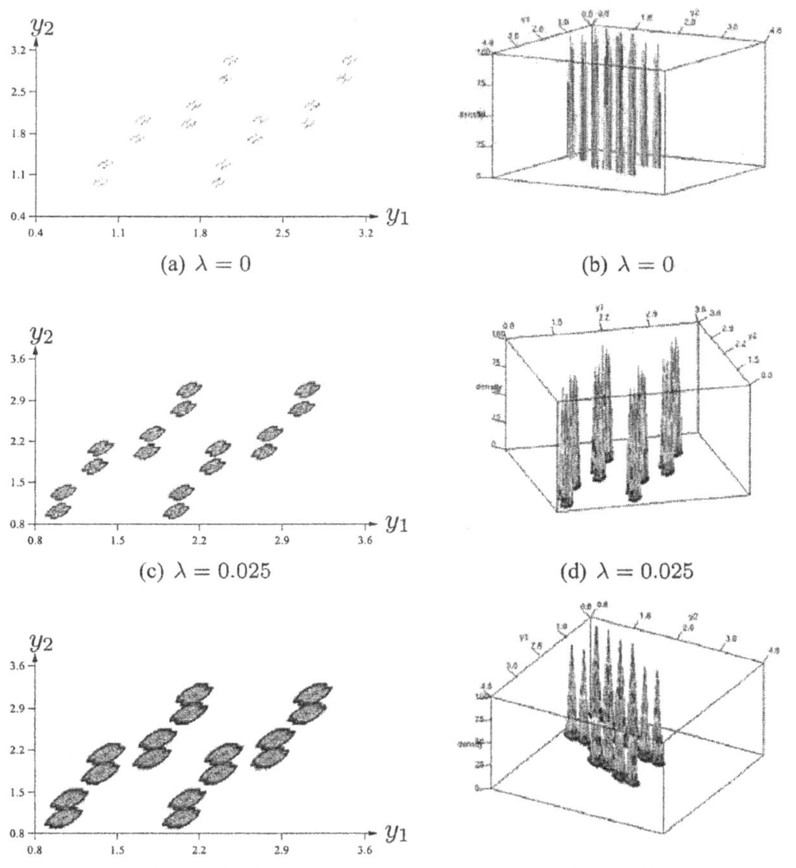

(a) $\lambda = 0$ (b) $\lambda = 0$

(c) $\lambda = 0.025$ (d) $\lambda = 0.025$

(e) $\lambda = 0.05$ (f) $\lambda = 0.05$

Figure 8: *Low accelerator:* $v = 0.25$; $m_0 \sim \{0, 1\}$; $\xi \sim [0, 2\lambda]$; $m = .5$.

modes. Figures 8 and 9 display the change of the attractor and the invariant measure as the continuous noise increases from $\lambda = 0$ to $\lambda = 0.5$.

The sensitivity of these features with respect to the multiplier and the accelerator is quite different. It is a remarkable fact, that the appearance of the 'gaps' is more frequent for low values of the accelerator. As in the case with smooth additive noise alone, it appears again that the increase in the rotation caused by complex eigenvalues is the reason for this phenomenon. Therefore, a high value of the accelerator may create sufficient rotation by

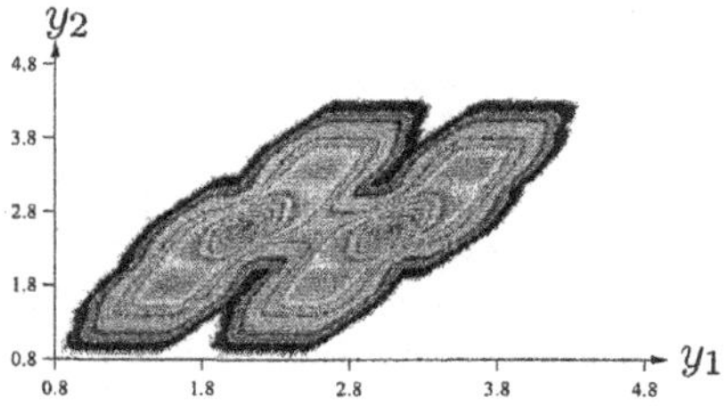

(a) $\lambda = 0.3$

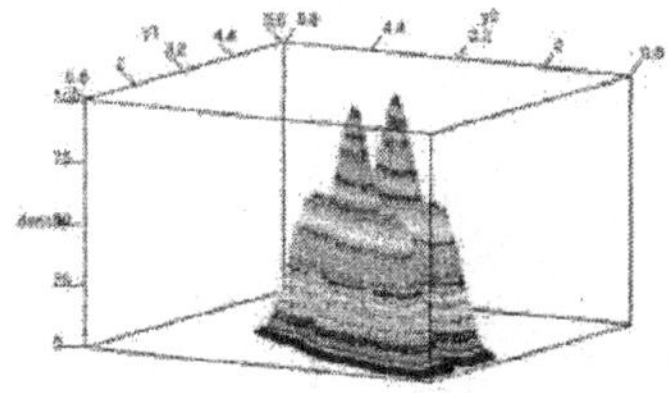

(b) $\lambda = 0.3$

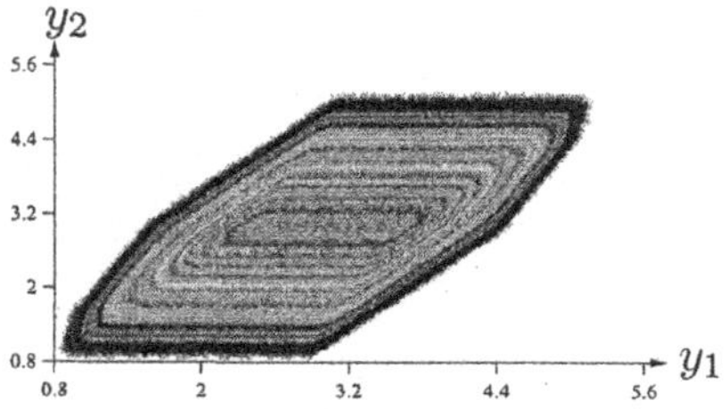

(c) $\lambda = 0.5$

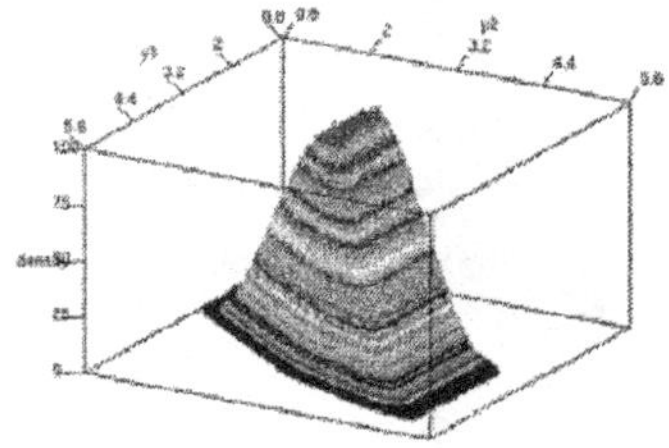

(d) $\lambda = 0.5$

Figure 9: *Low accelerator:* $v = 0.25$; $m_0 \sim \{0, 1\}$; $\xi \sim [0, 2\lambda]$; $m = .5$.

itself, so that even for $\lambda = 0$, no gaps appear. As a consequence, for all small positive values of λ, the long run behavior induces essentially the same invariant distribution as for $\lambda = 0$, as can be seen in Figure 10.

Figures 11 displays the results of bifurcations of the accelerator under different levels of noise for aggregate demand. The v-bifurcation shows quite clearly the disconnected attractor for low values of the accelerator while its mean remains at the same level. In contrast, any m-bifurcation displays the joint effect of the multiplier on rotation and on the position of the attractor. In both cases, the invariant measure will have multiple modes of different order.

Summarizing the results of the experiments with additive demand shocks, one finds that the attractor may consist of a symmetric collection of disconnected subsets of the state space provided the perturbation is discrete (with small smooth noise) and the accelerator is low. In such a situation, the unique stationary solution fluctuates in a random fashion between the disconnected subsets inducing multi modal invariant distributions on the symmetric disconnected subsets of the attractor without regularity or periodicity. If the smooth additive noise becomes larger or the accelerator becomes large, the

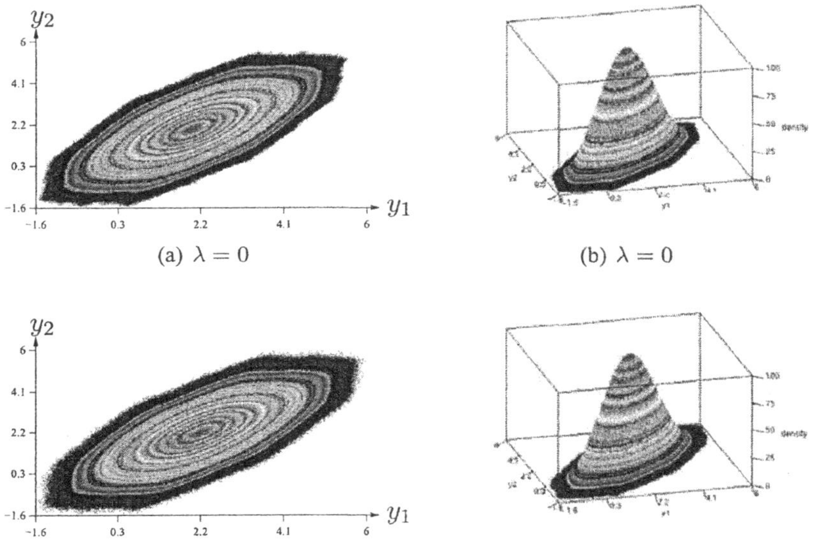

(a) $\lambda = 0$ (b) $\lambda = 0$

(c) $\lambda = 0.1$ (d) $\lambda = 0.1$

Figure 10: *High accelerator:* $v = 0.75$; $m_0 \sim \{0, 1\}$; $\xi \sim [0, 2\lambda]$; $m = 0.5$.

attractor is always a connected compact set. The multi modality disappears as the noise and/or the accelerator increase. Then, the stationary distribution exhibits the typical features of a VAR(1) model with an AR(2) delay structure with high rotation, an invariant distribution with support similar to an ellipsoid and with positive cross correlation, as presented in section 4.5. Thus, the statistical properties of smooth additive noise with high accelerators may not be distinguishable from those of a mixed perturbation scenario with low accelerators. However, from a time series perspective, much of the regularity of the smooth case is lost. Sample paths will reveal clustering, moment reversion, and slow convergence of moments. From the perspective of time series analysis or estimating procedures, little seems to be known about the theoretical properties of the invariant distributions or methods to estimate parameters of an affine system under discrete noise[6].

[6]For some preliminary results see Böhm & Jungeilges (2004).

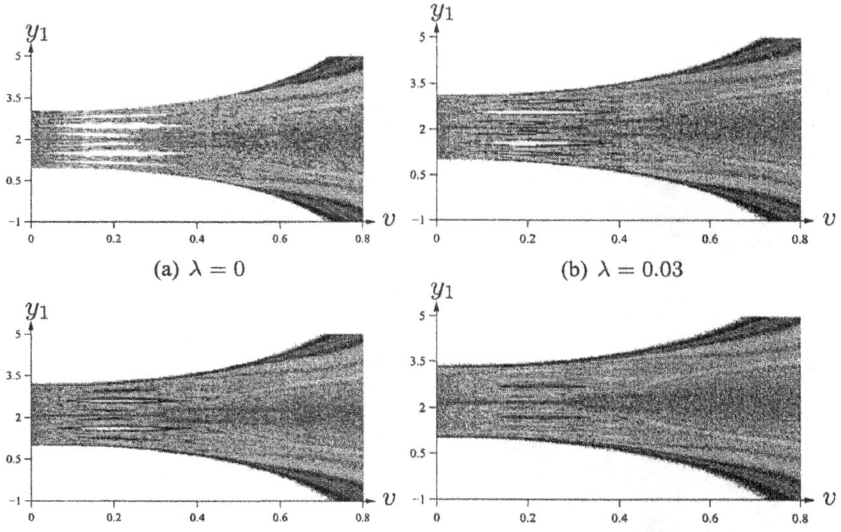

(a) $\lambda = 0$ (b) $\lambda = 0.03$ (c) $\lambda = 0.05$ (d) $\lambda = 0.1$

Figure 11: v - *Bifurcations;* $m_0 \sim \{0, 1\}$; $\xi \sim [0, 2\lambda]$; $m = 0.5$.

4.7 Random Multiplier and Random Accelerator

Finally, consider a discrete perturbation of the multiplier or the accelerator combined with small additive noise $\xi \sim [0, 2\lambda]$ on aggregate demand. In such a case, the system becomes a Markov switching model and is no longer a VAR(1), since the noise acts in a multiplicative way on the delay equation. Due to Proposition 4.1, there exists a unique asymptotically stable random fixed point (stationary solution) whose statistical properties can be derived from the empirical statistics of a single sample path. The multiplicative random effects change the local stability property of the mappings implying a *random* change of the type of rotation. As a consequence, the attractor will not be symmetric any longer implying also that the stationary solution may show reversion of moments, volatility clustering or alike. However, while the random accelerator leaves the steady state unchanged (for $\lambda = 0$), the random multiplier has both an effect on the rotation and on steady states. Therefore, in the latter case, one would expect larger attractors (higher variance) than with a random accelerator alone, a feature which is confirmed by the numerical experiments.

In general, one finds qualitatively that multiplicative discrete noise reduces the occurrence of "gaps" but it often induces non symmetric attractors.

Discrete random multipliers generate less smooth invariant distributions than discrete random accelerators (compare Figures 13 and 14). Random accelerators increase the rotation inducing more symmetry of the attractor. In the latter case, the data may be indistinguishable from the situation with continuous additive noise (VAR1). In particular, autocorrelations will be indistinguishable.

4.8 Two Special Cases with Discrete Noise

Consider a model with simultaneous discrete switching of the accelerator *and* aggregate demand as characterized by Table 2 while keeping the multiplier constant. Four mappings which involve one real root and three complex roots are chosen with equal probability. The table lists the set of parameters but also the four associated fixed points and their eigenvalues λ_j.

The resulting dynamics, however, leads to an overall low rotation with an asymmetric attractor (see Figure 15). The time series indicates effects of mean reversion and of volatility clustering, while there does not appear any

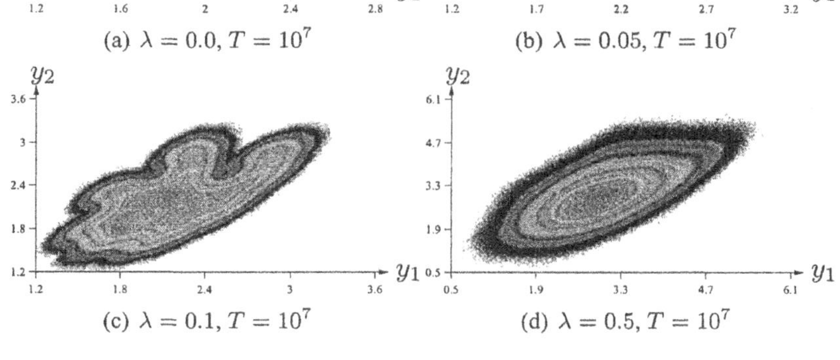

(a) $\lambda = 0.0, T = 10^7$

(b) $\lambda = 0.05, T = 10^7$

(c) $\lambda = 0.1, T = 10^7$

(d) $\lambda = 0.5, T = 10^7$

Figure 12: *Random Multiplier:* $m \sim \{0.4, 0.6\}$; $m_0 + \xi$; $\xi \sim [0, 2\lambda]$; $v = .5$.

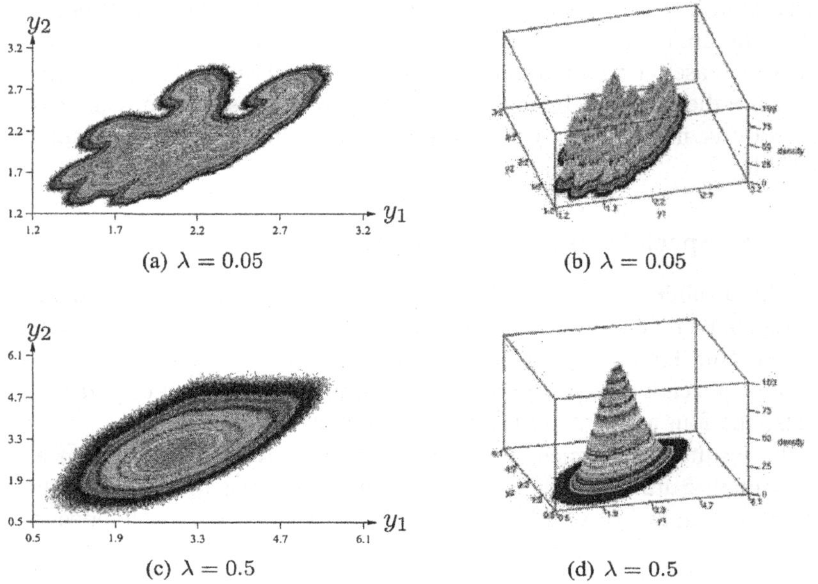

(a) $\lambda = 0.05$ (b) $\lambda = 0.05$

(c) $\lambda = 0.5$ (d) $\lambda = 0.5$

Figure 13: *Random multiplier:* $m \sim \{0.4, 0.6\}$; $v = .5$; $m_0 + \xi$; $\xi \sim [0, 2\lambda]$.

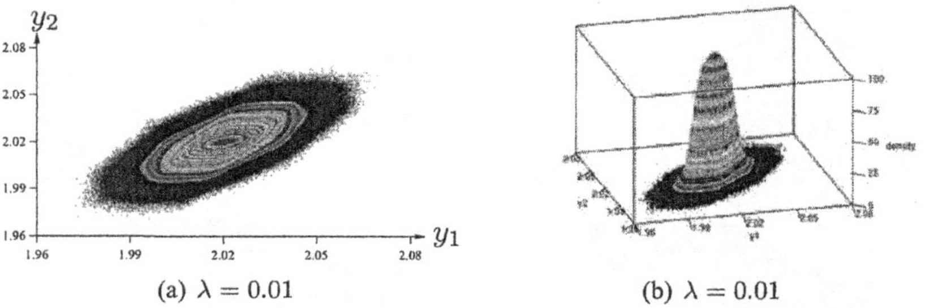

(a) $\lambda = 0.01$ (b) $\lambda = 0.01$

Figure 14: *Random Accelerator:* $v \sim \{0.25, 0.75\}$; $m = 0.5$; $m_0 + \xi$; $\xi \sim [0, 2\lambda]$.

substantial correlation of higher order. The fixed points of the four deterministic mappings are contained in the asymmetric attractor which is stretched out along the diagonal. The invariant distribution is highly skewed with high

i	m_i	v_i	A_i	m_0^i	$\lambda_j(A_i)$	$\bar{y}_i$	p_i
1	.80	**.10**	$\begin{pmatrix} 0 & 1 \\ -.1 & .9 \end{pmatrix}$	$\begin{pmatrix} 0 \\ \mathbf{.5} \end{pmatrix}$	$\begin{pmatrix} .77 \\ .13 \end{pmatrix}$	$\begin{pmatrix} 2.5 \\ 2.5 \end{pmatrix}$	$\frac{1}{4}$
2	.80	**.31**	$\begin{pmatrix} 0 & 1 \\ -.31 & 1.1 \end{pmatrix}$	$\begin{pmatrix} 0 \\ \mathbf{1} \end{pmatrix}$	$\begin{pmatrix} .55 \\ .085i \end{pmatrix}$	$\begin{pmatrix} 5 \\ 5 \end{pmatrix}$	$\frac{1}{4}$
3	.80	**.80**	$\begin{pmatrix} 0 & 1 \\ -.8 & 1.6 \end{pmatrix}$	$\begin{pmatrix} 0 \\ \mathbf{0.5} \end{pmatrix}$	$\begin{pmatrix} .8 \\ .4i \end{pmatrix}$	$\begin{pmatrix} 10 \\ 10 \end{pmatrix}$	$\frac{1}{4}$
4	.80	**1.0**	$\begin{pmatrix} 0 & 1 \\ -1 & 1.8 \end{pmatrix}$	$\begin{pmatrix} 0 \\ \mathbf{1} \end{pmatrix}$	$\begin{pmatrix} .9 \\ .436i \end{pmatrix}$	$\begin{pmatrix} 15 \\ 15 \end{pmatrix}$	$\frac{1}{4}$

Table 2: *Parameters of Model SAM5.*

statistic	time series SAM5
mean	8.12587
variance	6.88639
standard deviation	2.62419
skewness	1.41137
kurtosis	2.80578
quantile (0.55)	7.72191

Table 3: *Statistics of Model SAM5.*

frequency occurring near the two lower fixed points and a high kurtosis. Table 3 provides empirical estimates of the basic statistics only. Theoretical values of the true moments seem to be unaccessible and not known for Markov switching models.

Finally, consider the model SAM4 describing a situation with simultaneous discrete switching of the multiplier, the accelerator, and of aggregate demand as given by Table 4.

This corresponds to a pure Markov switching model. The two mappings which are chosen with equal probability have fixed points with complex eigenvalues. The time series also shows the typical moment reversion and clustering as the previous model.

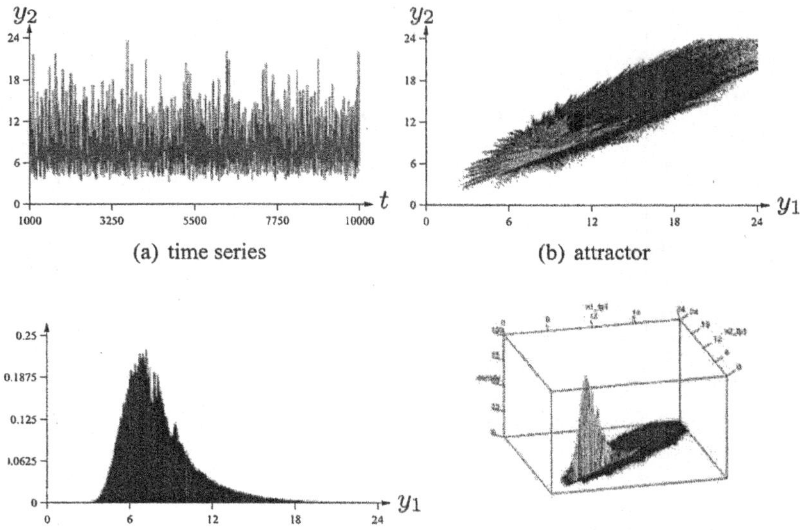

(a) time series

(b) attractor

(c) histogram

(d) attractor with histogram

Figure 15: *Characteristics of Model SAM5* ($T = 10^6$).

i	m_i	v_i	A_1	m_0^i	$\lambda_j(A_i)$	$\bar{y}_i$	p_i
1	**.40**	**.31**	$\begin{pmatrix} 0 & 1 \\ -.31 & 0.71 \end{pmatrix}$	$\begin{pmatrix} 0 \\ \mathbf{1} \end{pmatrix}$	$\begin{pmatrix} .355 \\ .429i \end{pmatrix}$	$\begin{pmatrix} 1.7 \\ 1.7 \end{pmatrix}$	$\frac{1}{2}$
2	**.60**	**.80**	$\begin{pmatrix} 0 & 1 \\ -.8 & 1.4 \end{pmatrix}$	$\begin{pmatrix} 0 \\ \mathbf{0.5} \end{pmatrix}$	$\begin{pmatrix} .7 \\ .557i \end{pmatrix}$	$\begin{pmatrix} 5 \\ 5 \end{pmatrix}$	$\frac{1}{2}$

Table 4: *Parameters of Model SAM4.*

In contrast to the previous situation SAM5, however, the resulting dynamics shows a high degree of rotation with a less connected attractor than in Model SAM5, which points to a 'fractal' structure. Observe that the two stationary points are $(1.7, 1.7)$ and $(5, 5)$ most likely are not in the attractor. The invariant measure is much less smooth and less skewed. However, the autocorrelation is not distinctly different than in Model SAM5.

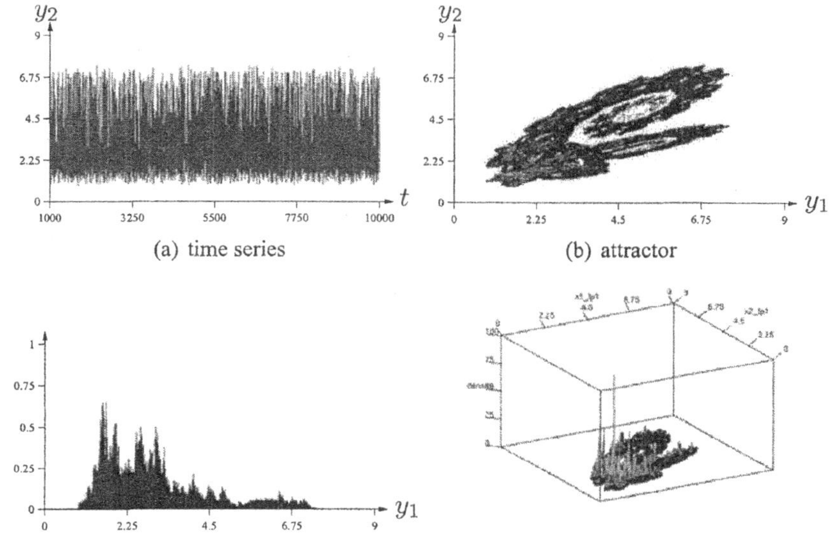

(a) time series (b) attractor

(c) histogram (d) attractor with histogram

Figure 16: *Characteristics of Model SAM4 ($T = 10^6$).*

4.9 Summary and Conclusions

The random multiplier accelerator model can be described as a parameterized family of random affine mappings, induced by a random family of second order delay equations. If the multiplier and the accelerator are restricted to be strictly between zero and one, i. e. the stable case, every Multiplier-Accelerator map is a contraction. Applying a result on existence, uniqueness, and asymptotic stability of a random fixed point for invertible affine random maps due to Arnold (1998), it was shown that for stationary and ergodic compact valued noise processes, the dynamics of the random Multiplier-Accelerator model has a well defined *unique, stationary* and *stable* long run random behavior, satisfying the following properties:

1. (almost all) random orbits/sample paths converge to a unique stationary solution which induces a unique invariant distribution on a unique attractor;

2. time averages converge to the invariant distribution according to the Mean Ergodic Theorem;

statistic	time series SAM4
mean	3.00249
variance	2.0681
standard deviation	1.43809
skewness	1.10593
kurtosis	0.578912
quantile (0.55)	2.8285

Table 5: *Statistics of Model SAM4.*

3. when perturbations are discrete (finite) and i. i. d. , the random multiplier-accelerator map corresponds to a Hyperbolic Iterated Function System (IFS).

4. In this case, the unique attractor (the support of the invariant measure) may be a complex ('fractal') set or a Cantor set, and

5. the invariant measure (distribution) may be very complex (with discontinuous distribution functions).

With i. i. d. perturbations, the random multiplier accelerator model belongs to the class of generalized two dimensional Vector Autoregressive Systems of Order 1 (VAR1) including so called Markov switching models. A numerical analysis with different i. i. d. perturbations showed that

1. additive uniform i. i. d. perturbations alone lead to symmetric attractors and distributions

2. on ellipsoidal attractors for high accelerators and on rectangular attractors for low attractors;

3. fractal attractors and distributions under discrete additive noise are more frequent for low than for high accelerators;

4. adding small/continuous additive noise reduces/eliminates the 'fractal' structure of the attractor implying a multi modal invariant distribution on a finite collection of disjoint compact sets which make up the support/attractor;

5. random accelerators as well as random multipliers typically lead to stationary solutions which can show a variety of complex time series phenomena, like moment reversion and clustering;

6. while the attractors and invariant distributions are typically non symmetric;
7. these features seem less prevalent under a discrete random accelerator than under random multipliers or random aggregate demand.

Since the mathematical result is applicable to general invertible affine random dynamical systems, the above features would be expected to appear as properties of unique stationary stable solutions also in random affine delay equations of any finite order as well as in more general affine economic models. Therefore, even with i. i. d. perturbations alone, these models represent a rich structure for interesting complex business cycle features.

References

Arnold, L. (1998): *Random Dynamical Systems.* Springer-Verlag, Berlin.

Barnsley, M. (1988): *Fractals Everywhere.* Academic Press, New York.

Böhm, V. & J. Jungeilges (2004): "Estimating Affine Economic Models with Discrete Random Perturbations", Discussion Paper 513, Department of Economics, University of Bielefeld.

Borovkov, A. A. (1998): *Ergodicity and Stability of Stochastic Processes.* John Wiley & Sons, New York.

Brandt, A. (1986): "The Stochastic Equation $Y_{t+1} = A_t Y_t + B_t$ with Stationary Coefficients", *Advances in Applied Probability,* 18, 211–220.

Duffie, D., J. Geanakoplos, A. Mas-Colell & A. McLennan (1994): "Stationary Markov Equilibria", *Econometrica,* 62(4), 745–781.

Hamilton, J. D. (1994): *Time Series Analysis.* Princeton University Press.

Hicks, J. (1950): *A Contribution to the Theory of the Trade Cycle.* Oxford University Press, Oxford.

Kesten, H. (1973): "Random Difference Equations and Renewal Theory for Products of Random Matrices", *Acta Math.*, 131, 207–248.

Lasota, A. & M. Mackey (1994): *Chaos, Fractals, and Noise: Stochastic Aspects of Dynamics*, vol. 97 of *Applied Mathematical Science.* Springer-Verlag, New York.

Samuelson, P. A. (1939): "Interaction between the Multiplier Analysis and the Principle of Acceleration", *Review of Economics and Statistics*, 21, 75–78.

Schmalfuß, B. (1996): "A Random Fixed Point Theorem Based on Lyapunov Exponents", *Random and Computational Dynamics*, 4(4), 257–268.

Schmalfuß, B. (1998): "A Random Fixed Point Theorem and the Random Graph Transformation", *Journal of Mathematical Analysis and Application*, 225(1), 91–113.

5 Non-Autonomous Business Cycle Model

José S. Cánovas Peña and Manuel Ruiz Marín

5.1 Introduction

In previous chapters we have considered different versions of the Hicksian business cycle model. This model, as well as the original linear Samuelson model, was stated on the base that savings (S), consumption (C) and capital stock (K) at t are proportional to the income (Y) at $t-1$, and these proportions do not depend on time, that is

$$S_t = sY_{t-1}; \quad C_t = Y_{t-1} - S_t = (1-s)Y_{t-1} = cY_{t-1}; \quad K_t = aY_{t-1} \tag{1}$$

and therefore the income formation equation remains

$$Y_t = C_t + I_t = C_t + (K_t - K_{t-1}) = (a+c)Y_{t-1} - aY_{t-2}, \tag{2}$$

where I_t denote the investments at the instant t.

In this chapter we propose to modify this assumption by introducing non constant coefficients in the difference equation (2). More concretely we propose a model rewriting equations (1) as follows:

$$S_t = s_tY_{t-1}; \quad C_t = c_tY_{t-1}; \quad K_t = a_tY_{t-1}, \tag{3}$$

that is, the savings, consumption and capital stock in the period of time t are proportional to the income at $t-1$ and these proportions depend on t. This new assumption makes sense because these proportions could depend on many factors, even on random factors.

Hence equation (2) remains as

$$Y_t = (a_t + c_t)Y_{t-1} - a_tY_{t-2}. \tag{4}$$

and if we also consider autonomous expenditures A (as stated in Chapter 3), one obtain the following difference equation:

$$Y_t - (a_t + c_t)Y_{t-1} + a_t Y_{t-2} = A. \tag{5}$$

Notice that there is no a general solution in closed form for (5). In order to study it, we introduce a new variable $X_t := Y_{t-1}$. Then we can write

$$\begin{cases} X_t = Y_{t-1}, \\ Y_t = -a_t X_{t-1} + (c_t + a_t)Y_{t-1} + A, \end{cases}$$

or in term of matrices

$$\begin{pmatrix} X_t \\ Y_t \end{pmatrix} = \begin{pmatrix} 0 & 1 \\ -a_t & c_t + a_t \end{pmatrix} \begin{pmatrix} X_{t-1} \\ Y_{t-1} \end{pmatrix} + \begin{pmatrix} 0 \\ A \end{pmatrix}.$$

So,

$$(X_t, Y_t) = F_t(X_{t-1}, Y_{t-1}), \tag{6}$$

where

$$F_t(X, Y) = (Y, -a_t X + (c_t + a_t)Y + A).$$

We are going to study the system given in (6) under different assumptions on the parameters a_t and c_t, by using the notion of non-autonomous discrete system. We call the sequence (F_t), denoted by $F_{1,\infty}$, a non-autonomous cycle.

The next section will be devoted to introduce some notions and results concerning non-autonomous discrete systems.

5.2 Non-Autonomous Discrete Systems

Let X be a metric space with metric d and let $f_n : X \to X$, $n \in \mathbb{N}$, be a sequence of continuous maps. The pair $(X, f_{1,\infty})$, where $f_{1,\infty}$ denotes the sequence $(f_1, f_2, ..., f_n, ...)$, is a non-autonomous discrete system. Throughout this chapter we are going to denote

$$f_n^k = f_{n+k} \circ f_{n+k-1} \circ \ldots f_n.$$

If $x \in X$, then the trajectory (also orbit) of x under $f_{1,\infty}$ is given by the sequence

$$\mathrm{Orb}(x, f_{1,\infty}) = (x, f_1(x), f_1^2(x), ..., f_1^n(x), ...),$$

where $f_1^n = f_n \circ ... \circ f_2 \circ f_1$, $n \geq 1$, and f_1^0 denotes the identity on X. Notice that when $f_{1,\infty}$ is the constant sequence $(f, f, ..., f, ...)$, then the pair $(X, f_{1,\infty}) = (X, f)$ is a classical discrete dynamical system. The notion of non-autonomous discrete system can be found in Kolyada et al. 1996.

One of the main goals in the study of autonomous and non-autonomous systems is to characterize the set of limit points of trajectories, that is, to characterize the set $\omega(x, f_{1,\infty})$ of accumulation points of the orbit $\mathrm{Orb}(x, f_{1,\infty})$. The set $\omega(x, f_{1,\infty})$ is called the ω–limit set of x under $f_{1,\infty}$. In this setting, only partial results have been stated for the particular case of X being the compact unit interval $[0, 1]$ (see Kolyada et al. 1995 and Kempf 2002). When discrete dynamical systems are concerned the following result gives an useful property satisfied by the ω–limit set.

Theorem 1 *[Sharkovsky et al. 1997] Let X be a compact set, let $f : X \to X$ be a continuous map and $x \in X$. Then the ω–limit set $\omega(x, f)$ is closed and strictly invariant by f, that is, $f(\omega(x, f)) = \omega(x, f)$.*

In general, the study of non-autonomous systems is rather complicated. However, there are two special classes of non-autonomous systems which can be deeply analyzed.

In the first one we consider the sequence $f_{1,\infty}$ such that f_n converges to a continuous map f as n goes to infinity. Then the non-autonomous system can be studied as a discrete dynamical system as follows. Let $Y = \{1/n : n \in \mathbb{N}\} \cup \{0\}$ be a compact set and define the map $T : Y \times X \to Y \times X$ by

$$T(1/n, x) := \begin{cases} (1/(n+1), f_n(x)) & \text{if } n \neq 0, \\ (0, f(x)) & \text{if } n = 0. \end{cases} \tag{7}$$

Then T is continuous and the pair $((\mathbb{N} \cup \{0\}) \times X, T)$ is a discrete dynamical system called triangular. This is so because usually the map T is called a triangular map.

The second case is when the sequence $f_{1,\infty}$ is periodic, that is, there is $k \in \mathbb{N}$ such that $f_{n+k} = f_n$ for any positive integer n. The smallest positive integer k satisfying this condition is called the period of $f_{1,\infty}$. Hence the sequence $f_{1,\infty}^{[k]} = (f_1^k, f_{k+1}^k, ...)$ is constant and then $(X, f_{1,\infty}^{[k]})$ is a discrete dynamical system.

The following result involves the first special type of non autonomous systems.

Proposition 1 *Let X be a compact metric space and let $f_n : X \to X$ be a sequence of continuous maps such that (f_n) converges to a continuous map*

$f : X \to X$ as n goes to infinity. Fix $x \in X$. Then $\omega(x, f_{1,\infty})$ is strictly invariant by f (that is $f(\omega(x, f_{1,\infty})) = \omega(x, f_{1,\infty})$).

Proof. Let $T(n, x)$ be the map defined in equation (7). Since T moves $1/n$ to $1/(n+1)$, then any ω–limit set of T is contained in the set $\{0\} \times X$. Let $\pi_2 : Y \times X \to Y \times X$ be the projection map on the second component, that is $\pi_2(y, x) = x$. Notice that $\pi_2(T^n(1, x)) = f_1^n(x)$ for any $x \in X$ and $n \in \mathbb{N}$. On the other hand, it is straightforward to check that $y \in \omega(x, f_{1,\infty})$ if and only if $(0, y) \in \omega((1, x), T)$ and hence $\{0\} \times \omega(x, f_{1,\infty}) = \omega((1, x), T)$. Moreover, since by Theorem 1, $\omega((1, x), T)$ is strictly invariant by T, on one hand we have that

$$T(\omega((1, x), T)) = \omega((1, x), T) = \{0\} \times \omega(x, f_{1,\infty}), \tag{8}$$

and on the other hand,

$$T(\omega((1, x), T)) = T(\{0\} \times \omega(x, f_{1,\infty})) = \{0\} \times f(\omega(x, f_{1,\infty})), \tag{9}$$

Therefore by comparing equations (8) and (9) we have that

$$f(\omega(x, f_{1,\infty})) = \omega(x, f_{1,\infty}),$$

which finishes the proof. ∎

Remark 1 An alternative proof of the above proposition can be seen in Kempf 2002 without using triangular maps. However, the use of triangular maps helps in shorten the proof.

As we mentioned before we also are interested in studying the special case in which the sequence $f_{1,\infty}$ is periodic. To this end consider

$$f_{1,\infty} = (f_1, f_2, ..., f_k, f_1, f_2, ..., f_k, ...)$$

that is $f_{1,\infty}$ is a periodic sequence of continuous maps with period k. In this case, the ω–limit sets of $f_{1,\infty}$ can be computed as the next result shows.

Proposition 2 *Let $f_{1,\infty} = (f_1, f_2, ..., f_k, f_1, f_2, ..., f_k, ...)$ be a periodic sequence of continuous maps of period k and fix $x \in X$. Then*

$$\omega(x, f_{1,\infty}) = \omega(x, f_1^n) \cup \omega(f_1(x), f_2^n) \cup ... \cup \omega(f_1^{n-1}(x), f_{n-1}^n).$$

Proof. First notice that the sequences $f_{i,\infty}^{[k]}$ for $i = 1, 2, ..., k-1$ are the constant sequences f_i^k, respectively. Then, for any $x \in X$, the set $\omega(x, f_{i,\infty}^{[k]}) = \omega(x, f_i^k)$ for $i = 1, 2, ..., k-1$. In order to prove the equality of the statement first we prove the following inclusion

$$\omega(x, f_{1,\infty}) \subseteq \omega(x, f_1^n) \cup \omega(f_1(x), f_2^n) \cup ... \cup \omega(f_1^{n-1}(x), f_{n-1}^n).$$

To this end, let $y \in \omega(x, f_{1,\infty})$. Therefore there is a strictly increasing sequence of integers (n_i) such that $\lim_{i\to\infty} f_1^{n_i}(x) = y$. For any i we have that there exist $m_i, r_i \in \mathbb{N}$ such that $n_i = k \cdot m_i + r_i$ with $r_i \in \{0, 1, \ldots, k-1\}$. Therefore there exists $j_0 \in \{0, 1, \ldots, k-1\}$ such that $j_0 = r_i$ for infinitely many i's. Then

$$y = \lim_{i\to\infty} f_1^{n_i}(x) = \lim_{i\to\infty} f_{j_0+1}^{n_i - j_0}(f_1^{j_0}(x)) = \lim_{i\to\infty} (f_{j_0+1}^k)^{m_i}(f_1^{j_0}(x)),$$

which shows that $y \in \omega(f_1^{j_0}(x), f_{j_0+1}^k)$, and the inclusion is proved. Since it is straightforward to see that $\omega(f_{j_0}(x), f_{j_0+1}^k) \subseteq \omega(x, f_{1,\infty})$ then the equality holds and the proof concludes. ∎

The following notation will be used in what follows. Given two sequences of continuous maps $f_{1,\infty} = (f_1, f_2, ...)$ and $g_{1,\infty} = (g_1, g_2, ...)$, we construct the sequence $(f, g)_{1,\infty} = (f_1, g_1, f_2, g_2, ...)$. In this setting, it will be useful the next result.

Proposition 3 *Let $f_{1,\infty} = (f_n)$ and $g_{1,\infty} = (g_n)$ be two sequences of continuous maps that converge uniformly to f and g respectively. Then $(f, g)_{1,\infty}^{[2]}$ converges uniformly to $g \circ f$.*

Proof. First notice that the nth term of the sequence $(f, g)_{1,\infty}^{[2]}$ is $g_n \circ f_n$. Fix $\varepsilon > 0$. Since (g_n) converges uniformly to g there is $n_0 \in \mathbb{N}$ such that

$$d(g_n(x), g(x)) < \varepsilon$$

for all $x \in X$ and $n \geq n_0$. Also, since g is uniformly continuous there is $\delta > 0$ such that if $d(x, y) < \delta$, then $d(g(x), g(y)) < \varepsilon$. On the other hand, Since (f_n) converges uniformly to f there is $n_1 \in \mathbb{N}$ such that

$$d(f_n(x), f(x)) < \delta$$

for all $x \in X$ and $n \geq n_1$. Then if $n > \max\{n_0, n_1\}$, we have that

$$\begin{aligned} d((g_n \circ f_n)(x), (g \circ f)(x)) &\leq d(g_n(f_n(x)), g(f_n(x))) \\ &+ d(g(f_n(x)), g(f(x))) < 2\varepsilon \end{aligned}$$

for any $x \in X$, which finishes the proof of the proposition. ∎

In the next section we wonder about the ω–limit sets of sequences of maps F_n which define the non-autonomous cycle. Proposition 1 states that when the maps F_n converge to a map F, then this set is invariant by F. To improve the result we will need some definitions which can be found in Aoki et al. 1994.

Definition 1 *Let $\delta, \varepsilon > 0$. Let (X, d) be a metric space, $f : X \to X$ be a continuous map and $(x_n) \in X$ be a sequence.*

- *(a) We say that the sequence (x_n) is a δ–pseudo orbit of f if it is held that $d(x_{n+1}, f(x_n)) < \delta$ for $n \geq 1$.*
- *(b) We say that* $\mathrm{Orb}(x, f)$ *ε–shadows (x_n) if $d(x_n, f^n(x)) < \varepsilon$ for $n \geq 1$.*
- *(c) The map f has the shadowing property, also called pseudo orbit tracing property, if for any $\varepsilon > 0$ there is $\delta > 0$ such that any δ–pseudo orbit is ε–shadowed by an orbit of f.*

An interesting problem related with the dynamics of the sequence $f_{1,\infty}$, when this sequence is periodic of period 2, is the so called *Parrondo's paradox*. The Parrondo's paradox can be stated as follows. Consider two continuous maps $f, g : X \to X$ and a sequence $(\alpha_n) \in \{0,1\}^{\mathbb{N}}$. Define the sequence $f_{1,\infty} = (f_n)$ by the rule $f_n = f$ if $\alpha_n = 0$ and $f_n = g$ if $\alpha_n = 1$. Notice that the map f_1^n is constructed by the composition of the maps f and g depending on the sequence (α_n). We say that the Parrondo's paradox (see Almeida et al. 2005, Arena et al. 2003, Parrondo et al. 2002, or Harmer et al. 2000 for additional information on the Parrondian phenomena) occurs when the dynamical systems (X, f) and (X, g) are complicated (respectively simple) and the system $(X, f_{1,\infty})$ is simple (respectively complicated). We will analyze whether a Parrondo phenomena occurs for non-autonomous cycles generated by two maps F_1 and F_2.

5.3 A First Approach to the Model

Recall that the model presented in Section 5.1 is given by the following sequence of homeomorphisms

$$F_t(X,Y) = (Y, -a_tX + (c_t + a_t)Y + A), \tag{10}$$

where (c_t) and (a_t) are sequences of real numbers such that $0 < c_t < 1$ and $a_t > 0$ for any $t \geq 1$. The non-autonomous cycle is given by the sequence $F_{1,\infty} = (F_t)$. We always assume that $(a_t + c_t)^2 - 4a_t < 0$ for any $t > 0$, in order to have complex eigenvalues.

For any $t \geq 1$, the sequence of fixed points of the map F_t is given by

$$(X_t^*, Y_t^*) = \left(\frac{A}{1-c_t}, \frac{A}{1-c_t}\right).$$

Notice that if $c_t = c$ for every $t \geq 1$, then the above sequence is constant.

The following result shows that if we do not impose additional conditions on a_t and c_t then the behavior of the sequence $F_{1,\infty}$ can be complicated.

Proposition 4 *Fix $(X_0, Y_0) \in (\mathbb{R}^+)^2$. Then there is a sequence $((a_t, c_t))$ with $a_t > 0$ and $0 < c_t < 1$ such that* $\mathrm{Orb}((X_0,Y_0), F_{1,\infty})$ *is dense on $\mathbb{R}^2$. Then $\omega((X_0,Y_0), F_{1,\infty}) = \mathbb{R}^2$.*

Proof. Let D be a dense and countable subset of $\mathbb{R}$ such that $X_0, Y_0 \in D$. Then $D \times D = D^2$ is dense on $\mathbb{R}^2$. Now, fix $X_1 = X_0 \in D$ and consider

$$(X_1, Y_1) = F_1(X_0, Y_0) = (Y_0, -aX_0 + (c+a)Y_0 + A),$$

which gives us the equation

$$Y_1 = -aX_0 + (c+a)Y_0 + A. \tag{11}$$

Then a straightforward computation shows that

$$c = \frac{Y_1 - A + a(X_0 - Y_0)}{Y_0}.$$

Then fixing $Y_1 \in D$ and a such that

$$0 < \frac{Y_1 - A + a(X_0 - Y_0)}{Y_0} < 1$$

one deduces that there are infinitely many c such that equation (11) holds. Choose a_1 and c_1 such that (11) holds. Now, we take $(X_2, Y_2) \in D^2$ such that $X_2 = Y_1$, and arguing as before we can find a_2 and c_2 such that $Y_2 = -a_2X_1+(c_2+a_2)Y_1+A$. Since D^2 is a countable set, repeating this process we get that $D^2 = \mathrm{Orb}((X_0, Y_0), F_{1,\infty})$, and the proof concludes. ∎

Remark 2 The existence of a dense orbit is known as transitivity of the system. Although transitivity is not enough to provide chaos (consider, for instance, irrational rotations on the circle), notice that one can choose Y_n in a random way and thus, the behavior of the orbit would be unpredictable.

Then by Proposition 4 it is clear that to obtain some order in the model, the values of a_t and c_t can not be arbitrary, they have to be chosen following some rules. We are going to consider different cases for the sequence $((a_t, c_t))$. In the next section we are going to assume that the sequence $((a_t, c_t))$ converges to (a, c). Afterwards we will study the proposed model when the sequence $((a_t, c_t))$ is not converging.

5.4 The Convergent Case

Assume that $((a_t, c_t))$ converges to (a, c), $c < 1$, as t goes to infinity. Then the sequence F_t converges to the map F, where

$$F(X, Y) = (Y, -aX + (a + c)Y + A). \qquad (12)$$

In addition, the sequence of fixed points (X_t^*, Y_t^*) converges to the fixed point of F, denoted by (X^*, Y^*). Since $X_t^* = Y_t^* = \frac{A}{1-c_t}$ for all $t \geq 0$ we obtain that $X^* = Y^* = \frac{A}{1-c}$. Now, we need some information on when the orbits of the non-autonomous system are bounded. To this end, we introduce the following technical computations.

Let $||(x, y)|| = \sqrt{x^2 + y^2}$ be the Euclidean norm defined on $\mathbb{R}^2$. This norm induces a norm on $M_2(\mathbb{R})$ as follows (see Serre 2002, page 65). Let $A \in M_2(\mathbb{R})$ and let A^T be the transpose matrix. Denote by

$$\rho(A) = \max\{|\lambda|; \lambda \text{ is an eigenvalue of } A\}.$$

Then

$$||A|| := \sqrt{\rho(A \cdot A^T)}. \tag{13}$$

Consider the sequence of fixed points (X_t^*, Y_t^*) (recall that $X_t^* = Y_t^*$). In order to get some information concerning the orbit of the point (X, Y), we are going to estimate

$$||F_1^t(X,Y) - (X_t^*, Y_t^*)||.$$

Notice that if $F_t = F$ for all $t \geq 0$, with fixed point (X^*, Y^*), then

$$||F_1^t(X,Y) - (X_t^*, Y_t^*)|| = ||F^t(X,Y) - (X^*, Y^*)||$$

measures the distance between any point of the orbit of (X, Y) and the fixed point. Under this assumption, as it was stated in Chapter 3, if $a < 1$ any orbit converges to the fixed point of F, and therefore

$$\lim_{t \to \infty} ||F^t(X,Y) - (X^*, Y^*)|| = 0.$$

On the other hand if $a = 1$ then $||F^t(X,Y) - (X^*, Y^*)||$ is bounded and finally if $a > 1$ then $||F^t(X,Y) - (X^*, Y^*)||$ is unbounded if $(X, Y) \neq (X^*, Y^*)$.

Now fix $t \geq 0$. We begin by estimating $||F_t(X,Y) - (X_t^*, Y_t^*)||$. Let

$$W = \begin{pmatrix} 0 & 1 \\ -a_t & c_t + a_t \end{pmatrix}.$$

Notice that a property of matrix norms are $||AB|| \leq ||A||||B||$. For the matrix W, after a straightforward calculation, we have that $\rho(W \cdot W^T) = a_t^2$ (recall that $(a_t + c_t)^2 - 4a_t < 0$).

Therefore by the previous paragraph we obtain that

$$\begin{aligned} ||F_t(X,Y) - (X_t^*, Y_t^*)|| &= ||F_t(X,Y) - F_t(X_t^*, Y_t^*)|| \\ &= \left\| \begin{pmatrix} 0 & 1 \\ -a_t & c_t + a_t \end{pmatrix} \begin{pmatrix} X - X_t^* \\ Y - Y_t^* \end{pmatrix} \right\| \\ &\leq a_t ||(X,Y) - (X_t^*, Y_t^*)||. \end{aligned}$$

Then

$$\begin{aligned} ||F_1^t(X,Y) - (X_t^*, Y_t^*)|| &\leq a_t ||F_1^{t-1}(X,Y) - (X_t^*, Y_t^*)|| \\ &\leq a_t ||F_1^{t-1}(X,Y) - (X_{t-1}^*, Y_{t-1}^*)|| \\ &\quad + a_t ||(X_{t-1}^*, Y_{t-1}^*) - (X_t^*, Y_t^*)|| \\ &\leq a_{t-1} a_t ||F_1^{t-2}(X,Y) - (X_{t-1}^*, Y_{t-1}^*)|| \\ &\quad + a_t ||(X_{t-1}^*, Y_{t-1}^*) - (X_t^*, Y_t^*)||. \end{aligned}$$

Hence, in an inductive way, we obtain

$$\begin{aligned}||F_1^t(X,Y)-(X_t^*,Y_t^*)|| &\leq \sum_{n=2}^{t}||(X_{n-1}^*,Y_{n-1}^*)-(X_n^*,Y_n^*)||\prod_{j=n}^{t}a_j \\ &+||(X,Y)-(X_t^*,Y_t^*)||\prod_{n=1}^{t}a_n. \end{aligned} \tag{14}$$

Now, we can prove the following result.

Theorem 2 *Let $F_{1,\infty}=(F_t)$ be a non-autonomous cycle defined as in (10) converging to the continuous function F defined as in (12). Then*

(a) If $a<1$, then for all $(X,Y)\in\mathbb{R}^2$ the ω–limit set

$$\omega((X,Y),F_{1,\infty})=\{(X^*,Y^*)\}=\omega((X,Y),F).$$

(b) If $a>1$, then for all $(X,Y)\in\mathbb{R}^2$ the orbit $\mathrm{Orb}((X,Y),F_{1,\infty})$ is not bounded or converges to the fixed point (X^*,Y^*).

Proof. First, assume that (a_t) converges to $a<1$. By inequality (14) we obtain

$$\begin{aligned}||F_1^t(X,Y)-(X^*,Y^*)|| &\leq ||F_1^t(X,Y)-(X_t^*,Y_t^*)|| \\ &+||(X_t^*,Y_t^*)-(X^*,Y^*)|| \\ &\leq ||(X_t^*,Y_t^*)-(X^*,Y^*)|| \\ &+||(X,Y)-(X_t^*,Y_t^*)||\prod_{n=1}^{t}a_n \\ &+\sum_{n=2}^{t}||(X_{n-1}^*,Y_{n-1}^*)-(X_n^*,Y_n^*)||\prod_{j=n}^{t}a_j.\end{aligned}$$

On the other hand, there are $t_0\in\mathbb{N}$ and $0<\beta,\alpha<1$ such that if $t\geq t_0$, then $a_t+\beta<\alpha<1$. Let

$$D=\max\{||(X_{t-1}^*,Y_{t-1}^*)-(X_t^*,Y_t^*)||,||(X^*,Y^*)-(X_t^*,Y_t^*)||:t\in\mathbb{N}\},$$

and

$$S=\max\{\prod_{n=1}^{t}a_n:t=1,2,...,t_0\}.$$

So, if $t > t_0$, we have

$$\begin{aligned} ||F_1^t(X,Y) - (X^*,Y^*)|| &\leq D + DS\alpha^{t-t_0} + t_0DS + \sum_{n=t_0+1}^{t} D\alpha^{t-n} \\ &\leq D\left(1 + S\alpha^{t-t_0} + t_0S + \sum_{n=t_0+1}^{t} \alpha^{t-n}\right). \end{aligned}$$

Since the serie

$$\sum_{n=1}^{t} \alpha^n,$$

converges, we deduce that $\text{Orb}((X,Y), F_{1,\infty})$ is bounded and then, there is a compact subset $K \subset \mathbb{R}^2$ such that $\text{Orb}((X,Y), F_{1,\infty}) \subset K$. Since F_t converges uniformly over K, for a fixed $\delta > 0$ there is $t_0 \in \mathbb{N}$ such that

$$||F_t(F_1^{t-1}(X,Y)) - F(F_1^{t-1}(X,Y))|| < \delta, \tag{15}$$

for all $t \geq t_0$. We claim that the sequence

$$(F_1^{t+t_0}(X,Y) = F_{t_0+1}^t(F_1^{t_0}(X,Y)))$$

is a δ–pseudo orbit of F. To see this notice that by (15) $||F_1^{t+t_0}(X,Y) - F(F_1^{t+t_0-1}(X,Y))|| = ||F_{t+t_0}(F_1^{t+t_0-1}(X,Y)) - F(F_1^{t+t_0-1}(X,Y))|| < \delta$ for all $t \geq 1$, which proves the claim.

By Aoki et al. 1994, page 86, the limit map F has the shadowing property. Then, there are $\varepsilon > 0$ and $(Z_\varepsilon, T_\varepsilon) \in \mathbb{R}^2$ such that if $t \geq 1$, then

$$||F_1^{t+t_0}(X,Y) - F^t(Z_\varepsilon, T_\varepsilon)|| < \varepsilon \tag{16}$$

Since $a < 1$, there is $t_1 \in \mathbb{N}$ such that

$$||F^t(Z_\varepsilon, T_\varepsilon) - (X^*,Y^*)|| < \varepsilon \tag{17}$$

for all $t > t_1$. Therefore, if $t > t_0 + t_1$ by applying inequalities (16) and (17) we obtain that

$$\begin{aligned} ||F_1^t(X,Y) - (X^*,Y^*)|| &\leq ||F_1^t(X,Y) - F^{t-t_0}(Z_\varepsilon, T_\varepsilon)|| \\ &\quad + ||F^{t-t_0}(Z_\varepsilon, T_\varepsilon) - (X^*,Y^*)|| < 2\varepsilon. \end{aligned}$$

Since ε was arbitrarily chosen, the sequence $(F_1^n(X,Y))$ converges to the fixed point (X^*,Y^*).

Now we assume that (a_t) converges to $a > 1$. If $\mathrm{Orb}((X,Y), F_{1,\infty})$ is not bounded, there is nothing to prove. Otherwise, we are going to assume that $\mathrm{Orb}((X,Y), F_{1,\infty})$ is bounded. Then, there is a compact subset $K \subset \mathbb{R}^2$ containing the orbit. Since F_t converges uniformly over K and the limit map F has the shadowing property (see Aoki et al. 1994, page 86). Therefore there are t_0, δ, ε and $(Z_\varepsilon, T_\varepsilon)$ as above. Then proceeding as in the previous case $(Z_\varepsilon, T_\varepsilon) = (X^*, Y^*)$ for any $\varepsilon > 0$ (otherwise $\mathrm{Orb}((Z_\varepsilon, T_\varepsilon), F)$ would be unbounded) and hence, again by (16), $\omega((X,Y), F_{1\infty}) = \{(X^*, Y^*)\}$. ∎

Theorem 2 states that when $a \neq 1$, the dynamical behavior of any orbit of the non-autonomous cycle is similar to an orbit of the dynamical system generated by the limit map F. Here three different possibilities can be analyzed. Firstly if $a_t < 1$ for all $t \geq 1$, intuition tells us that any orbit should go to the fixed point of the limit map. To see this we have to go through simulations. In all the simulations we assume that $A = 1$. The initial condition is always the same for all simulations $(X_0, Y_0) = (0.25, 0.189)$. In Figure 1 we simulate the income traces and the orbit $\mathrm{Orb}((0.25, 0.189), F_{1\infty})$ when $a_t = 0.9 - 1/t$ and $c_t = 0.5$ is constant and when $c_t = 0.45 + 1/t$ is variable with the time t, respectively, for all t. Notice that in the first case, since $c_t = 0.5$ for all t then there is a unique fixed point in the real plane $\mathbb{R}^2$.

Secondly if $a_t > 1$ for all $t \geq 1$ an unbounded orbit appears. This situation is simulated in Figure 2, (similar pictures are shown when $c_t = 0.5$ is constant for all t, that is why we only show the case in which $c_t = 0.5 + 1/t$ is variable with the time t).

In Figure 3, the cycle starts with $a_t > 1$, but finally it converges to $a = 0.99 < 1$.

There is not clear intuitions about what happens if a_t can be arbitrarily greater than, equal to or less than 1 depending on the instant on time t. To investigate this, we only have inequality (14) to prove the following result, in which convergence is not assumed.

Theorem 3 *Let $F_{1,\infty} = (F_t)$ be a non-autonomous cycle defined as in (10). Assume (X^*, Y^*) is the only fixed point in $\mathbb{R}^2$ of F_t for all $t \in \mathbb{N}$. Then for all $(X,Y) \in \mathbb{R}^2$*

(a) If $\lim_{t \to \infty} \prod_{n=1}^{t} a_n = 0$, *then* $\omega((X,Y), F_{1,\infty}) = \{(X^*, Y^*)\}$.

(b) If $\limsup_{t \to \infty} \prod_{n=1}^{t} a_n = \alpha$, *then* $\mathrm{Orb}((X,Y), F_{1,\infty})$ *is bounded.*

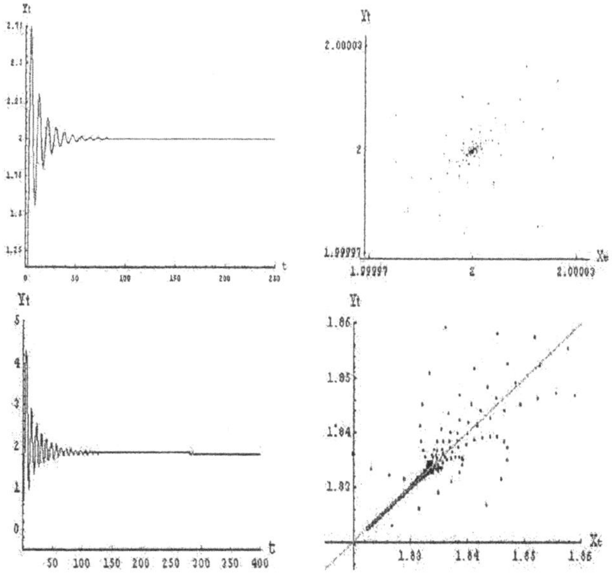

Figure 1: *We simulate in the upper part income traces (left) and orbit (right) where* $a_t = 0.9 - 1/t$ *and* $c_t = 0.5$ *with initial condition* $(X_0, Y_0) = (0.25, 0.189)$ *and in the lower part income traces (left) and orbit (right) where* $a_t = 0.95 - 1/t$ *and* $c_t = 0.45 + 1/t$ *with the same initial condition. The orbit converges to the limit fixed point* $(2, 2)$ *and* $(1.81.., 1.81..)$, *respectively, as Theorem 2 points out.*

Proof. Notice that in this particular case inequality (14) reads as follows

$$||F_1^t(X,Y) - (X^*,Y^*)|| \leq ||(X,Y) - (X^*,Y^*)|| \prod_{n=1}^{t} a_n.$$

Therefore, if $\lim\limits_{t\to\infty} \prod_{n=1}^t a_n = 0$, we have that

$$\lim_{t\to\infty} ||F_1^t(X,Y) - (X^*,Y^*)|| = 0,$$

which proves the first statement.

To prove the second statement, since $\limsup\limits_{t\to\infty} \prod_{n=1}^t a_n = \alpha$, for a fix $\varepsilon > 0$ there exists $t_0 \in \mathbb{N}$ such that $\prod_{n=1}^t a_n < \alpha + \varepsilon$ if $t > t_0$. Then, again

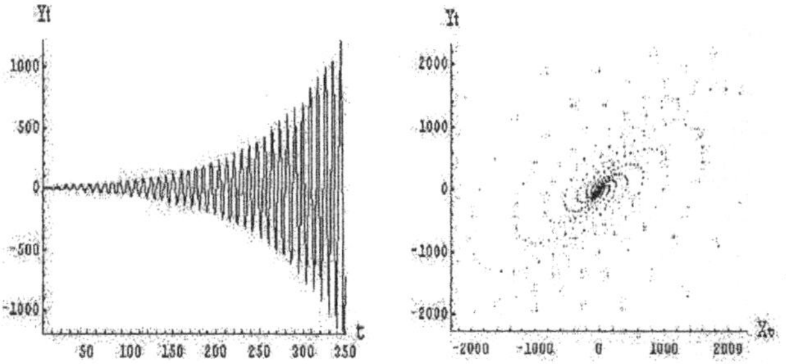

Figure 2: *Income traces (left) and orbit (right) where* $a_t = 1.02 + 1/t$ *and* $c_t = 0.5 + 1/t$ *with initial condition* $(X_0, Y_0) = (0.25, 0.189)$. *As it is expected, by Theorem 2, the orbit is not bounded.*

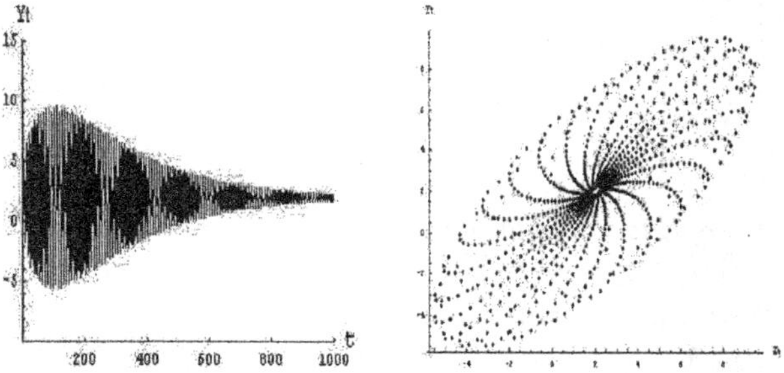

Figure 3: *Income traces (left) and orbit (right) where* $a_t = 0.99 + 1/t$ *and* $c_t = 0.5$ *with initial condition* $(X_0, Y_0) = (0.25, 0.189)$. *The limit map holds that* $a = 0.99 < 1$ *and it is expected, by Theorem 2, that the orbit goes to the fixed point* $(2, 2)$. *However,* $a_t > 1$ *at the beginning of the orbit and therefore the convergence is slow. In fact, if one looks at the first iterations, it could be thought that the orbit diverges.*

by (14) we obtain that

$$\begin{aligned} ||F_1^t(X,Y) - (X^*,Y^*)|| &\leq ||(X,Y) - (X^*,Y^*)|| \prod_{n=1}^{t} a_n \\ &\leq ||(X,Y) - (X^*,Y^*)||(\alpha + \varepsilon). \end{aligned}$$

Since the previous inequality has been proved for an arbitrary $\varepsilon > 0$, then the proof of the second statement finishes. ∎

Notice that (X^*, Y^*) is the only fixed point of all maps F_t if either $c_t = c$ is constant or $A = 0$, that is, the model does not include autonomous expenditures. Next result also gives us some conditions to have bounded orbits, even when the fixed point changes with time.

Theorem 4 *Let $F_{1,\infty} = (F_t)$ be a non-autonomous cycle defined as in (10) which converges to F defined as in (12). Assume $a_t = 1$ for all $t \in \mathbb{N}$. If the series*

$$\sum_{n=2}^{\infty} ||(X_{n-1}^*, Y_{n-1}^*) - (X_n^*, Y_n^*)||$$

converges then $\text{Orb}((X,Y), F_{1,\infty})$ *is bounded for all* $(X,Y) \in \mathbb{R}^2$.

Proof. Let (X^*, Y^*) be the fixed point of the limit function F. Then, inequality (14) reads as

$$\begin{aligned} ||F_1^t(X,Y) - (X_t^*, Y_t^*)|| &\leq ||(X,Y) - (X_t^*, Y_t^*)|| \\ &\quad + \sum_{n=2}^{t} ||(X_{n-1}^*, Y_{n-1}^*) - (X_n^*, Y_n^*)||. \end{aligned}$$

Since

$$\begin{aligned} ||F_1^t(X,Y) - (X^*, Y^*)|| &\leq ||F_1^t(X,Y) - (X_t^*, Y_t^*)|| \\ &\quad + ||(X_t^*, Y_t^*) - (X^*, Y^*)|| \end{aligned}$$

then

$$\begin{aligned} ||F_1^t(X,Y) - (X^*, Y^*)|| &\leq ||(X_t^*, Y_t^*) - (X^*, Y^*)|| \\ &\quad + ||(X,Y) - (X_t^*, Y_t^*)|| \\ &\quad + \sum_{n=2}^{t} ||(X_{n-1}^*, Y_{n-1}^*) - (X_n^*, Y_n^*)|| \quad (18) \end{aligned}$$

Let

$$\alpha = \lim_{t\to\infty} ||(X,Y) - (X_t^*, Y_t^*)||$$

and

$$\beta = \sum_{n=2}^{\infty} ||(X_{n-1}^*, Y_{n-1}^*) - (X_n^*, Y_n^*)||.$$

Therefore, since the sequence $((X_t^*, Y_t^*))$ converges to (X^*, Y^*), by (18) for any $\varepsilon > 0$ there exists $t_0 \in \mathbb{N}$ such that if $t > t_0$, then

$$||F_1^t(X,Y) - (X^*, Y^*)|| \leq \varepsilon + \alpha + \beta,$$

which finishes the proof of this theorem. ∎

In Figure 4 we simulate the situation presented in Theorem 4. Notice that since $a_t = 1$ for all $t \geq 1$, the only thing we may say about the orbit is that it is bounded, but we cannot say anything concerning the ω–limit set of the orbit. Although the orbit is bounded, we cannot say anything about the complexity of the orbit. For instance, when $F_t = F$ for all $t \geq 1$, that is the sequence of maps is constant, the orbit is quasiperiodic (see Chapter 2) and hence no complex dynamics appear. Nothing can be said in the general case.

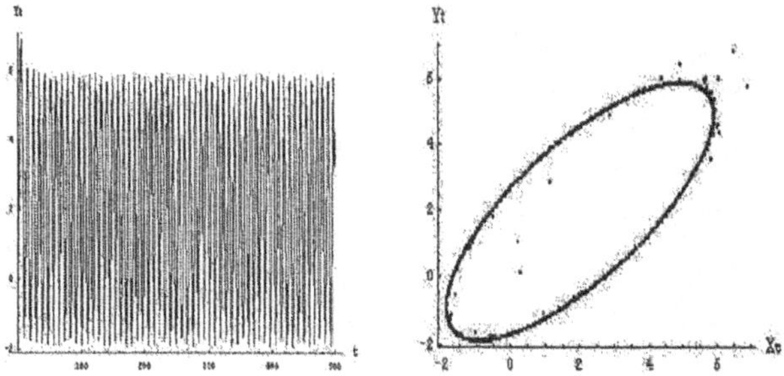

Figure 4: *Income traces (left) and orbit (right) where* $a_t = 1$ *and* $c_t = 0.5 + 1/t$ *with initial condition* $(X_0, Y_0) = (0.25, 0.189)$. *Since* $A = 1$, *notice that the series* $\sum_{n=2}^{\infty} ||(X_{n-1}^*, Y_{n-1}^*) - (X_n^*, Y_n^*)|| = 4\sqrt{2}$ *and hence the orbit* $\mathrm{Orb}((X,Y), F_{1,\infty})$ *is bounded.*

When a_t converges to 1 and $a_t \neq 1$ for all t we have to go through simulations to see that in this case also the orbit $\mathrm{Orb}((X,Y), F_{1,\infty})$ is bounded for all $(X,Y) \in \mathbb{R}^2$. In Figure 5 we simulate this situation when $a_t \leq 1$, $a_t \geq 1$ and a_t is randomly alternating ≥ 1 and ≤ 1 for all t. Roughly speaking, if $a_t > 1$ the map F_t gives unbounded orbits (we say that F_t is expansive) and if $a_t < 1$ all orbits converges to the fixed point. Using the idea that F_t expands the orbit when $a_t > 1$ and contracts it when $a_t < 1$ we can "explain" some simulations which cannot be explained by using the results proved in this chapter. These simulations point out that the condition $a \neq 1$

in Theorem 2 is necessary and it cannot be avoided. It is also interesting to emphasize how the behavior of the orbit of the non-autonomous system and the orbit of the limit map can be totally different.

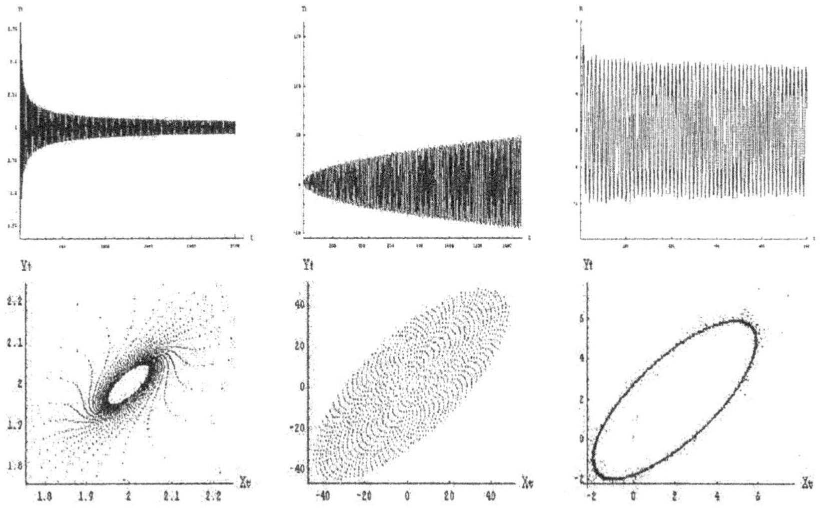

Figure 5: *For the initial condition* $(X_0, Y_0) = (0.25, 0.189)$ *we simulate the following cases from left to right: (1) income traces and orbit where* $a_t = 1 - 1/t$ *and* $c_t = 0.5$. *Notice that according to Theorem 3 the orbit goes to the fixed point* $(2, 2)$, *although the convergence is very slow because* a_t *grows up to* 1. *(2) Income traces and orbit where* $a_t = 1 + 1/t$ *and* $c_t = 0.5$. *Here one can expect unbounded orbits because* $a_t > 1$ *and hence any map* F_t *is expansive. (3) Income traces and orbit where* $a_t = 1 + (-1)^r/t$ *where* r *is a random integer between 1 and t and* $c_t = 0.5 + 1/t$. *These simulations show how the hyphotesis* $a \neq 1$ *in Theorem 2 is neccesary.*

5.5 Non-Autonomous Cycles Generated by Two Maps F_1 and F_2

In this section, we study non-autonomous cycles which are generated by two maps F_1 and F_2. The simplest way in which we can obtain a non-autonomous cycle generated by two maps is with a periodic sequence $F_{1,\infty} = (F_1, F_2, F_1, F_2, ...)$. In this case, the second iterate of the cycle is given by a constant sequence $F_{1,\infty}^{[2]} = (F_2 \circ F_1, F_2 \circ F_1, ...)$. Moreover, given $(X, Y) \in \mathbb{R}^2$, its orbit $\mathrm{Orb}((X, Y), F_{1,\infty})$ is equal to

$$\mathrm{Orb}((X, Y), F_2 \circ F_1) \cup \mathrm{Orb}(F_1(X, Y), F_1 \circ F_2). \qquad (19)$$

The above equality holds because

$$F_1^n(X, Y) = (F_2 \circ F_1)^{n/2}(X, Y)$$

if $n \in \mathbb{N}$ is even and

$$F_1^n(X, Y) = (F_1 \circ F_2)^{n/2}(F_1(X, Y))$$

if $n \in \mathbb{N}$ is odd. Then, it is easy to derive from (19) and Proposition 2 that

$$\omega((X, Y), F_{1,\infty}) = \omega((X, Y), F_2 \circ F_1) \cup \omega(F_1(X, Y), F_1 \circ F_2).$$

Recently, there are several papers which deals with the following question. If F_1 and F_2 are chaotic (or simple) in some sense, is it true that $F_{1,\infty}$, or more precisely $F_2 \circ F_1$ is chaotic (or simple)? (see for instance the references Almeida et al. 2005, Harmer et al. 2000, Parrondo et al. 2002, Arena et al. 2003, Klic et al. 1996 and Klic et al. 2002). As we stated in Section 5.2, this phenomenon is known as Parrondo's paradox.

As we have done in the previous sections, the aim of this section is to analyze the asymptotic behavior of the orbit $\mathrm{Orb}((X, Y), F_{1,\infty})$. If we translate this into the present context, the problem reads as follows: *can two stable (resp. unstable) cycles provide an unstable (resp. stable) cycle?*

In order to give an answer to the previous question we have to take into account that we have two compositions $F_1 \circ F_2$ and $F_2 \circ F_1$, which play a role in the orbit of the non-autonomous cycle. In general, if the composition $f \circ g$ of two continuous functions f and g has a dynamical property (say, stability, chaos in any context,...) it is not true that the converse composition map $g \circ f$ has the same property. In fact, it can be seen in Linero et al. 2002, that, there are two continuous maps f and g on the interval $[0, 1]$, such that $f \circ g$ is chaotic in the sense of Devaney while $g \circ f$ is not. From the point of view of non-autonomous cycles, we have to answer the following question: *do the maps $F_1 \circ F_2$ and $F_2 \circ F_1$ have the same dynamical properties, let us say for instance, stability?*

Consider the maps

$$F_i(X,Y) = \begin{pmatrix} 0 & 1 \\ -a_i & c_i + a_i \end{pmatrix} \begin{pmatrix} X \\ Y \end{pmatrix} + \begin{pmatrix} 0 \\ A \end{pmatrix}, i = 1,2. \tag{20}$$

Then, we construct the compositions

$$(F_2 \circ F_1)(X,Y) = \mathcal{A}_1 \begin{pmatrix} X \\ Y \end{pmatrix} + \begin{pmatrix} A \\ A(1 + c_2 + a_2) \end{pmatrix},$$

and

$$(F_1 \circ F_2)(X,Y) = \mathcal{A}_2 \begin{pmatrix} X \\ Y \end{pmatrix} + \begin{pmatrix} A \\ A(1 + c_1 + a_1) \end{pmatrix}$$

where

$$\mathcal{A}_1 = \begin{pmatrix} -a_1 & c_1 + a_1 \\ -a_1(c_2 + a_2) & (c_2 + a_2)(c_1 + a_1) - a_2 \end{pmatrix}$$

and

$$\mathcal{A}_2 = \begin{pmatrix} -a_2 & c_2 + a_2 \\ -a_2(c_1 + a_1) & (c_1 + a_1)(c_2 + a_2) - a_1 \end{pmatrix}.$$

A simple calculation gives us that in the case in which the eigenvalues of both matrices are complex (this is the case of interest), the modulus of the eigenvalues coincide and its value is

$$\sqrt{a_1 a_2}.$$

Then, we obtain stability if $a_1 a_2 < 1$ and unstability if $a_1 a_2 > 1$. Moreover, if both maps are stable, that is $\max\{a_1, a_2\} < 1$, then the compositions are also stable, while if they are unstable, $\min\{a_1, a_2\} > 1$, then the composition is unstable. But notice that we can get stability even when one of the maps is unstable.

When $a_1 a_2 = 1$, we consider for instance the map $F_2 \circ F_1$. The characteristic equation

$$\begin{aligned} 0 &= \begin{vmatrix} -a_1 - \lambda & a_1 + c_1 \\ -a_1(c_2 + a_2) & -a_2 + (c_1 + a_1)(c_2 + a_2) - \lambda \end{vmatrix} \\ &= \lambda^2 + [a_1 + a_2 - (c_1 + a_1)(c_2 + a_2)]\lambda + a_1 a_2. \end{aligned}$$

Since $a_1 a_2 = 1$, we put $a = a_1$ and $1/a = a_2$. Then the solutions of the above equation are

$$\frac{-K \pm \sqrt{K^2 - 4}}{2},$$

where

$$K = a(1 - c_1) + \frac{1}{a}(1 - c_2) - (1 + c_1 c_2).$$

Now, if $|K| < 2$, then the roots are complex with modulus 1, and hence the orbits are periodic or quasiperiodic (for instance when $c_1 = c_2 = 0.5$ and $a = 2$). By other hand, if $|K| \geq 2$, the roots are real, but in this case one of the roots has modulus greater that one because $|-K - \sqrt{K^2 - 4}| > 2$ and hence, in the real case we cannot have stable maps but unstable maps (for instance when $c_1 = c_2 = 0.5$ and $a = 8$). In a similar way it can be proved the same for the composition $F_1 \circ F_2$.

When the compositions are stable we can enunciate the next result whose proof is a direct consequence of Proposition 2.

Theorem 5 *Let $F_{1,\infty} = (F_1, F_2, F_1, F_2, ...)$ be a periodic sequence of continuous functions defined as in (20). Assume that $a_1 a_2 < 1$. Then for any $(X, Y) \in \mathbb{R}^2$ we have*

$$\omega((X,Y), F_{1,\infty}) = \{(X_{21}^*, Y_{21}^*), (X_{12}^*, Y_{12}^*)\},$$

where (X_{21}^*, Y_{21}^*) and (X_{12}^*, Y_{12}^*) are the unique fixed point in $\mathbb{R}^2$ of $F_2 \circ F_1$ and $F_1 \circ F_2$, respectively.

The periodic sequence described above is the simplest way of constructing a non-autonomous cycle with two maps. A general way of doing this is the following. Let $(\alpha_t) \in \{1,2\}^{\mathbb{N}}$ be an infinite sequence of 1 's and 2's. Let $F_{1,\infty} = (F_{\alpha_1}, F_{\alpha_2}, ...)$. If (α_t) is the periodic sequence $(1, 2, 1, 2, ...)$, then we obtain the periodic sequence of Theorem 5. When (α_t) is constant, for instance $(1, 1, 1, ...)$, then we obtain an autonomous cycle defined by F_1. Basically the same happens when (α_t) is eventually constant, that is, there is $n_0 \in \mathbb{N}$ such that $\alpha_t = \alpha_{t_0}$ for all $t \geq t_0$. Now we are interested in sequences with infinitely many 1's and 2's.

Then under the previous assumptions we are going to estimate

$$||F_1^t(X,Y) - (X_1^*, Y_1^*)||,$$

where (X_1^*, Y_1^*) is the fixed point of F_1 in order to find conditions for obtaining bounded and convergent orbits. To this end, notice that by inequality

(14), $||F^t_{\alpha_1}(X,Y) - (X^*_{\alpha_t}, Y^*_{\alpha_t})||$ is smaller or equal to

$$||(X,Y) - (X^*_{\alpha_t}, Y^*_{\alpha_t})|| \prod_{n=1}^{t} a_{\alpha_n}$$
$$+ \sum_{n=2}^{t} ||(X^*_{\alpha_{n-1}}, Y^*_{\alpha_{n-1}}) - (X^*_{\alpha_n}, Y^*_{\alpha_n})|| \prod_{j=n}^{t} a_{\alpha_j} \leq$$

$$\leq ||(X,Y) - (X^*_{\alpha_t}, Y^*_{\alpha_t})|| \prod_{n=1}^{t} a_{\alpha_n} + ||(X^*_2, Y^*_2) - (X^*_1, Y^*_1)|| \sum_{n=2}^{t} \prod_{j=n}^{t} a_{\alpha_j},$$

because there are only two fixed points. Then, we can prove the following result.

Theorem 6 *Let* $(\alpha_t) \in \{1,2\}^{\mathbb{N}}$ *be an infinite sequence. Let* $F_{1,\infty} = (F_{\alpha_t})$ *where* F_{α_t} *is defined as in (20). Assume that* $\sum_{n=2}^{t} \prod_{j=n}^{t} a_{\alpha_j}$ *converges. Then any orbit,* $\mathrm{Orb}((X,Y), F_{1,\infty})$*, of the non-autonomous sequence is bounded. If in addition* F_1 *and* F_2 *has the same fixed point* (X^*, Y^*) *and the product* $\prod_{n=1}^{t} a_{\alpha_n}$ *converges to zero, then any orbit converges to the fixed point* (X^*, Y^*).

Proof. If $\sum_{n=2}^{t} \prod_{j=n}^{t} a_{\alpha_j}$ converges, then $\prod_{n=1}^{t} a_{\alpha_n}$ converges to zero. Now proceed as in the proof of Theorem 3 to obtain the result. ∎

Notice that the sequence (α_t) can be generated in several ways. Here we propose some of them which, in our opinion, have a special interest. The first one is to choose the sequence (α_t) is in a random way. For instance, we consider that a probabilty measure μ on $\{1,2\}$ such that $\mu(\{1\}) = \mu(\{2\}) = 1/2$. In this case one could make himself the following questions: *is there a common behavior, for almost all sequence* (α_t)*?* or *is that common behaviour similar to that of* $F_1 \circ F_2$ *and* $F_2 \circ F_1$*?*. By other hand, *what happens if the measure* μ *changes?* Figures 6 to 11 show simulations in which the sequence (α_t) is chosen in a random way.

To end this section, notice that we can combine the results obtained here jointly with those obtained in section 5.4 to construct non-autonomous cycles. Basically, we are going to construct non-autonomous cycles which are

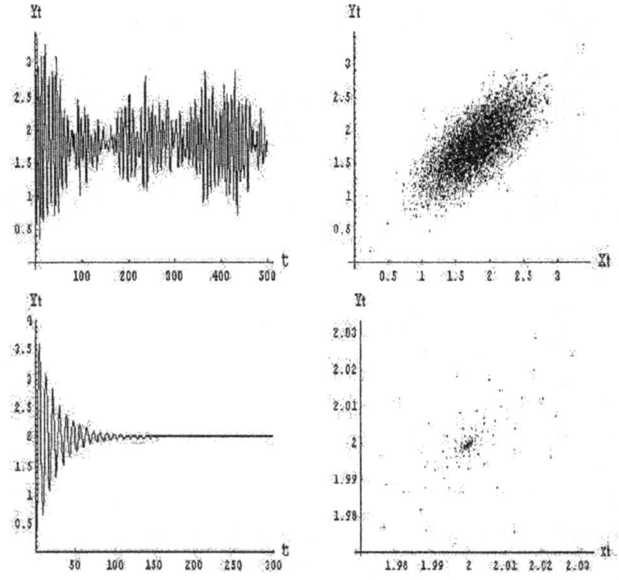

Figure 6: *Income traces (left) and orbit (right) where* $a_1 = 0.9$, $a_2 = 0.95$ *with initial condition* $(X_0, Y_0) = (0.25, 0.189)$. *In the upper part of the figure* $c_1 = 0.4$ *and* $c_2 = 0.5$, *while in the lower part* $c_1 = c_2 = 0.5$, *that is* F_1 *and* F_2 *have the same fixed point. Both maps are contractive, but in the first case the existence of different fixed points for* F_1 *and* F_2 *produces a non-convergent orbit, while in the second case, the existence of a common fixed point, jointly with Theorem 3, implies the convergence of the orbit to the common fixed point. The example shows a situation in which the existence of non common fixed points generates a complicated behaviour. It seems to be difficult to obtain a mathematical explanation of this fact.*

given by two sequences which converge to the maps $F^{(1)}$ and $F^{(2)}$ in the following way.

Let

$$F_t^{(1)}(X,Y) = (Y, -a_t^1 X + (a_t^1 + c_t^1)Y) \tag{21}$$

and

$$F_t^{(2)}(X,Y) = (Y, -a_t^2 X + (a_t^2 + c_t^2)Y) \tag{22}$$

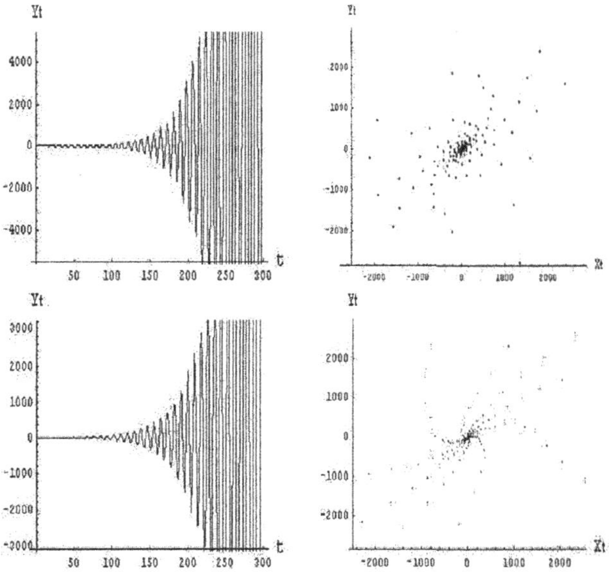

Figure 7: *Income traces (left) and orbit (right) where* $a_1 = 1.09$, $a_2 = 1.05$ *with initial condition* $(X_0, Y_0) = (0.25, 0.189)$. *In the upper part of the figure* $c_1 = 0.4$ *and* $c_2 = 0.5$, *while in the lower part* $c_1 = c_2 = 0.5$, *that is* F_1 *and* F_2 *have the same fixed point. Since both maps* F_1 *and* F_2 *are expansive, it is expected an unbounded orbit. Since the orbit is expanding out, it seems that it is not important the fact that the maps share the fixed point, because both simulations are similar. Notice that the same does not happens when the maps are contractive.*

be two sequences of cycles which converge to

$$F^{(1)}(X,Y) = (Y, -a^1 X + (a^1 + c^1)Y)$$

and

$$F^{(2)}(X,Y) = (Y, -a^2 X + (a^2 + c^2)Y),$$

respectively. Consider the non-autonomous cycle defined by the sequence

$$F_{1,\infty}^{(1,2)} = (F_1^{(1)}, F_1^{(2)}, F_2^{(1)}, F_2^{(2)}, \dots).$$

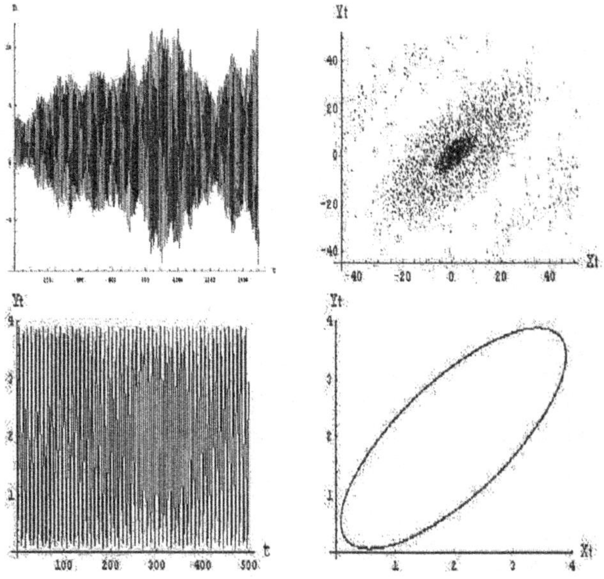

Figure 8: *Income traces (left) and orbit (right) where* $a_1 = a_2 = 1$ *with initial condition* $(X_0, Y_0) = (0.25, 0.189)$. *In the upper part of the figure* $c_1 = 0.4$ *and* $c_2 = 0.5$, *while in the lower part* $c_1 = c_2 = 0.5$, *that is* F_1 *and* F_2 *have the same fixed point and hence* $F_1 = F_2$. *In both cases we obtain bounded orbits, but the existence of different fixed points in the first case gives us a more complicated orbit. Theorem 4 proves that the second case is bounded.*

If $a^1 a^2 \neq 1$, then by Aoki et al. 1994, page 86, both maps $F^{(1)} \circ F^{(2)}$ and $F^{(2)} \circ F^{(1)}$ have the shadowing property. Hence, by Propositions 2 and 3 and proceeding as in the proof of Theorem 2, we can enunciate the next result.

Theorem 7 *Let* $F^{(1)}_{1,\infty}$ *and* $F^{(2)}_{1,\infty}$ *be two non-autonomous cycles defined as (21) and (22) respectively, converging to*

$$F^{(1)}(X,Y) = (Y, -a^1 X + (a^1 + c^1)Y)$$

and

$$F^{(2)}(X,Y) = (Y, -a^2 X + (a^2 + c^2)Y),$$

respectively. Then for any $(X,Y) \in \mathbb{R}^2$ *the following statements hold:*

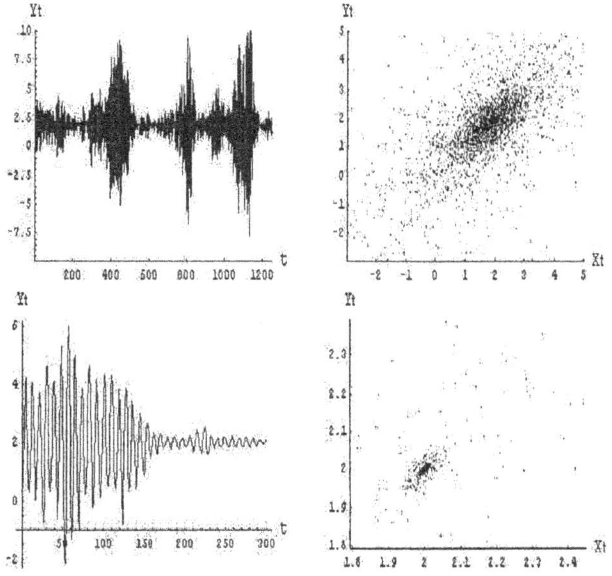

Figure 9: *Income traces (left) and orbit (right) where* $a_1 = 1.2$, $a_2 = 0.79$ *with initial condition* $(X_0, Y_0) = (0.25, 0.189)$. *In the upper part of the figure* $c_1 = 0.4$ *and* $c_2 = 0.5$, *while in the lower part* $c_1 = c_2 = 0.5$, *that is* F_1 *and* F_2 *have the same fixed point. Notice that* $a_1 a_2 < 1$ *and then roughly speaking, if the number of times in which* a_1 *and* a_2 *appear is approximately the same, according to Theorem 13, we have bounded and convergent orbits. That is what it seems that happens in these simulations. Notice that the existence of different fixed points implies a greater complexity.*

(a) If $a^1 a^2 < 1$, *then* $\omega((X,Y), F_{1,\infty}^{(1,2)}) = \{(X_{21}^*, Y_{21}^*), (X_{12}^*, Y_{12}^*)\}$, *with* (X_{12}^*, Y_{12}^*) *and* (X_{21}^*, Y_{21}^*) *the fixed points in* $\mathbb{R}^2$ *of* $F^{(1)} \circ F^{(2)}$ *and* $F^{(2)} \circ F^{(1)}$, *respectively.*

(b) If $a^1 a^2 > 1$, *then the orbit* $\mathrm{Orb}((X,Y), F_{1,\infty}^{(1,2)})$ *is unbounded.*

Figures 12 to 15 are simulations of different situations for the income traces and orbits of the non-autonomous cycle $F_{1,\infty}^{(1,2)}$ depending on the parameters of the model. Notice that when $a^1 a^2 \neq 1$, then all the simulations can be rigorously explained by Theorem 14.

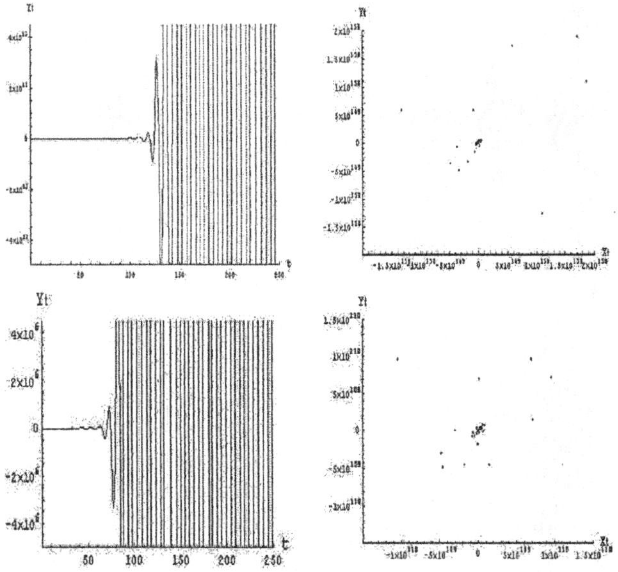

Figure 10: *Income traces (left) and orbit (right) where* $a_1 = 2.19$ *and* $a_2 = 0.9$ *with initial condition* $(X_0, Y_0) = (0.25, 0.189)$. *In the upper part of the figure* $c_1 = 0.4$ *and* $c_2 = 0.5$, *while in the lower part* $c_1 = c_2 = 0.5$, *that is* F_1 *and* F_2 *have the same fixed point. Since* $a_1 a_2 > 1$, *one would expect that the modulus of the points in the orbit grows. Indeed the simulations show unbounded orbits.*

5.6 A Naive Approach to the General Case

As we saw in Section 5.3, if a_t and c_t can be chosen without any restriction, then the orbit of the non-autonomous cycle can be a dense subset of $\mathbb{R}^2$. In this section we are going to choose a_t and c_t in three different ways which have not been studied before. In the cases we analyze we always randomly choose c_t and a_t from a bounded closed interval. Three cases appear because degenerate intervals, that is a single point, are taking into account, but they cannot appear simultaneously. We can think that always either a_t

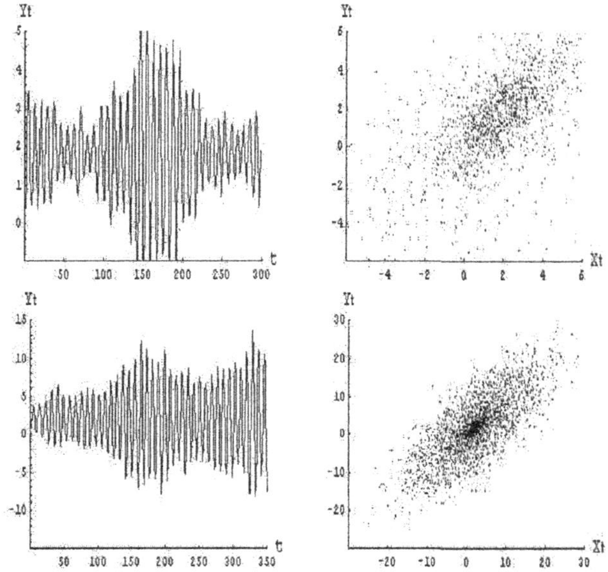

Figure 11: *Income traces (left) and orbit (right) where* $a_1 = 1/0.9$ *and* $a_2 = 0.9$ *with initial condition* $(X_0, Y_0) = (0.25, 0.189)$. *In the upper part of the figure* $c_1 = 0.5$ *and* $c_2 = 0.4$, *while in the lower part* $c_1 = c_2 = 0.5$, *that is* F_1 *and* F_2 *have the same fixed point. Notice that* $a_1 a_2 = 1$, *and then one can expect bounded orbits. As before, the more complicated situation appears when the fixed points of* F_1 *and* F_2 *are different.*

or c_t or both are chosen from a bounded closed interval following a uniform probabilistic distribution.

So first, we consider that $a_t = a$ for all $t \geq 0$ and $c_t \in [\underline{c}, \overline{c}]$ is randomly chosen. We are going to estimate $||F_1^t(X,Y) - (X_t^*, Y_t^*)||$ in order to characterize bounded orbits. Now, inequality (14) reads as

$$||F_1^t(X,Y) - (X_t^*, Y_t^*)|| \leq \sum_{n=2}^{t} a^{t-n+1} ||(X_{n-1}^*, Y_{n-1}^*) - (X_n^*, Y_n^*)|| + a^t ||(X,Y) - (X_t^*, Y_t^*)||. \quad (23)$$

Then we can prove the following result.

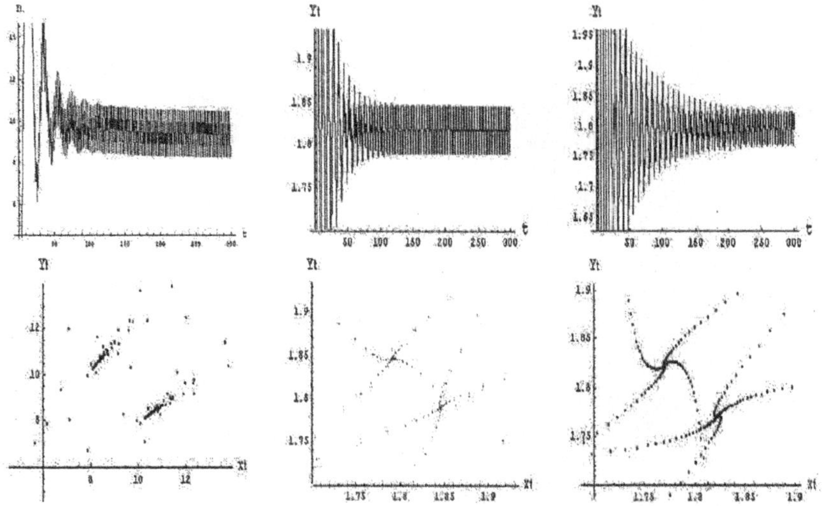

Figure 12: *From left to right we simulate income traces and orbit in the following cases: (1)* $a_t^1 = 0.9 - 1/t$, $a_t^2 = 0.95 - 1/t$, $c_t^1 = 0.5 + 1/t$ *and* $c_t^2 = 0.4 + 1/t$, *(2)* $a_t^1 = 0.9 - 1/t$, $a_t^2 = 0.95 - 1/t$, $c_t^1 = 0.5$ *and* $c_t^2 = 0.4$ *and (3)* $a_t^1 = 1.2 - 1/t$, $a_t^2 = 0.79 - 1/t$, $c_t^1 = 0.5$ *and* $c_t^2 = 0.4$ *with initial condition* $(X_0, Y_0) = (0.25, 0.189)$, *respectively. For the limit maps we have that* $a^1 a^2 < 1$ *and then, by Theorem 14 it is expected that the orbits converges to the fixed points of the composition of the maps* $F^{(1)}$ *and* $F^{(2)}$.

Theorem 8 *Let* $F_{1,\infty} = (F_t)$ *be a non-autonomous cycle defined as in (10). Assume that* $a_t = a$ *and* $c_t \in [\underline{c}, \overline{c}]$ *with* $\overline{c} < 1$ *for all* $t \geq 1$. *Then the following statements hold:*

(a) If $a < 1$, *then any orbit,* $\mathrm{Orb}((X, Y), F_{1,\infty})$, *of the non-autonomous cycle is bounded.*

(b) If $a = 1$ *and the series*

$$\sum_{n=2}^{\infty} \|(X_{n-1}^*, Y_{n-1}^*) - (X_n^*, Y_n^*)\|$$

converges, then for all $(X, Y) \in \mathbb{R}^2$ *the orbit,* $\mathrm{Orb}((X, Y), F_{1,\infty})$, *of the non-autonomous cycle is bounded.*

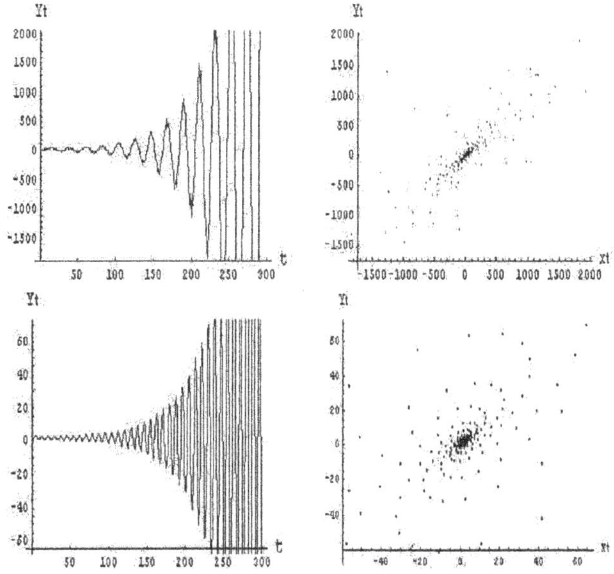

Figure 13: *First we simulate income traces (left) and orbit (right) where* $a_t^1 = 1.09 - 1/t$, $a_t^2 = 1.02 - 1/t$, $c_t^1 = 0.5 + 1/t$ *and* $c_t^2 = 0.4 + 1/t$ *and second income traces (left) and orbit (right) where* $a_t^1 = 1.09 - 1/t$, $a_t^2 = 1.02 - 1/t$, $c_t^1 = 0.5$ *and* $c_t^2 = 0.4$, *in both cases with initial condition* $(X_0, Y_0) = (0.25, 0.189)$. *Since* $a^1 a^2 > 1$, *it is natural to expect unbounded orbits, which is what the simulations show.*

Proof. Since $\bar{c} < 1$, the sequence of fixed points $((X_t^*, Y_t^*))$ are bounded because $X_t^* = Y_t^* \leq A/(1-\bar{c})$. The proof of the first statement is analogous to the proof of Theorem 3. For the second statement by (23) we have that

$$\begin{aligned} ||F_1^t(X,Y) - (X_t^*, Y_t^*)|| &\leq ||(X,Y) - (X_t^*, Y_t^*)|| \\ &+ \sum_{n=2}^{t} ||(X_{n-1}^*, Y_{n-1}^*) - (X_n^*, Y_n^*)||. \end{aligned}$$

Now proceeding as in the proof of Theorem 3 we obtain the required result. ∎

Below, in Figure 16 we simulate conditions 1 and 2 of Theorem 8 respectively.

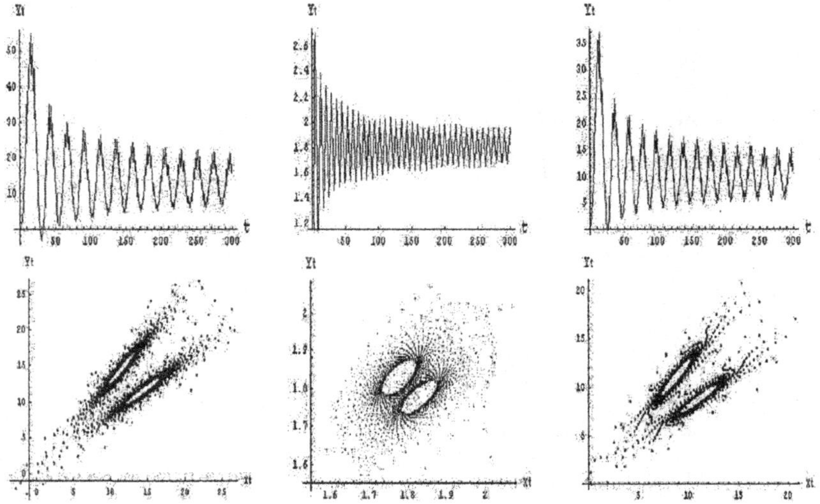

Figure 14: *For the initial condition* $(X_0, Y_0) = (0.25, 0.189)$ *from left to right we simulate income traces and orbit in the following cases: (1)* $a_t^1 = 1/0.9 - 1/t$, $a_t^2 = 0.9 - 1/t$, $c_t^1 = 0.5 + 1/t$ *and* $c_t^2 = 0.4 + 1/t$, *(2)* $a_t^1 = 1/0.9 - 1/t$, $a_t^2 = 0.9 - 1/t$, $c_t^1 = 0.5$ *and* $c_t^2 = 0.4$ *and (3)* $a_t^1 = 1 - 1/t$, $a_t^2 = 1 - 1/t$, $c_t^1 = 0.5 + 1/t$ *and* $c_t^2 = 0.4 + 1/t$. *Notice that* $a^1 a^2 = 1$ *and then Theorem 14 does not give any information about the simulations. Since* $a_t^1 a_t^2 < 1$, *one would expect the convergence of the orbit, which is what happens in the simulations.*

Notice that if $\overline{c} = 1$, then the sequence of fixed points is not bounded and then, even when $a < 1$ the orbits of the non-autonomous cycle could be unbounded as the simulations of Figure 17 shows.

Secondly, we fix $c_t = c$ for all $t \geq 0$ and assume that a_t is bounded by $\underline{a}, \overline{a} \in \mathbb{R}$ and such that $a_t \in [\underline{a}, \overline{a}]$ is randomly chosen. Again, the only thing we are able to do is to characterize bounded orbits. To this end, we consider

$$||F_1^t(X, Y) - (X^*, Y^*)||,$$

where (X^*, Y^*) denotes the unique fixed point in $\mathbb{R}^2$ of the sequence $F_{1,\infty}$, and we will try to obtain an upper bound. Then we use inequality (14) which

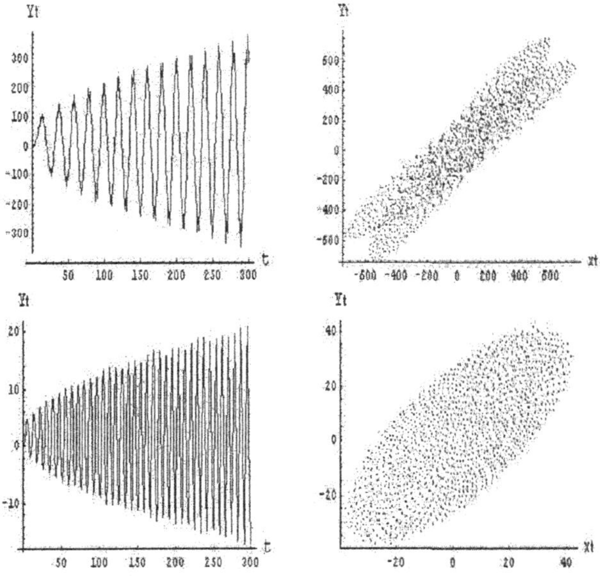

Figure 15: *For the initial condition* $(X_0, Y_0) = (0.25, 0.189)$ *we simulate income traces (left) and orbit (right) in the following cases: in the upper* $a_t^1 = 1 + 1/t$, $a_t^2 = 1 + 1/t$, $c_t^1 = 0.5 + 1/t$ *and* $c_t^2 = 0.4 + 1/t$ *and in the lower* $a_t^1 = 1 + 1/t$, $a_t^2 = 1 + 1/t$, $c_t^1 = 0.5$ *and* $c_t^2 = 0.4$. *Since* $a^1 a^2 = 1$, *Theorem 14 does not help us to see if simulations are right. Anyway,* $a_t^1 a_t^2 > 1$ *and then one can expect that the orbits will be unbounded, which is what simulations show.*

in this setting reads as follows

$$
\begin{aligned}
||F_1^t(X,Y) - (X^*,Y^*)|| &\leq ||(X,Y) - (X_t^*, Y_t^*)|| \prod_{n=1}^{t} a_n \\
&\quad + \sum_{n=2}^{t} ||(X_{n-1}^*, Y_{n-1}^*) - (X_n^*, Y_n^*)|| \prod_{j=n}^{t} a_j \\
&= ||(X,Y) - (X^*,Y^*)|| \prod_{n=1}^{t} a_n,
\end{aligned}
$$

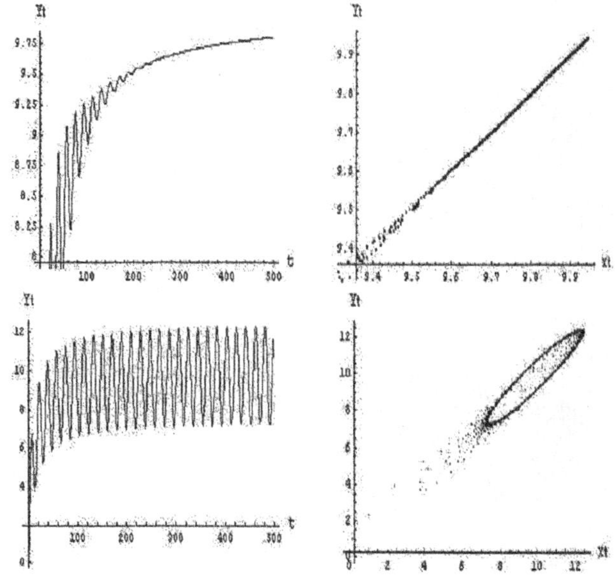

Figure 16: *In the upper part we show income traces (left) and orbit (right) where* $a_t = .95$ *and* $c_t = 0.9 - 1/t$ *with initial condition* $(X_0, Y_0) = (0.25, 0.189)$ *and in the lower part income traces (left) and orbit (right) where* $a_t = 1$ *and* $c_t = 0.9 - 1/t$ *with the same initial condition. Here, notice that the series* $\sum_{n=2}^{\infty} ||(X_{n-1}^*, Y_{n-1}^*) - (X_n^*, Y_n^*)|| = \sum_{n=2}^{\infty} \sqrt{2}/(0.81n^2 - 18n + 0.1)$*, which is convergent and then the orbit is bounded (cf. Theorem 8).*

because $||(X_{n-1}^*, Y_{n-1}^*) - (X_n^*, Y_n^*)|| = 0$. Then, following the proof of Theorem 3, it can be proved the next result which establishes conditions to have bounded and convergent orbits.

Theorem 9 *Let* $F_{1,\infty} = (F_t)$ *be a non-autonomous cycle defined as in (10). Assume that* $c_t = c$ *for all* $t \geq 0$ *and* $a_t \in [\underline{a}, \overline{a}]$ *is randomly chosen. Then the following statements hold:*

(a) If $\lim_{t\to\infty} \prod_{n=1}^{t} a_n = 0$*, then* $\omega((X,Y), F_{1,\infty}) = \{(X^*, Y^*)\}$ *for all* $(X,Y) \in \mathbb{R}^2$.

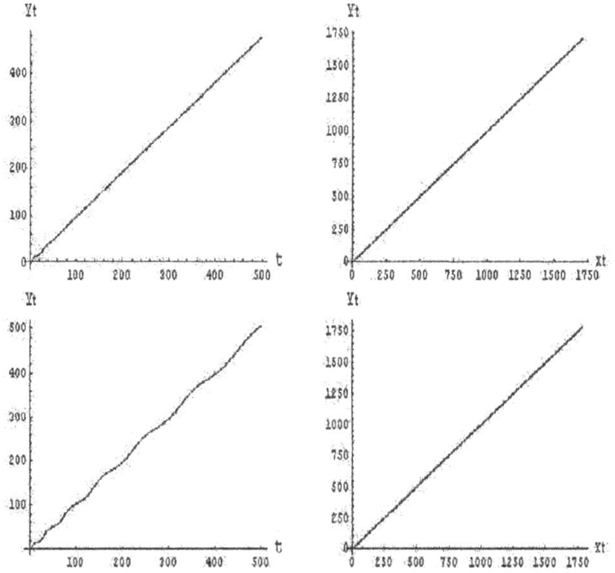

Figure 17: *We simulate income traces (left) and orbit (right) in the following cases: in the upper part* $a_t = .95$ *and* $c_t = 1 - 1/t$ *and in the lower part* $a_t = 1$ *and* $c_t = 1 - 1/t$ *with initial condition* $(X_0, Y_0) = (0.25, 0.189)$. *Since* c_t *converges to* 1, *the modulus of the fixed points are growing up and then, even when* $a_t < 1$ *we have an unbounded orbit, although in this case it seems that its behaviour is simple.*

(b) If $\limsup_{t\to\infty} \prod_{n=1}^{t} a_n = a \in \mathbb{R}$, *then for all* $(X,Y) \in \mathbb{R}^2$ *the orbit* $\mathrm{Orb}((X,Y), F_{1,\infty})$ *is bounded.*

Notice that the first case in Figure 5 is a simulations for (a) in Theorem 9. In case (1) of Figure 5 we have that $a_t = 1 - 1/t$ and hence $\lim_{t\to\infty} \prod_{n=1}^{t} 1 - 1/n = 0$.

Finally, we may assume that both parameters $a_t \in [\underline{a}, \overline{a}]$ and $c_t \in [\underline{c}, \overline{c}]$ are randomly chosen. We distinguish two cases: $\overline{c} < 1$ and $\overline{c} = 1$. In the first case, the sequence of fixed points is bounded, and then $s = \sup\{||(X,Y) - (X_t^*, Y_t^*)|| : t \in \mathbb{R}\}$ and $r = \sup\{||(X_{t+1}^*, Y_{t+1}^*) - (X_t^*, Y_t^*)|| : t \in \mathbb{R}\}$ are finite (recall that $X_t^* = Y_t^* = A/(1 - c_t)$) and hence inequality (14) can be rewritten as follows

$$\begin{aligned} ||F_1^t(X,Y) - (X_t^*, Y_t^*)|| &\leq ||(X,Y) - (X_t^*, Y_t^*)|| \prod_{n=1}^{t} a_n \\ &\quad + \sum_{n=2}^{t} ||(X_{n-1}^*, Y_{n-1}^*) - (X_n^*, Y_n^*)|| \prod_{j=n}^{t} a_j \\ &\leq s \prod_{n=1}^{t} a_n + r \sum_{n=2}^{t} \prod_{j=n}^{t} a_j, \end{aligned} \tag{24}$$

The inequality (24) allows us to enunciate the following result whose proof is similar to the proof of Theorem 4.

Theorem 10 *Let* $F_{1,\infty} = (F_t)$ *be a non-autonomous cycle defined as in (10). Assume that both* $a_t \in [\underline{a}, \overline{a}]$ *and* $c_t \in [\underline{c}, \overline{c}]$ *are randomly chosen, with* $\overline{c} < 1$. *If the sequence* $\sum_{n=2}^{t} \prod_{j=n}^{t} a_j$ *converges then any orbit,* $\text{Orb}((X,Y), F_{1,\infty})$, *is bounded for all* $(X,Y) \in \mathbb{R}^2$.

Notice that when $\overline{c} = 1$ the sequence of fixed points is not bounded. In Figure 17 we simulate this situation.

Conclusions

In a classical model of business cycle, we introduce parameters depending on time, producing a non-autonomous linear second order difference equation, which is analyzed in the setting of non-autonomous discrete systems. Roughly speaking, one could think on a linear model whose parameters are pertubed is some way, for instance a random way.

The stability and limit set of the orbits of the non-autonomous system associated to the difference equation are studied. When all the maps of the system are contractive, then the system is stable, producing bounded orbits. In other cases, some simulations shows that when we have expansive maps in the system, unbounded orbits and some type of chaotic behaviour may appear. It must be pointed out that the chaotic behaviour appear when both, contractive and expansive maps are in the system infinitely many times.

It is an interesting question to analyze these type of "chaotic orbits", that is: are they really chaotic in some theoretical sense?

References

Almeida, J., Peralta–Salas, D. and Romera, M., 2005, "Can two chaotic systems make an order?", *Physica D* 200:124-132.

Aoki, N., and Hiraide, K., 1994, *Topological theory of dynamical systems: recent advances*, North–Holland.

Arena, P. Fazzino, S. Fortuna, L. and Maniscalco, P., 2003, "Game theory and non–linear dynamics: the Parrondo Paradox case study", *Chaos, Solitons & Fractals* 17:545–555.

Buceta, J., Lindenberg, K. and Parrondo, J. M. R., 2002, "Pattern formation induced by nonequilibrium global alternation of dynamics", *Phys. Rev. E* 66:36216-36227.

Cánovas, J. S. and Linero, A., 2002, "On topological entropy of commuting interval maps", *Nonlinear Analysis* 51:1159–1165.

Harmer, G. P., Abbott, D. and Taylor, P. G., 2000, "The paradox of Parrondo's games", *R. Soc. Lond. Proc. Ser. A Math. Phys. Eng. Sci.* 456:247–259.

Kempf, R., 2002, "On Ω–limit sets of discrete–time dynamical systems", *Journal of Difference Equations and Applications* 8:1121–1131.

Kolyada, S. and Snoha, L'., 1995, "On topological dynamics of sequences of continuous maps", *Internat. J. Bifur. Chaos Appl. Sci. Engrg.* 5:1437–1438.

Kolyada, S. and Snoha, L'., 1996, "Topological entropy of nonautononous dynamical systems", *Random and Comp. Dynamics* 4:205–233.

Klíc, A. and Pokorny, P., 1996, "On dynamical systems generated by two alternating vector fields", *Internat. J. Bifur. Chaos Appl. Sci. Engrg.* 6:2015–2030.

Klíc, A., Pokorny, P. and Rehácek, J., 2002, "Zig-zag dynamical systems and the Baker-Campbell-Hausdorff formula", *Math. Slovaca* 52:79–97.

Serre, D., 2002, *Matrices. Theory and applications,* Graduate text in Mathematics 216, Springer Verlag.

Sharkovsky, A. N. , Kolyada, S. F., Sivak, A. G. and Fedorenko, V. V., 1997, *Dynamics of one–dimensional maps*, Kluwer Academic Publishers.

6 The Hicksian Model with Investment Floor and Income Ceiling

Laura Gardini, Tönu Puu and Iryna Sushko

6.1 Introduction

As we saw in Chapter 3, Hicks (1950) modified the Samuelson (1939) linear multiplier-accelerator model through introducing two constraints. The linear multiplier-accelerator model itself only has two options: Exponentially explosive or damped motion. According to Hicks, only the explosive case is interesting, as only this produces persistent motion endogenously, but it had to be limited through two (linear) constraints for which Hicks gave factual explanations.

When the cycle is in its depression phase it may happen that income decreases so fast that more capital can be dispensed with than what disappears through depreciation, i.e., natural wear and aging. As a result, the linear accelerator would predict not only negative investments (disinvestments), but to an extent that implies active destruction of capital. To avoid this, Hicks introduced his floor to disinvestment at the natural depreciation level.

When the cycle is in its prosperity phase, then it may happen that income would grow at a pace which does not fit available resources. Hicks has a discussion about what then happens, in terms of inflation, but he contended himself with stating that (real) income could not grow faster than available resources which put a ceiling on the income variable.

Hicks never formulated his final model with floor and ceiling mathematically, it seems that this was eventually done by Rau (1974), where the accelerator-generated investments were limited downwards through the natural depreciation floor, and where the income is limited upwards through the ceiling, determined by available resources. Formally:

$$I_t = \max(a(Y_{t-1} - Y_{t-2}), -I^f);$$

$$C_t = cY_{t-1};$$
$$Y_t = \min(C_t + I_t, Y^c).$$

Eliminating C_t and I_t, one has the single recurrence equation:

$$Y_t = \min(cY_{t-1} + \max(a(Y_{t-1} - Y_{t-2}), -I^f), Y^c). \tag{1}$$

It remains to say that Hicks's original discussion included an exponential growth in autonomous expenditures, combined with the bounds I^f and Y^c growing at the same pace, but taking the bounds as constant and deleting the autonomous expenditures, gives a more clear-cut version. It was this that was originally analyzed in detail by Hommes (1991), and the notation above comes from Hommes. However, there were some pieces missing in his discussion, such as two-dimensional bifurcation diagrams, which makes it motivated to make a new attack on this model.

6.2 Description of the Map

Let $x_t := Y_t$, $y_t := Y_{t-1}$, $d := I^f$ and $r := Y^c$. Then the model given in (1) can be rewritten as a two-dimensional piecewise linear continuous map $F : \mathbb{R}^2 \to \mathbb{R}^2$:

$$F : \begin{pmatrix} x \\ y \end{pmatrix} \mapsto \begin{pmatrix} \min(cx + \max(a(x-y), -d), r) \\ x \end{pmatrix}, \tag{2}$$

which depends on four real parameters: $a > 0$, $0 < c < 1$, $d > 0$, $r > 0$.

The map F is given by three linear maps F_i, $i = 1, 2, 3$, defined, respectively, in three regions R_i of the phase plane:

$$\begin{aligned} F_1 &: \begin{pmatrix} x \\ y \end{pmatrix} \mapsto \begin{pmatrix} (c+a)x - ay \\ x \end{pmatrix}; \\ R_1 &= \{(x, y) : (1 + c/a)x - r/a \le y \le x + d/a\}; \end{aligned} \tag{3}$$

$$\begin{aligned} F_2 &: \begin{pmatrix} x \\ y \end{pmatrix} \mapsto \begin{pmatrix} cx - d \\ x \end{pmatrix}; \\ R_2 &= \{(x, y) : y > x + d/a, x \le (d + r)/c\}; \end{aligned} \tag{4}$$

$$\begin{aligned} F_3 &: \begin{pmatrix} x \\ y \end{pmatrix} \mapsto \begin{pmatrix} r \\ x \end{pmatrix}; \\ R_3 &= \mathbb{R}^2 / R_1 / R_2. \end{aligned} \tag{5}$$

Three half lines denoted LC_{-1}, LC'_{-1} and LC''_{-1} are boundaries of the regions R_i:

$$\begin{aligned} LC_{-1} &: \ y = x + d/a, \ x \leq (r+d)/c, \\ LC'_{-1} &: \ y = (1 + c/a)x - r/a, \ x < (r+d)/c, \\ LC''_{-1} &: \ x = (r+d)/c, \ y > (r+d)/c + d/a. \end{aligned}$$

Their images by F are called critical lines:

$$\begin{aligned} LC_0 &: \ y = (x+d)/c, \ x \leq r, \\ LC'_0 &: \ x = r, \ y < (r+d)/c. \end{aligned}$$

The image of LC''_{-1} by F is a point $(r, (r+d)/c)$. A qualitative view of the phase plane of the map F for $a > 1$, $d < r$ and $a > c^2/(1-c)$ is shown in Fig.1 (the last inequality indicates that the intersection point of LC'_{-1} and LC_0 is in the negative quadrant).

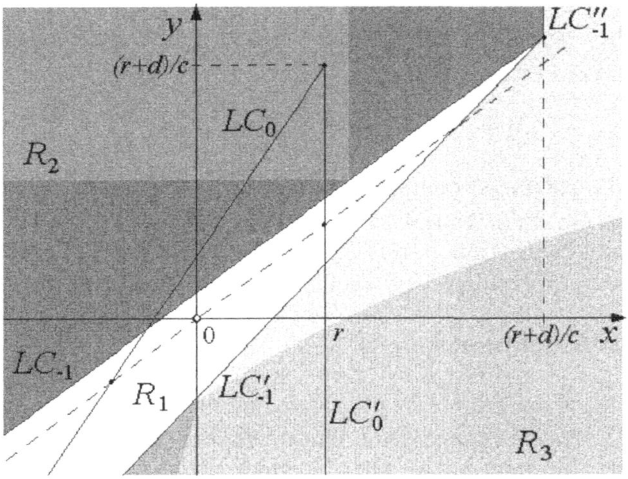

Figure 1: *Critical lines of the map F for $a > 1$, $d < r$, $a > c^2/(1-c)$.*

As it was mentioned in the introduction, an analogous model has been studied by Hommes (1991). Main conclusions of this paper hold also for the map F, namely, for $a > 1$ the map F has an attracting set C homeomorphic to a circle and all the trajectories of F (except for the fixed point) are attracted to this set. It was also proved that the dynamics of the map F on $\mathcal{C}$ are either periodic or quasiperiodic. In our consideration we show how the set $\mathcal{C}$ appears relating this to the center bifurcation described in detail in Chapter 2. We also discuss the structure of the two-dimensional bifurcation diagram in the (a, c)-parameter plane.

First note that the maps F_2 and F_3 have simple dynamics: The eigenvalues of F_2 are $\mu_1 = c$, $0 < c < 1$, $\mu_2 = 0$, so that any initial point $(x_0, y_0) \in R_2$ is mapped into a point of LC_0, while the map F_3 has two zero eigenvalues, and any $(x_0, y_0) \in R_3$ is mapped into a point of the straight line $x = r$. In such a way the whole phase plane is mapped in one step to the straight line $x = r$ and a cone $D = \{(x, y) : y \leq (x + d)/c,\ x \leq r\}$ (see Fig.1). Thus, the map F is a noninvertible map of so-called $(Z_\infty - Z_1 - Z_0)$ type: Any point belonging to the critical lines or to the half line $x = r$, $y > (r + d)/c$, has infinitely many preimages, any inner point of D has one preimage and any other point of the plane has no preimages.

The map F has a unique fixed point $(x^*, y^*) = (0, 0)$ which is the fixed point of the map F_1 (while the fixed points of the maps F_2 and F_3 belong to R_1, thus, they are not fixed points for the map F). The eigenvalues of the Jacobian matrix of F_1 are

$$\lambda_{1,2} = (a + c \pm \sqrt{(a + c)^2 - 4a})/2, \tag{6}$$

so that for the parameter range considered the fixed point (x^*, y^*) is a node if $(c+a)^2 > 4a$, and a focus if $(c+a)^2 < 4a$, being attracting for $a < 1$ and repelling for $a > 1$. Thus, for $a < 1$ the fixed point (x^*, y^*) is the unique global attractor of the map F (given that F_2 and F_3 are contractions).

6.3 Center Bifurcation $(a = 1)$

At $a = 1$ the fixed point (x^*, y^*) loses stability with a pair of complex-conjugate eigenvalues crossing the unit circle, that is the center bifurcation occurs. First we describe the phase portrait of the map F exactly at the bifurcation value $a = 1$. Analogous description is presented in Section 2.2 of Chapter 2 for a two-dimensional piecewise linear map defined by two linear maps, which for the particular parameter value $b = 0$ are the maps F_1 and F_2 given in (3) and (4). It is proved that for the parameter values corresponding to the center bifurcation there exists an invariant region in the phase plane, which either is a polygon bounded by a finite number of images of a proper segment of the critical line, or the invariant region is bounded by an ellipse and all the images of the critical line are tangent to this ellipse (see Propositions 1 and 2 of Chapter 2). In the following we use these results for the considered map F specifying which critical lines are involved in the construction of the invariant region.

The map F_1 at $a = 1$ is defined by a rotation matrix. Moreover, if

$$c = c_{m/n} \overset{def}{=} 2\cos(2\pi m/n) - 1, \tag{7}$$

then the fixed point (x^*, y^*) is locally a center with rotation number m/n, so that any point in some neighborhood of (x^*, y^*) is periodic with rotation number m/n, and all points of the same periodic orbit are located on an invariant ellipse of the map F_1. Note that from $c > 0$ it follows that $m/n < 1/6$. Denote

$$c = c^* \overset{def}{=} 1 - (d/r)^2. \tag{8}$$

Proposition 1. *Let $a = 1$, $c = c_{m/n}$, then in the phase space of the map F there exists an invariant polygon P such that*

- *if $c_{m/n} < c^*$ then P has n edges which are the generating segment $S_1 \subset LC_{-1}$ and its $n - 1$ images $S_{i+1} = F_1(S_i) \subset LC_{i-1}$, $i = 1, ..., n - 1$;*
- *if $c_{m/n} > c^*$ then P has n edges which are the generating segment $S'_1 \subset LC'_{-1}$ and its $n - 1$ images $S'_{i+1} = F_1(S'_i) \subset LC'_{i-1}$;*
- *if $c_{m/n} = c^*$ then P has $2n$ edges which are the segments S_i and S'_i, $i = 1, ..., n$.*

Any initial point $(x_0, y_0) \in P$ is periodic with rotation number m/n, while any $(x_0, y_0) \notin P$ is mapped in a finite number of steps into the boundary of P.

The proof of the proposition is similar to the one presented in Section 2.2 of Chapter 2. The value c^* is obtained from the condition of an invariant ellipse of F_1 to be tangent to both critical lines LC_{-1} and LC'_{-1}. It can be shown that for $c_{m/n} < c^*$ only the upper boundary LC_{-1} is involved in the construction of the invariant region, while if $c_{m/n} > c^*$ we have to iterate the generating segment of the lower boundary LC'_{-1} to get the boundary of the invariant region. An example of the invariant polygon P in the case $c_{m/n} = c^*$ is presented in Fig.2, where $a = 1$, $d = 10$, $r = 10/\sqrt{2 - \sqrt{2}}$, $c = c_{1/8} = c^* = \sqrt{2} - 1$. For such parameter values the polygon P has 16 edges, which are the segments $S_i \subset LC_{i-2}$ and $S'_i \subset LC'_{i-2}$, $i = 1, ..., 8$.

Any point of P is periodic with rotation number $1/8$ (in Fig.2 the points of two such cycles belonging to the boundary of P are shown by black and gray circles), while any point $(x_0, y_0) \notin P$ is mapped to the boundary of P.

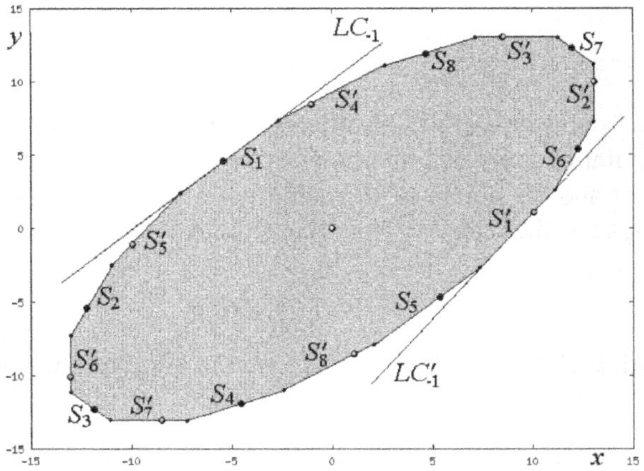

Figure 2: *The invariant polygon P with* 16 *edges at* $a = 1$, $c = c_{1/8} = \sqrt{2} - 1 = c^*$, $d = 10$, $r = 10/\sqrt{2 - \sqrt{2}}$.

Consider now the case in which the map F_1 is defined by the rotation matrix with an irrational rotation number ρ, which holds if

$$c = c_\rho \stackrel{def}{=} 2\cos(2\pi\rho) - 1, \tag{9}$$

where $\rho < 1/6$. Then any point in some neighborhood of the fixed point (x^*, y^*) is quasiperiodic, and all points of the same quasiperiodic orbit are dense on the corresponding invariant ellipse of the map F_1. Using the Proposition 2 of Chapter 2 and the values c^* given in (8) we can state the following

Proposition 2. *Let* $a = 1$, $c = c_\rho$. *Then in the phase space of the map* F *there exists an invariant region* Q, *bounded by an invariant ellipse* $\mathcal{E}$ *of the map* F_1 *which is tangent to* LC_{-1} *(and to all its images) if* $c < c^*$, *to* LC'_{-1} *if* $c > c^*$, *and to both critical lines* LC_{-1} *and* LC'_{-1} *if* $c = c^*$. *Any initial point* $(x_0, y_0) \in Q$ *belongs to a quasiperiodic orbit dense in the corresponding invariant ellipse of* F_1, *while any initial point* $(x_0, y_0) \notin Q$ *is mapped to* $\mathcal{E}$.

Note that from (8) it follows that if $d > r$ then the inequality $c^* < 0$ holds, thus, given $c > 0$, for $d > r$ only the lower boundary LC'_{-1} is involved in the construction of the invariant region of the map F at $a = 1$.

6.4 Bifurcation Structure of the (a, c)-Parameter Plane

In this section we describe the dynamics of the map F after the center bifurcation, that is for $a > 1$. In short, an initial point (x_0, y_0) from some neighborhood of the unstable fixed point (x^*, y^*) moves away from it under the map F_1 and in a finite number k of iterations it necessarily enters either the region R_2, or R_3 (in the case in which (x^*, y^*) is a focus the statement is obvious, while if (x^*, y^*) is a repelling node this can be easy verified using the eigenvalues $\lambda_{1,2}$ given in (6) and the corresponding eigenvectors). If $(x_k, y_k) \in R_2$, then the map F_2 is applied: $F_2(x_k, y_k) = (x_{k+1}, y_{k+1}) \in LC_0$. All consequent iterations by F_2 give points on LC_0 approaching the attracting fixed point of F_2 (which belongs to R_1), until the trajectory enters R_1 where the map F_1 is applied again. If $(x_k, y_k) \in R_3$, then the map F_3 is applied: $F_3(x_k, y_k) = (x_{k+1}, y_{k+1}) \in LC'_0$. We have that either $(x_{k+1}, y_{k+1}) \in R_1$, or $(x_{k+1}, y_{k+1}) \in R_3$ and one more application of F_3 gives its fixed point $(r, r) \in R_1$, so, the map F_1 is applied to this point. In such a way the dynamics appear to be bounded.

Indeed, it was proved in Hommes (1991), that for $a > 1$ any trajectory of F rotates with the same rotation number around the unstable fixed point, and it is attracted to a closed invariant curve $\mathcal{C}$ homeomorphic to a circle. It was also proved that the dynamics of F on $\mathcal{C}$, depending on the parameters, are either periodic or quasiperiodic. We can state that such a curve $\mathcal{C}$ is born due to the center bifurcation of the fixed point, described in the previous section: Namely, the bounded region P (or Q), which is invariant for $a = 1$, exists also for $a > 1$, but only its boundary remains invariant, and this boundary is the curve $\mathcal{C}$.

We refer as well to Chapter 2 in which it is shown that also in a more generic case of a two-dimensional piecewise linear map, defined by two linear maps, the center bifurcation can give rise to the appearance of a closed invariant attracting curve $\mathcal{C}$, on which the map is reduced to a rotation with rational or irrational rotation number. Recall that in the case of a rational rotation number m/n the map has an attracting and a saddle m/n-cycle on $\mathcal{C}$, so that the curve $\mathcal{C}$ is formed by the unstable set of the saddle cycle, approaching the points of the attracting cycle. While in the case of an irrational rotation number the map has quasiperiodic orbits on $\mathcal{C}$. In Section 2.3 of Chapter 2 the curve $\mathcal{C}$ is described in detail for the map defined by the linear maps F_1 and F_2 given in (3) and (4). So, we can use these results for the considered map F if the curve $\mathcal{C}$ belongs to the regions R_1, R_2 and has no intersection with the region R_3, thus, only the maps F_1 and F_2 are involved in the asymptotic dynamics. Obviously, we have a qualitatively similar case if the curve $\mathcal{C}$ has no intersection with the region R_2 and, thus, only the maps F_1 and F_3 are applied to the points on $\mathcal{C}$. One more possibility is the case in which the curve $\mathcal{C}$ belongs to all the three regions R_i, $i = 1, 2, 3$. We can state that in the first and second cases the curve $\mathcal{C}$ can be obtained by iterating the generating segment of LC_{-1} and LC'_{-1}, respectively, while in the third case both generating segments can be used to get the curve $\mathcal{C}$.

To see which parameter values correspond to the cases described above we present in Fig.3 a two-dimensional bifurcation diagram in the (a, c)-parameter plane for fixed values $d = 10$, $r = 30$. Different gray tonalities indicate regions corresponding to attracting cycles of different periods $n \leq 41$ (note that regions related to the attracting cycles of the same period n, but with different rotation numbers are shown by the same gray tonality). The white region in Fig.3 is related either to periodic orbits of period $n > 41$, or to quasiperiodic orbits.

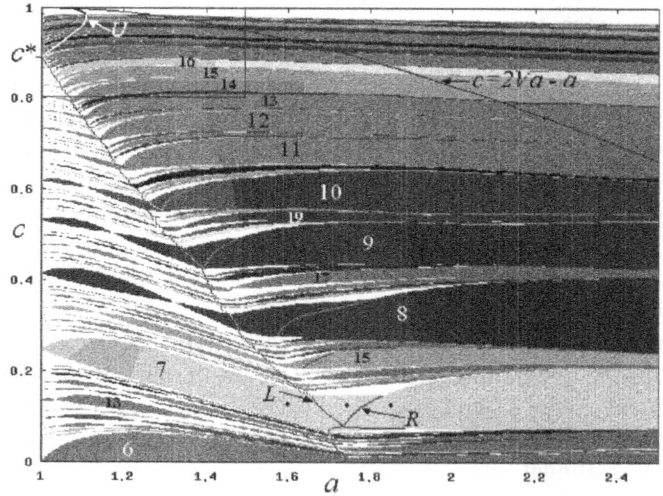

Figure 3: *Two-dimensional bifurcation diagram of the map F in the (a, c)-parameter plane at $d = 10$, $r = 30$. Regions corresponding to attracting cycles of different periods $n \leq 41$ are shown by various gray tonalities.*

Let us first comment on some particular parameter values of the bifurcation line $a = 1$. As described in the previous section, at $a = 1$, $c = c_{m/n}$ given in (7), in the phase plane of F there exists an invariant polygon P such that any point of P is periodic with the rotation number m/n. So, the points $a = 1$, $c = c_{m/n}$, for different $m/n < 1/6$, are starting points for the corresponding periodicity tongues. For example, $a = 1$, $c = c_{1/8} = \sqrt{2} - 1$ is the point from which the 8-periodicity tongue starts, corresponding to the attracting cycle with the rotation number $1/8$. Recall that according to the summation rule (see Hao and Zheng (1998)), between any two rotation numbers m_1/n_1 and m_2/n_2 there is also the rotation number $m'/n' = (m_1+m_2)/(n_1+n_2)$, so that $a = 1$, $c = c_{m'/n'}$ is the starting point for the corresponding periodicity region. If the (a, c)-parameter point is taken inside the periodicity region, then the map F has the attracting and saddle cycles with corresponding rotation number, and the unstable set of the saddle cycle form the closed invariant attracting curve $\mathcal{C}$. Note that in the case in which both constrains are involved in the asymptotic dynamics, the map F may have two attracting cycles and two saddles of the same period coexisting on the invariant curve[1] (as it occurs, for example, inside the 7-periodicity tongue at $a = 2.9$, $c = 0.136$, $d = 10$, $r = 30$). While if the (a, c)-parameter point belongs to the boundary of the periodicity region, then the border-collision bifurcation occurs (see Nusse and Yorke (1995)) for the attracting and saddle cycles, giving rise to their merging and disappearance (see Chapter 2).

The parameter points $a = 1$, $c = c_\rho$ given in (9), for different irrational numbers $\rho < 1/6$ correspond to the case in which any point of the invariant region Q is quasiperiodic. Such parameter points are starting points for the curves related to quasiperiodic orbits of the map F.

At $a = 1, c = c^* = 8/9$, (which is the value c^* given in (8) at $d = 10$ and $r = 30$) there exists an invariant ellipse of F_1 tangent to both critical lines LC_{-1} and LC'_{-1}, so that for $c < c^*$ the boundary of the invariant region can be obtained by iterating the generating segment of LC_{-1}, while for $c > c^*$ we can iterate the segment of LC'_{-1}. Thus, after the center bifurcation for $c < c^*$ at first only LC_{-1} is involved in the asymptotic dynamics, and then increasing a there is a contact of the curve $\mathcal{C}$ with the lower boundary LC'_{-1}. And vice versa for $c > c^*$. For example, the curve denoted by L inside the 7-periodicity region in Fig.3 indicates a collision of the curve $\mathcal{C}$ with the lower boundary LC'_{-1}. The curves related to similar collision are shown also inside some other periodicity regions. Before this collision the

[1] The authors wish to note that the first example of bistability in this model was notified by Professor V. Böhm.

dynamics of F on $\mathcal{C}$ is as described in Proposition 3 of Chapter 2, while after both boundaries LC_{-1} and LC'_{-1} are involved in the asymptotic dynamics. One more curve shown inside the periodicity regions (for example, the one denoted by R inside the 7-periodicity region) indicates that the point $(x, y) = (r, r)$ becomes a point of the corresponding attracting cycle.

To clarify, let us present examples of the phase portrait of the map F corresponding to three different parameter points inside the 7-periodicity region, indicated in Fig.3. Fig.4 shows the closed invariant attracting curve $\mathcal{C}$ at $a = 1.6$, $c = 0.125$, when $\mathcal{C}$ has no intersection with the region R_3, being made up by 7 segments of the images of the generating segment of LC_{-1}.

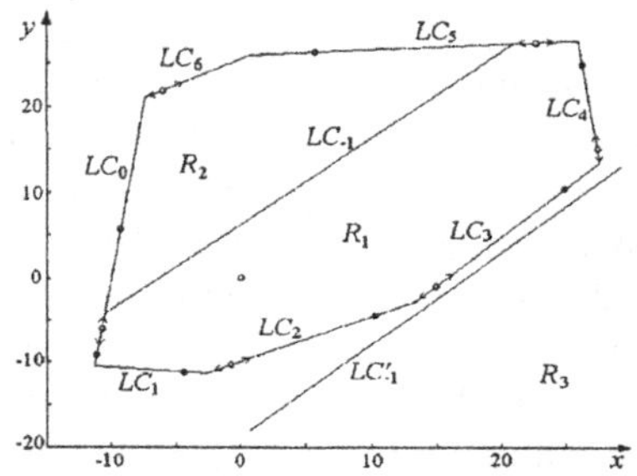

Figure 4: *The attracting closed invariant curve* $\mathcal{C}$ *with the attracting and saddle cycles of period* 7 *at* $a = 1.6$, $c = 0.125$, $d = 10$, $r = 30$.

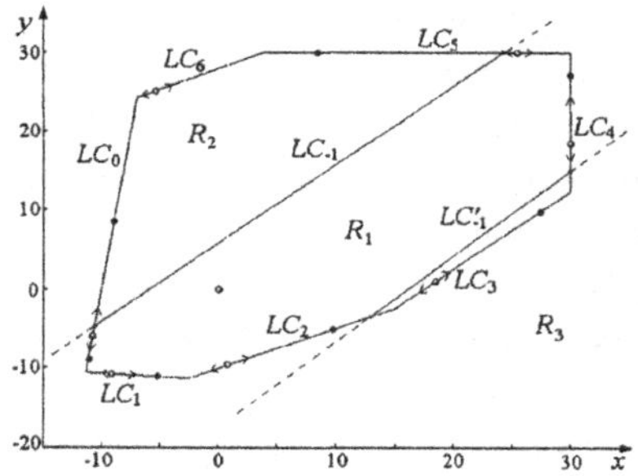

Figure 5: *The attracting closed invariant curve* $\mathcal{C}$ *with the attracting and saddle cycles of period* 7 *at* $a = 1.75$, $c = 0.125$, $d = 10$, $r = 30$.

The closed invariant curve C corresponding to the parameter values $a = 1.75$, $c = 0.125$, is shown in Fig.5. In such a case both boundaries LC_{-1} and LC'_{-1} are involved in the dynamics. It can be easily seen that images of the generating segments of LC_{-1} and LC'_{-1} form the same set, so it does not matter which segment is iterating to get the curve C.

Fig.6 presents an example of C at $a = 1.85$, $c = 0.125$, when two consequent points of the attracting cycle belong to the region R_3, so that $(x, y) = (r, r)$ is a point of the attracting cycle.

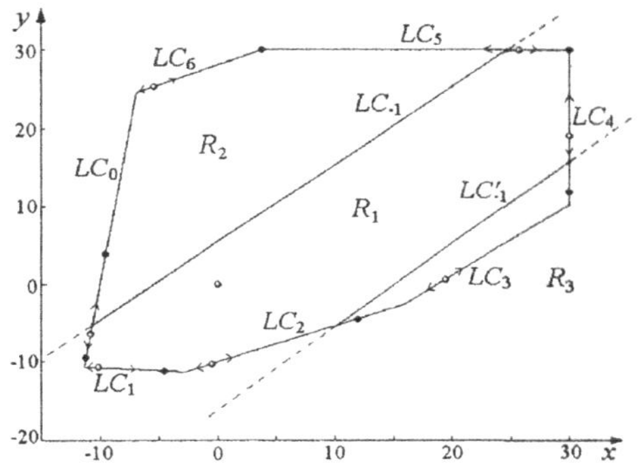

Figure 6: *The attracting closed invariant curve C at* $a = 1.85$, $c = 0.125$, $d = 10$, $r = 30$.

In Fig.7 we show the enlarged window of the bifurcation diagram presented in Fig.3 in order to indicate the (a, c)-parameter region corresponding to the case in which only the lower boundary is involved in the asymptotic dynamics. The curve denoted by U indicates the contact of the trajectory with the upper boundary LC_{-1}, so that just after the center bifurcation, for $c > c^*$ at first only the lower boundary LC'_{-1} is involved in the asymptotic dynamics (see Fig.8 with an example of the attracting closed invariant curve C at $a = 1.05$, $c = 0.94$). Then, increasing a the trajectory has a contact also with the upper boundary LC_{-1}. Note that for the main periodicity tongues (those related to the rotation number $1/n$) just after the center bifurcation the point (r, r) immediately becomes a point of the attracting cycle, because after the bifurcation two points of the attracting cycle must be in the region R_3, but we know that two successive applications of F_3 give the point (r, r). In Hommes (1991) it was proved that if and only if the attracting set C contains the point (r, r), then the restriction of the map F to C is topologically conjugate to a piecewise linear nondecreasing circle map f, and there exists a unique circle arc I on which f is constant being strictly increasing on the complement of I. From this statement it follows that in such a case the map F cannot have quasiperiodic trajectory, but only periodic ones.

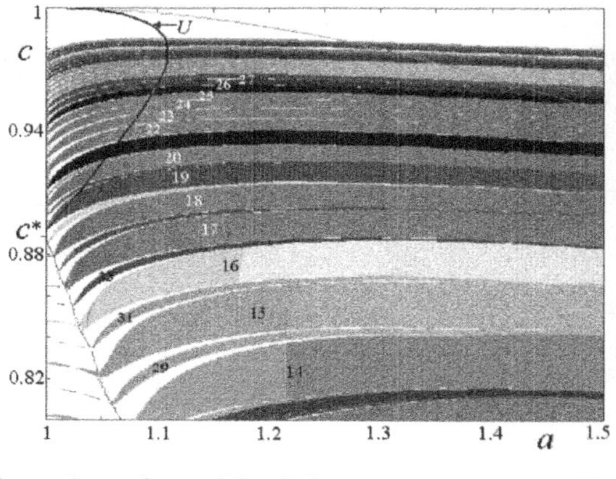

Figure 7: *Enlarged window of the bifurcation diagram of the map F shown in Fig.3.*

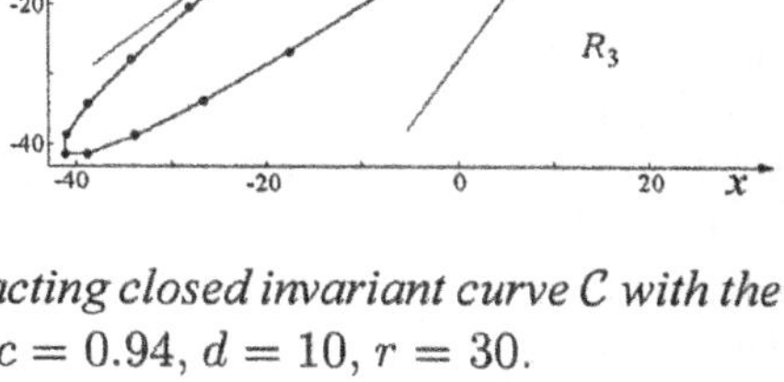

Figure 8: *The attracting closed invariant curve C with the attracting* 23-*cycle on it at* $a = 1.05$, $c = 0.94$, $d = 10$, $r = 30$.

Summarizing, we state that for $c < c^*$ (or $c > c^*$) given in (7), increasing the values of a from $a = 1$, the closed invariant attracting curve C at first is made up by a finite number of images of LC_{-1} (or LC'_{-1}, respectively), then a contact with LC'_{-1} (or LC_{-1}) occurs after which to get the curve C we can iterate the generating segment either LC_{-1} or LC'_{-1}. As long as the curve C does not contain the point (r, r), the dynamics of F on C are either periodic, or quasiperiodic, while if (r, r) belongs to C then dynamics are only periodic.

References

Gallegati, M., Gardini, L., Puu, T., and Sushko, I., 2003, "Hicks's trade cycle revisited: cycles and bifurcations", *Mathematics and Computers in Simulations* 63, pp. 505-527.

Hao, B.-L., Zheng, W.-M., 1998, *Applied Symbolic Dynamics and Chaos*, World Scientific.

Hicks, J.R., 1950, *A Contribution to the Theory of the Trade Cycle*, Clarendon Press, Oxford.

Hommes, C.H., 1991, *Chaotic Dynamics in Economic Models: Some Simple Case Studies*, Thesis University of Groningen, Wolters-Noordhoff Groningen.

Nusse, H. E. and Yorke, J. A., 1995, "Border-collision bifurcation for piecewise smooth one-dimensional maps", *International Journal of Bifurcation and Chaos 5,* 11, pp. 89-207.

Rau, N., 1974, *Trade Cycle: Theory and Evidence*, Macmillan, London.

Samuelson, P.A., 1939, "Interactions between the multiplier analysis and the principle of acceleration", *Review of Economics and Statistics* 21, pp. 75-78.

7 Growth Cycles in a Modified Hicksian Business Cycle Model

Tönu Puu

7.1 Introduction

We are now going to discuss a version of the Hicksian floor and ceiling model, where the floor is related to actual depreciation on capital, and the ceiling is deleted altogether. This version with floor only was briefly stated in Chapter 3, and has been presented in two previous publications, Puu *et al.* (2005) and Sushko *et al.* (2004). A further development, with the ceiling as well related to capital stock in its capacity of a limiting production factor, was presented in Puu (2005), but will not be discussed at present.

Tying the floor to capital stock requires that we include capital as an additional variable in the multiplier-accelerator model, but, as was argued in Chapter 3, this is no problem, because the model already contains a theory for investments, and hence also for the formation of capital as the sum of cumulated investments. It is just a matter of making this explicit.

The deletion of the ceiling is no big problem, because, whenever the solution is oscillatory, we get *bounded motion* with floor alone. This was realized by James Duesenberry (1950) in his review of Hicks's book. Allen (1956) gave a very clear account of the argument: *"On pursuing this point, as Duesenberry does, it is seen that the explosive nature of the oscillations is largely irrelevant, and no ceiling is needed. A first intrinsic oscillation occurs, the accelerator goes out in the downswing, and a second oscillation starts up when the accelerator comes back with new initial conditions. The explosive element never has time to be effective - and the oscillations do not necessarily hit a ceiling".*

Of course, the argument applies only to the case with a fixed floor. Once we tie the floor through depreciation to a growing stock of capital, the floor is no longer fixed. Due to the growing capital stock, a growth trend with growth cycles around it is created. Hence, nothing is bounded in the present model variation. This results in both problems and advantages.

The primary advantage is that, to the liking of economists, the model produces economic growth endogenously along with cyclic growth rate deviations, and that it does this without any need to introduce exogenous growing autonomous expenditures. This is the only model of the multiplier-accelerator variety presented until now which is able to explain growth and cycles on its own. It is an advantage in terms of scientific procedure, because any exogenous element is something having a flavour of *ad hoc* sticking to it.

The problem is in terms of analysis. Methods of nonlinear dynamics are suited to analyse fixed points, periodic and quasiperiodic motions, and chaos, but all applicable to stationary time series! There are no similar methods to analyse growing systems! In the Gandolfo (1985) format with growing autonomous expenditures, floor and ceiling, there is an externally given unexplained growth rate. Using this growth rate trends can be eliminated, and the remaining motion reduced to a stationary one, but we have no such thing in the present case.

We have to *construct* some new variables *within the model* which display stationary motion, even though the original ones are growing. A clue to this can be found in a publication by the present author over 40 years ago. See Puu (1963). The method suggested there applies to the original multiplier accelerator model, but can be easily adapted to be applied to the present model.

7.2 Relative Dynamics

To see the idea, let us reconsider the original Samuelson model, stated in its reduced form as (25) in Chapter 3:

$$Y_{t+1} = (a+c) \cdot Y_t - a \cdot Y_{t-1} \tag{1}$$

In Puu (1963) there was defined a new variable:

$$y_{t+1} := \frac{Y_{t+1}}{Y_t} \tag{2}$$

This is the relative growth factor for income, which transforms (1) into:

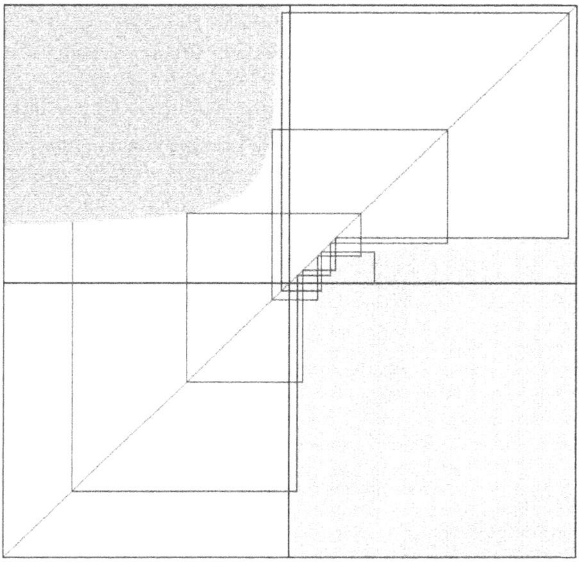

Figure 1. *"Cobweb" for the nonlinear iteration of relative dynamics.*

$$y_{t+1} = (a + c) - \frac{a}{y_t} \tag{3}$$

Unlike (1), (3) is *first order*, but *nonlinear*. The denominator, which can become zero, may present some technical problems, but in case the model produces stable growth, or periodic growth cycles, then (3) indeed goes to a fixed point, or to a periodic cycle, which the model (1) in original variables does *not*. We know from Chapter 3 that there are no periodic solutions in the original linear model, but, once periodicity, due to the introduction of the floor, becomes main frame, the method of defining relative variables will show up as most useful.

The method using relative variables was originally introduced as a pedagogical device, to the end of reducing the order of the recurrence equation and to make the iteration suited for a simple graphical analysis. To give a flavour of it we reproduce one of the original diagrams as Fig. 1.

The graphical method is the same as that used for iterative first order systems in current chaos studies, and ages earlier, by economists in the context of dynamic multiplier analyses, and in "cobweb" price dynamics. In Fig. 1 we see a pair of hyperbolas, representing the right hand side of equation (3).

Further, there is a 45 degree line through the origin, which is used to shift any new iterate of (3) as initial condition for the next iteration. We also see the "cobweb" trace resulting from repeating this over and over. Should we choose parameters a, c so as to hit a *periodic* solution, we would eventually see a web connecting a *finite* number of points visited over and over. As we know, this is an unlikely case, so the general scenario is quasiperiodic, i.e., a web that fills the entire space. This is deceptive, as there are still infinitely many gaps, representing rational rotations, which we cannot see in the finite screen resolution.

Equation (1) has the closed form solution:

$$Y_t = A\lambda_1^t + B\lambda_2^t \tag{4}$$

where

$$\lambda_{1,2} = \frac{a+c}{2} \pm \frac{1}{2}\sqrt{(a+c)^2 - 4a} \tag{5}$$

are the eigenvalues. As noted in Chapter 3, when the expression under the root sign is negative, i.e., when $(a+c)^2 < 4a$, the eigenvalues become complex conjugates, and the solution is better written in the form (28) of Chapter 3, which we reproduce here for convenience:

$$Y_t = \rho^t \left(A\cos\omega t + B\sin\omega t \right) \tag{6}$$

where

$$\rho = \sqrt{a} \tag{7}$$

and

$$\omega = \arccos\frac{a+c}{2\sqrt{a}} \tag{8}$$

The solution (6) is the product an exponential growth factor, increasing (decreasing) whenever $a > 1$ ($a < 1$), and a simple harmonic oscillation. The reason why the oscillatory factor is not periodic is that, from (8), as a rule, the frequency of oscillation ω fails to be a *rational* multiple of 2π, so the oscillatory motion is quasiperiodic in terms of our basic predefined unit time period.

The only exception, as we saw in Chapter 3, is when it happens that:

$$\frac{a+c}{2\sqrt{a}} = \cos\frac{2\pi m}{n} \tag{9}$$

holds with m and n *integers*. Then the oscillatory part of the solution is indeed periodic. We saw that this happens on thin curves in the parameter plane displayed in Fig. 6 of Chapter 3.

When we know the closed form solution (6) to (1), we can, of course, using definition (2), also construct the solution to (3):

$$y_{t+1} = \frac{\rho^{t+1}\cos(\omega(t+1))}{\rho^{t}\cos(\omega t)} \tag{10}$$

which simplifies to

$$y_{t+1} = \rho(\cos\omega - \sin\omega \cdot \tan(\omega t)) \tag{11}$$

Unlike (6), which contains a multiplicative power function, (11) only contains constants and pure trigonometric functions, and is hence *stationary*, as a rule quasiperiodic, or, should (9) happen to hold, periodic.

In Fig. 2 we display an illustrative case with $a = 1.25$ and $c = 0.225$. According to (8), this parameter combination results in $\omega \approx 0.85$, which is relatively close to $2\pi/7 \approx 0.90$, so the oscillation is about, but not quite, 7-periodic.

Of course, we could find much better rational approximations to the true rotation number, for instance $2\pi \cdot 16/59 \approx 0.85$, to pick just one example, but for the point we want to make it is better to use as low a periodicity as possible. Later, in the nonlinear model we will be concerned with an example where we indeed have exact 7-periodicity, so it is good to prepare for it.

In the picture we show two continuous time traces, the gray including the growth factor, i.e., $\rho^{t}\cos(\omega t)$, and the black, stationary, just $\cos(\omega t)$. On these continuous curves we marked the points in discrete time $t = 0, 1, 2$, etc., which are the only relevant points in the discrete time setting. We also indicated the discrete time intervals through the vertical strips in different shade. The points for $t = 7, 14, 21$ etc., marked by larger dots, unlike the point for t

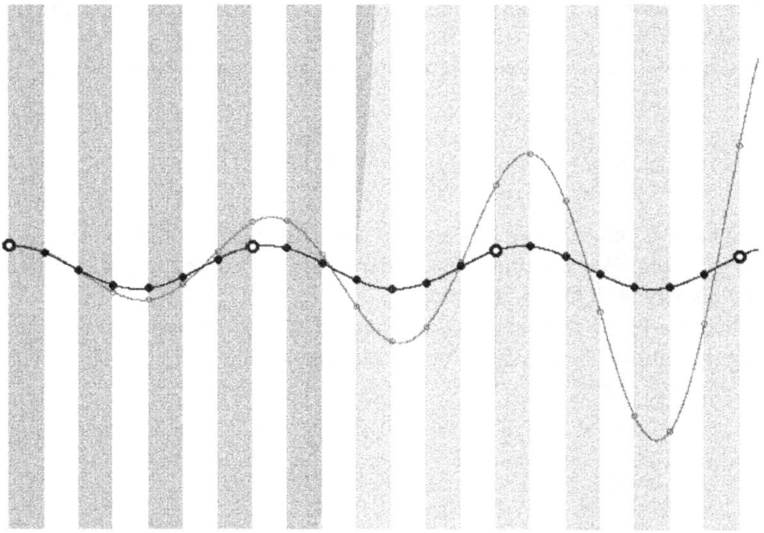

Figure 2. *Time traces for income and for its quasiperiodic oscillatory part.*

= 0, are not quite at the top of the oscillating trace, but slide more and more down to the left. Therefore, there is no exact recurrence, and the time series is *not* periodic. It is just this noncommensurability of the period of the trace with the period 2π that quasiperiodicity means in our context.

As a companion to Fig. 2, which shows the solution for income (6), we also display Fig. 3, which shows the evolution of the relative income ratio variable according to (11). The continuous curves represent (11), and contain tangents, which, unlike the sine and cosine, have branches which go to $\pm\infty$ with regular intervals. However, again, only the marked points are relevant in the discrete time setting, and we would have to be really unlucky to hit exactly an infinite branch. As in Fig. 2, we find that the big points at 7-period intervals slide successively to the left, as an indication of the fact that the sequence of points is *not* exactly 7-periodic.

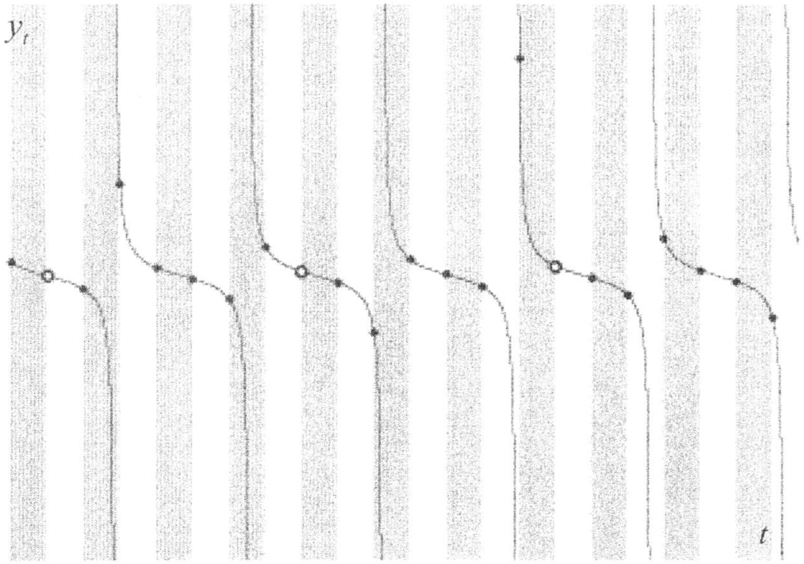

Figure 3. *Relative dynamics for the income growth rate.*

7.3 Growth in the Relative Dynamics System

To anticipate the nonlinear model, suppose that we indeed have an exact periodicity, for instance 7-periodicity, which we are close to. Then, given the rational rotation 1/7, or any other m/n, (11) can be written

$$y_{t+1} = \rho\left(\cos\frac{2\pi m}{n} - \sin\frac{2\pi m}{n}\cdot\tan\left(\frac{2\pi m}{n}t\right)\right) \tag{12}$$

with $m = 1$ and $n = 7$. It is then easy to calculate that for any t:

$$\prod_{i=1}^{n}\left(\cos\frac{2\pi m}{n} - \sin\frac{2\pi m}{n}\cdot\tan\left(\frac{2\pi m}{n}(t+i)\right)\right) \equiv 1 \tag{13}$$

t	y_t	Y_t
0	1.764263	1.000000
1	0.685839	0.685839
2	-0.392585	-0.269250
3	4.453809	-1.199190
4	1.100000	-1.319109
5	0.271678	-0.358372
6	-3.082132	1.104550
7	1.764263	1.948717

Table 1. *Growing income with 7-periodic cycle in the growth rate.*

From (12)-(13), we get:

$$\prod_{i=1}^{n} y_{t+i} = \rho^n \tag{14}$$

whenever the solution is *n-periodic*. Accordingly, from (2) and (14):

$$Y_{t+n} = \rho^n Y_t \tag{15}$$

As an example, put $m = 1$, $n = 7$, as already indicated. Hence, $\omega = 2\pi/7$. Further put $\rho = 1.1$. Then from (7) we have $a = 1.21$, and further from (9) $c = 2.2 \cdot \cos(2\pi/7) - 1.21 \approx 0.16$. Note that we could never choose this exact numerical value for the computer to produce an exactly 7-periodic cycle. In terms of Fig. 6 in Chapter 3, the case corresponds to the intersection point of the parabola labelled 7, and the first vertical line to the right of $a = 1$.

From equation (12) we can now easily calculate the orbit for relative income growth ratios $y_{t+1} = 1.1 \cdot (\cos(2\pi/7) - \sin(2\pi/7) \cdot \tan(2\pi t/7))$. The results are listed in Table 1.

The entries in the column for y_t, for $t = 0, \ldots 7$, are calculated from the formula just stated. As we see, $y_7 = y_0$, which confirms periodicity. After that entry, the column, if continued, is just a repetition of the seven entries over and over. The entries in the column for Y_t, can be obtained in two different ways:

(i) They have *actually* been calculated as continued products $Y_0 \prod_{\tau=1}^{t} y_\tau$, (using $Y_0 = 1$) from the previous column.

(ii) They *could* also be calculated from the formula $Y_t = 1.1^t \cdot \cos(2\pi t / 7)$. We can check that $Y_7 = 1.1^7 \cdot Y_0 \approx 1.948717$, so the growth rate over one complete cycle is about 95%. The unit entry Y_0 is chosen arbitrarily. The table shows us how the time series for income can be retrieved as a continued product of the income ratios, the initial income remaining arbitrary. We can hence use a value Y_0 different from unity and scale the whole income series up or down in proportion.

Note also that, whereas y_t is periodic, Y_t is *not*, it is *growing*! This is the point in defining the relative variable for a growing system. In the linear model periodicity is, as we know, an unlikely phenomenon, but these facts become interesting once nonlinearity is introduced and periodic solutions become mainframe. Further, note that, whenever y_t is periodic, then there must be an *even* number of negative entries in order that the product over a cycle be equal to unity, as stated in (13).

Given the fact that, for any periodic motion, there is always an even number of negative entries of y_t over a complete period, we can reformulate (14) as: $\sum_{i=1}^{n} \ln|y_{t+i}| = n \ln \rho$, or even better, as:

$$\ln \rho = \frac{1}{n} \sum_{i=1}^{n} \ln|y_{t+i}| \tag{16}$$

which is a convenient formula for calculating the growth factor from a series of relative variables whenever the solution is periodic.

7.4 Capital Accumulation

As the principle of acceleration governs investment, the original Samuelson model *actually contains an implicit process for capital accumulation*. From definition we have $I_{t+1} = K_{t+1} - K_t$. Hence, just rearranging:

$$K_{t+1} = K_t + I_{t+1} \tag{17}$$

However, from the principle of acceleration we have $I_{\tau+1} = a(Y_\tau - Y_{\tau-1})$, so using this recursively, we obtain: $\sum_{\tau=1}^{\tau=t} I_{\tau+1} = a(Y_t - Y_0)$, or

$$K_{t+1} = K_1 + a(Y_t - Y_0) \tag{18}$$

Given we know the initial capital, and the development of income, we can calculate the orbit for capital as well. If income grows exponentially according to (6), then it is obvious that capital does so as well.

Suppose that an oscillatory solution applies according to (6), and assume amplitude and phase such that $A = 1$, $B = 0$, i.e., such that $Y_0 = A = 1$. As a consequence:

$$K_{t+1} = K_1 + a(\rho^t \cos(\omega t) - Y_0) \tag{19}$$

In the right hand side of (19) there are two components, the compound constant $K_1 - aY_0$, which indicates the amount to which initial capital exceeds, or falls short of the optimal, as required by the acceleration principle, and the time dependent term $a\rho^t \cos(\omega t)$, where $\rho = \sqrt{a}$. Provided $a > 1$, we also have $\rho > 1$, so that the oscillations are growing.

Suppose now that we deal with the (presently unlikely) case of an n-periodic solution, i.e., that $\omega = 2\pi m / n$. Then, $\omega n = 2\pi m$, so, generalizing slightly, for any initial t, we get the simple formula:

$$K_{t+n} = K_t + a(\rho^n - Y_{t-1}) \tag{20}$$

The right hand side in (20) is *always growing* when $a > 1$, so, in case of periodicity, capital accumulates over *each* cycle. Further, putting $t = 1$, recalling that $Y_0 = A = 1$, and assuming nonnegative initial capital, i.e. $K_1 \geq 0$, we conclude that *capital never becomes negative*, which is reassuring. If it is zero from the start, then it becomes positive after only one period, and, as we saw, just goes on accumulating.

7.5 Depreciation and Gross Investment

If there is depreciation on capital, then gross investments are different from and larger than net investments which we dealt with up to now. Suppose that depreciation is just some proportion r of total capital. Then gross investments become $I_{t+1}+D_{t+1}=a(Y_t-Y_{t-1})+rK_t$, where the capital accumulation equations are as stated in (19) and (20).

We have thus seen that there is a capital accumulation theory implicit in the original multiplier-accelerator model, *though it does not feed back in any way into the model*, and therefore it is a sort of separate system, which depends on, but does not itself influence the development of income.

As we will see, it is natural to relate the Hicksian "floor" to actual depreciation, and thus provide the missing feedback. The whole system then becomes nonlinear, and one of the effects of this will be seen to make periodicity, which, as we saw, was a rare phenomenon in the original model, the dominant scenario.

We have thus commented a seldom mentioned fact about the original multiplier-accelerator model, i.e., that it actually contains a capital formation theory through the principle of acceleration. If we want to introduce the Hicksian floor in the investment function, we will also have to change the capital formation theory accordingly, but this is quite straightforward.

7.6 Hicksian Floor

Let us so recall some basic facts from Chapter 3 about the Hicksian reformulation of Samuelson's model. As noted, Hicks (1950) proposed that the principle of acceleration be limited in its downward action through the condition $I_{t+1}\geq -I^f$, where superscript f alludes on "floor". The well known argument was that capital owners do not actively destroy capital when income decreases at such a speed that more capital can be dispensed with than what disappears through natural wear and aging.

Obviously, this negative limit to net investments corresponds to a zero limit to gross investments. The floor limit to net investment is the maximum *dis*investment that takes place when no worn out capital is replaced at all. It can be considered as fixed, or varying over time, so to be completely general we write I^f_{t+1}. It was interpreted as a fixed number by Hommes (1991), and as exponentially growing by Gandolfo (1985). In Chapter 3 we saw that the latter is a rather problematic assumption to retain.

One particular problem pertains to the assumed *growing* floor case as preferred by Gandolfo and others. The floor should delimit disinvestment to the amount of depreciation on current capital. When capital accumulates, then maximum depreciation on it increases. Accordingly, as a consequence, the floor $-I^f_{t+1}$ should be *decreasing* over time (in absolute value), *not growing*.

Including the floor, the acceleration principle, as we saw in Chapter 3, has to be reformulated to the nonlinear (piecewise linear) format (33) of Chapter 3, which we restate here for convenience:

$$I_{t+1} = \max\left\{a(Y_t - Y_{t-1}), -I^f_{t+1}\right\} \tag{21}$$

By assuming depreciation to be a given fraction of total capital, as suggested above, we could calculate depreciation, and formally relate the floor to the stock of capital, i.e., put $I^f_{t+1} = D_{t+1} = rK_t$. Accordingly the investment function (21) changes to:

$$I_{t+1} = \max\left\{a(Y_t - Y_{t-1}), -rK_t\right\} \tag{22}$$

The stock of capital now feeds back into the investment function. We therefore need a theory for capital accumulation, but, fortunately, as we saw in Section 7.4, there is implicit a theory for capital formation in Samuelson's model, and hence also in the Hicksian model. This tiny change closes the model in a most natural way, and, as we will see, introduces a fundamental change to how the model works.

As for the ceiling, we skip it altogether. As we saw in the introduction to this Chapter, Duesenberry (1950) suggested that both floor and ceiling would not be needed for bounded motion. He obviously took for granted the case of fixed bounds.

Given we model the investment function as in (22), the floor is *not* fixed, but, as we will see, the argument applies to a reformulation in terms of relative variables. We already introduced the relative income ratio in (2), and will introduce a companion for capital below. Then Duesenberry's argument is still valid in the sense that income *growth rate cycles* have limited amplitude even if we skip the ceiling.

7.7 The Reformulated Model

It is now time to assemble the bits and pieces of our reformulation of the original Hicks model. Some of its properties were already discussed in Puu *et al.* (2005) and Sushko *et al.* (2004).

Given the consumption function $C_t = cY_{t-1}$, and the income formation identity $Y_t = C_t + I_t$, we can state the equation for income generation:

$$Y_{t+1} = cY_t + I_{t+1} \tag{23}$$

and, we can rewrite the definition $I_{t+1} = K_{t+1} - K_t$ as a capital updating equation:

$$K_{t+1} = K_t + I_{t+1} \tag{24}$$

It only remains to plug (22) into (23)-(24) and we finally have our system:

$$Y_{t+1} = cY_t + \max\{a(Y_t - Y_{t-1}), -rK_t\} \tag{25}$$

$$K_{t+1} = K_t + \max\{a(Y_t - Y_{t-1}), -rK_t\} \tag{26}$$

Note that equation (25) is just the original Hicksian multiplier-accelerator model with a floor, where the only new element is that the floor is determined by capital stock. As for equation (26), it is just the original Hicksian definition of investments, restated as a capital updating equation, using the same determinant for investments as in (25).

Tying the investment floor to the stock of capital converts (25)-(26) into one interdependent system, where (25) can no longer be studied independently. Given we know Y_t, Y_{t-1}, and K_t, we can calculate Y_{t+1} and K_{t+1}. Note that then we also automatically advance Y_{t-1} to Y_t. As a matter of fact the system (25)-(26) is *third* order. We could have introduced a new symbol for lagged income Y_{t-1}, such as Z_t, with definition $Z_{t+1} = Y_t$ as a third equation, but, the traditional way of stating the original multiplier-accelerator model is through one single equation, so we preferred to keep this style of presentation. Further, through the strategy of converting to relative variables, as already indicated in Section 7.2, the order of the system will actually be lowered from third to second.

Observe further that the system (25)-(26) has three parameters: the propensity to consume c, the rate of capital depreciation r, and the accelerator or capital coefficient a. Obviously c and r are positive fractions less than unity, whereas a is just positive. It must exceed unity in order to create sufficient instability to keep the dynamical process going, and past empirical measurements, for whatever they are worth, estimate a to the interval 2 to 4. As for r, it depends on the durability of capital, the more durable capital is, the lower is r. In the sequel the condition $c+r<1$ plays an important role. It is fulfilled when the space left for investments by the consumers is not less than capital depreciation, and we consider it rather likely that it is fulfilled.

It is now more convenient to state (25)-(26) as two different systems, defined in two different regions of phase space. In order to achieve this we first define a constraint whose sign decides whether the first or the second argument in the investment function (22) applies. To this end put:

$$R_t := a\left(Y_t - Y_{t-1}\right) + rK_t \tag{27}$$

It is obvious that, whenever $R_t > 0$, investments will be accelerator generated in the next time period, so the first argument in (22) applies. Whenever $R_t \le 0$, the floor is activated, and the second argument applies. Note that when $R_t = 0$, then the arguments of the investment function are equal, so it does not really matter in which case we include the weak inequality.

We thus get:

$$F_1: \quad \begin{cases} Y_{t+1} = cY_t + a\left(Y_t - Y_{t-1}\right) \\ K_{t+1} = K_t + a\left(Y_t - Y_{t-1}\right) \end{cases} \qquad R_t > 0 \tag{28}$$

and

$$F_2: \quad \begin{cases} Y_{t+1} = cY_t - rK_t \\ K_{t+1} = \left(1 - r\right)K_t \end{cases} \qquad R_t \le 0 \tag{29}$$

Observe that (28) gives us the original multiplier-accelerator model back, with the first equation an autonomous (second order) iteration in income alone, and the second a dependent companion for the updating of capital stock. In the system (29) the roles are reversed. Here it is the second equation for capital which stands on its own, and just means a proportional decay of capital, as if it were a radioactive substance. The disinvestments implicit in this decay are fed back into the first equation, which, except for this, is just a multiplier process in consumption alone.

A common feature shared by (28) and (29) is linearity. As we will see (29) is always a contraction, whereas (28) can be a contraction or an expansion. In the case which interests us, we deal with an expansion. The process is kept going through jumping between the regions, and this is also what provides for nonlinearity in the model.

7.8 Fixed Points, Stability, and Bifurcation

There exist fixed points for both maps (28) and (29). In the case of (28), we note that there is just one fixed point for income, i.e., $Y_{t+1} = Y_t = Y_{t-1} = 0$. On the other hand $K_{t+1} = K_t = K$ can then take any (positive) value. Substituting the equilibrium values into the definition (27) we see that $R_{t+1} > 0$ indeed holds (given that capital is positive). Hence the fixed point with zero income and arbitrary positive capital indeed belongs to the definition region for the map (28).

As for (29) we easily find that there is just the fixed point $Y_{t+1} = Y_t = 0$, and $K_{t+1} = K_t = 0$. Under the weak inequality in the definition range for (29), this fixed point with zero income and capital again belongs to the definition range for the map.

Stability is easiest to check for this latter fixed point of (29), because this map is truly two-dimensional. We can linearize, and write down its Jacobian matrix:

$$\begin{bmatrix} c & -r \\ 0 & (1-r) \end{bmatrix} \tag{30}$$

Given that $0 < c < 1, 0 < r < 1$, the determinant is positive and less than unity, so the fixed point is stable. Note that, due to the form of (29), we do not need to substitute for the variable values at the fixed point. The matrix and its determinant are independent of where in phase space we are. As the Jacobian matrix is in triangular form, we can read the eigenvalues directly from its main diagonal elements, i.e. c and $(1 - r)$ respectively. As both eigenvalues are positive and less than unity, the map (29) is a simple contraction in the entire range of its definition.

From the dynamics point of view this stable fixed point could be a big problem. However, things are not that bad. The second equation of (29) has the closed form solution $K_{t+1} = (1-r)^t K_1$, so the process (starting from any positive amount of capital) indeed implies that the fixed point is approached, but, *it takes infinite time* for $(1-r)^t$ to really get down to zero. As we will show below, the process of iterating (29) is, however, *in a finite number of steps*, mapped into the region where (29) is no longer defined, whereas (28) is working. This map may, on the contrary, be unstable, as we will now see.

From (28) we find that the first equation is autonomous in income alone. However, it is *second order*, and the whole map is order three. We can write down the characteristic equation for this first equation right away:

$$\lambda^2 - (a+c)\lambda + a = 0 \tag{31}$$

Again, the map (28) is linear, so we do not need to substitute for the phase variables. Note that this also holds with respect to the equilibrium stock of capital, which we saw was arbitrary. The, solutions to (31), i.e., the eigenvalues, were written in (5) above for the original multiplier-accelerator model, but we repeat them here for convenience:

$$\lambda_{1,2} = \frac{a+c}{2} \pm \frac{1}{2}\sqrt{(a+c)^2 - 4a} \tag{32}$$

It is easy to check that $\lambda_1 \lambda_2 = a$, so, like the case of the original model, $a = 1$ is a borderline for stability. The fixed point with zero income and arbitrary capital is stable for $a < 1$, and unstable for $a > 1$.

Note that, for $a = 1$, the expression under the root sign becomes $(1+c)^2 - 4$, which is negative for $c < 1$.

Hence, the eigenvalues are complex conjugates with unit modulus for $a = 1$, i.e., at the moment the fixed point loses stability, and can hence be written:

$$\lambda_{1,2} = \cos\omega \pm \mathrm{i} \sin\omega \tag{33}$$

where, as usual, $\mathrm{i} = \sqrt{-1}$, and:

$$\cos\omega = \frac{a+c}{2} \qquad \sin\omega = \frac{1}{2}\sqrt{4a - (a+c)^2} \tag{34}$$

Suppose now that the fixed point bifurcates to a periodic solution, i.e., that $\omega = 2\pi m / n$. Substituting for ω in the first equation of (34) along with $a = 1$, and solving, we get:

$$c = 2\cos\left(2\pi \frac{m}{n}\right) - 1 \tag{35}$$

If we want to check the lowest fundamental resonances, i.e., putting $m = 1$, then, for $n = 1, 2, 3, 4, 5$, and 6, we get: $c = 1, -3, -2, -1, \left(\sqrt{5} - 3\right)/2 \approx -0.38$, and 0 respectively. Only for $n > 6$ do we get bifurcations from fixed point to some periodic cycle with admissible parameter values $0 < c < 1$.

It is interesting to refer back to Fig. 6 of Chapter 3. The calculated c values, as a matter of fact, coincide with the points where the correspondingly numbered periodicity curves intersect the bifurcation line $a = 1$. In the present model these curves will be seen to set out from the just calculated bifurcation points, not as curves, but as thick tongues, as we see in Fig. 6 below.

It would be tempting to speak of a Neimark bifurcation, and of Arnol'd tongues. But, this terminology applies to stationary systems, periodic, quasiperiodic, or chaotic. Our system, however, is not stationary, it is growing, and only after reduction to relative variables, are we able to calculate the tongues. So at most can we speak of a Neimark-like bifurcation in our non-standard model.

We did not yet speak of the stability of the second equation of (28), but this is quite trivial. Capital is just neutral, so any previous K_t is just perpetuated as K_{t+1}, and the stability/instability issue completely hangs on the stability of the income generating process - if the latter is stable, then capital approaches some neutral equilibrium value, if not, then capital accumulation is as unstable as the income generation process.

It should also be emphasized that we focus on oscillatory motion, i.e., where the eigenvalues (32) are indeed complex conjugates. We just saw that on the bifurcation line $a = 1$ nothing else can happen. If we look at Fig. 6 in Chapter 3 (or Fig. 6 in this Chapter), we see why this is so. The curve for emergence of complex eigenvalues, i.e. where the expression under the root sign in (32) becomes zero, has its maximum for $a = 1$, so the entire admissible segment $0 < c < 1$ is contained in the area for complex roots. But, this does not hold to the right (or left) of the bifurcation line. Then for sufficiently large c, though less than unity, the eigenvalues can become real. To the right of the bifurcation line, the process then settles on pure unlimited growth without oscillations. To the left of the line the system goes to the fixed point, again without oscillations.

Suppose now that we deal with an oscillatory solution, i.e. that $(a+c)^2 < 4a$, and that the fixed point is unstable, i.e. $a > 1$. Then (28) is an expansion, whereas (29) is a contraction, and we will see how the process keeps going, alternating between the definition regions for the two maps. This was proved already in Puu *et al.* (2005), more elegantly than in the following, though using some "higher" mathematics.

7.9 Why the Map Leaves the Floor

Suppose that the system for a while has been in the region of phase space where (29) applies, i.e. where (27) is nonpositive. Let us then substitute $Y_t = cY_{t-1} - rK_{t-1}$, and $Y_{t-1} = cY_{t-2} - rK_{t-2}$ from (29) in (27). Then:

$$R_t = a\left(c\left(Y_{t-1} - Y_{t-2}\right) - r\left(K_{t-1} - K_{t-2}\right)\right) + rK_t \tag{36}$$

But, from (29) $K_{t-1} - K_{t-2} = -rK_{t-2}$, and $K_t = (1-r)^2 K_{t-2}$, so:

$$R_t = c\left(a\left(Y_{t-1} - Y_{t-2}\right)\right) + \left(ar^2 + r(1-r)^2\right)K_{t-2} \tag{37}$$

From (27) we also have $a\left(Y_{t-1} - Y_{t-2}\right) = R_{t-1} - rK_{t-1}$, so substituting and using $K_{t-1} = (1-r)K_{t-2}$, we get:

$$R_t = cR_{t-1} + \left(ar^2 + r(1-r)(1-r-c)\right)K_{t-2} \tag{38}$$

Obviously, capital is positive, and further the coefficient of the second term:

$$\kappa = ar^2 + r(1-r)(1-r-c) \tag{39}$$

is positive as well. Note that we assumed $a > 1$ as a condition for instability for the fixed point. Hence $\kappa > r^2 + r(1-r)(1-r-c)$. Suppose the contrary of what we want to prove, i.e. that $\kappa < 0$. Then $r^2 + r(1-r)(1-r-c) < 0$ must hold. Dividing through by the common factor r, which is positive, and by $(1 - r)$, which is positive as well, we conclude that $c > 1 + r / (1-r)$. As the second term is positive, we conclude that c, the propensity to consume, would have to exceed unity in order to result in a negative κ. This is contrary to assumption, and hence we have $\kappa > 0$, as a result of $a > 1$, $c < 1$, and $0 < r < 1$.

Using (39), the recurrence relation (38) looks particularly simple:

$$R_t = cR_{t-1} + \kappa K_{t-2} \tag{40}$$

The second term is a product of two positive numbers, so, as we consider $R_{t-1} \leq 0$, we are looking for the possibility to get $R_t > 0$ due to the added positive term, and also due to the fact that the nonpositive number is scaled down through successive multiplication by $c < 1$.

To find this out, we have to use (40) iterated over a sequence of periods. So, suppose we start with $t = 2$, for which $R_2 = cR_1 + \kappa K_0$, and iterate according to (40) $t - 1$ times. Then:

$$R_{t+1} = c^t R_1 + \kappa \sum_{\tau=0}^{t-1} c^\tau (1-r)^{t-1-\tau} K_0 \tag{41}$$

Assume now $c < 1 - r$. Then obviously $c^\tau (1-r)^{t-1-\tau} > c^{t-1}$ holds. Further, as $c < 1$, we have $c^{t-1} > c^t$. Hence, as everything in the second term of (41) is positive, we obtain:

$$R_{t+1} > c^t (R_1 + t\kappa K_0) \tag{42}$$

We assumed that $R_1 \leq 0$, whereas $\kappa K_0 > 0$. The latter is multiplied by the number t, i.e., the number of terms in the sum in (41), so, in a finite number of steps, the positive term is bound to dominate, and produce $R_{t+1} > 0$. The positive factor c^t, of course, decreases with time as $c < 1$, but it stays finite in finite time.

Now this is what we wanted to prove: When the process sticks to the floor, it is bound to leave this constraint in a finite number of iterations, so that the accelerator starts working again, and the process is kept going.

It is worth noting that the condition $c<1-r$ is a *sufficient* condition for the process to leave the floor region. It is by no means necessary. When the series in equation (41) is evaluated, we find that the whole expression boils down to a sum of two power functions. In case they have opposite sign, then (41) as a function of time attains a maximum. Only if this maximum is negative does the process never leave the floor region.

7.10 Why the Map Hits the Floor

Once we know that, whenever the process sticks to the floor, approaching the zero equilibrium, it will in a finite number of steps liberate itself from the floor and return to a working accelerator, we also know that the process will go on for ever. This is true, of course, only provided that the multiplier-accelerator process itself is unstable, i.e. provided $a > 1$ holds. For the sake of completeness we will also show that the unstable process hits the floor again and again, in spite of the fact that capital is accumulating, and the floor constraint hence slackens during the accumulation process.

Suppose the map (28) has been active for some while, which means that R_t has been positive. Then we can substitute for Y_t and Y_{t-1} from the first equation of (33), and obtain:

$$R_t = a(a+c)(Y_{t-1}-Y_{t-2})-a^2(Y_{t-2}-Y_{t-3})+rK_t \tag{43}$$

Next, let us eliminate the income differences, using (27) for periods t - 1 and t - 2. Hence:

$$R_t = (a+c)(R_{t-1}-rK_{t-1})-a(R_{t-2}-rK_{t-2})+rK_t \tag{44}$$

We now have to deal with the capital entries in equation (44). The formation of capital while the accelerator is working is described in the second equation of (28). But we already have the result of its repeated application stated above in (18), i.e. $K_{t+1}=K_1+a(Y_t-Y_0)$. So, let us apply this for t -1, t -2, and t - 3 in (44). The result is:

$$R_t = (a+c)R_{t-1}-aR_{t-2}+r(1-c)(K_1-aY_0)+ra(Y_{t-1}-(a+c)Y_{t-2}+aY_{t-3}) \tag{45}$$

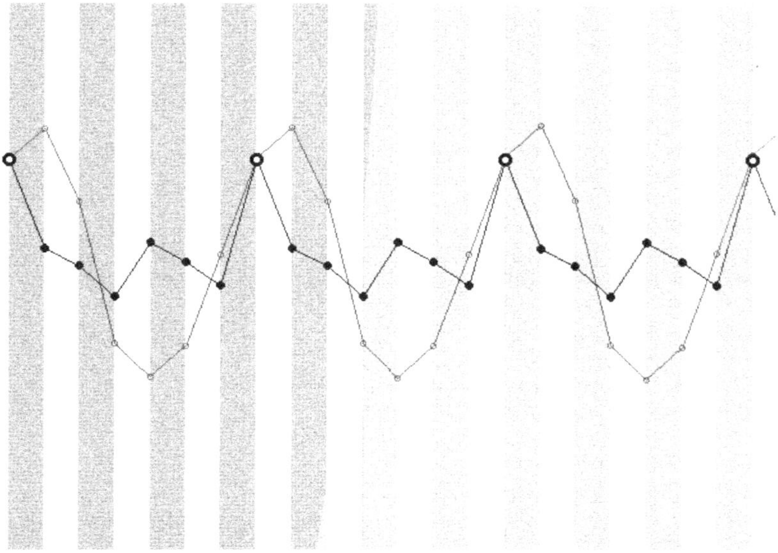

Figure 4. *Trace for income (gray and growing), and for its growth factor (black and stationary).*

While (28) is working, its first equation states that $Y_{t-1} = (a+c)Y_{t-2} - aY_{t-3}$, so (45) loses its last term and simplifies to:

$$R_t = (a+c)R_{t-1} - aR_{t-1} + r(1-c)(K_1 - aY_0) \tag{46}$$

where $r(1-c)(K_1 - aY_0)$ can be positive or negative depending on whether initial capital K_1 exceeds or falls short of initial optimal capital according to the accelerator, i.e., aY_0.

The important fact about (46) is that the last term is a constant. Putting:

$$R_t = R_{t-1} = R_{t-2} = R = r(K_1 - aY_0) \tag{47}$$

in (46), we find that it is reduced to an identity. Hence, $R = r(K_1 - aY_0)$ is a particular solution to the nonhomogenous difference equation (46). We can hence restate it as:

$$(R_t - R) = (a+c)(R_{t-1} - R) - a(R_{t-2} - R) \tag{48}$$

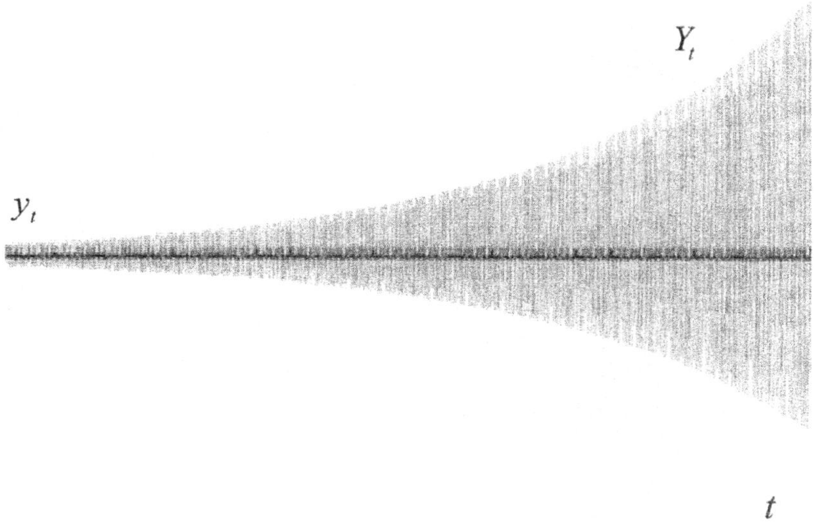

Figure 5. Trace for income, and for its growth factor over a prolonged period.

and note that it is a difference equation of exactly the same form as (1) above, even if we now stated it for the branch constraint (27).

Accordingly, we already know the solution to (48). It is the product of a growth factor, and a trigonometric oscillatory factor. We already said that we are just interested in the oscillatory and growing cases, with $(a+c)^2 < 4a$ and $a > 1$. Due to the growth factor, $R_t - R$ is bound to recurrently exceed any negative value, and hence R_t is bound to become negative, even when R happens to be positive.

7.11 Periodic Solutions

This completes the proof. Provided $c < 1-r$, $a > 1$, and $(a+c)^2 < 4a$ hold, the model keeps going for ever, growing with oscillating growth rates for

t	y_t	Y_t
0	5.207056	1.000000
1	1.259941	1.259941
2	0.507890	0.639912
3	-0.868097	-0.555505
4	1.525107	-0.847205
5	0.680385	-0.576425
6	-0.337195	0.194368
7	5.207056	1.012083

Table 2. *Growing income with 7-periodic cycle for the modified model.*

income and capital, visiting the floor constraint over and over, and leaving it again. We will now see how this fact fundamentally changes the working of the model, producing periodic growth cycles, which did not occur in the original model. Unfortunately, analytic methods are no longer of any use, so we have to rely on numerical work at the computer.
We present a picture for the case $a = 1.25$, $c = 0.25$, and $r = 0.01$ in Fig. 4. It is easy to check that the three constraints stated above are fulfilled, though the propensity to consume is unrealistically low. The reason for this choice is that it is then easy to pick a fundamental resonance of low periodicity. As we see in Fig. 4, we hit a 7-periodic cycle. The gray trace represents the development of income, the black trace the ratio of income to that of the previous period. The gray income trace is actually growing, and hence not periodic, though it is difficult to see this over just three cycles, because the growth rate is now so low. This *lowering of growth rates* is another consequence of the modified model. To convince ourselves that the gray trace is at all growing, we show Fig. 5, of the same traces over a *prolonged* period. Though we no longer can identify the cycles in the compressed picture, we clearly see that the black trace is stationary, whereas the gray grows exponentially.

Figs. 2 and 4 are different, not only because the latter has nothing of the smooth sinoid shape of the former. What is really interesting is that, whereas the black trace in Fig. 2 was only *approximately* 7-periodic, its counterpart in Fig. 4 is *exactly* 7-periodic. Not only is it now easy to pick the above stated parameter combination to produce exact 7-periodicity, but we could find infinitely many nearby, or even more distant parameter combinations within a so called resonance tongue, that produce the same. As stated above, the thin resonance curves of Fig. 6 in Chapter 3 are replaced by thick resonance tongues in Fig. 6 below.

We can also present the difference in terms of Table 2, to be compared to Table 1 above. Both are numerical calculations of 7-period cycles. However, to get the exact 7-periodicity for Table 1, we cheated by choosing the rational rotation $\omega = 2\pi / 7$, as we could not have picked this through choosing the parameter values.

Further, the way of calculation is different. In Table 1 we calculated y_t, and then obtained Y_t as continued products of the former. Now we do the reverse, i.e. calculate Y_t, and then obtain the y_t as quotients Y_t / Y_{t-1} according to the definition (2). To tell the complete story, in order to make the nonlinear system converge upon cyclicity in growth rates, we first run a couple of thousand transient iterations, which we trash. Through this, the initial Y_0 of the cycle displayed, would not equal unity, but we can rescale the time series, in order to make the Tables comparable, and in order to be able to easily read off the growth rate over a cycle. Note that this does not affect the entries of the y_t column, because any such rescaling constant appears in both numerator and denominator of Y_t / Y_{t-1} and hence cancels.

Another interesting fact is the low growth factor, 1.012083 over a 7-period cycle, i.e. $1.012083^{1/7} \approx 1.001823$ for one period. Suppose that we did not have the floor constraint. Then we know that the growth factor, given $a = 1.25$, would be $\sqrt{1.25} \approx 1.118034$ for one period, or $\sqrt{1.25}^7 \approx 2.183660$ over a complete cycle. So, despite the fact that the floor constraint slackens with accumulating capital, its existence lowers the growth rate to about one hundredth of what it is in the original model without the floor. As we will see, this property holds over the entire parameter space.

7.12 Conversion to Relative Dynamics

For further studies of the multiplier-accelerator model with floor dependent on accumulated capital, as formulated in (28)-(29), we now introduce the relative variables, y_t and k_t the first already defined in (2), but restated here for convenience:

$$y_{t+1} := \frac{Y_{t+1}}{Y_t} \tag{49}$$

$$k_{t+1} := \frac{K_{t+1}}{Y_t} \tag{50}$$

The most convenient relative variable transformation for capital is the ratio of capital stock to income in the previous period. This may seem a bit arbitrary, but we must recall that capital is a *stock* concept, dated through attribution to a *time point*, whereas income is a *flow* concept, dated through attribution to a *time period*. Setting up a time scale is always a bit arbitrary, as we realise even from everyday language by denoting the same hundred years as "Cinquecento" (in Italian) but as 16th Century (in English). We chose t to denote the time period between time points t and $t+1$, and so (50) is as logical as anyone may want.

We now need to restate R_t in the branch condition (27), in terms of the relative variables. So, for a start, divide (27) through by Y_{t-1}, thus obtaining:

$$\frac{R_t}{Y_{t-1}} = a(y_t - 1) + rk_t \tag{51}$$

from definitions (27) and (49)-(40). There is, however, a problem with using the right hand side of (51) as choice condition between the branches of the map (28)-(29). The choice condition is stated in terms of inequalities, and, as we know, Y_{t-1} may take on negative values, hence *changing the sense of the inequality*. We therefore have to neutralize this effect, for instance by multiplying (51) through by a variable which takes the same sign as Y_{t-1}. We only have two to choose from, y_t and k_t, but the latter indeed is a suitable variable according to (50). Multiplication through by $k_t = K_t / Y_{t-1}$ results in:

$$\rho_t = \frac{K_t R_t}{Y_{t-1}^2} = a(y_t - 1)k_t + rk_t^2 \tag{52}$$

where ρ_t *always* takes the sign of R_t, because capital is positive, and income is squared.

It now remains to convert (28)-(29). Dividing the first equation of (28) through by Y_t, results in $y_{t+1} = c + a(1 - 1/y_t)$. Doing the same with the second equation, results in the quotient K_t / Y_t in the right hand side, which is not one of our new relative variables. But $K_t / Y_t = (K_t / Y_{t-1})(Y_{t-1} / Y_t) = k_t / y_t$, so $k_{t+1} = k_t / y_t + a(1 - 1/y_t)$. Collecting facts, we have the first map:

$$f_1: \begin{cases} y_{t+1} = c + a\left(1 - \dfrac{1}{y_t}\right) \\ k_{t+1} = \dfrac{k_t}{y_t} + a\left(1 - \dfrac{1}{y_t}\right) \end{cases} \qquad \rho_t \geq 0 \tag{53}$$

Doing the same transformation to (29), again using what we just found out about $K_t / Y_t = k_t / y_t$, we transform the first equation to $y_{t+1} = c - rk_t / y_t$, and the second to $k_{t+1} = (1-r)k_t / y_t$. Hence the other map becomes:

$$f_2: \begin{cases} y_{t+1} = c - r\dfrac{k_t}{y_t} \\ k_{t+1} = (1-r)\dfrac{k_t}{y_t} \end{cases} \qquad \rho_t < 0 \tag{54}$$

The map (53)-(54) represents the same model as (28)-(29) above, though the fact that it is stated in relative variables makes the solutions predominantly periodic, which is not the case with the original absolute variables. As we recall, y_t is the income growth factor, and k_t is the capital/income ratio.

7.13 Numerical Study

We will now take a closer look at the case where the roots are conjugate complex, i.e. $(a+c)^2 < 4a$, but (28) is not damped, i.e. $a > 1$. Geometrically this means below the parabola, and to the right of the vertical line at unit accelerator in Fig. 6, Chapter 3.

Fig. 6 of this Chapter is a direct companion to Fig. 6 of Chapter 3, though for the nonlinear model with floor linked to depreciation on accumulated

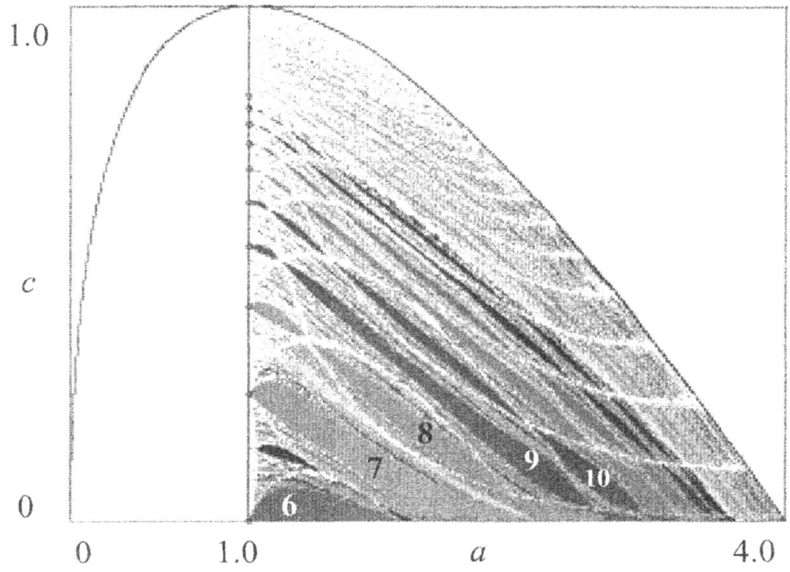

Figure 6. *Bifurcation diagram with periodic Arnol'd tongues.*

capital stock. We see the same box $(a,c)\in[0,4]\times[0,1]$ in parameter space, the same vertical line at $a = 1$, the threshold of instability of the zero fixed point for the model in original (i.e. not relative) variables, and the parabola $(a+c)^2 = 4a$, the watershed between oscillatory (below) and steady (above) solutions.

What we see in Fig. 6 is a set of periodicity tongues, so called Arnol'd tongues, which almost completely fill out the right part of the space below the parabola, though only periodicities up to 45 were computed. The method used was to run the system (53)-(54) on the computer, skipping the first thousand iterates, belonging to the transient, and then check for the lowest periodicity among the 45 selected. The tongues corresponding to each parameter combination were then coloured according to the lowest periodicity which would fit the time series computed. Two remarks are in place.

First, by checking for the lowest periodicity, we do not catch the existence of multistability, i.e., coexistence of different periodicities for one and the same parameter combination. Such multistability may exist also in terms of different coexisting solutions of the same periodicity. This cannot be seen at all in a bifurcation diagram such as Fig. 6. To see multistability, we would

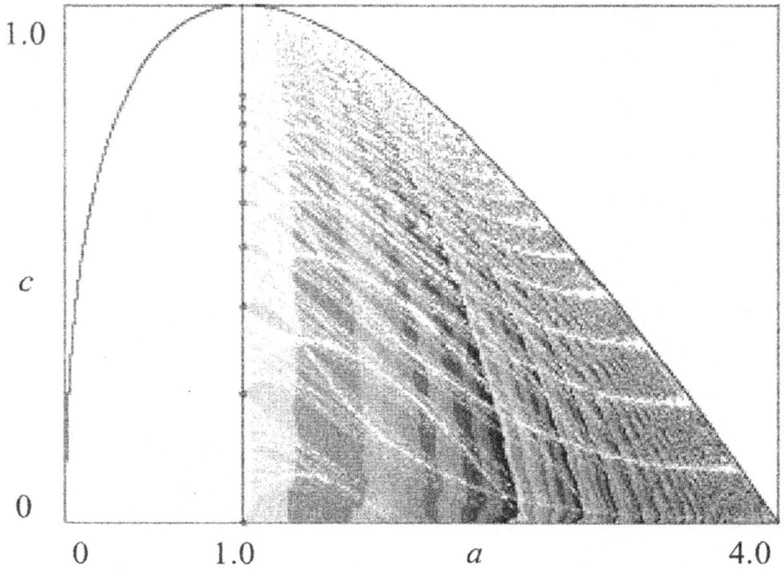

Figure 7. *Growth rates for periodic solutions. Band width 0.2 %.*

have to select one parameter point, and then produce a picture of the phase plane with different attractors and their basins of attraction.

Second, as already mentioned, almost the whole picture is filled with periodicity tongues of the lowest 45 periodicities. In reality there exist all periodicities, so there are more tongues for higher periods, but they must be thin because there is not much space left. It is likely that, had we proceeded with higher periods, a little more space would be filled, but the clear pattern of white streaks would remain. Probably they represent cycles of infinite period, i.e. quasiperiodic orbits.

Note that we have three parameters, so we have to fix one, i.e. r in order to produce a plane picture. We chose $r = 0.01$.

Comparing Fig. 6 to Fig. 6 from Chapter 3, we see that, in the nonlinear model, it is quasiperiodicity that has become a rare phenomenon, whereas the reverse held for the original linear multiplier-accelerator model. However, there is a relation: The periodicity tongues of Fig. 6 start out from exactly the points on the $a = 1$ line, where the thin periodicity curves in Fig. 6 of Chapter 3 intersect that line. Accordingly, we do not find any 5-period tongue, as it does not intersect this line at a positive value of c. Running the computer program for $a < 1$, does not produce any periodic tongues, because the model restated in relative variables is divergent for those parameter values.

The lowest tongue is 6-period, and we also find the rest of the periodicities displayed in Fig. 6 of Chapter 3, in Fig. 6 of this Chapter as well, further in approximately the regions we would expect them to be located.

Note the peculiar shape of the periodicity tongues, like twisted bands, or strings of "sausages", 3 pieces for the 8- and 9-period tongues, four pieces for the 10-period tongue. This depends on different orders of application of the component maps, and was explained in Sushko *et al.* (2004).

7.14 Growth

Fig. 7 presents some different aspects of the same bifurcation diagram as Fig. 6. We see the same pattern of white streaks, and can identify the tongues, though the gray scale shading is different. We now chose colouring according to the growth rates. The numerical procedure was exactly as illustrated in Table 2, with the only difference that we did not calculate y_t as a ratio from Y_t and Y_{t-1}, but directly from the relative dynamics model (53)-(54). After checking for periodicity, we calculated the growth factor as the geometric average of the calculated y_t values over a complete cycle.

The width of each band represents a growth rate of 0.002 per period. As we see, these bands recur in bundles of 15. (This is due to the fact that the picture was produced by a DOS program, where only 15 (nonblack) colours are available.) This is actually helpful, because we can easily see where one bundle ends and the next begins. So, by the end of the first we have a growth rate of 0.03, by the end of the second 0.06, etc. Note that the first bundle ends at approximately $a \approx 2.5$, where the growth rate according to the original linear model would have been $\sqrt{2.5} \approx 1.58$, i.e. 58% compared to 3% in the nonlinear model. This lowering of growth rates was mentioned above, and we now see that indeed this holds over the entire parameter plane. It hardly needs saying that we by the procedure described only can calculate growth rates for cyclic processes.

References

Allen, R.G.D., 1956, *Mathematical Economics*. Macmillan, London.

Duesenberry, J., 1950, "Hicks on the trade cycle". *The Quarterly Journal of Economics* 64:464-76

Frisch R. "Propagation problems and impulse problems in dynamic economics". *Economic Essays in Honour of Gustav Cassel*. Allen & Unwin, London; 1933

Gallegati, M., Gardini, L., Puu, T., and Sushko, I., 2003, "Hicks's Trade Cycle Revisited: Cycles and Bifurcations", *Mathematics and Computers in Simulations*, 63:505-527

Gandolfo, G., 1985, *Economic Dynamics: Methods and Models*. North-Holland, Amsterdam.

Hicks, J.R., 1950, A *Contribution to the Theory of the Trade Cycle*. Oxford University Press, Oxford.

Hommes, C.H., 1991, *Chaotic Dynamics in Economic Models*. Wolters-Noordhoff, Groningen.

Puu, T., 1963. A graphical solution of second-order homogeneous difference equations. Oxford Economic Papers 15, 54-58

Puu, T., Gardini, L. and Sushko, I., 2005, "A multiplier-accelerator model with floor determined by capital stock", *Journal of Economic Behavior and Organization*, 56:331-348

Puu, T. and Sushko, I., 2004, "A business cycle model with cubic nonlinearity", *Chaos, Solitons & Fractals* 19:597-612

Puu, T., 2005, "The Hicksian Trade Cycle with Floor and ceiling dependent on Capital Stock", *Journal of Economic Dynamics and Control* (submitted)

Rau, N., 1974, *Trade Cycle: Theory and Evidence*. Macmillan, London.

Sushko, I., Gardini, L. and Puu, T., 2004, "Tongues of periodicity in a family of two-dimensional maps of real Möbius type", *Chaos, Solitons & Fractals*, 21:403-412

Samuelson, P.A., 1939, "Interactions between the multiplier analysis and the principle of acceleration", *Review of Economics and Statistics* 21:75-8.

8 Coexistence of Attractors and Homoclinic Loops in a Kaldor-Like Business Cycle Model

Anna Agliari and Roberto Dieci

8.1 Introduction

Coexistence of attractors is often a characteristic feature of economic models represented by nonlinear dynamic systems [see, among others, Agliari *et al.* (2002), Bischi & Kopel (2001), Dieci *et al.* (2001), Agliari *et al.* (2000)]. Generally speaking, when multiple attractors coexist in the phase-space for a particular choice of the parameters of the model, a crucial question is about the role played by the initial conditions in determining the asymptotic behavior of the system. Moreover, in order to perform a proper bifurcation analysis with respect to some specific parameters it is necessary to take into account that parameter variations determine in general both qualitative changes (including appearance/disappearance) of the attractors, and structural changes of the basins of attraction of the coexisting attractors. The latter point has been less emphasized in the economic literature. In general, typical features of such qualitative changes of the basins are the following: (a) they are due to *global* bifurcations (not associated with the eigenvalues of the linearized system around a particular steady state) and (b) they may bring about a kind of "complexity" which is different from the one usually reported in the literature (associated with "strange attractors", and "sensitivity to initial conditions"): Namely, simple attractors (steady states, cycles of low period, attracting closed curves) may have basins with complex structures.

In recent years, several studies have pointed out particular mechanisms of basin bifurcations, which are associated with contacts between basin boundaries and "critical sets", in the case of dynamical systems represented by the iteration of *noninvertible maps* [Mira *et al.* (1996), Agliari *et al.* (2002), Agliari (2001)]. Other possible mechanisms, which may occur in the case of *invertible maps* as well, are associated with homoclinic tangencies of the stable and unstable manifolds of saddles. The present Chapter illustrates the latter type of phenomena, in situations of coexisting attractors that arise from a particular version of Kaldor's business cycle model in discrete time, described by a nonlinear two-dimensional dynamical system.

The particular Kaldor-like model at hand, where consumption is modelled as an S-shaped function of income, and investment is a linear increasing function of output (and a linear decreasing function of capital), has been developed in Herrmann (1985), and studied also in Lorenz (1992, 1993), Dohtani *et al.* (1996), mainly in order to prove the emergence of chaotic dynamics in Kaldor-like models under extreme values of the output adjustment parameter. However, the particular parameter constellation which is assumed within the present Chapter (under which multiple equilibria exist) has been excluded from the analysis carried out in earlier work, though it corresponds to economically meaningful situations. We will show that for this choice of parameters, business fluctuations along a stable closed curve (which typically arise in Kaldor model), coexist with alternative dynamic outcomes (stable steady states, or stable periodic orbits of low period), which the system may reach in the long-run depending on the initial state. Furthermore, we will explain the bifurcation mechanisms which determine such situations of coexistence, the appearance or disappearance of attractors and the qualitative changes of the basins of attraction. The global dynamic phenomena which are detected in this Chapter are described in Chapter 1 and have also been detected in a different version of the Kaldor model in discrete-time [see Bischi *et al.* (2001) and Agliari *et al.* (2005b)], where investment is an increasing S-shaped function of output (and depends negatively on capital stock) and savings depend linearly on income. Therefore such dynamic phenomena seem to be very persistent ones, and their occurrence seems to be ultimately related to the following basic assumptions: (i) investment or consumption have sigmoid shaped graphs, in a way that the marginal propensity to invest is larger (smaller) than the marginal propensity to save for normal (extreme) levels of income, and (ii) the investment schedule shifts downwards (upwards) as output increases (decreases) as a result of a negative dependence on accumulated stock of capital. Both these assumptions are essential qualitative features of Kaldor's original model. On the other hand, very similar dynamic phenomena have been detected also in Agliari *et al.* (2005a), where a two-dimensional map with a "minimal" structure qualitatively similar to that in Agliari *et al.* (2005b), and to the one being studied here, has been analyzed in details. Further examples are shown in this book, Chapters 9 and 11.

The Chapter is organized as follows. In Section 8.2 we present the business cycle model, perform useful changes of coordinates, and reduce it to a two-dimensional map. Section 8.3 presents some general properties of the map, namely the symmetry, the steady states and local asymptotic stability conditions, and the conditions for invertibility. Section 8.4 focuses on particular global bifurcations, involving qualitative changes of the basins of attraction, occurring in a particular regime of parameters where three equilibria exist, and relates these phenomena to the behavior of the stable and unstable manifolds of saddles.

8.2 The Model

Let us consider the following discrete-time version of the Kaldor (1940) nonlinear model of the business cycle

$$\begin{cases} Y_{t+1} = Y_t + \alpha\left(I_t - (Y_t - C_t)\right) \\ K_{t+1} = I_t + (1-\delta)\, K_t \end{cases} \tag{1}$$

where the dynamic variables Y_t and K_t represent the income (or output) level and the capital stock in period t, respectively, and both the investment I_t and the consumption C_t (or equivalently the savings $S_t = Y_t - C_t$) are assumed to depend in general on Y_t and K_t.

The first equation in (1) views the output level as reacting over time to the excess demand or, put differently, to the difference between ex-ante investment (I_t) and saving ($S_t = Y_t - C_t$). The *speed of adjustment* is measured by the parameter α ($\alpha > 0$), where a value of α smaller than 1 means a prudent reaction by firms, while a value of α greater than 1 denotes rash reactions and coordination failure.

The second equation in (1) models the capital stock as being increased by realized investment (here assumed to coincide with ex-ante investment) $I_t = I_t\left(Y_t, K_t\right)$, and decreased by depreciation δK_t, where δ ($0 < \delta < 1$) represents the *capital stock depreciation rate*.

The discrete dynamical equations (1) (or, alternatively, their continuous-time counterparts) provide the common structure of several versions of the Kaldor model, which have been proposed in the literature up to now [see Dana & Malgrange (1984), Herrmann (1985), Grasman & Wentzel (1994), Bischi *et al.* (2001), among others]. Such models are able to produce both periodic or quasi-periodic trajectories and further dynamic scenarios, ranging from chaotic fluctuations to coexistence of different attractors, once the investment and the savings function I_t and S_t are specified in a way consistent with Kaldor's original qualitative assumptions, namely (a): $\partial I/\partial Y >$

$\partial S/\partial Y$ (i.e. propensity to invest higher than the propensity to save) for "normal" levels of income, but $\partial I/\partial Y < \partial S/\partial Y$ for extreme income levels, below and above the "normal" range; (b) $\partial I/\partial K < 0$, i.e. a negative relationship between investment and capital stock, or $\partial S/\partial K > 0$, i.e. a positive relationship between savings and capital stock. In particular, assumption (a) has been illustrated by Kaldor using an S-shaped investment function, or equivalently a savings function characterized by an inverted S-shape. The present Chapter is a dynamical exercise on the particular version of the Kaldor model introduced in Herrmann (1985), which has been studied also in Lorenz (1992, 1993), and in Dohtani *et al.* (1996). While in the aforementioned papers the focus was on chaotic dynamics, in our analysis we will explore different regimes of parameters, where the dynamical behavior is characterized by coexistence of attractors.

Our assumptions about consumption (C_t) and investment (I_t), which are the same as in Herrmann (1985), are stated and discussed below.

- **Consumption**

  At each time t, the consumption is a sigmoid shaped function of income:

$$C_t = c_0 + \frac{2}{\pi} c_1 \arctan\left(\frac{\pi c_2}{2c_1}(Y_t - Y^*)\right) \tag{2}$$

  where Y^* denotes the exogenously assumed equilibrium (or normal) level of income and c_0, c_1, c_2 are positive parameters. A qualitative plot of the consumption function (2) is given in Fig.1. The consumption is therefore an increasing function of income (ranging between $c_0 - c_1$ and $c_0 + c_1$):However, while for extreme values of income

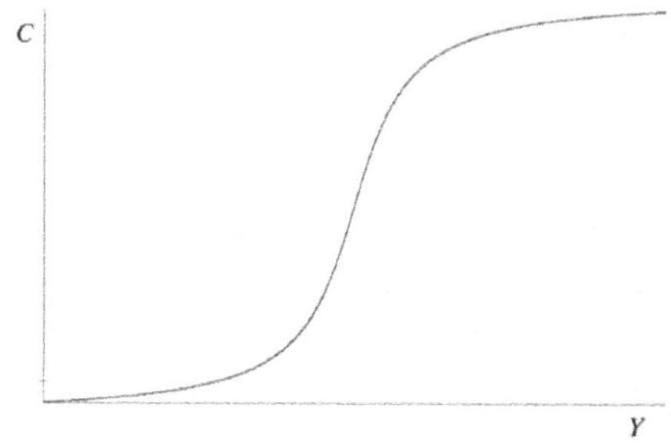

Figure 1: *Qualitative consumption function.*

consumption remains nearly constant, there exists a region around the normal level Y^* where consumption increases rapidly at a rate close to c_2, which represents the consumption propensity at Y^* (we assume $0 < c_2 < 1$).[1] The consumption function (2), or equivalently the inverted S-shaped savings function $S_t = Y_t - C_t$, reflects the view that the proportion of income which is saved is higher in non-ordinary periods, when Y_t is far from Y^*, because in such periods people perceive a larger portion of their income as being transitory[2].

- **Investment**

  At each time t, the investment is a linear function of income and capital stock. Precisely it is assumed that (gross) investment responds to a gradual adjustment of the actual capital stock to the desired capital stock, i.e.,

$$I_t = b\left(K_t^d - K_t\right) + \delta K_t$$

  where K_t^d is the desired stock of capital at time t, assumed linear in current output, that is $K_t^d = kY_t$, with k representing the desired *capital-output ratio* (which here will be considered as an exogenous parameter) and b, $0 < b < 1$, is the capital stock adjustment parameter. Therefore the investment function can be rewritten as a linear function of income and capital, as follows

$$I_t = bkY_t - (b - \delta)K_t \tag{3}$$

  where the Kaldorian negative relationship between investment and capital stock is fulfilled provided that $b > \delta$.

Substituting the consumption and investment functions (2)-(3) in model (1) we get

$$\begin{cases} Y_{t+1} = (1 - \alpha + \alpha bk)\,Y_t + \left(\alpha c_0 + \frac{2}{\pi}c_1 \arctan\left(\frac{\pi c_2}{2c_1}\left(Y_t - Y^*\right)\right) - \right. \\ \left. \qquad\qquad - (b-\delta)\,K_t\right) \\ K_{t+1} = b\,(kY_t - K_t) + K_t \end{cases} \tag{4}$$

[1] Given that Y^* is the turning point of the function (2), c_2 is the maximum propensity to consume.

[2] See Gallegati & Stiglitz (1993) for a model of business fluctuations where a similar consumption function is involved.

from which the coordinates of the exogenous steady state can be easily obtained

$$\begin{cases} Y^* = \frac{c_0}{1-k\delta} \\ K^* = kY^* = \frac{kc_0}{1-k\delta} \end{cases}$$

In order to simplify the analysis of the model (4), we normalize the steady state to $(0,0)$, by reformulating the model in terms of deviations

$$\begin{cases} x_t = K_t - kY^* \\ y_t = Y_t - Y^* \end{cases} \tag{5}$$

With the new coordinates (5), the dynamical system (4) is represented by the following map

$$T : \begin{cases} x' = (1-b)\,x + bky \\ y' = \alpha\,(\delta - b)\,x + (1-\alpha+\alpha bk)\,y + \frac{2}{\pi}\alpha c_1 \arctan\left(\frac{\pi c_2}{2c_1}y\right) \end{cases} \tag{6}$$

where the symbol $'$ denotes the unit time advancement operator. Note first that the map T is independent on c_0, that is c_0 is only a "location" parameter and does not affect the asymptotic behavior of the system. Second, though the map T depends on 6 parameters, in our analysis we will assume b, k, δ, c_1 as fixed parameters, and we will perform stability and bifurcation analysis in the parameter space

$$\Omega = \{(\alpha, c_2) : \alpha > 0 \text{ and } 0 < c_2 < 1\}$$

8.3 General Properties of the Map

In this section we analyze some general properties of the map T in (6), which will play a role in the analysis of the global dynamics. Precisely we will discuss a symmetry property, the steady states and their local asymptotic stability, and the conditions of invertibility or noninvertibility of the map.

8.3.1 Symmetry Property

It can be easily checked that the map T is symmetric with respect to the origin $(0,0)$. This means that two points which are symmetric (with respect to the origin) are mapped into points which are also symmetric. This has important implications for attractors and basins of attraction of T. An immediate consequence is that any invariant set of T either is symmetric with respect to the origin, or it admits a symmetric invariant set. In particular this holds for the fixed points and cycles of T. Thus, whenever further fixed points exist besides $(0,0)$, they must be in symmetric positions, and any cycle of T of odd period necessarily coexists with a symmetric one having the same characteristics. Moreover, the basins of attraction of the attracting sets of T either are symmetric or symmetric basins also exist.

8.3.2 Fixed Points and Local Stability Analysis

The equilibrium points of the model (6) are the fixed points of T, solutions of the system

$$\begin{cases} x = ky \\ \alpha\,(\delta - b)\,x + \alpha\,(bk-1)\,y + \frac{2}{\pi}\alpha c_1 \arctan\left(\frac{\pi c_2}{2c_1}y\right) = 0 \end{cases}$$

Besides the trivial solution $E^* = (0,0)$, the map T may have further fixed points, whose y-coordinates satisfy

$$(1-k\delta)\,y = \frac{2}{\pi}c_1 \arctan\left(\frac{\pi c_2}{2c_1}y\right)$$

Since the straight line of equation $z = (1-k\delta)\,y$ and the sigmoid-shaped graph of the function $z = \frac{2}{\pi}c_1 \arctan\left(\frac{\pi c_2}{2c_1}y\right)$ intersect in three points if the slope of the straight line is positive and lower than that of the curve evaluated at the origin, we obtain the following

Proposition 1 *The map T in (6) has*

- *the unique fixed point $E^* = (0,0)$, if $(1-k\delta) \le 0$ or $c_2 \le (1-k\delta)$*
- *three fixed points, $E^* = (0,0)$ and two further points, P^* and Q^*, symmetric with respect to E^*, if $c_2 > (1-k\delta) > 0$.*

The condition for the existence of further equilibria, stated in Proposition 1, has a straightforward interpretation, in that it can be rewritten as

$$(1-c_2)Y^* < \delta k Y^* = \delta K^*$$

where the quantity $(1-c_2)Y^*$ represents the savings at the exogenously assumed normal equilibrium, while δK^* is the amount of depreciation at the same equilibrium. Therefore further equilibria exist if the equilibrium savings are insufficient to replace capital depreciation at the "normal" stationary state.

Let us now consider the local stability of the fixed point $E^* = (0,0)$. As usual, the analysis of local stability of a fixed point is obtained through the localization, in the complex plane, of the eigenvalues of the Jacobian matrix evaluated at the fixed point, and their dependence on the parameters of the model.

The Jacobian matrix of the map T in (6) is

$$J(x,y) = \begin{bmatrix} 1-b & bk \\ \alpha(\delta - b) & 1+\alpha(bk-1)+\frac{\alpha c_2}{1+\left(\frac{\pi c_2}{2c_1}y\right)^2} \end{bmatrix} \qquad (7)$$

and at E^* it specializes to

$$J^* = \begin{bmatrix} 1-b & bk \\ \alpha(\delta-b) & 1+\alpha(bk-1+c_2) \end{bmatrix}$$

Observe that J^* does not depend on the parameter c_1: Then only five parameters are relevant in this context. To localize the eigenvalue of J^*, denoting by Tr its trace and by Det its determinant, we use the following well known necessary and sufficient condition [see e.g. Gumoswki & Mira (1980), Medio & Lines (2001)]:

i) $1 - Tr + Det = b\alpha(1-c_2-k\delta) > 0$

ii) $1 + Tr + Det = 2(2-b) - \alpha(2-b)(1-c_2) + \alpha bk(2-\delta) > 0$

iii) $1 - Det = b + \alpha(1-b)(1-c_2) - \alpha bk(1-\delta) > 0$

For fixed values of δ, k, b we can determine the region of local asymptotic stability of the steady state E^*, in the plane (α, c_2), as stated in the following

Proposition 2 *Assume* $\delta k < 1$, $b < 1$.

- *If* $b > \delta$ *and* $(2-b)^2 \geq bk(4-4\delta+\delta b)$ *the fixed point* $E^* = (0,0)$ *is locally asymptotically stable if the parameters* α *and* c_2 *belong to the region OABCD of the plane* (α, c_2), *with vertices* $O = (0,0)$, $A = \left(\frac{2(2-b)}{2-b-bk(2-\delta)}, 0\right)$, $B = \left(\frac{(b-2)^2}{bk(b-\delta)}, \frac{(2-b)^2-bk(\delta b-4\delta+4)}{(-2+b)^2}\right)$, $C =$

$\left(\frac{b}{k(b-\delta)}, 1-\delta k\right)$, $D = (0, 1-\delta k)$, where the sides AB, BC and CD belong to the hyperbola of equation

$$c_2 = c_{2f}(\alpha) = \frac{\alpha - 2}{\alpha} - \frac{bk(2-\delta)}{2-b} \tag{8}$$

to the hyperbola of equation

$$c_2 = c_{2N}(\alpha) = 1 + \frac{b - \alpha bk(1-\delta)}{\alpha(1-b)} \tag{9}$$

and to the line $c_2 = 1 - \delta k$, respectively;

- *if $b > \delta$ and $(2-b)^2 < bk(4 - 4\delta + \delta b)$ the fixed point $E^* = (0,0)$ is locally asymptotically stable if the parameters α and c_2 belong to the region OBCD of the plane (α, c_2), with vertices $O = (0,0)$, $B = \left(\frac{b}{bk(1-\delta)-(1-b)}, 0\right)$, $C = \left(\frac{b}{k(b-\delta)}, 1-\delta k\right)$, $D = (0, 1-\delta k)$, where the sides BC and CD belong to the hyperbola of equation*

$$c_2 = c_{2N}(\alpha) = 1 + \frac{b - \alpha bk(1-\delta)}{\alpha(1-b)}$$

  and to the line $c_2 = 1 - \delta k$, respectively;

- *if $b < \delta$ the fixed point $E^* = (0,0)$ is locally asymptotically stable if the parameters α and c_2 belong to the region OABD of the plane (α, c_2), with vertices $O = (0,0)$, $A = \left(\frac{2(2-b)}{2-b-bk(2-\delta)}, 0\right)$, $B = \left(\frac{2-b}{k(\delta-b)}, 1-\delta k\right)$, $D = (0, 1-\delta k)$, where the sides AB and BD belong to the hyperbola of equation*

$$c_2 = c_{2f}(\alpha) = \frac{\alpha - 2}{\alpha} - \frac{bk(2-\delta)}{2-b}$$

  and to the line $c_2 = 1 - \delta k$, respectively.
  If $b = \delta$ the vertex B is missing, because the hyperbola of equation $c_2 = c_{2f}(\alpha)$ approaches asymptotically the straight line of equation $c_2 = 1 - \delta k$ for $\alpha \to \infty$.

Moreover if the point (α, c_2) exits the stability region by crossing the side AB, then a supercritical flip bifurcation occurs at which E^* becomes a saddle point and a period 2 attracting cycle appears; if the *point* (α, c_2) *exits the stability region by crossing the side BC, then a Neimark bifurcation occurs at which* E^* *is transformed into an unstable focus; if the point* (α, c_2) *exits the stability region by crossing the side CD, then a supercritical pitchfork bifurcation occurs at which two stable fixed points are created close to* E^**, which becomes a saddle.*

Proposition 2 confirms analytically that the non-Kaldorian case $b \leq \delta$ (where the condition of inverse dependence of investment on capital stock is not fulfilled) cannot produce a Neimark bifurcation followed by self-sustained fluctuations of output and capital stock along a stable closed curve. On the other hand, in the opposite case $\delta < b$, self-sustained oscillatory behavior around the unstable steady state E^* occurs for sufficiently small values of c_2[3], i.e. when the propensity to save $1 - c_2$ is large enough, whereas for high values of c_2 the typical situation is that of two stable steady states P^* and Q^* and an unstable steady state E^*, located in the middle, i.e. a situation of *bi-stability* (without oscillations). For sufficiently small values of c_2, if condition $(2-b)^2 > bk(4 - 4\delta + \delta b)$ is fulfilled, also cycles of low period are possible, as a consequence of a flip bifurcation. This is what can be immediately deduced from the local analysis carried out in Proposition 2. However, global analysis will point out that long-run oscillatory behavior is possible even for high values of c_2 (beyond the pitchfork boundary), in parameter ranges where two further equilibria P^* and Q^* exist and are stable, or where they exist unstable but further stable periodic orbits exist. This will reveal phenomena of coexistence of the Kaldorian business cycle with other possible long-run dynamic outcomes, where the role played by the initial condition will be crucial.

8.3.3 Invertibility of the Map

Under particular parameters constellations, the map T in (6) is a noninvertible map of the plane. This means that while starting from an initial condition (x_0, y_0) the forward iteration of (6) uniquely defines the trajectory $(x_t, y_t) = T^t(x_0, y_0)$, $t = 1, 2, ...$, the backward iteration of (6) may not exist, or whenever it exists, may not be unique. Recent economic literature dealing with cases of multiple attractors in two-dimensional discrete-time dynamical systems represented by noninvertible maps [see e.g. Bischi & Kopel (2001), Dieci *et al.* (2001), Agliari *et al.* (2000)], has pointed out the

[3] Based on numerical evidence, we claim the supercritical nature of the Neimark bifurcation in this case.

role played by noninvertibility in bringing about bifurcations and complex structures of the basins of attraction. Complexity of the basins of attraction is also detected within the present model, though we must stress that in our case this is not due to the noninvertibility of the map. The goal of the present subsection is therefore to determine the regions of the space of parameters where the map is invertible (and noninvertible), in order to prove that the particular parameter constellation which will be adopted for our numerical simulation is one belonging to the invertibility region. Considering again the (α, c_2)-plane (for fixed values of the remaining parameters) so that the ranges of invertibility or noninvertibility of the map T can be compared with the local bifurcation curves, we can state the following proposition

Proposition 3 *The map T is invertible for any parameter combination (α, c_2) if $1 - b \leq bk(1-\delta)$. In the opposite case $1 - b - bk(1-\delta) > 0$, the noninvertibility region is an unbounded set defined by*

$$\begin{aligned} \alpha &> \frac{1-b}{1-b-bk(1-\delta)} \\ c_2 &> \frac{(\alpha-1)(1-b)-\alpha bk(1-\delta)}{(1-b)\alpha} \end{aligned} \tag{10}$$

Such a region has a vertex on the α-axis, given by $Z = \left(\frac{1-b}{1-b-bk(1-\delta)}, 0\right)$.

Proof. The rank-1 preimages of a point (u, v) are the solutions of the system

$$\begin{cases} u = (1-b)x + bky \\ v = \alpha(\delta - b)x + (1 - \alpha + \alpha bk)y + \frac{2}{\pi}\alpha c_1 \arctan\left(\frac{\pi c_2}{2c_1}y\right) \end{cases}$$

in the unknown variables x and y. Rearranging the two equations of such a system we obtain

$$\begin{cases} x = \frac{u-bky}{1-b} \\ v - \alpha(\delta-b)\frac{u}{1-b} + \frac{(\alpha-1)(1-b)-\alpha bk(1-\delta)}{1-b}y = \frac{2}{\pi}\alpha c_1 \arctan\left(\frac{\pi c_2}{2c_1}y\right) \end{cases}$$

Then the y-coordinates of the rank-1 preimages of the points (u, v) must satisfy the equation

$$q(u, v) + my = \frac{2}{\pi}\alpha c_1 \arctan\left(\frac{\pi c_2}{2c_1}y\right) \tag{11}$$

where $q(u,v) = v - \alpha(\delta - b)\frac{u}{1-b}$ and $m = \frac{(\alpha-1)(1-b)-\alpha bk(1-\delta)}{1-b}$.
It is simple to verify that if $m < 0$ or $m \geq \alpha c_2$, equation (11) has a unique solution for any given (u,v). Therefore if

$$\left\{\begin{array}{l} \frac{(\alpha-1)(1-b)-\alpha bk(1-\delta)}{1-b} < 0 \\ \frac{(\alpha-1)(1-b)-\alpha bk(1-\delta)}{1-b} \geq \alpha c_2 \end{array}\right.$$

holds, the map T is invertible, i.e. has a unique inverse. If $m = 0$, then a unique solution of (11) exists if $-\alpha c_1 < q(u,v) < \alpha c_1$, otherwise no solution exists.

In the case $0 < m < \alpha c_2$, one, two or three solutions of the equation (11) may exist depending on the value of $q = q(u,v)$. In particular, for a given m, two solutions exists if the straight line at the left side of (11) is tangent to the S-shaped curve $f(y) = \frac{2}{\pi}\alpha c_1 \arctan\left(\frac{\pi c_2}{2c_1}y\right)$, that is if

$$m = \frac{\alpha c_2}{1 + \left(\frac{\pi c_2}{2c_1}y\right)^2}$$

We obtain that the equation (11) admits two solutions if $q(u,v)$ becomes equal to q_1 or q_2, where

$$\begin{aligned} q_1 &= \frac{2c_1}{\pi c_2}\left[\sqrt{m(\alpha c_2 - m)} - \alpha c_2 \arctan\left(\frac{1}{m}\sqrt{m(\alpha c_2 - m)}\right)\right] \\ q_2 &= \frac{2c_1}{\pi c_2}\left[\alpha c_2 \arctan\left(\frac{1}{m}\sqrt{m(\alpha c_2 - m)}\right) - \sqrt{m(\alpha c_2 - m)}\right] \end{aligned}$$

Moreover, if $q(u,v) < q_1$ or $q(u,v) > q_2$ the equation (11) has a unique solution, while if $q_1 < q(u,v) < q_2$ three solutions exist.$\Diamond$

From Proposition 3 we deduce that, if

$$\left\{\begin{array}{l} \frac{(\alpha-1)(1-b)-\alpha bk(1-\delta)}{1-b} > 0 \\ \frac{(\alpha-1)(1-b)-\alpha bk(1-\delta)}{1-b} < \alpha c_2 \end{array}\right. \tag{12}$$

the map T is noninvertible and, following the notation used in Mira *et al.* (1996), it is a $Z_1 - Z_3 - Z_1$ map, which means that the phase plane is subdivided in different region Z_1 and Z_3, whose points have one and three different rank-1 preimages, respectively. Such regions, or *zones*, are separated by the *critical line LC*, i.e. the locus of points having two merging rank-1 preimages.

Thanks to the above computation, it is easy to obtain that the critical line is given by two distinct branches, that is $LC = L^a \cup L^b$ with

$$\begin{aligned} L^a &: \ y = \frac{\alpha(\delta - b)}{1-b}x + q_1 \\ L^b &: \ y = \frac{\alpha(\delta - b)}{1-b}x + q_2 \end{aligned} \tag{13}$$

The locus of the merging preimages of the points belonging to the set LC, is the rank-0 critical line LC_{-1} and it is given by $L_{-1}^a \cup L_{-1}^b$, where

$$\begin{aligned} L_{-1}^a &: \ y = -\frac{2c_1}{m\pi c_2}\sqrt{m(\alpha c_2 - m)} \\ L_{-1}^b &: \ y = \frac{2c_1}{m\pi c_2}\sqrt{m(\alpha c_2 - m)} \end{aligned}$$

i.e. the points which satisfy the tangency condition.

Such critical lines can be also obtained from the Jacobian matrix of the map T, indeed LC_{-1} is the locus of point at which the determinant of the Jacobian matrix (7) vanishes, and $LC = T(LC_{-1})$.

In particular, we are interested in the intersection of the noninvertibility region with the region of local stability of E^*. We restrict our analysis on the case $b > \delta$, which is the one of interest from the point of view of the dynamic analysis. Proposition 2 suggests that two different cases need to be considered.

- Case 1: $(2-b)^2 > bk(4 - 4\delta + \delta b)$. In such a case it is simple to show that the noninvertibility region (10) intersects the stability region of E^*, since the vertex B belongs to that region. In fact, the α- and c_2-coordinates of the vertex B satisfy the first and second inequality in (10), respectively.

- Case 2: $(2-b)^2 \leq bk(4 - 4\delta + \delta b)$. In such a case the map is invertible. In fact the condition $(2-b)^2 \leq bk(4 - 4\delta + \delta b)$ implies $1 - b - bk(1-\delta) < 0$.[4]

[4]This result is derived by observing that in this case the intersection point between flip and Neimark bifurcation curves belongs to the half-plane $c_2 \leq 0$, and therefore the horizontal asymptote of the Hopf bifurcation curve must be negative, i.e. $1 - bk(1-\delta)/(1-b) < 0$. Given that $b < 1$, the latter condition implies $1 - b - bk(1-\delta) < 0$.

In our analysis we shall consider constellations of parameters belonging to Case 2, under which the map T is invertible: The corresponding stability region of E^* is shown in Fig.2.

8.4 Global Dynamics Under Coexistence of Equilibria

As we have seen in Section 8.3, the local bifurcation curves of the "normal" steady state E^* suggest the existence of at least two different qualitative dynamic scenarios, outside the region of local asymptotic stability (see Fig.2). The first scenario, where α is small enough and c_2 is located just beyond its

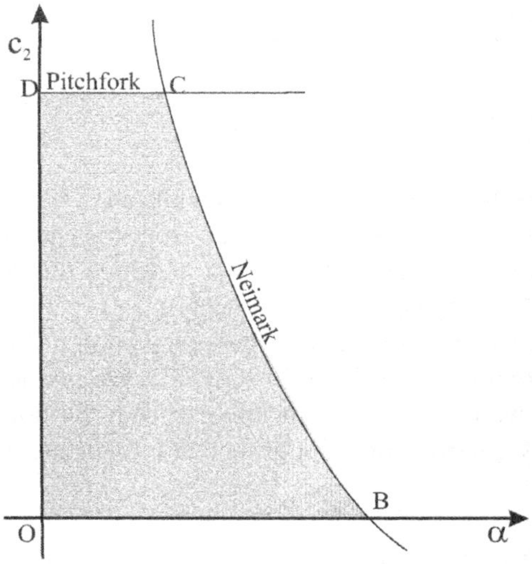

Figure 2: *Stability region of* E^*.

pitchfork bifurcation value $\widehat{c}_2 = 1 - \delta k$, is one where E^* is a saddle point and two further attracting steady states exist in the phase-space xy, on the line $y = x/k$, in symmetric positions with respect to E^* (bi-stability). The second scenario, where $c_2 < \widehat{c}_2$ and α is just larger than its Neimark bifurcation value, is one where the unique steady state E^* is an unstable focus and an attracting invariant closed curve exists around it in the phase space. As it is well known, however, the above results have only a local validity. In particular, nothing can be said in general about the survival of the attracting curve far from the Neimark bifurcation curve in the space of parameters: In principle, it is possible that the attracting curve born via Neimark bifurcation is still surviving even for parameters far from the local stability region where in particular $c_2 > \widehat{c}_2$, i.e. where two further equilibria exist. This is precisely what happens in the case of the present model. Of course in similar cases [see also Agliari *et al.* (2005a,b)] a number of interesting questions are about the mechanisms which lead to the coexistence of an attracting closed curve with two further equilibria, the qualitative changes and the fate of the coexisting attractors (in particular the attracting curve) when the parameters are moved away from the region of stability, and the effects of changes of the parameters on the basins of attraction. These questions are the main topic of the present Section.

As we have also remarked in Section 8.3, other general properties of the map T in (6) may play a crucial role in the asymptotic behaviour of the system. One of this properties is the noninvertibility, which holds in the region (10) of the space of parameters: This may be in general at the origin of complex structures of the attractors and the basins of attraction (see the textbook Mira *et al.* (1996) and Chapter 1, Section 1.4). We rule out this possibility here, by choosing a regime of parameters under which the map T is invertible, in order to simplify as much as possible our understanding of the dynamic phenomena that we are going to analyze. Precisely, our analysis will be restricted to the region of invertibility of the map, and will follow a path in the parameter space through the region of existence of three fixed points, characterized by increasing values of α for a fixed value of $c_2 > \widehat{c}_2 = 1 - \delta k$. We will drive our attention to two different situations of coexistence of attractors, and to the associated bifurcations of attractors and basins: In the first one the two (locally) stable steady states born at the pitchfork bifurcation coexist with endogenous self-sustained oscillatory motion on an attracting closed curve; in the second one, where all the three steady states are unstable, the attracting curve coexists with periodic orbits of low period. A remarkable fact about the following examples is that they represent phenomena which occur when the selected parameters are far from the local bifurcation curves and therefore are due to global mechanisms. A second fact is that, though the two situations to be analyzed are apparently quite different from each other, they are ultimately determined by very similar mechanisms, associated with saddle connections and homoclinic tangles of some saddle cycle as described in Chapter 1 (to which we refer for technical details and symbolisms).

In the following we shall consider fixed values for the parameters k, b, δ, and c_1, given by $k = 1$, $b = 0.8$, $\delta = 0.25$, $c_1 = 2$. With these parameters, the pitchfork bifurcation occurs at $\widehat{c}_2 = 1 - \delta k = 0.75$. Therefore we consider $c_2 > 0.75$, so that three fixed points exist, and increase α starting from $\widehat{\alpha} = \frac{16}{11} = 1.4545$, which is the α-coordinate of the vertex C in Fig.2.

8.4.1 Three Coexisting Attractors and Homoclinic Bifurcation of E*

Immediately after the pitchfork bifurcation of the exogenous steady state E^*, two attracting fixed points, the nodes P^* and Q^*, appear, located at symmetric positions with respect to the saddle E^*. Their basins of attraction are separated by the stable manifold $W^S(E^*)$. The unstable set $W^U(E^*)$ reaches the two fixed points: More precisely, a branch, say α_1, tends to P^* whereas the other one, say α_2, goes to Q^*.

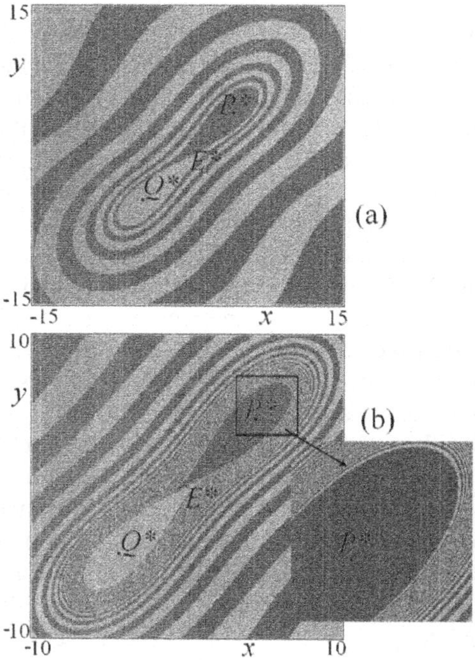

Figure 3: (a) $\alpha = 1.5; c_2 = 0.98$: *Basins of attraction of* P^* *and* Q^*. (b) $\alpha = 1.55; c_2 = 0.98$: *More and more convolutions of* $W^S(E^*)$ *appear.*

The phase portrait of Fig.3a shows an example of this situation: It has been obtained at $\alpha = 1.5$ and $c_2 = 0.98$, then quite far from the bifurcation.

Indeed at this parameter values the two nodes have turned into stable foci and the stable set of the saddle exhibits some convolutions separating the basins of attraction of P^* and Q^*, $\boldsymbol{B}(P^*)$ and $\boldsymbol{B}(Q^*)$ respectively (represented in Fig.3 with different gray tonalities).

As the speed of adjustment α increases, the set $W^S(E^*)$ involves more and more winging around the fixed points P^* and Q^*, as shown in Fig.3b. Consequently, the basin boundary appear to be more complicated and a trajectory starting from the region where the convolutions become thicker is subject to greater uncertainty about its long run behavior. In fact, a slight perturbation of an initial condition taken in such a region (see enlargement of Fig.3b) may cause a crossing of the basin boundary and consequently the convergence to a different equilibrium.

Moreover this basin structure suggests that some global bifurcation is about to occur. Indeed, when α is slightly increased, as in Fig.4a, an attracting closed curve Γ appears in the area where there was many convolutions of $W^S(E^*)$. This means that long-run quasi-periodic self-sustaining fluctuations are now a possible outcome, as well as dampened oscillations converging to the fixed points: Three typical trajectories, starting from initial condition taken in the three different basins, are represented versus time in Fig.4b.

The basins of attraction of P^* and Q^* are still separated by the stable manifold of the saddle E^*, but, differently from the case illustrated in Fig.3, now the preimages of the points of $W^S(E^*)$ accumulate on a repelling closed curve $\widetilde{\Gamma}$, appeared with Γ and very close to it (see enlargement in Fig.4a). The appearance of Γ and $\widetilde{\Gamma}$ could be due in principle to a "saddle-node" bifurcation for closed curves, given that the two curves are very close to each other, but we know that such a bifurcation is very quite rare in discrete maps. Then a mechanism similar to that described in Section 1.7 may be conjectured in this case: A saddle cycle appears via saddle-node bifurcation together with a repelling (or attracting) node cycle of the same period, then a saddle connection made up by the merging of two branches of the stable and unstable manifolds of the saddle gives rise to an attracting (or repelling) closed curve and to a heteroclinic connection between the periodic points of the two cycles made up by the stable (or unstable) set. These two invariant closed curves appear very close to each other and if the period of the cycle is very high they look like those of Fig.4a.

Whichever is the underlying mechanism, the appearance of the two invariant closed curves, one attracting and one repelling, has a noticeable effect on the asymptotic behaviour of the model, since three attractors now coexist (the two equilibria, $P^*$and Q^*, and the closed curve Γ), the basins $\boldsymbol{B}(P^*)$ and $\boldsymbol{B}(Q^*)$ are strongly reduced and the majority of the trajectories are quasi-periodic (or periodic of very high period), since the curve $\widetilde{\Gamma}$ is now the basin boundary of Γ.

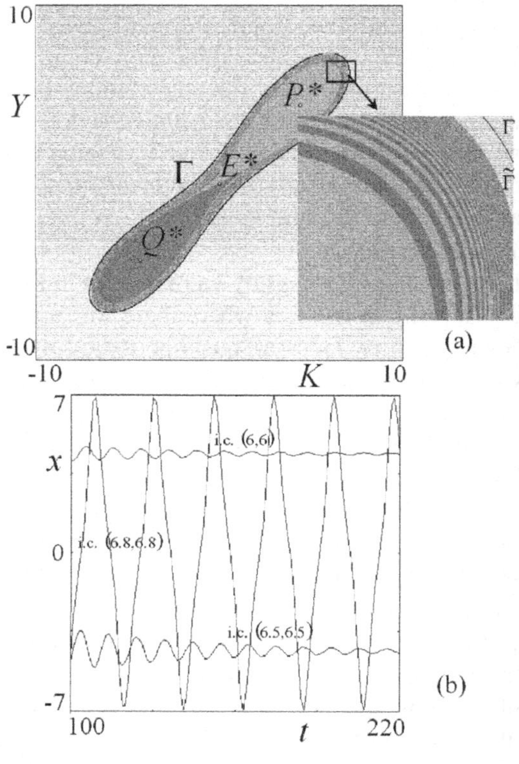

Figure 4: $\alpha = 1.552; c_2 = 0.98$: *Three coexisting attractors.* (a) *Phase space.* (b) *Three typical trajectories versus time.*

Moreover the repelling closed curve $\widetilde{\Gamma}$ is involved in other important qualitative changes in the structure of the basins of attraction as the adjustment speed is increased further. Indeed, as we can see in Fig.5a, it progressively reduces in size and shrinks in proximity of the saddle E^*. Up to now, initial conditions taken close to the exogenous equilibrium have produced trajectories converging to P^* or Q^*, but this is no longer true in the parameter constellation of Fig.5b, where trajectories starting close to E^* exhibit self-sustaining oscillations.

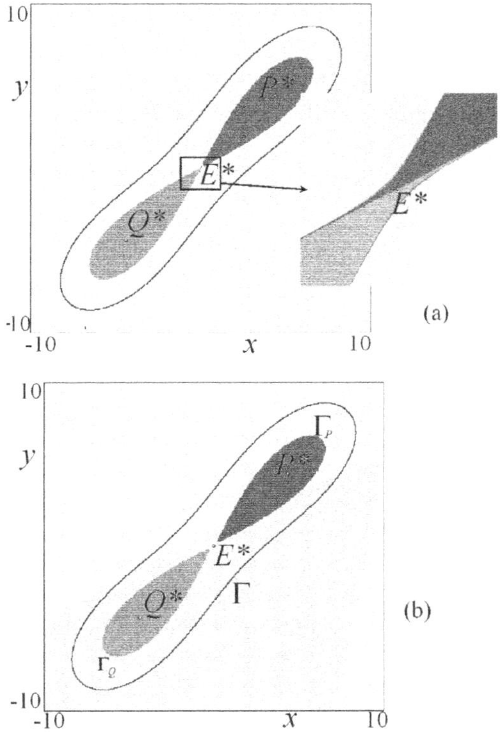

Figure 5: (a) $\alpha = 1.568; c_2 = 0.98$: *The repelling curve* $\widetilde{\Gamma}$ *shrinks in the proximity of* E^*. (b) $\alpha = 1.57; c_2 = 0.98$: $\widetilde{\Gamma}$ *is splitted into two repelling closed curves.*

This means that the points of the unstable manifold of E^* no longer reach the two equilibria but converge to Γ. This change in the asymptotic behaviour of $W^U(E^*)$ proves that a global bifurcation has occurred, involving both the unstable branches of the saddle E^*. Indeed in the phase portrait of Fig.5b we can observe the splitting of $\widetilde{\Gamma}$ into two repelling closed curves, Γ_P and Γ_Q, each one bounding the basin of the corresponding fixed point. These two repelling closed curves are the α-limit sets of the points of the two branches ω_1 and ω_2 of the stable set $W^S(E^*)$, which have modified their behavior as well. Then we deduce that when the parameter α ranges from 1.568 to 1.57, a homoclinic bifurcation of E^* occurs, whose effect is the transition from one "large" repelling closed curve, basin boundary of the attracting set $\{P^*, Q^*\}$, to two "small" repelling closed curves, basin boundaries of $\boldsymbol{B}(P^*)$ and $\boldsymbol{B}(Q^*)$ respectively. This situation has been classified as *double homoclinic loop* in Chapter 1, since it involves both the branches of the stable and unstable sets of E^*: Its evolution, qualitatively described in Section 1.9 of that Chapter, is represented in Fig.6, where some enlargements of the phase space as well as of the stable and unstable sets of E^* are shown.

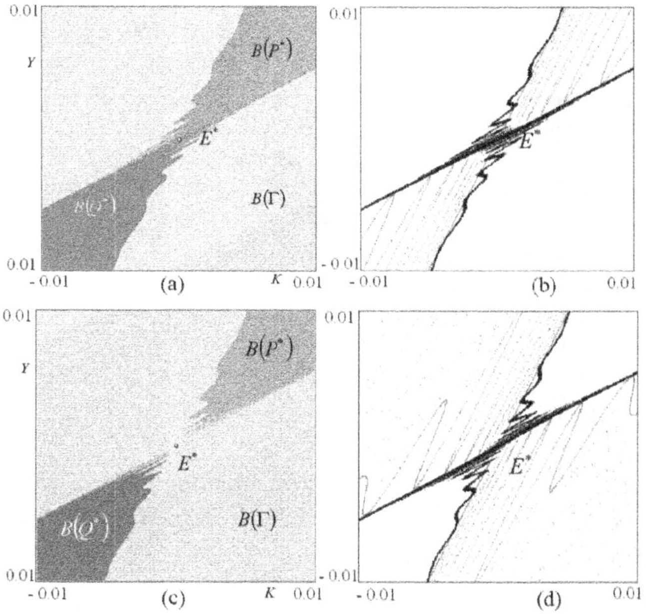

Figure 6: (a) $\alpha = 1.56855; c_2 = 0.98$: *Enlargement of the basins of attraction in the proximity of* E^*. (b) $\alpha = 1.56855; c_2 = 0.98$: *Stable (black) and unstable (gray) manifolds of* E^* *at the first tangency.* (c) $\alpha = 1.56855051; c_2 = 0.98$: *Enlargement of the basins of attraction in the proximity of* E^*. (d) $\alpha = 1.56855051; c_2 = 0.98$: *Stable (black) and unstable (gray) manifolds of* E^* *at the second tangency.*

The first homoclinic tangency is shown in Fig.6a,b, obtained at $\alpha = 1.56855$: The branch α_1 of $W^U(E^*)$ converges to P^* and it is completely contained in its basin of attraction; the same is true for α_2 with respect to the fixed point Q^*. The stable branches have a complex structure: The repelling closed curve Γ is replaced by a strange repellor, generated at the tangency and separating the basins of $\{P^*, Q^*\}$ and Γ. After the transversal crossing of $W^S(E^*)$ and $W^U(E^*)$, at which more and more homoclinic points of E^* are created, the second homoclinic tangency occurs at $\alpha = 1.5685501$, as shown in Fig.6c,d, and closes the tangle. The homoclinic points of E^* disappear as well as the chaotic repellor, leaving the two disjoint curves Γ_P and Γ_Q as boundaries of the basins of attraction of P^* and Q^*, respectively. After the homoclinic tangle both the branches of $W^U(E^*)$ converge to the attracting closed curve Γ and those of the stable set $W^S(E^*)$ come from the repelling closed curves Γ_P and Γ_Q.

A different illustration of this homoclinic tangle, occurring in a very narrow range of the parameter α, is proposed in Fig.7, where we show the as-

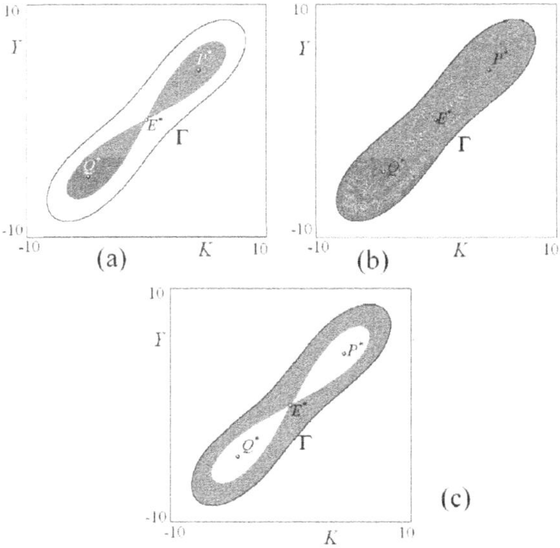

Figure 7: *The asymptotic behaviour of the unstable manifold of E^* at* (a) $\alpha = 1.56855; c_2 = 0.98$. (b) $\alpha = 1.5685503; c_2 = 0.98$. (c) $\alpha = 1.5685501; c_2 = 0.98$.

ymptotic behavior of the whole unstable set of the saddle E^*. In Fig.7a, obtained at the same parameter value as Fig.6a corresponding to the first homoclinic tangency, the points of $W^U(E^*)$ converge to the two equilibria, forming an eight-shaped structure; then, in fig.7b the unstable set $W^U(E^*)$ enters the basin of attraction of the attracting closed curve Γ as well as that of the attracting set $\{P^*, Q^*\}$: The separator of the three basins of attraction is a chaotic repellor, associated with the infinitely many periodic points existing close to the homoclinic trajectories. As α is further increased, more and more points of $W^U(E^*)$ converge to Γ until at the second homoclinic tangency, shown in Fig.7c, no points of the unstable set converge to the two stable foci.

As the parameter α further increases, the two repelling closed curves Γ_P and Γ_Q become smaller and smaller, until a new bifurcation value $\alpha = \widetilde{\alpha}_N$ is reached at which a Neimark subcritical bifurcation occurs: The two repelling closed curves collapse in P^* and Q^* respectively and at $\alpha > \widetilde{\alpha}_N$ the attracting closed curve Γ is the unique surviving attractor, since the two fixed points become unstable foci.

8.4.2 Coexistence of Cyclical and Quasi-Cyclical Trajectories and Homoclinic Loop of a Saddle Cycle

After the subcritical Neimark bifurcation of P^* and Q^*, the saddle E^* coexists with two repelling foci, from which the stable set $W^S(E^*)$ comes. The points of the unstable manifold $W^U(E^*)$ converges to the attracting closed curve Γ surrounding the three unstable fixed points.

This situation persists until at a certain value of α, say α_{sn}, a saddle-node bifurcation occurs, causing the appearance of two cycles of period 8, a saddle, S, and a stable node, C, which turns into a stable focus cycle immediately after. The two cycles are located outside the attracting closed curve and, as α increases from α_{sn}, a larger and larger portion of trajectories exhibits period-8 oscillations, as shown in Fig.8a, where the basins of attraction of the two attractors are represented in different gray tones. The points close to the exogenous equilibrium E^* still give rise to quasi-periodic fluctuations.

The phase portrait shown in Fig. 8b is completely different: Quasi-periodic and period-8 trajectories still coexist, but now the attracting closed curve $\widetilde{\Gamma}$ surrounds the stable focus cycle C and the majority of the trajectories exhibit quasi-periodic motion. Moreover the long run behaviour of trajectories starting in the area close to E^* is no longer predictable, since a small shock on them may have strong consequences given the many and many convolution of the separatrix of the two basins in this area.

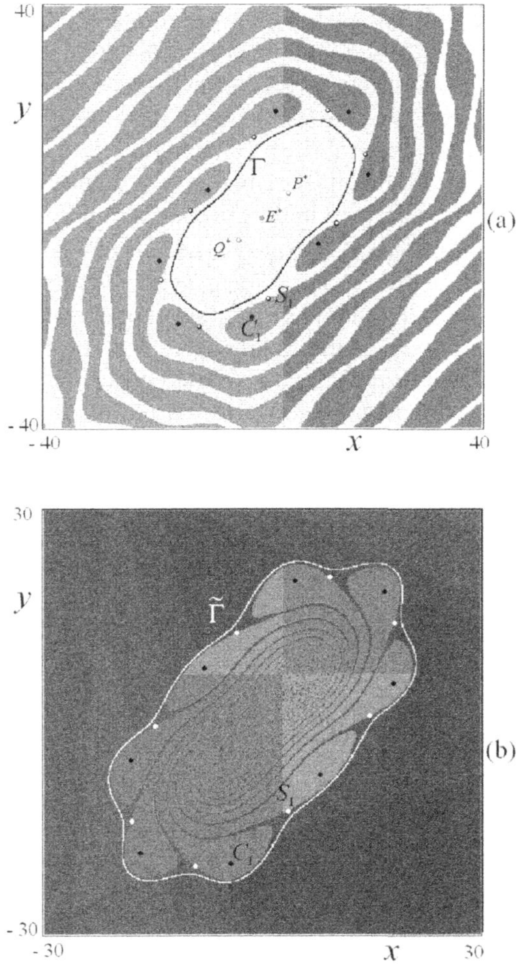

Figure 8: (a) $\alpha = 1.7; c_2 = 0.98$: *The attracting curve* Γ *coexists with a stable cycle* C *of period 8 and a saddle cycle* S *of the same period.* (b) $\alpha = 1.745; c_2 = 0.98$: *A new curve* $\widehat{\Gamma}$ *surrounds the attracting period 8 cycle.*

The aim of this subsection is to explain the global mechanisms which cause this important modification in the basin structures, transforming an attracting closed curve, coexisting with a stable cycle external to it, into a larger one, surrounding the stable cycle. As we shall see, the global bifurcation involved in this transition is of the same type of those described in Section 1.8, involving the invariant manifolds of the saddle cycle 8. Moreover, despite the different dynamic situation described here, the bifurcation mechanisms are similar to the ones analyzed in the previous section.

Let us start from Fig.8a, obtained at $\alpha = 1.7 > \alpha_{sn}$: Two attractors exist, the closed curve Γ and a focus cycle C, surrounding the curve, while the two basins, $\boldsymbol{B}(C)$ and $\boldsymbol{B}(\Gamma)$, are separated by the stable manifold $W^S(S) = \omega_1 \cup \omega_2$ of the saddle cycle S. The branches of the unstable one $W^U(S)$ reach the attracting closed curve (α_1) and the stable focus cycle (α_2). As the parameter α is increased, the two branches ω_1 and α_1 start to oscillate until a homoclinic tangency occurs. More precisely, at

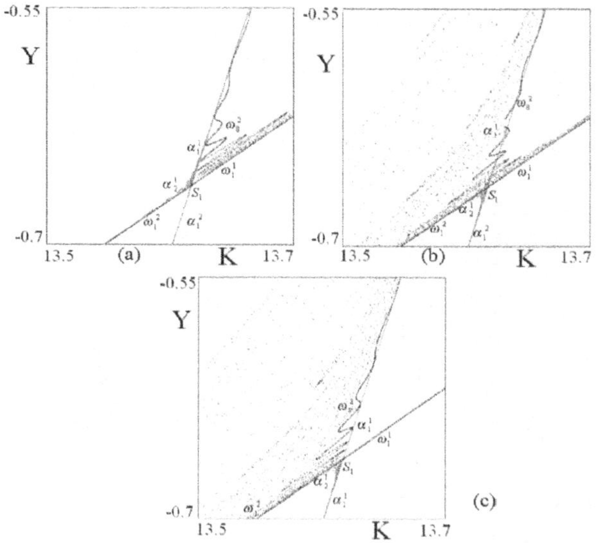

Figure 9: *Heteroclinic tangle involving the inner branches of stable and unstable manifolds of the cycle* S. (a) $\alpha = 1.7102384; c_2 = 0.98$: *First homoclinic tangency.* (b) $\alpha = 1.7102386; c_2 = 0.98$: *Transversal crossing.* (c) $\alpha = 1.7102387; c_2 = 0.98$: *Second homoclinic tangency.*

$\alpha = 1.7102384$ the stable branch $\alpha_{1,i}$ of the periodic point S_i has a tangential contact with the unstable branch $\omega_{1,j}$ of a different periodic point S_j (see Fig.9a) and this occurs cyclically for all the periodic points of the saddle S. This contact is the starting point of a heteroclinic tangle, which develops into a transversal crossing of the involved inner branches (Fig.9b) and closes at $\alpha = 1.7102387$, when a second cyclical homoclinic tangency occurs (Fig.9c). Observe that at the end of the heteroclinic tangle, the two branches α_1 and ω_1 have inverted they reciprocal position with respect to that of Fig.9a.

Approaching the heteroclinic tangle, the curve Γ exhibits more and more oscillations, as in Fig.10a obtained at the same parameter values of Fig.9a,

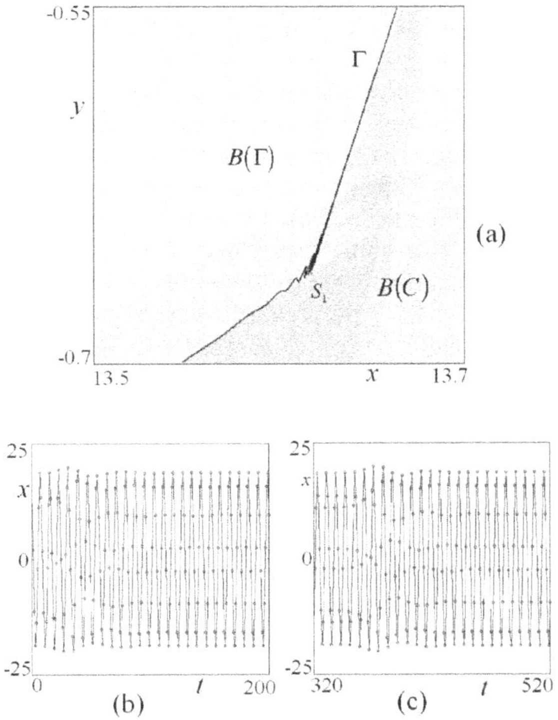

Figure 10: $\alpha = 1.7102384; c_2 = 0.98$. (a) *Oscillations of the attracting closed curve* Γ. (b-c) $\alpha = 1.7102386; c_2 = 0.98$: *Two different trajectories with initial conditions* (13.7,-0.7) *and* (13.5,-0.6) *respectively.*

before coming into resonance with the cycle, forming an attracting set with the saddle S and the focus cycle C, with C the attractor within it. Moreover during the tangle a chaotic repellor $\mathcal{R}$ is created in the area occupied by the transversal crossing of the two manifolds: The existence of $\mathcal{R}$ has important effects on the long run behaviour of the trajectories, as we can observe in Figs.10b,c, obtained at the same value of Fig.9b.

In such figures, two trajectories of the variable x are represented versus time and both converge to the cycle of period 8: In Fig.10b only a few iterations are needed to reach the period 8 oscillations whereas in Fig.10c a longer transient part exists (note that the first 320 iterations have been dropped in Fig.10c). This difference in the transient part is due to the initial conditions: The one of Fig.10c is taken in the area occupied by the chaotic repellor, and the existence of the infinitely many unstable cycle causes its particular behavior.

The effects of the observed heteroclinic tangle are illustrated in Fig.11: The attracting closed curve Γ has disappeared, leaving the focus cycle C as unique attractor (Fig.11b). More precisely, Γ has been replaced by the heteroclinic connection of the periodic points of the cycles, made up by the unstable manifold of the saddle S which reach the periodic points of the focus cycle (Fig.11a).With a similar mechanism the final situation of Fig.8b is obtained. Indeed, increasing α the two outer branches α_2 and ω_2 approach each other, oscillating. This is the prelude to a new heteroclinic tangle, again occurring in a very small range of the parameter α: The first tangential contact between the unstable branch $\alpha_{2,i}$ of the periodic point S_i and the stable branch $\omega_{2,j}$ of a different periodic point S_j is followed by their transversal crossing and then by the homoclinic tangency occurring at the opposite side with respect to the previous one (as illustrated in Fig.12a,b,c). A chaotic repellor appears at the first homoclinic tangency, persists during the transversal crossing phase and disappears at the closure of the tangle: Consequently, the trajectories starting close to it have a longer transient part before converging to the period 8 cycle. But the main effect of this global bifurcation is the appearance of an attracting closed curve $\widetilde{\Gamma}$, which replaces the heteroclinic connection between the periodic points of the cycles S and C. As soon as it has appeared, it exhibits many oscillations, as shown in Fig.13 obtained at the same parameter value as in Fig.12c, and surrounds the periodic points of the attracting cycle. As α increases, $\widetilde{\Gamma}$ becomes smoother and smoother reaching the shape of Fig.8b.

In order to discuss the results of our numerical analysis carried out in the last two sections, let us first remark that the original Kaldor's (1940) busi-

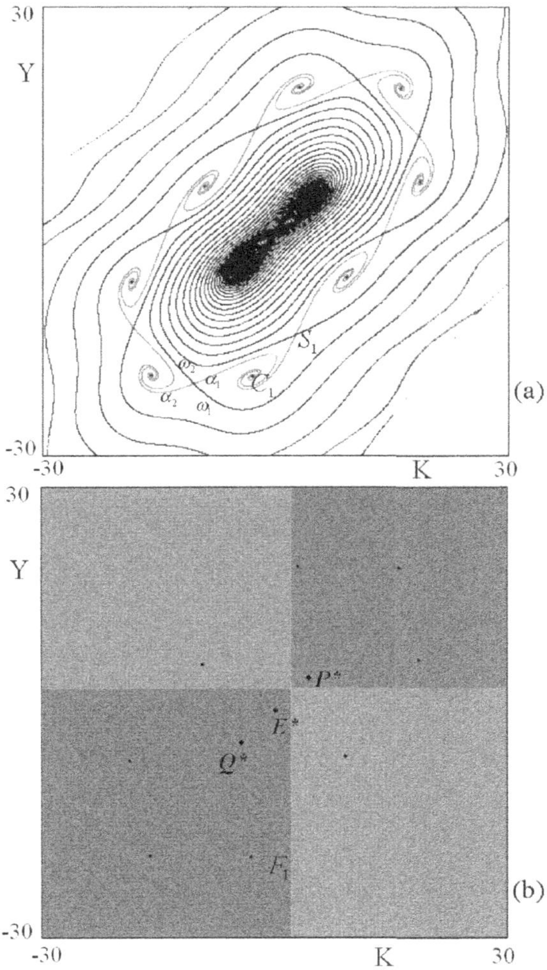

Figure 11: $\alpha = 1.72; c_2 = 0.98$: (a) *Heteroclinic connection made up by the unstable manifold of the saddle cycle S.* (b) *The period 8 focus cycle C is the unique attractor.*

ness cycle model - in spite of its simplicity and though it has been criticized on a number of grounds - is still present in modern treatments of business cycle theory and continues to stimulate pedagogical and methodological research (see e.g. Gabisch & Lorenz (1989)); such research is mainly oriented

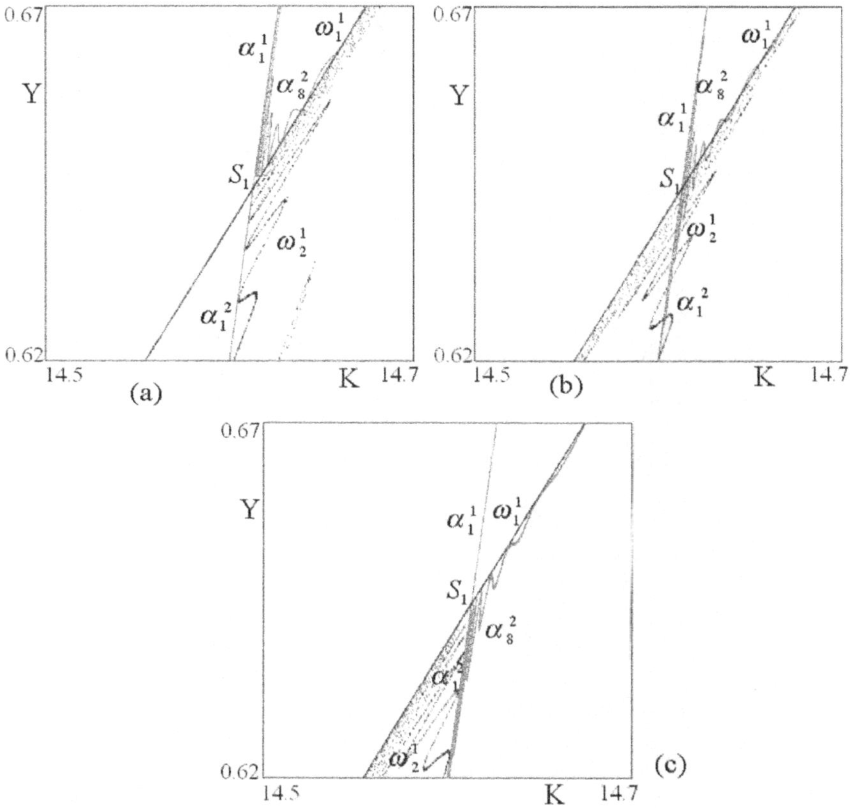

Figure 12: *Heteroclinic tangle involving the outer branches of stable and unstable manifolds of the cycle S.* (a) $\alpha = 1.74265991; c_2 = 0.98$: *First homoclinic tangency.* (b) $\alpha = 1.74266; c_2 = 0.98$: *Transversal crossing.* (c) $\alpha = 1.742660085; c_2 = 0.98$: *Second homoclinic tangency.*

to achieve a deeper understanding of the full range of dynamic outcomes compatible with the key qualitative assumptions of the model. Our contribution belongs to this stream of research, and focuses on particular phase-space transitions that determine two characteristic dynamic scenarios:

(i) the coexistence of two stable steady states and a stable closed curve, and the qualitative changes of their basins of attraction, in a regime of parameters where the exogenous, "normal" equilibrium is unstable (a saddle point);

(ii) the change of size and location of an attracting invariant curve with respect to a coexisting stable periodic orbit, in a parameter range where the map admits three unstable equilibria.

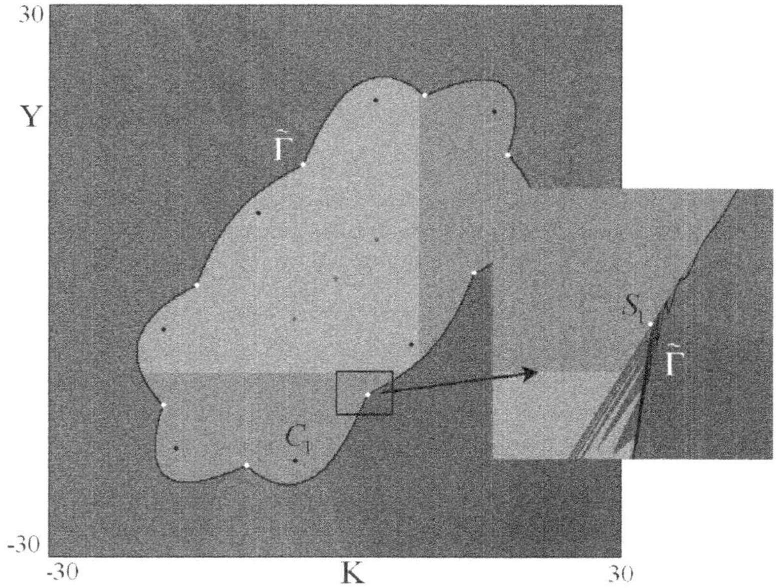

Figure 13: $\alpha = 1.742660085; c_2 = 0.98$: *The oscillations of the curve* $\widetilde{\Gamma}$ *at its appearance.*

The main insight gained from our numerical and graphical investigation of such scenarios is that - though these phenomena look very different from each other at first sight - they are ultimately determined by the same kind of behavior of the stable and unstable set of the saddle point (in the first case), or of a saddle cycle (in the second case). Following the qualitative changes of stable and unstable manifolds closely, we have been able to detect numerically particular ranges of the parameter where transversal intersections and homoclinic tangles exist, which proves the existence of chaotic behavior, and explains the complex structures of the basins of attraction in those particular situations. We remark once again that very similar dynamic phenomena have been detected also in a quite different version of the Kaldor model [Agliari *et al.* (2005b)], for plausible values of the parameters: This leads us to conjecture that such kinds of dynamic behavior might be ultimately related to the essential qualitative features of the original Kaldor model.

References

Agliari, A., 2001, "Global bifurcations in the basins of attraction in noninvertible maps and economic applications", *Nonlinear Analysis* 47, pp. 5241-5252.

Agliari, A., Bischi, G.I., Dieci, R., and Gardini, L., 2005a, "Global bifurcations of closed invariant curves in two-dimensional maps: A computer assisted study", *International Journal of Bifurcation and Chaos* 15, pp. 1285-1328.

Agliari, A., Bischi, G.I., and Gardini, L., 2002, "Some methods for the Global Analysis of Dynamic Games represented by Noninvertible Maps", Chapter 3 in *Oligopoly and Complex Dynamics: Tools & Models*, T. Puu and I. Sushko (eds.), Springer Verlag

Agliari, A., Dieci, R., and Gardini, L., 2005b, "Homoclinic tangles in a Kaldor-like business cycle model", *Journal of Economic Behavior & Organization*, to appear.

Agliari, A., Gardini, L., Delli Gatti, D., and Gallegati, M., 2000, "Global dynamics in a nonlinear model for the equity ratio", *Chaos, Solitons and Fractals* 11, pp. 961-985,

Bischi, G.I., Dieci, R., Rodano, G., and Saltari, E., 2001, "Multiple attractors and global bifurcations in a Kaldor-type business cycle model", *Journal of Evolutionary Economics* 11, pp. 527-554.

Bischi, G.I., and Kopel, M., 2001, "Equilibrium Selection in a Nonlinear Duopoly Game with Adaptive Expectations", *Journal of Economic Behavior and Organization* 46/1, pp. 73-100.

Dana, R.A., and Malgrange, P., 1984, "The dynamics of a discrete version of a growth cycle model", in *Analyzing the structure of economic models*, J.P. Ancot (Ed.), The Hague: Martinus Nijhoff, pp. 205-222.

Dieci R., Bischi, G.I., and Gardini, L., 2001, "Multistability and role of noninvertibility in a discrete-time business cycle model", *Central European Journal of Operation Research* 9, pp. 71-96.

Dohtani, A., Misawa, T., Inaba, T., Yokoo, M., and Owase, T., 1996, "Chaos, complex transients and noise: Illustration with a Kaldor model", *Chaos Solitons & Fractals* 7, pp. 2157-2174.

Gabisch, G., and Lorenz, H.W., 1989, *Business Cycle Theory*, 2nd edition, Springer-Verlag, New York.

Gallegati, M., and Stiglitz, J.E., 1993, "Stochastic and deterministic fluctuations in a nonlinear model with equity rationing", *Giornale degli Economisti e Annali di Economia* Anno LI (Nuova Serie) - Fasc. 1/4, pp. 97-108.

Grasman, J., and Wentzel, J.J., 1994, "Coexistence of a limit cycle and an equilibrium in a Kaldor's business cycle model and its consequences", *Journal of Economic Behavior and Organization* 24, pp. 369-377.

Gumowski, I., and Mira, C., 1980, *Dynamique Chaotique*, Cepadues Ed., Toulouse.

Herrmann, R., 1985, "Stability and chaos in a Kaldor-type model", DP22, Department of Economics, University of Gottingen.

Kaldor, N., 1940, "A model of the Trade Cycle", *Economic Journal* 50, pp.78-92, reprinted in *Essays on Economic Stability and Growth*, London, Duckworth, 1964, pp. 177-192.

Lorenz, H.W., 1992, "Multiple attractors, Complex Basin Boundaries, and Transient Motion in Deterministic Economic Systems", in *Dynamic Economic Models and Optimal Control*, G. Feichtinger (Ed.), North-Holland, Amsterdam, pp. 411-430

Lorenz, H.W., 1993, *Nonlinear Dynamical Economics and Chaotic Motion*, Second Edition, Springer-Verlag, New York.

Medio, A., and Lines, M., 2001, *Nonlinear Dynamics*, Cambridge University Press, Cambridge (UK).

Mira, C., Gardini, L., Barugola, A., and Cathala, J.C., 1996, *Chaotic Dynamics in Two-dimensional Noninvertible Map*, World Scientific, Singapore.

9 Expectations and the Multiplier-Accelerator Model

Marji Lines and Frank Westerhoff

9.1 Introduction

In this paper we investigate how a simple expectations mechanism modifies the basic dynamical structure of the multiplier-accelerator model due to Samuelson (1939). Consumption depends on the expected value of present income rather than lagged income. National income is determined as a nonlinear mix of extrapolative and reverting expectations formation rules (prototypical predictors used in recent literature on financial markets). The total level of economic activity depends endogenously on the proportion of agents using the predictors.

The very simplicity of Samuelson's descriptive macroeconomic model makes it an excellent candidate for studying the effects of introducing expectations without changing the emphasis of the formalization. That is, agents' expectations are not part of an optimization problem and the resulting framework remains in the class of descriptive models. (For bibliographical references of past and recent extensions to Samuelson's model see Westerhoff (2005) and the bibliographies in other chapters of this volume.)

The expectations hypotheses follow in the style of Kaldor. Some destabilizing force exists for values near the equilibrium but the economy neither explodes nor contracts indefinitely due to a global stabilizing mechanism that is activated when the economy deviates too much from its equilibrium. These interacting forces permit a greater variety of attracting sets including point equilibria above and below the (unique) Samuelsonian equilibrium and closed curves on which lie both quasiperiodic and periodic cycles. Moreover, under realistic values for the multiplier and coefficient of acceleration, a larger area of the parameter space is characterized by stable limit sets and much of that is dominated by solutions with persistent fluctuations.

The remainder of the paper is organized as follows. Section 2 reconsiders Samuelson's business cycle model. In section 3, we discuss the hypotheses introduced to describe expectations formation and aggregation rules. In section 4 we study the properties of the model using the local linear approximation. In section 5 we use analysis and numerical simulations to study the global properties of the model. In section 6 conclusions are offered.

9.2 The Multiplier and the Accelerator

Samuelson's seminal model incorporates the Keynesian multiplier, a multiplicative factor that relates expenditures to national income and the accelerator principle whereby induced investment is proportional to increases in consumption. An increase in investment therefore leads to an increase in national income and consumption (via the multiplier effect) which in turn raises investment (via the accelerator process). This feedback mechanism repeats itself and may generate an oscillatory behavior of output. It may also lead to explosive oscillation, monotonic convergence to an equilibrium point or monotonic divergence, depending on the values of the marginal propensity to consume and the acceleration coefficient (See Gandolfo 1996 for a complete treatment of the dynamics over parameter space).

The assumptions are well-known. Consumption in period t depends on national income in period $t-1$

$$C_t = bY_{t-1} \qquad 0 < b < 1 \tag{1}$$

where b is the propensity to consume out of previous period income. Investment is partly autonomous and independent of the business cycle, denoted I_a, and partly induced, proportional to changes in consumption with acceleration coefficient, k:

$$I_t = I_a + k(C_t - C_{t-1}) \qquad k > 0. \tag{2}$$

The equilibrium condition for a closed economy is

$$Y_t = C_t + I_t. \tag{3}$$

Combining (1), (2) and (3), we obtain a second-order linear difference equation, in the income variable:

$$Y_t = I_a + b(1+k)Y_{t-1} - bkY_{t-2}. \tag{4}$$

That is, current national income depends on autonomous investment and on the output of the previous two periods. The fixed point of (4), the long-run equilibrium output, is determined as

$$\bar{Y} = \frac{1}{1-b} I_a \tag{5}$$

with $1/(1-b)$ the multiplier. It follows from (1) and (2) that the other equilibrium values are $\bar{C} = b\bar{Y}$ and $\bar{I} = I_a$. It can be shown that stability of the fixed point requires

$$b < \frac{1}{k}. \tag{6}$$

It can also be shown that no improper oscillations occur and that the flutter boundary, between monotonic and oscillatory solutions, is $b = 4k/(1+k)^2$. With only two parameters the dynamics over parameter space are easily determined. Damped oscillations occur only in the area with $b < 1/k$ and $b < 4k/(1+k)^2$. In that case temporary business cycles arise due to the interplay of the multiplier and the accelerator, increased investment increases output which, in turn, induces increased investment.

A major criticism of linear business cycle theory is that changes in economic activity either die out or explode (persistent cycles only occur for a nongeneric boundary case). In reaction to this deficiency the nonlinear theory of business cycle has developed. In particular, in the seminal work of Hicks (1950) the evolution of an otherwise explosive output path was limited by proposing upper and lower bounds for investment, so-called ceilings and floors. These simple frameworks of Samuelson and Hicks are still used as workhorses to study new additional elements that may stimulate business cycles (see, besides the current monograph, Hommes 1995 and Puu, et al. 2004).

9.3 Expectations

As argued by Simon (1955), economic agents are boundedly rational in the sense that they lack knowledge and computational power to derive fully optimal actions. Instead, they tend to use simple heuristics which have proven to be useful in the past (Kahneman, Slovic and Tversky 1986). Survey studies reveal that agents typically use a mix of extrapolative and reverting expectation formation rules to forecast economic variables (Ito 1990, Takagi 1991). Similar results are observed in asset pricing experiments. For instance, Smith (1991) and Sonnemans et al. (2004) report that financial market participants typically extrapolate past price trends or expect a reversion of the price towards its long-run equilibrium value. Indeed, the dynamics of group expectations have successfully been modeled for financial markets. Contributions by Day and Huang (1990), Kirman (1993), de Grauwe et al. (1993), Brock and Hommes (1998) or Lux and Marchesi (2000) demonstrate that interactions between heterogeneous agents who rely on heuristic forecasting rules may cause complex financial market dynamics, as observed in actual markets.

Our goal is to investigate the importance of expectations for the variability of output. Our main modification of Samuleson's model is that the agents' consumption depends on their expected current income (and not on their past realized income). Note that Flieth and Foster (2002) and Hohnisch et al. (2005) model socioeconomic interactions between heterogeneous agents to explain the evolution of business confidence indicators. Both papers are able to replicate typical patterns in the German business-climate index (the so-called Ifo index), yet refrain from establishing a link between expectations and economic activity. We believe, however, that mass psychology, expressed via expectations and visible in business confidence indicators, is a major factor that may cause swings in national income. For example, new era thinking may lead to optimistic self-fulfilling prophecies (e.g. the New Economy hype) while general pessimism may cause economic slumps (Shiller 2000).

Then, with respect to Samuelson's hypothesis that consumption depends on last period's income (1), we assume that consumption depends on the expected value of current income, which is based on information available last period:

$$C_t = bE_{t-1}[Y_t] \tag{7}$$

The aggregate expectation $E_{t-1}[Y_t]$ is formed as a weighted average of extrapolative (denoted 1) and reverting (denoted 2) expectations:

$$E_{t-1}[Y_t] = w_t E^1_{t-1}[Y_t] + (1 - w_t) E^2_{t-1}[Y_t] \quad 0 < w < 1. \tag{8}$$

Expectations are formed with reference to a "long-run" equilibrium which is taken to be the fixed point of Samuelson's linear model, denoted in what follows as $\mathcal{Y} = I_a/(1-b)$. In the extrapolative expectation, or trend, formation rule, agents either optimistically believe in a boom or pessimistically expect a downturn. Such expectations are formalized as

$$E^1_{t-1}[Y_t] = Y_{t-1} + \mu_1(Y_{t-1} - \mathcal{Y}) \quad \mu_1 > 0. \tag{9}$$

If output is above (below) its long-run equilibrium value, $\mathcal{Y}$, people think that the economy is in a prosperous (depressed) state and thus predict that national income will remain high (low) (a similar assumption has been applied by Day and Huang 1990).

Equilibrium-reverting expectations are formed as

$$E^2_{t-1}[Y_t] = Y_{t-1} + \mu_2(\mathcal{Y} - Y_{t-1}) \qquad 0 < \mu_2 < 1 \tag{10}$$

where μ_2 captures the agents' expected adjustment speed of the output towards its long-run equilibrium value.

The more the economy deviates from $\mathcal{Y}$, the less weight the agents put on extrapolative expectations. Agents believe that extreme economic conditions are not sustainable. Formally, the relative impact of the extrapolative rule depends on the deviation of income from equilibrium at the time that expectations are formed:

$$w_t = \frac{1}{1 + \left(\gamma\left(\frac{Y_{t-1} - \mathcal{Y}}{\mathcal{Y}}\right)\right)^2} \qquad \gamma > 0 \tag{11}$$

with γ as a scale factor. The percentage gap is typically less than one which, when squared, results in a small number. Setting $\gamma > 1$ increases the weight factor, resulting in a more realistic distribution between extrapolative and equilibrium-reverting expectations. (For example, if $\gamma = 10$ and the percentage gap is 10%, the proportion of agents using E^1 is 50%; the proportion is 99% for $\gamma = 1$.) Extrapolative and reverting expectations are linear functions of the previous level of national income, but the expectation operator, combining the heterogeneous expectations through a nonlinear weighting function, is not. In Figure 1 w_t and $1 - w_t$, the weights given to each type of expectation are plotted against national income ($\gamma = 10$, $b = 0.8$, $\mathcal{Y} = 5000$). Close to equilibrium the trend-following expectation dominates (and at $Y_t = \mathcal{Y}$, $w_t = 1$), acting as a destabilizing force for any small deviation from the long-run equilibrium. Expectations are equally distributed (with $\gamma = 10$) at a 10% gap between actual and long-run values of income. At further distances from $\mathcal{Y}$ the reverting expectation dominates, acting as a global stabilizing force.

Other weighting functions and other basic types of expectation formation rules can be found in, e.g., Brock and Hommes (1997, 1998). The former paper explores the expectation formation of heterogeneous producers in cobweb markets while the latter paper investigates the selection of forecasting rules among financial market participants. However, the essential idea is the same. For similar states of the current economy (market) agents have differing expectations about the future state, these expectations feed-back through the economy (market), but the aggregate expected value is not necessarily equal to the (deterministic) value of that future state. It is also typically assumed that extremes will be considered unsustainable, providing a global mechanism for stability. This new approach to modeling how agents incorporate future uncertainty in their decision-making process breaks with both the rational expectations hypothesis and with earlier homogeneous, aggregate expectation hypotheses that R.E. criticized. Of course, assumptions about agent's expectations must be coherent with the particular context, but we argue that for business cycle theory our approach may provide a reasonable alternative.

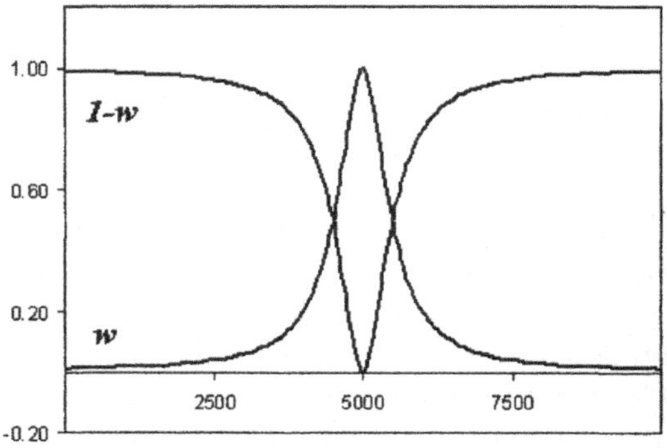

Figure 1: *Weights against national income: w extrapolative, $1-w$ reverting.*

Substituting (2) and (7) into (3) we derive the expectations version of (4) as

$$Y_t = I_a + b(1+k)E_{t-1}[Y_t] - bkE_{t-2}[Y_{t-1}] \tag{12}$$

Then using (8)-(11) we arrive at a second-order nonlinear difference equation $Y_t = f(Y_{t-1}, Y_{t-2})$. For the analysis we introduce an auxiliary variable $Z_t = Y_{t-1}$, deriving a first-order system in (Y_t, Z_t) (see the Appendix for full system and Jacobian)

$$\begin{aligned} Y_t &= I_a + b(1+k)E_{t-1}[Y_t] - bkE_{t-2}[Z_t] \\ Z_t &= Y_{t-1} \end{aligned} \tag{13}$$

with Jacobian matrix

$$J(Y,Z) = \begin{pmatrix} b(1+k)\frac{dE_{t-1}[Y_t]}{dY_{t-1}} & -bk\frac{dE_{t-2}[Z_t]}{dZ_{t-1}} \\ 1 & 0 \end{pmatrix}$$

9.4 Local Dynamics

In this section we consider fixed points and the conditions for which local stability is lost. It can be shown that the equilibrium value for Samuelson's multiplier-accelerator model is also an equilibrium for the modified model. At $\mathcal{Y}$ the trend followers are predicting perfectly, $w_1 = 1$ and the Jacobian, calculated at that value, simplifies to:

$$J(\mathcal{Y}) = \begin{pmatrix} b(1+k)(1+\mu_1) & -bk(1+\mu_1) \\ 1 & 0 \end{pmatrix} \tag{14}$$

with trace tr$J = b(1+k)(1+\mu_1)$ and determinant det$J = bk(1+\mu_1)$. We can use the stability conditions for a two-dimensional system to help understand how the equilibrium might lose its local stability:

$$\begin{aligned} 1 + \text{ tr } J(\mathcal{Y}) + \text{ det } J(\mathcal{Y}) &> 0 \quad (i) \\ 1 - \text{ tr } J(\mathcal{Y}) + \text{ det } J(\mathcal{Y}) &> 0 \quad (ii) \\ 1 - \text{ det } J(\mathcal{Y}) &> 0. \quad (iii) \end{aligned}$$

The first condition holds always and we should not expect to see flip bifurcations. The second condition and third conditions, which reduce to, respectively:

$$b < \frac{1}{1+\mu_1} \quad \text{and} \quad b < \frac{1}{k(1+\mu_1)} \tag{15}$$

are not necessarily satisfied, leaving open the possibility of both fold and Neimark-Sacker bifurcations. The parameter assumptions are simply that $\mu_1, k > 0$ and the binding inequality is condition (ii) if $k < 1$, condition (iii) if $k > 1$.

In Samuelson's linear model the stability conditions are satisfied always, except for the third which requires $b < 1/k$. In the linear case, of course, there is only one equilibrium set and it is a fixed point, so that when stability is lost the system itself is unstable. In the nonlinear case a fixed point may lose stability at the parameter value for which some other limit set becomes an attractor or there may be co-existing attractors which are limit sets for different collections of initial conditions. In the case of the Neimark-Sacker bifurcation, when the third condition is broken, global stability may continue in the form of an attractor which is a sequence of points lying on a closed curve. If attracting (and we see below that they are), these sequences represent endogenous fluctuations which are a generic feature of the dynamics (rather than the particular case of constant amplitude oscillations in Samuelson's model).

If the accelerator coefficient is less than unity, the breaking of the second condition leads to a pitchfork bifurcation, that is, as $\mathcal{Y}$ loses stability 2 new (stable) fixed points appear. These are determined by returning to the second order difference equation (12) which, setting $Y_{t-1} = Z_t = \bar{Y}$ becomes

$$\bar{Y} = \mathcal{Y} + \frac{b}{1-b}(\bar{Y} - \mathcal{Y})\big(\bar{w}(\mu_1 + \mu_2) - \mu_2\big) \tag{16}$$

with equilibrium weight

$$\bar{w} = \frac{\mathcal{Y}^2}{\mathcal{Y}^2 + \gamma^2(\bar{Y} - \mathcal{Y})^2}.$$

Expanding and simplifying (16) gives

$$(\bar{Y} - \mathcal{Y})^2 = \frac{\mathcal{Y}^2\big(b(1+\mu_1) - 1\big)}{\gamma^2\big(b(\mu_2 - 1) + 1\big)}. \tag{17}$$

These two fixed points are complex-valued for $b < 1/(1+\mu_1)$ and become real and equal in value to $\mathcal{Y}$ at the critical value $b = 1/(1+\mu_1)$. For $b > 1/(1+\mu_1)$ there are two positive, real equilibria determined by (17), one larger and one smaller than $\mathcal{Y}$, respectively $\bar{Y}_1$, $\bar{Y}_2$, each attracting over a given basin, a situation of bi-stability. With these basics in mind we now turn to a study of the global dynamics using a combination of analysis and numerical simulations.

9.5 Global Dynamics

Consider first a comparison of the dynamics over the parameter space (k, b). In Figure 2, left, Samuelson's linear model is characterized by a single fixed point, stable to the left of the stability frontier $b = 1/k$, unstable to the right. At the boundary crossing the fixed point is a focus, adjacent to the left are damped oscillations (in gray), adjacent to the right explosive fluctuations (in black). The existence of any kind of persistent fluctuations is guaranteed only for those combinations of parameter values that are on the stability frontier itself, that is for $bk = 1$.

In Figure 2, right, we have the same parameter space for the expectations version of the multiplier-accelerator with standard constellation $\mu_1 = \mu_2 = 0.5$, $I_a = 1000$, $\gamma = 10$, $(Y_0, Z_0) = (4000, 4000)$ and infinity set at 10^{10}, transients at 5000 with maximal period 24 and precision epsilon set at 0.01. This and all following plots were produced with the open-source software iDMC - Copyright Marji Lines and Alfredo Medio, available at www.dss.uniud.it/nonlinear.

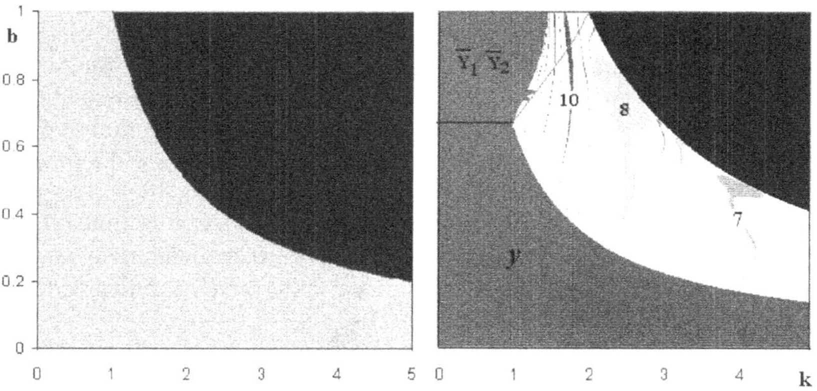

Figure 2: *Parameter space* (k, b)*: left, linear model; right, with expectations.*

The black area again represents the lack of any attracting finite limit set, and the gray area on the left again represents stable fixed points. The lighter area in the middle section is characterized by quasi-periodic or high-order periodic fluctuations, in white, and cycles of the given periods in grays. For both the original and the expectation models higher values of the multiplier and the accelerator lead to instability. An economy with high demand resulting from spending most of its income on consumption encourages entrepreneurs to invest in order to keep up the supply of these goods and services. As a consequence the economy heats up. The acceleration coefficient is a reaction parameter, how strongly investment responds to changes in demand. It can also be interpreted as the capital-output ratio, how much new capital will be necessary to produce the increased output. When Samuelson was modeling the interaction between the multiplier analysis and the principle of acceleration in the late thirties the propensity to consume was much lower (and not only due to the Great Depression but also to spending habits), as was the capital-output ratio. Consumption out of income in the United States today has almost reached the upper bound of $b = 1$, creating growth not only in the US but in the economies that supply it with goods and services such as China and India. Of course there are other issues involved, but if these interactions are fundamental and their dynamics are well-approximated by the models, the sustainability of the current situation in the U.S. is doubtful.

A noticeable difference in the model dynamics is that the area of attractors is much larger for the expectations version and that there is a significant area of attractors characterized by fluctuations (a pertinent issue for business cycle models). On the other hand, the area for which $\mathcal{Y}$ is stable (below the second condition, the line $b = 0.6\bar{6}$, and to the left of the third condition, $b = 0.6\bar{6}/k_{ns}$) is smaller than that of Samuelson's model. In both models there is some trade-off between the accelerator coefficient and the propensity to consume out of income for maintaining stability, and high values are de-stabilizing for both. The extreme simplicity of the dynamics in the linear version ($\mathcal{Y}$ is stable or unstable) is replaced by more challenging dynamics, but $\mathcal{Y}$ (through its stable and unstable manifolds) remains crucial to their explanation.

For $b < 0.6\bar{6}$ stability of $\mathcal{Y}$ is lost through a Neimark-Sacker bifurcation. Fixing b a constant and increasing k so as to cross through the curve of the stability frontier at $b_{ns} = 0.6\bar{6}/k$, we have $\mathcal{Y}$ changing from a stable focus to an unstable focus as, simultaneously, an invariant closed curve is created (denoted, generically, as Γ). As k is further increased the periodic or quasiperiodic limit sets on Γ continue to be attracting over a large interval until the stability frontier for Γ is reached, after which no attractors exist.

For $b \in (0.6\bar{6}, 1)$, stability of $\mathcal{Y}$ is lost through a pitchfork bifurcation at the critical value $b_p = 0.6\bar{6}$ which has been traced in Figure 2, right to separate the subspace characterized by stable fixed point $\mathcal{Y}$ from that characterized by stable fixed points $\bar{Y}_1, \bar{Y}_2$. The bifurcation scenario moving right from the upper sub-space is more relevant for economics as a typical range for the propensity to consume out of expected income is $b \in (0.75, 1)$. For small k there are the two co-existing fixed points which are attractors, each with its own basin of attraction, $B(\bar{Y}_1)$, $B(\bar{Y}_2)$ (that is, initial conditions determine on which point the trajectory comes to rest). These lose stability as k is increased and a region of periodic or quasiperiodic attractors gives way to no attractors at all for larger values of the acceleration coefficient.

Using the standard constellation the (k, b) combination at which $\bar{Y}_1$ and $\bar{Y}_2$ lose stability due to a Neimark- Sacker bifurcation can be calculated as $k(1.5b - 3 + \frac{2}{b}) = 1$. These critical values are represented in Figure 2, right, by the curve extending from $(1, 0.66\bar{7})$ to $(2, 1)$.

Let $b = 0.8$. Given the standard parameter values, local properties of the fixed points can be calculated. First, $\mathcal{Y}$ is a saddle point and remains so for at least up to $k = 5$, let $\lambda_1 > 1$ and $\lambda_2 < 1$. The two equilibria of the pitchfork bifurcation also exist and we have, increasing from $k = 0$: $\bar{Y}_1, \bar{Y}_2$ are stable nodes, then (near $k = 0.3$) they become stable foci. These fixed points lose stability through a Neimark-Sacker bifurcation at $k = 1/b$, $\Phi \approx 1.43$.

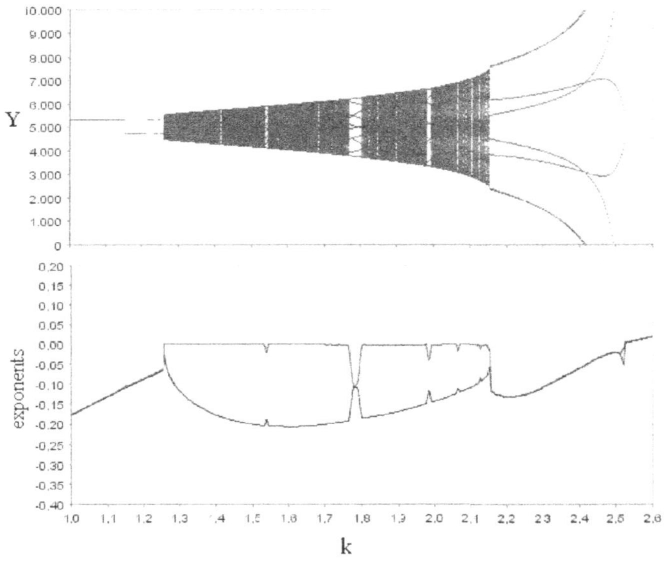

Figure 3: *Above, bifurcation diagram; below, Lyapunov exponents.*

Numerical simulations of the dynamics of the economy, with these parameter values, are provided in Figure 3; the single parameter bifurcation diagram for $k \in (1, 2.6)$, above; the Lyapunov exponents over the same interval, below. Both figures suggest that there are three basic types of long-run dynamics and that for trajectories beginning at (4000, 4000) the changes occur at around $k = 1.26$ and $k = 2.13$. For small values of the acceleration coefficient the economy experiences bi-stability. The weight in the economy-wide expectation operator is not a function of k and, for the given parameter values, 75% expect the trend to continue while 25% expect reversion. The economy moves toward one of the two fixed points, far from the Samuelsonian equilibria, and switching between high and low equilibrium values increases with k. Over the next interval, approximately $k \in (1.26, 2.13)$ the economy is characterized by persistent fluctuations over a range of values symmetrical around $\mathcal{Y}$. For some values the recurrent behavior seems cyclical (cycles of 10 are evident), but for most the motion is quasiperiodic or periodic of order greater than 24. The last type of behavior is found in the tentacles of the octopus, period-8 cycles that cover a wider span of national income than the invariant cycle that preceded it. The periodic cycle loses stability at around $k = 2.55$ after which no attractor exists.

There are 3 puzzles to explain in this bifurcation scenario: the increased switching between $\bar{Y}_1$ and $\bar{Y}_2$; the attracting curve appearing before the critical value; the period-8 cycle which does not seem to derive from frequency-locking.

The switching behavior of the economy occurs because of the pitchfork bifurcation and bi-stability that exists for k small. The switching between long-run behavior increases because as k changes the separatrix, the boundary separating basins of attraction, becomes increasingly entwined. This phenomena can be seen in Figure 4 which presents the basins of attraction for the fixed points in the state space $Y \in (4000, 6000)$ under the standard constellation.

Moving clockwise from upper-left k increases through 0.2 ($\bar{Y}_1$, $\bar{Y}_2$ stable nodes), 0.9, 1.1, 1.255 ($\bar{Y}_1$, $\bar{Y}_2$ stable foci). Recall that initial conditions used in Figure 2 are (4000, 4000), the lower-left hand corner of the basin plots. The other dynamical puzzles are not so clear. In fact, on the basis of local evidence and the single and double parameter bifurcation diagrams alone, we cannot explain the large curve Γ appearing at a value of k less than the critical value of the Neimark-Sacker bifurcation of $\bar{Y}_1$, $\bar{Y}_2$ and the origin of the period-8 cycle, lying as it does outside the bounds of the invariant circle. The global bifurcation scenarios that answer these questions are described by Agliari, Bischi and Gardini in Chapter 1, to which we refer the reader (see, also, the business cycle application by Agliari and Dieci in Chapter 8). We consider each of these puzzles in turn.

From foci to invariant curve. An important point to note is that, although over the interval of interest the Samuelsonian fixed point has already lost local stability through a pitchfork bifurcation, the saddle point $\mathcal{Y}$ is still a significant factor in the global dynamics through its stable and unstable manifolds. In fact, it is the stable manifold $w^s(\mathcal{Y})$ (associated with λ_2) that plays the role of separatrix for the basins of attraction of the stable foci $\bar{Y}_1, \bar{Y}_2$. The unstable manifold $w^u(\mathcal{Y})$ (associated with λ_1) has two branches, each exiting $\mathcal{Y}$ and connecting to either $\bar{Y}_1$ or $\bar{Y}_2$ until the basins become disjoint.

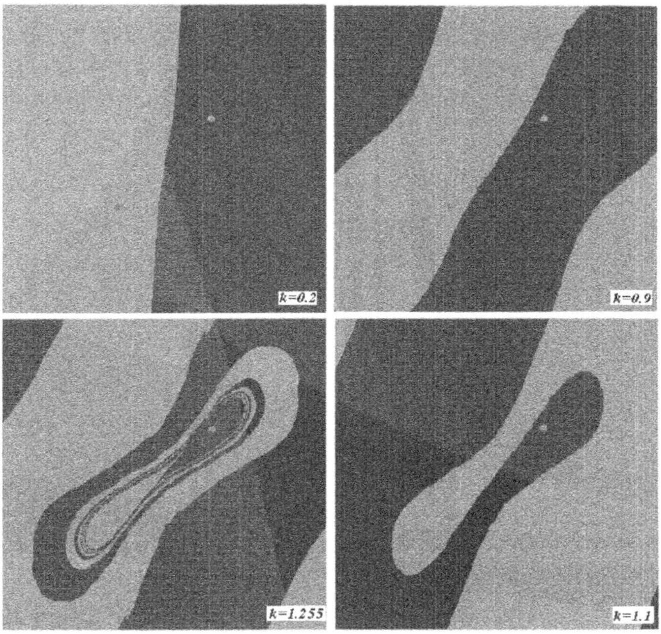

Figure 4: *Basins of attraction in state space as k increases.*

Another point is that when there are co-existing attractors and global changes in the dynamics, bifurcation diagrams calculated on the basis of a single initial condition cannot tell the whole story. In Figure 5 we use a series of simulations of the state space to help describe what is happening over the interval $k \in (1.25, 1.43)$, moving clockwise as k increases, $k = 1.25, 1.27, 1.35, 1.42$. Again both axes are $Y \in (4000, 6000)$, symmetric around $\mathcal{Y} = 5000$, and the initial conditions used in Figure 3 simulations are in the lower axes' intersection. In the upper-left figure the separatrix $w^s(\mathcal{Y})$ separates the state space into basins of attraction for $\bar{Y}_1, \bar{Y}_2$. The convolutions of the stable manifold form a ring of entwined basins around the fixed points where, increasing k, an attracting invariant closed curve appears. At the creation of the attracting curve, call it Γ_s, a second curve, Γ_u, also appears which is repelling. Γ_u belongs to the area bounded by Γ_s. The latter forms the separatrix between collections of initial conditions with trajectories tending to one or other of the stable foci and initial conditions with trajectories tending to the attracting Γ. As k is further increased the radius of Γ_s increases while that of Γ_u decreases and the basins of $\bar{Y}_1, \bar{Y}_2$ contract. Between upper and lower right the basins become disjoint through a homoclinic bifurcation. Finally, the subcritical Neimark-Sacker bifurcation for $\bar{Y}_1$, $\bar{Y}_2$ occurs for a value of k just beyond that in Figure 5, lower left, and the basins disappear altogether.

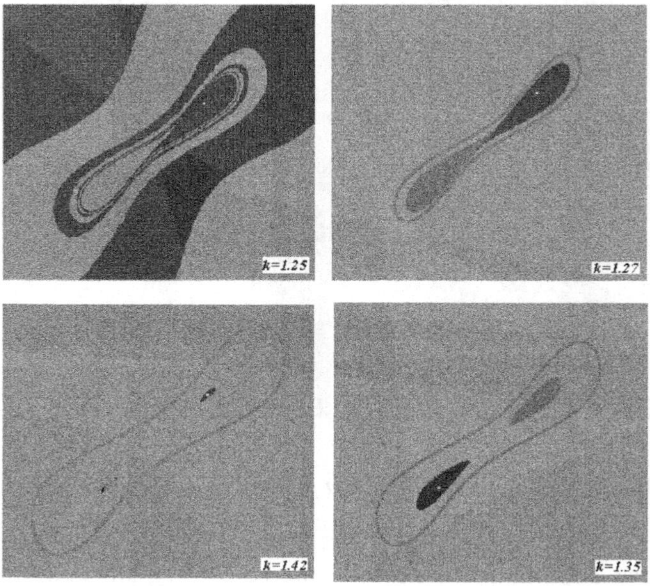

Figure 5: *Basins from upper-left, clockwise:* $k = 1.244, 1.27, 1.35, 1.42$.

There are a number of global bifurcations involved in this interval. First, and most mysterious, is the creation of the attractor Γ_s, which comes to co-exist with the stable foci, and the separatrix Γ_u defining its basin of attraction. The likely sequence leading to the formation of Γ_s is that proposed in Chapter 1, Section 7 which we summarize as follows. In the vicinity of the tightly woven basins, where the stable manifold is coiled like yarn on a spindle, at a certain parameter value (in this case around $k = 1.259$) a saddle-node bifurcation leads to a saddle cycle of high period along with a node cycle of the same period. The periodic points of the node immediately become repelling foci. In quick succession, over a narrow interval of k, we have the following changes. The periodic points are joined through a saddle connection of the outwards branches of stable manifolds of point i and unstable manifolds of point j forming an unstable saddle-focus connection Γ_u surrounded by an attracting invariant curve Γ_s. Γ_u is destroyed as a second heteroclinic loop forms from the connection of the inward stable branches of point j and the inward unstable branches of point i and this unstable saddle-focus connection becomes Γ_u, the separatrix in Figure 5.

All initial conditions outside of Γ_u are attracted to the invariant curve and any economy beginning from these values (or after being disturbed to them) is destined to a recurrent fluctuation, even though there are three equilibria within the closed curve, two of which are stable. Only trajectories with initial conditions on the inside of Γ_u, a small area of the state space, tend to $\bar{Y}_1$ or $\bar{Y}_2$ with damped oscillations. Looking back at Figure 3 it can be observed that at this bifurcation the Lyapunov exponents separate, the largest at 0, representing motion on the invariant curve, the other negative, representing the attracting property of the curve.

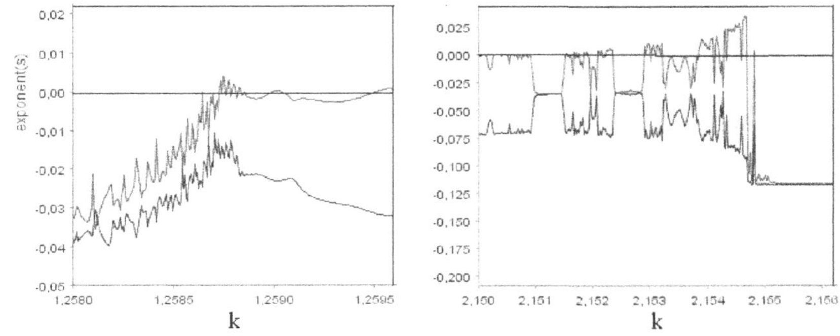

Figure 6: *Lyapunov exponents: left,* $k \in (1.258, 1.2595)$*; right,* $k \in (2.15, 2.156)$.

In Figure 6, left $k \in (1.258, 1.2595)$, the exponents are calculated over 500 iterations. There seems to be some evidence of chaotic transients, as we would expect for the saddle connection, but these disappear before reaching 5000 iterations (the time range used in Figure 2).

The next change occurs between upper right and lower right, in which a homoclinic bifurcation of $\mathcal{Y}$ gives rise to a double homoclinic loop and Γ_u breaks into two repelling curves forming the disjoint basin boundaries $B(\bar{Y}_1)$, $B(\bar{Y}_2)$. In this bifurcation, over a narrow interval of parameter values a homoclinic tangency (in which $w^u(\mathcal{Y})$ comes to touch $w^s(\mathcal{Y})$) is followed by a transversal crossing of the manifolds and a second homoclinic tangency ($w^u(\mathcal{Y})$ is tangent on the opposite side of $w^s(\mathcal{Y})$). Recall that the stable manifold is the separatrix for the basins of $\bar{Y}_1$ and $\bar{Y}_2$. The unstable manifold branches of $w^u(\mathcal{Y})$ are provided in Figure 7 for the standard parameter constellation and $k = 1.289$, left; $k = 1.29$, right. Between these values $w^u(\mathcal{Y})$ becomes tangent, then crosses, and becomes tangent again to $w^s(\mathcal{Y})$. After the homoclinic bifurcation, trajectories with initial conditions close to $\mathcal{Y}$ converge to Γ_s rather than $\bar{Y}_1$ or $\bar{Y}_2$. That is, economies starting close to the Samuelsonian equilibrium move away and fluctuate around it.

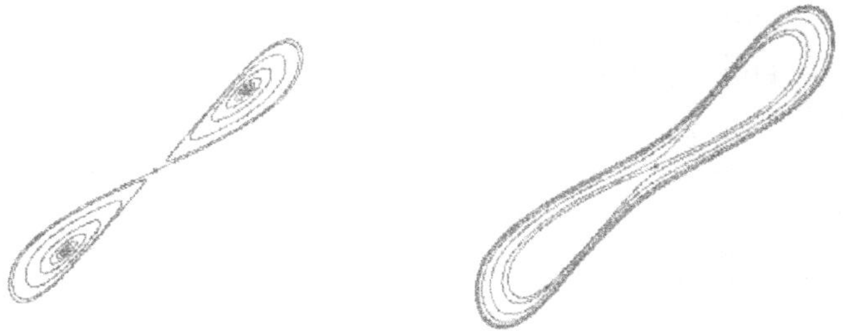

Figure 7: *Unstable manifold of Y: left, $k = 1.289$; right, $k = 1.29$.*

Finally, the two loops of Γ_u shrink around $\bar{Y}_1$ and $\bar{Y}_2$ as k is increased until, at $k = 1.429$ (just beyond the value used in Figure 5, lower left), the fixed points lose stability through subcritical Neimark-Sacker bifurcations as the modulus of the complex, conjugate eigenvalues reaches one. From this value until just before $k = 2.13$ all attractors lie on the increasing amplitude invariant curve, Γ_s, to which all initial conditions are attracted.

From invariant curve to period-8 cycle. The last type of periodic behavior becomes visible at around $k = 2.13$. We describe the scenario with reference to Figure 8, where the basins of attraction are simulated as k increases, starting upper-left and moving clockwise: $k = 2.128, 2.13, 2.15, 2.17$. The state space has been enlarged with respect to previous figures to $Y \in (0, 10000)$, as the invariant curve has blown up considerably. The initial conditions for Figure 2 are slightly southwest of center. A saddle-node bifurcation takes place between $k = 2.128$ and $k = 2.13$. In the upper-left there is still the single attracting invariant curve on which all trajectories eventually lie. After the bifurcation, upper-right, Γ_s is still attracting for all initial conditions within in it, but most others are attracted to a period-8 cycle which has appeared around the invariant circle. The basin pieces for the cycle $B(C)$ expand, the basin $B(\Gamma_s)$ shrinks until, by $k = 2.17$, the invariant curve has disappeared and all further attractors are periodic. For the propensity to consume out of expected income at $b = 0.8$ the last attractor, a period-8 cycle, becomes unstable around $k = 2.53$.

The invariant curve Γ_s is destroyed and the aperiodic fluctuations disappear through the heteroclinic loop sequence described earlier. Starting from coexistence in upper-right, the periodic points and associated saddle points are very near to each other and lie on the boundaries of the basin of attraction for the focus cycle $B(C)$. The branches of the stable manifolds of the saddle cycle serve as separatrix between $B(C)$ and $B(\Gamma_s)$. The outer branch of the unstable manifold of the saddle leads to the focus cycle, the inner branch leads to the invariant curve. As k is increased, the inner unstable branch of the saddle point i becomes tangential to the inner stable branch of nearby saddle point j, and this happens all around the cycle. This heteroclinic tangency starts a tangle, followed by a transversal crossing of these branches and another heteroclinic tangency. Transversal crossings are usually associated with chaotic repellers and long chaotic transients. A hint of this can be seen in Figure 3 as there is a slight rise in the Lyapunov characteristic exponent near the bifurcation interval, There are clearly chaotic transients evident in Figure 6, right, which are calculated over 5000 iterations and $k \in (2.15, 2.156)$. At the end of the tangle the branches are switched in position. The unstable branches of the saddle point i tend to the nearby stable foci (to the right and left, h and j) forming a heteroclinic saddle-focus connection that leaves no initial condition leading to Γ_s.

For $b = 0.8$ this is the end of the story. Had we fixed the propensity to consume at some other level, slightly above or below for example (refer again, to Figure 2, right), the sequence would have continued with another heteroclinic saddle-focus connection forming from the outer branches of the saddle points. This connection would be an invariant closed curve, enveloping and destroying the stable focus cycle. Still higher values of b would have avoided the period-8 cycle altogether and ended with the first invariant curve becoming unstable.

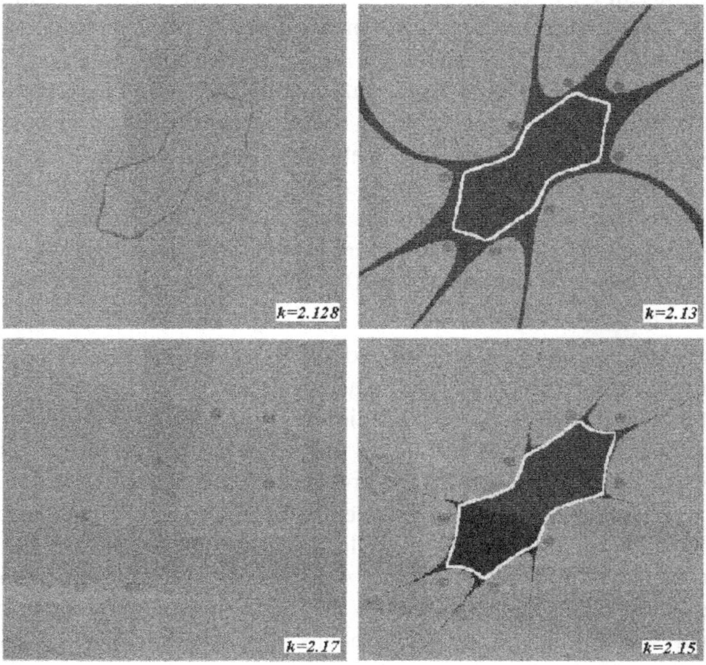

Figure 8: *Basins from upper-left, clockwise:* $k = 2.128, 2.13, 2.15, 2.17$.

9.6 Conclusions

Samuelson's linear multiplier-accelerator model is a classic example of a business cycle model based on the combined effects of the multiplier and accelerator principles. The equations are simple and the linear dynamics are completely understood. It is interesting to see how these dynamics change under a simple alteration to the consumption hypothesis: expenditures are a function of expected income rather than realized last period income and there are two types of expectations (each a linear function of last period income).

The aggregate expected income is a nonlinear combination of extrapolative and reverting expectation rules. The equilibrium of Samuelson's model is also a fixed point of the extended model, but other limit sets exist. A comparison of the dynamics of the linear multiplier-accelerator model and the nonlinear expectations-multiplier-accelerator model brings to light essential differences.

As regards the equilibrium of Samuelson's model, the stability conditions on $\mathcal{Y}$ are more restrictive in the nonlinear model. However, with nonlinear expectations, local stability of a fixed point may be lost while global stability continues in the form of: convergence to either of 2, co-existing stable fixed points; a periodic or quasiperiodic sequence of points lying on a closed curve.

In fact, over the parameter space (k, b) the nonlinear model has a much larger area characterized by attractors, under reasonable values for the extra parameters and persistent oscillations are a generic possibility in the nonlinear model. This characteristic is of special importance given that the phenomenon under study is the business cycle. Moreover this was accomplished by allowing consumption to depend on expectations and expectations to be heterogeneous, that is, by creating a more realistic economic context.

Appendix

Substituting the expectations formation hypotheses (9) and (10), the expectations weight hypothesis (11) into the aggregate expectations operator (8) the complete system (13) is

$$\begin{aligned}
Y_t &= I_a + b(1+k)\Bigg[\left(\frac{1}{1+\gamma^2\left(\frac{Y_{t-1}-\mathcal{Y}}{\mathcal{Y}}\right)^2}\right)(Y_{t-1}+\mu_1(Y_{t-1}-\mathcal{Y}))+ \\
&\qquad + \left(1-\frac{1}{1+\gamma^2\left(\frac{Y_{t-1}-\mathcal{Y}}{\mathcal{Y}}\right)^2}\right)(Y_{t-1}+\mu_2(\mathcal{Y}-Y_{t-1}))\Bigg] \\
&\quad -bk\Bigg[\left(\frac{1}{1+\gamma^2\left(\frac{Z_{t-1}-\mathcal{Y}}{\mathcal{Y}}\right)^2}\right)(Z_{t-1}+\mu_1(Z_{t-1}-\mathcal{Y}))+ \\
&\qquad + \left(1-\frac{1}{1+\gamma^2\left(\frac{Z_{t-1}-\mathcal{Y}}{\mathcal{Y}}\right)^2}\right)(Z_{t-1}+\mu_2(\mathcal{Y}-Z_{t-1}))\Bigg] \\
Z_t &= Y_{t-1}
\end{aligned}$$

The Jacobian matrix calculated in either of the fixed points $\bar{Y}_i$, $i = 1, 2$, is

$$J(\bar{Y}_i) = \begin{pmatrix} b(1+k)\Phi & -bk\Phi \\ 1 & 0 \end{pmatrix}$$

$$\Phi = \frac{-2\mathcal{Y}^2\gamma^2(\bar{Y}_i - \mathcal{Y})^2(\mu_1 + \mu_2)}{\left(\mathcal{Y}^2 + \gamma^2(\bar{Y}_i - \mathcal{Y})^2\right)^2} + \frac{\mathcal{Y}^2(\mu_1 + \mu_2)}{\mathcal{Y}^2 + \gamma^2(\bar{Y}_i - \mathcal{Y})^2} + 1 - \mu_2$$

References

Agliari, A., Bischi, G. and Gardini, L., 2006, "Some methods for the global analysis of closed invariant curves in two-dimensional maps". In *Business Cycle Dynamics. Models and Tools*, T. Puu, I.Sushko (Ed.s), Springer (to appear).

Agliari, A. and Dieci, R., 2006, "Coexistence of attractors and homoclinic loops in a Kaldor-like business cycle model". In *Business Cycle Dynamics. Models and Tools*, T. Puu, I.Sushko (Ed.s), Springer (to appear).

Brock, W. and Hommes. C., 1998, "Heterogeneous beliefs and routes to chaos in a simple asset pricing model", *Journal of Economic Dynamics and Control 22*, pp. 1235-2274.

Day, R. and Huang, W., 1990, "Bulls, bears and market sheep" *Journal of Economic Behavior and Organization 14*, pp. 299-329.

De Grauwe, P., Dewachter, H. and Embrechts, M., 1993, *Exchange Rate Theory - Chaotic Models of Foreign Exchange Markets*, Blackwell, Oxford.

Flieth, B. and Foster, J., 2002, "Interactive expectations", *Journal of Evolutionary Economics 12*, pp. 375-395.

Gandolfo, G., 1996, *Economic Dynamics*, 3rd edn. Springer-Verlag, New York.

Hicks, J.R., 1950, *A Contribution to the Theory of the Trade Cycle*, Oxford University Press, Oxford.

Hommes, C., 1995, "A reconsideration of Hicks' nonlinear trade cycle model", *Structural Change and Economic Dynamics 6*, pp. 435-459.

Hohnisch, M. Pittnauer, S., Solomon, S. and Stauffer D., 2005, "Socioeconomic interaction and swings in business confidence indicators", *Physica A 345*, pp. 646-656.

Ito, T., 1990, "Foreign exchange rate expectations: Micro survey data", *American Economic Review 80*, pp. 434-449.

Kahneman, D., Slovic, P. and Tversky, A, 1986, *Judgment under Uncertainty: Heur- istics and Biases*, Cambridge University Press, Cambridge.

Kirman, A., 1993, "Ants, rationality, and recruitment", *Quarterly Journal of Economics 108*, pp. 137-156.

Lines, M., ed., 2005, *Nonlinear dynamical systems in economics*, Springer-Wien, New York.

Lux, T. and Marchesi, M., 2000, "Volatility clustering in financial markets: A micro-simulation of interacting agents", *International Journal of Theoretical and Applied Finance 3*, pp. 675-702.

Medio, A. and Lines, M., 2001, *Nonlinear Dynamics: A Primer*, Cambridge University Press, Cambridge.

Puu, T., Gardini, L. and Sushko, I., 2005, "A Hicksian multiplier-accelerator model with floor determined by capital stock", *Journal of Economic Behavior and Organization 56*, pp. 331-348.

Samuelson, P., 1939, "Interactions between the multiplier analysis and the principle of acceleration", *Review of Economic Statistics 21*, pp. 75-78.

Simon, H., 1955, "A behavioral model of rational choice", *Quarterly Journal of Economics 9*, pp. 99-118.

Shiller, R., 2000, *Irrational Exuberance*, Princeton University Press, Princeton.

Smith, V., 1991, *Papers in Experimental Economics*, Cambridge University Press, Cambridge.

Sonnemans, J., Hommes, C., Tuinstra, J. and van de Velden, H., 2004, "The instability of a heterogeneous cobweb economy: a strategy experiment on expectation formation", *Journal of Economic Behavior and Organization 54*, pp. 453-481.

Takagi, S., 1991, "Exchange rate expectations: A survey of survey studies", *IMF Staff Papers 38*, pp. 156-183.

Westerhoff, F. ,2005, "Samuelson's multiplier-accelerator model revisited", *Applied Economics Letters* (in press).

10 'Floors' and/or 'Ceilings' and the Persistence of Business Cycles

Serena Sordi

10.1 Introduction

In chapters 3, 6, 7 and 12 of this book and in a number of other recent contributions (e.g. Gallegati *et al.* 2003) the dynamics of Hicks' (1950) discrete-time multiplier-accelerator model has been analysed in depth and the role played by 'floors' and/or 'ceilings' clarified. In this chapter we intend to tackle the same problem with reference to models formulated in continuos-time, in particular Goodwin's (1951) model of the interaction between the dynamic multiplier and the nonlinear accelerator. Of course, the choice of this model is not casual; rather, it is dictated by a number of factors. First, although Goodwin's article was published in January 1951, in the first issue of volume 19 of *Econometrica*, it was certainly already in 'incubation' and its main idea 'in the air' some years earlier. This is testified to by the fact that the paper (with the provisional title "The business cycle as a self-sustaining oscillation") had already been presented by Goodwin at the American Winter Meeting of the Econometric Society held in Cleveland, Ohio on 27-30 December 1948 (for a summary, see Goodwin 1949). Moreover, from what we read in a footnote contained in the second page of the published version of the paper, we can infer that Goodwin became aware of Hicks' contribution only at the end of his research on the topic, when he was making the final revision of his paper. In short, we can consider it as contemporaneous, if not antecedent, to Hicks' contribution. The second reason for our choice is that, at the same time as Duesenberry (1950), Goodwin (1950) also promptly wrote an important and well known review of Hicks' book. In it, as in Duesenberry's review, it is clearly stated and explained that "either the 'ceiling' or the 'floor' will suffice" (Goodwin 1950, p. 319) in order to maintain and perpetuate the cycle. The final reason for our choice is the fact that in the literature (e.g., Le Corbeiller 1958, 1960, de Figueiredo 1958, Sasakura 1996, Velupillai 1990, 1991, 1998, 2004), when reference is made to the 'Goodwin oscillator' (or 'oscillator with a Goodwin characteristic' or 'two-stroke oscillator' or 'one-sided oscillator' or 'two-straight-line oscillator') what is meant is the discovery by Goodwin of an oscillator capable of generating persistent fluctuations with only one barrier.

The analysis that follows is an attempt to clarify some of the issues raised in this literature. In order to prepare the ground for this, the next section is devoted to a concise presentation of the model.

10.2 The Multiplier-Nonlinear Accelerator Interaction

The final equation of Goodwin's (1951) model is the following second order differential equation with a forcing term:

$$\varepsilon\theta\ddot{y} + \{[\varepsilon + (1-\alpha)\theta]\dot{y} - \phi(\dot{y})\} + (1-\alpha)y = O_A(t+\theta) \qquad (1)$$

where y is income, $\phi(\dot{y})$ induced investment, $O_A(\cdot)$ the sum of the autonomous components of consumption $\beta(\cdot)$ and investment $l(\cdot)$, $0 < \alpha < 1$ the marginal propensity to consume, ε, $\theta > 0$ the time-lag of the dynamic multiplier and the time-lag between investment decisions and the resulting outlays respectively and where $\dot{y} = dy/dt$, $\ddot{y} = d^2y/dt^2$.

Goodwin arrives at equation (1) by means of a 'step by step' procedure that has the purpose of removing one by one the unrealistic aspects of the simple multiplier and accelerator principle. Leaving out the first step, which leads to a rather crude model in which there is either investment at the maximum rate allowed by the existing productive capacity ($\dot{k}^* > 0$) or disinvestment at the maximum rate allowed by not replacing capital goods which are being scrapped for depreciation ($\dot{k}^{**} < 0$),[1] such a procedure can be described as follows.

First, the instantaneous multiplier is replaced by the dynamic multiplier (Goodwin 1951, p. 9):[2]

$$y = c + \dot{k} - \varepsilon\dot{y} = \beta(t) + \alpha y + \dot{k} - \varepsilon\dot{y} \qquad (2)$$

where $c = \beta(t) + \alpha y$ is consumption, k the capital stock and $\dot{k} = dk/dt$, net investment.

[1]This is the only version of the model that is usually considered in textbooks. See, for example, Gandolfo (1997, pp. 464-465) and Gabisch and Lorenz (1989, pp. 118-122).

[2]See also Goodwin (1948), where this continuous-time formulation of the dynamic multiplier was first introduced.

Second, net investment is assumed to consist of an autonomous component $l(t)$ and an induced component $\phi(\dot{y})$:

$$\dot{k} = l(t) + \phi(\dot{y}) \tag{3}$$

The latter, in its turn, is assumed to be determined by the nonlinear accelerator, such that the simple acceleration principle (with an acceleration coefficient equal to $v > 0$) holds only over some middle range but passes to complete inflexibility at either extremity $\dot{k}^*$ and $\dot{k}^{**}$.

Fig.1 illustrates the case considered by Goodwin (1951, p. 7), namely, the case of an asymmetric nonlinear accelerator with $|\dot{k}^*| > |\dot{k}^{**}|$.

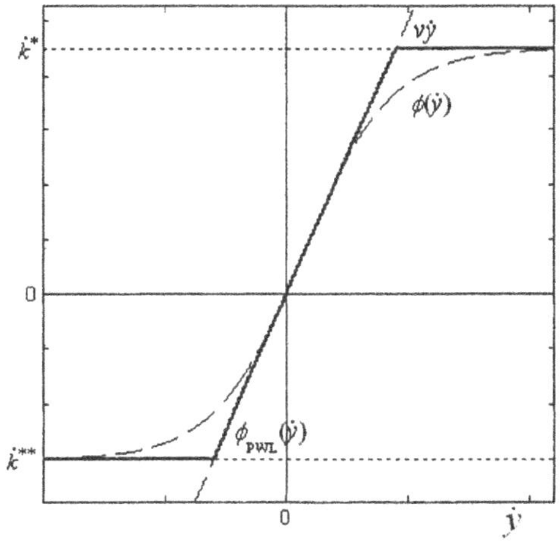

Figure 1: *The nonlinear asymmetric accelerator with* $|\dot{k}^*| > |\dot{k}^{**}|$.

As shown in the figure, $\phi(\dot{y})$ is well approximated by the following piecewise linear investment function:

$$\phi_{\mathrm{PWL}}(\dot{y}) = \begin{cases} \dot{k}^* & \text{if } \dot{y} > \dot{k}^*/v \\ v\dot{y} & \text{if } \dot{k}^{**}/v \leq \dot{y} \leq \dot{k}^*/v \\ \dot{k}^{**} & \text{if } \dot{y} < \dot{k}^{**}/v \end{cases} \tag{4}$$

that, for simplicity, is used in all the simulations that follow.

Finally, the time-lag θ between decisions to invest and the corresponding outlays is taken into account (Goodwin 1951, pp. 11-12), such that (3) becomes:

$$\dot{k}(t) = l(t) + \phi(\dot{y}(t-\theta)) \tag{5}$$

Introducing (5) into (2) and rearranging, we obtain:

$$\varepsilon\dot{y}(t+\theta) + (1-\alpha)\,y(t+\theta) - \phi(\dot{y}(t)) = O_A(t+\theta)$$

from which, expanding the two leading terms $\dot{y}(t+\theta)$ and $y(t+\theta)$ in a Taylor series and dropping all but the first two terms in each, (1) is readily obtained.

It is not too difficult to understand that the whole 'step by step' procedure, including the final approximation, is simply tantamount to assuming that (2) holds and that induced investment adjusts to its desired level, given by the nonlinear accelerator, with a time-lag of length equal to θ:

$$\dot{k} - l(t) = \phi(\dot{y}) - \theta\frac{d}{dt}\left[\dot{k} - l(t)\right] \tag{6}$$

Combining (6) in (2), we get:

$$\varepsilon\theta\ddot{y} + \{[\varepsilon + (1-\alpha)\theta]\,\dot{y} - \phi(\dot{y})\} + (1-\alpha)\,y = \left(\theta\frac{d}{dt} + 1\right)O_A(t) \tag{7}$$

that, as is easy to check, is nothing other than the original final equation (1) of Goodwin's model in the case in which the expansion in Taylor series and approximation is applied also to the leading term $O_A(t+\theta)$.

The subsequent analysis in Goodwin's article is based on the simplifying assumption that all autonomous expenditures are constant, so that[3]

$$O_A(t) = O_A^*,\ \forall t$$

Thus, equation (7), using the new variable $z = y - O_A^*/(1-\alpha)$, can be written in terms of deviations from equilibrium as:

$$\varepsilon\theta\ddot{z} + \{[\varepsilon + (1-\alpha)\theta]\,\dot{z} - \phi(\dot{z})\} + (1-\alpha)\,z = 0$$

or, choosing the time-unit so as to have $\theta = 1$:

$$\ddot{z} + \frac{1}{\varepsilon}\left[(\varepsilon + s)\,\dot{z} - \phi(\dot{z})\right] + \frac{s}{\varepsilon}z = 0 \tag{8}$$

where $0 < s = 1 - \alpha < 1$ is the marginal propensity to save.

[3] Clearly, in this case equations (1) and (7) are identical.

Equation (8) is a generalisation of a well known differential equation which, in physical applications, goes under the name of *Lord Raileigh equation* (see, for example, Le Corbeiller 1936, 1960). Using the terminology introduced by Le Corbeiller (1960), given any variable x, a *Lord Raileigh-Type* (LRT), is a differential equation of the type:

$$\ddot{x} + F(\dot{x}) + x = 0 \tag{9}$$

where the characteristic function (or, 'characteristic') $F(\dot{x})$ is such that (9) has a unique periodic solution (limit cycle). Thus, equation (8) – when $v > \varepsilon + s$ and, as a consequence, the origin is locally unstable – is a LRT equation with characteristic equal to:[4]

$$F(\dot{z}) = -\frac{1}{\varepsilon}\left[\phi(\dot{z}) - (\varepsilon + s)\,\dot{z}\right]$$

We then know (see Appendix 1) that, for given ε and s, (8) is either a so-called *two-stroke* or a *four-stroke* oscillator, depending on the degree of asymmetry of the investment function.

To appreciate fully and clarify the meaning of this, it is useful first to consider the case of a symmetric investment function, such that $|\dot{k}^*| = |\dot{k}^{**}|$. As shown in Fig.2(*ii*), in this case the model generates a symmetric limit cycle. Using the analogy with a physical system (see Le Corbeiller 1936 and Appendix 1 below), we can then describe it by saying that, over a full cycle, the total energy stored in the system increases along the arcs 2-3 and 4-1 and decreases along the arcs 1-2 and 3-4: this is exactly what is meant by the expression '*four*-stroke oscillator'.

This case, however, does not appear to be worth considering any further given that it implies a very unrealistic cycle such that, in an oscillation from peak to peak, the recession and the expansion are specularly identical and exactly of the same length (see Fig.2(*iii*)). Thus, it misses one of the main advantages of nonlinear modelling listed by Goodwin in his path-breaking

[4] Strictly speaking, (8) becomes a LRT equation only after it has been reduced to a dimensionless form (see Goodwin 1951, pp. 12-13). To avoid this complication, for illustrative purposes only, we assume that $s = \varepsilon$ in all simulations that follow. This assumption is unnecessary for the generation of the limit cycle, as long as $s + \varepsilon < v$. However, as we will see, it has the advantage of making straightforward the interpretation of the condition for a limit cycle in terms of exchanges of energy.

contribution, namely the capability of making "the depression as different from the boom as we wish" (Goodwin 1951, p. 4).[5]

To make sure that the model has this capability, we need an asymmetric accelerator such as, for example, the one drawn by Goodwin in his paper and that (choosing $\dot{k}^*$ and $\dot{k}^{**}$ arbitrarily such that $|\dot{k}^*| > |\dot{k}^{**})$ we have reproduced in Fig.1 above. Leaving unchanged all the remaining parameters we used to generate the symmetric cycle of Fig.2, it is not too difficult to understand what are the consequences of this change.

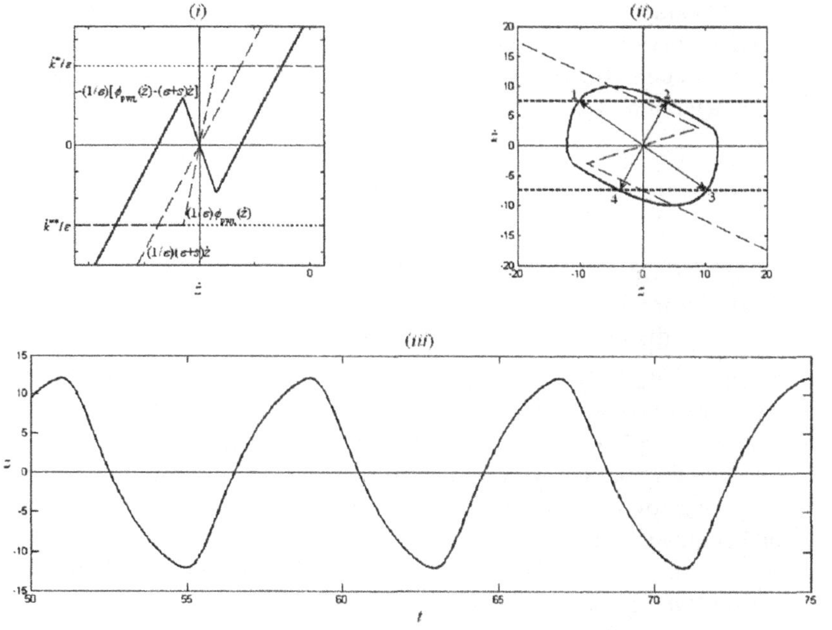

Figure 2: *The Goodwin symmetric (four-stroke) oscillator: (i) the characteristic function, (ii) the limit cycle in the phase plane and (iii) the periodic solution for* $z(t)$ *(*$\varepsilon = 0.4$, $s = 0.4$, $v = 2$, $\dot{k}^* = 6$, $\dot{k}^{**} = -6$*).*

As shown in Fig.3, the symmetric oscillator of Fig.2 becomes asymmetric and such that, over a cycle from peak to peak, the positive deviations of

[5]If, going on with the quotation, we accept Goodwin's view that such a capability is "one way of assessing the degree of nonlinearity" of a model, we can conclude that the model with a symmetric nonlinear accelerator has the lowest possible degree of nonlinearity.

national income from its equilibrium level are much larger than the negative ones. Moreover, the expansion is a smaller fraction of the period than the recession is.

This is due to the fact that, as shown in Fig.3(*i*), the 'ceiling' to investment spending is much less restrictive than the 'floor'. It can even happen, as with the values for $\dot{k}^*$ and $\dot{k}^{**}$ we have used in the simulation, that the 'ceiling' never becomes effective over the cycle (see Fig.3(*ii*)). In this case, the final dynamic equation of the model is said to be a *two-stroke* oscillator, namely, an oscillator such that the total energy stored in the system varies from a maximum to a minimum value (along the arc 1-2) and back again (along the arc 2-1) only once per cycle.[6]

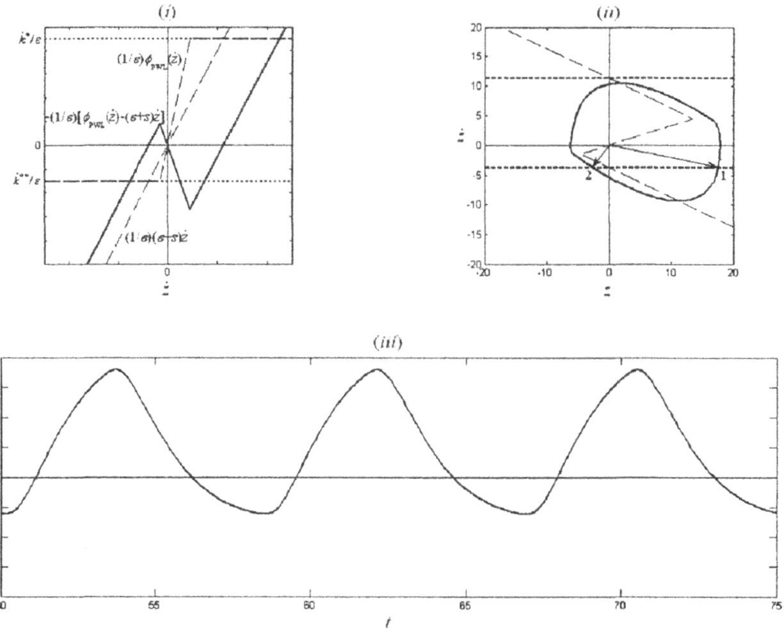

Figure 3: *The Goodwin asymmetric (two-stroke) oscillator with* $|\dot{k}^*| > |\dot{k}^{**}|$ *(*$\varepsilon = 0.4,\ s = 0.4, v = 2,\ \dot{k}^* = 9,\ \dot{k}^{**} = -3$*).*

[6]The transition from the one to the other type of oscillator as one of the parameters is varied is discussed in Appendix 1 where, for illustrative purposes, following Le Corbeiller (1960) and de Figueiredo (1958), a LRT equation with a cubic characteristic is considered.

For the sake of completeness, it should be noted that the result is exactly the opposite when we take $\dot{k}^* \neq \dot{k}^{**}$ such that $|\dot{k}^*\ | < |\dot{k}^{**}|$. As shown in Fig.4, in this case the final dynamic equation of the model is still a two-stroke oscillator, but now such that, over the stable limit cycle, the negative deviations from equilibrium dominate the positive ones. Moreover, it can happen, as in the case shown in the figure, that the 'floor' – rather than the 'ceiling' – never becomes effective over a cycle.

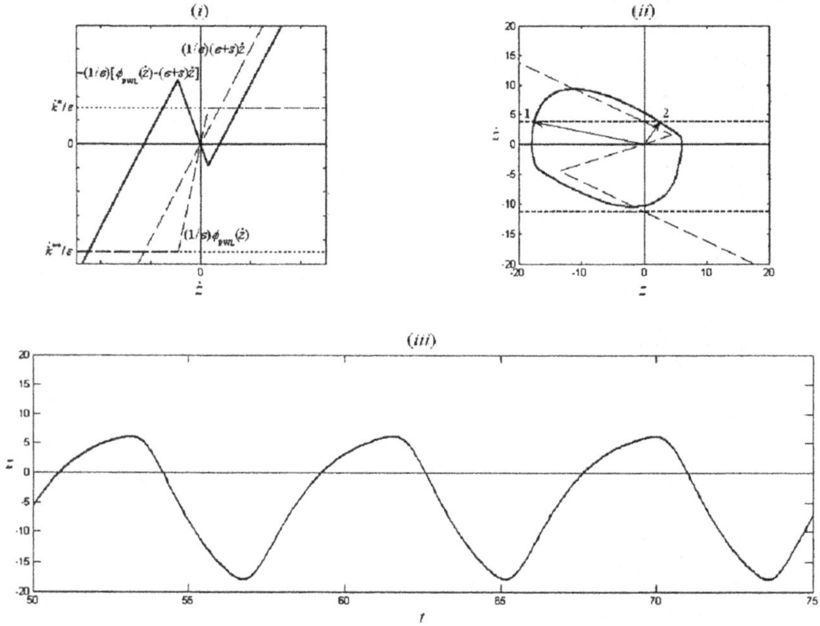

Figure 4: *The Goodwin asymmetric (two-stroke) oscillator with* $|\dot{k}^*| < |\dot{k}^{**}|$ *(*$\varepsilon = 0.4, s = 0.4, v = 2, \dot{k}^* = 3, \dot{k}^{**} = -9$*).*

In summary, we have confirmation of the claim made by both Goodwin (1950) and Duesenberry (1950) in their reviews of Hicks' (1950) book on the trade cycle, that either the 'ceiling' or the 'floor' may suffice to perpetuate the cycle.

Under the qualifications which will be given in the next section (see also Appendix 2), the two functions $F(\dot{z})$ pictured in Figs.3(i) and 4(i) are examples of the so-called '*Goodwin characteristic*'.

10.3 The 'Goodwin Characteristic' and the Persistence of the Cycle

The analysis we have developed in the previous section allows us to clarify some issues raised in the recent literature on the topic. To do so, a good starting point is the recent contribution by Sasakura (1996), where the existence of a unique stable limit cycle in Goodwin's model (for the general case of asymmetric nonlinearity of the investment function) is rigorously proved. In particular, it is interesting that, in a footnote at the very end of his paper – as if it were a secondary aspect (but it is not!) – Sasakura (1996, p. 1171) notes that the limit cycle in Goodwin's model is a two-stroke oscillator such that:

> ... it is the floor of investment that is essential to the persistence of business cycles. Goodwin (1982, pp. viii-ix) attaches importance to the ceiling, but his model works as an endogenous business cycle model without it (the Goodwin characteristic!)

Now, as we have seen, it is certainly true that, when $|\dot{k}^*| > |\dot{k}^{**}|$, depending on the relative values of $|\dot{k}^*|$ and $|\dot{k}^{**}|$, it may happen that the model works as an endogenous business cycle model without the 'ceiling'. However, on the basis of the analysis we have developed in the previous section, we know that this, as such, it is not an intrinsic feature of Goodwin's model. As we have shown, when $|\dot{k}^*| < |\dot{k}^{**}|$, exactly the opposite may happen, i.e., the model may endogenously generate a persistent cycle without the 'floor'. Thus, a more appropriate conclusion is to say that, although in his 1951 paper Goodwin considered the case in which $|\dot{k}^*| > |\dot{k}^{**}|$, it is the opposite case, in which $|\dot{k}^*| < |\dot{k}^{**}|$, that is closer to the view expressed by Goodwin (1982) and later fully worked out by him in the first part – on "Macrodynamics" – of Goodwin and Punzo (1987).

The fact is that, if we try to reconstruct the 'genesis' of the 'Goodwin characteristic',[7] we are in a position to arrive at an even more stunning conclusion.

Thanks to Le Corbeiller's (1958) reconstruction, we know that all the debate about the distinction between two- and four-stroke oscillators (and the related concept of the 'Goodwin characteristic') started in December 1950 or thereabouts, i.e., just a couple of weeks before Goodwin's (1951) paper (*with a 'floor' to investment more restrictive than the 'ceiling'*) was actually

[7] Some useful information in this regard is contained in various contributions by Velupillai (e.g., 1990, 1991, 1998 and 2004).

published. All started when Goodwin, at that time still at Harvard University, went to see Le Corbeiller in his office "in great elation" and showed him that an equation such as (9) with *a characteristic* $F(\dot{x})$ *made up of two straight lines* could have a periodic solution. That a characteristic of that type could generate a limit cycle was thought to be impossible at that time and this is the reason why Le Corbeiller named this kind of characteristic the 'Goodwin characteristic'. By 1960, thanks to de Figueiredo's Ph.D. thesis, discussed at Harvard in 1958, and to Le Corbeiller's article on "Two-Stroke Oscillators", the theory of this new type of oscillator had been fully developed.

It is not too difficult to understand how the multiplier-nonlinear accelerator interaction we have discussed in the previous section can originate a 'Goodwin characteristic' as rigorously defined in Le Corbeiller (1960). To do so, we must again consider separately the two basically different cases that may arise in the model, according to whether the 'ceiling' is more restrictive of the 'floor' or viceversa.

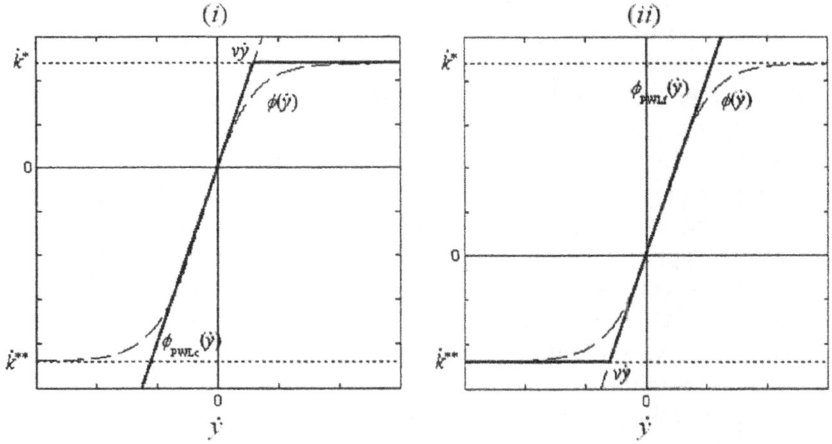

Figure 5: *The piecewise linear accelerator (i) with only the 'ceiling' and (ii) with only the 'floor'.*

As we have seen in the previous section, when the 'floor' is sufficiently less restrictive than the 'ceiling', it may happen that the former does not play any role in the generation of the stable limit cycle. When this happens, we can safely disregarded the 'floor' altogether and assume that the piecewise linear investment function is such that the linear accelerator always holds until the 'ceiling' is reached, after which investment remains at the maximum rate allowed by the existing productive capacity (see Fig. 5(*i*)); analytically:

$$\phi_{\text{PWL}}(\dot{y}) \approx \phi_{\text{PWLc}}(\dot{y}) = \begin{cases} v\dot{y} \text{ for } \dot{y} \le \dot{k}^*/v \\ \dot{k}^* \text{ for } \dot{y} > \dot{k}^*/v \end{cases} \tag{10}$$

Introducing (10) into (9), we get a LRT equation with the following characteristic (see Fig.6(*i*)):

$$F(\dot{z}) = \begin{cases} -(1/\varepsilon)\left[v - (\varepsilon + s)\right]\dot{z} & \text{for } \dot{z} \le \dot{k}^*/v \\ -(1/\varepsilon)\left[\dot{k}^* - (\varepsilon + s)\,\dot{z}\right] & \text{for } \dot{z} > \dot{k}^*/v \end{cases} \tag{11}$$

which is indeed a 'Goodwin characteristic', very similar to the one drawn by hand by Le Corbeiller in his 1958 letter to Goodwin with the intention to reproduce the one drawn by Goodwin at the blackboard during their 1950 meeting.

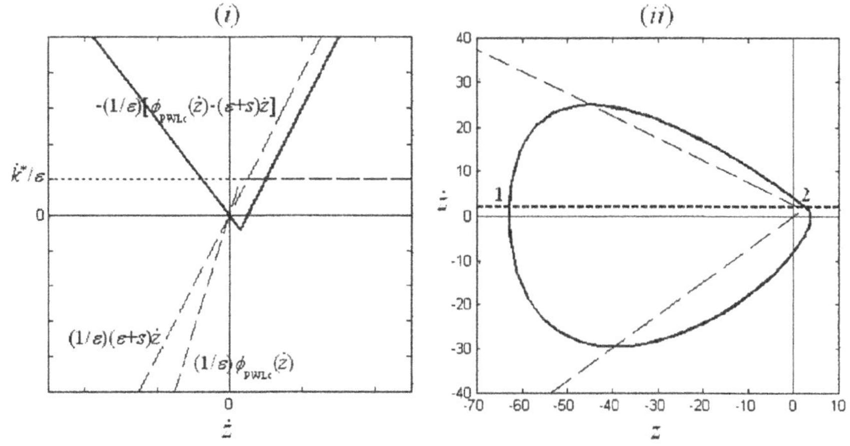

Figure 6: *The Goodwin piecewise linear (two-stroke) oscillator with only the 'ceiling' (*$\varepsilon = 0.6$*, *$s = 0.6$*, *$v = 2$*, *$\dot{k}^* = 3$*).*

In order to draw conclusions about the dynamics of the model when (11) is considered, we must study equation (9) separately for each regime (cfr. Appendix 2). In the first regime, where $\dot{z} \le \dot{k}^*/v$, equation (9) becomes:

$$\ddot{z} - \frac{1}{\varepsilon}\left[v - (\varepsilon + s)\right]\dot{z} + \frac{s}{\varepsilon}z = 0 \tag{12}$$

with characteristic equation given by

$$\lambda^2 - \frac{1}{\varepsilon}\left[v - (\varepsilon + s)\right]\lambda + \frac{s}{\varepsilon}z = 0$$

and eigenvalues

$$\lambda_{1,2} = \frac{1}{2\varepsilon}\left\{v - (\varepsilon + s) \pm \sqrt{\left[v - (\varepsilon + s)\right]^2 - 4s\varepsilon}\right\}$$

where, by assumption, $v > \varepsilon + s$. As a consequence, the unique equilibrium $z = 0$ is either an unstable node when:

$$v > \left(\sqrt{\varepsilon} + \sqrt{s}\right)^2$$

or an unstable focus when:

$$(\varepsilon + s) < v < \left(\sqrt{\varepsilon} + \sqrt{s}\right)^2$$

On the other hand, when the second regime applies, so that $\dot{z} > \dot{k}^*/v$, equation (9) becomes:

$$\ddot{z} + \frac{1}{\varepsilon}(\varepsilon + s)\dot{z} + \frac{s}{\varepsilon}z = \frac{1}{\varepsilon}\dot{k}^* \tag{13}$$

with singular point $z = \dot{k}^*/s$.

Writing the characteristic equation, we get:

$$\lambda^2 + \frac{1}{\varepsilon}(\varepsilon + s)\lambda + \frac{s}{\varepsilon}z = 0$$

from which

$$\lambda_{1,2} = \frac{1}{2\varepsilon}\left\{-(\varepsilon + s) \pm (\varepsilon - s)\right\}$$

Thus, since both eigenvalues are real and negative, the equilibrium for this regime is a stable node. Choosing values of the parameters such that in the first regime the equilibrium is an unstable focus, it is not too difficult to show by numerical simulation that the model has a stable limit cycle solution. The results of the simulation for this case are shown in Fig.6(*ii*) where, as was to be expected (cfr. Fig.4), a stable limit cycle – along which the negative deviations from equilibrium dominate the positive ones – is pictured. Needless to say, much importance in this case is attached to the 'ceiling' to investment spending that, by itself, accounts for the persistence of the cycle. The implication of all this is that Goodwin, in December 1950, at the time of his meeting with Le Corbeiller, already had in mind what he then explicitly theorised years later, namely that "(t)he basic, single, given, short-run nonlinearity is full employment, whether of capacity or of labour" (Goodwin 1982, p. *ix*).

The fact is that, in the article that appeared in *Econometrica* in the following month, exactly the opposite case is considered and pictured. To obtain the proper 'Goodwin characteristic' for this case, it is enough to notice that, if the 'ceiling' is so much less restrictive than the 'floor' that it does not play any role in the generation of the limit cycle, the former can be safely disregarded altogether (see Fig. 5(*ii*)) so that the investment function becomes:

$$\phi_{\text{PWL}}\left(\dot{y}\right) \approx \phi_{\text{PWLf}}\left(\dot{y}\right) = \begin{cases} \dot{k}^{**} \text{ for } \dot{y} < \dot{k}^{**}/v \\ v\dot{y} \text{ for } \dot{y} \geq \dot{k}^{**}/v \end{cases} \tag{14}$$

Introducing (14) into equation (9) we get a LRT equation with the following characteristic:

$$F\left(\dot{z}\right) = \begin{cases} -\left(1/\varepsilon\right)\left[\dot{k}^{**} - \left(\varepsilon + s\right)\dot{z}\right] & \text{for } \dot{z} < \dot{k}^{**}/v \\ -\left(1/\varepsilon\right)\left[v - \left(\varepsilon + s\right)\right]\dot{z} & \text{for } \dot{z} \geq \dot{k}^{**}/v \end{cases} \tag{15}$$

Also in this case, on the basis of an analysis similar to the one we have performed for the other case, it is not too difficult to find values of the parameters for which the equation generates a *stable* limit cycle (see Fig. 7). As we see, such a limit cycle is exactly specular with respect to the previous one; in particular, it is now the 'floor' to investment spending that, by itself, accounts for the existence and persistence of the cycle.

This result proves to be very useful in order to understand an aspect discussed in the literature (see, for example, Velupillai 1998, p. 11 and 2004, p. 36), but – we believe – never properly clarified.

Up to now, we have considered oscillators with piecewise-linear characteristics. However, more in general, we can say that a 'Goodwin characteristic' is any characteristic with only one bend and such that equation (9)

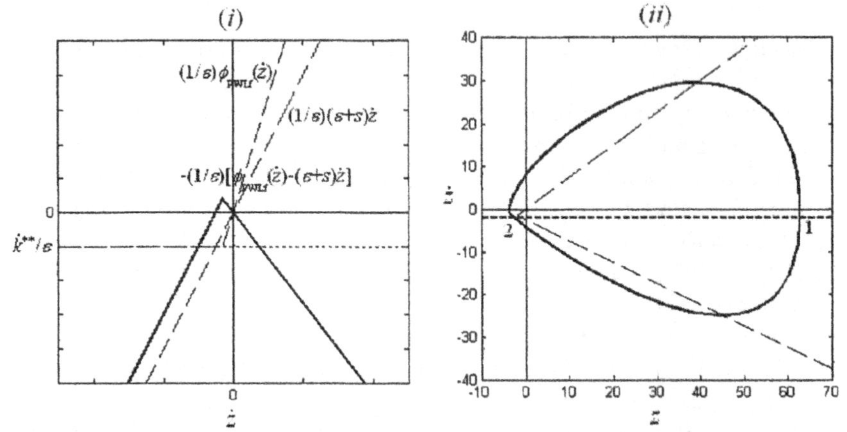

Figure 7: *The Goodwin piecewise linear (two-stroke) oscillator with only the 'floor' (*$\varepsilon = 0.6$*,* $s = 0.6$*,* $v = 2$*,* $\dot{k}^{**} = -3$*).*

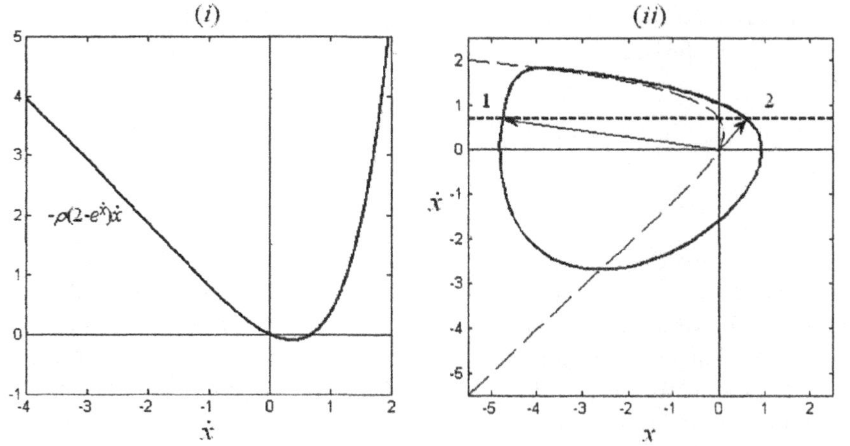

Figure 8: *The two-stroke oscillator with the exponential characteristic* $F(\dot{x}) = -\rho\left(2 - e^{\dot{x}}\right)\dot{x}$ *(*$\rho = 0.5$*).*

admits a unique periodic solution.[8] Some LRT equations with (exponential) characteristic functions which satisfy these conditions are suggested in Le Corbeiller (1960, pp. 390-391). It turns out that all of them, for example

$$\ddot{x} - \rho\left(2 - e^{\dot{x}}\right)\dot{x} + x = 0 \tag{16}$$

are two-stroke oscillators which generate limit cycles such that the negative amplitude of x is much greater than the positive amplitude (see Fig. 8).

It is possible, however, to imagine cases in which exactly the opposite happens. One of these is suggested by Le Corbeiller in his 1958 letter to Goodwin and is the following:

$$\ddot{x} - \rho\left(2 - e^{-\dot{x}}\right)\dot{x} + x = 0 \tag{17}$$

The resulting stable limit cycle for this two-stroke oscillator is shown in Fig. 9.

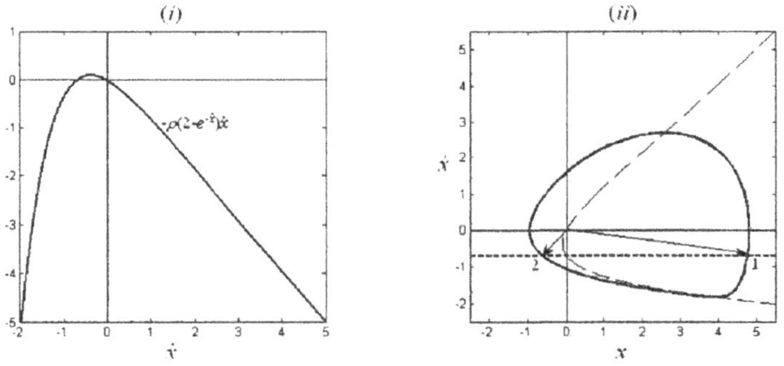

Figure 9: *The two-stroke oscillator with the exponential characteristic* $F(\dot{x}) = -\rho\left(2 - e^{-\dot{x}}\right)\dot{x}$ *(*$\rho = 0.5$*).*

This equation, however, is not included among the examples given in Le Corbeiller (1960), where it is replaced by (16). On the basis of the analysis we have developed in this chapter, we can conclude that, although both (16) and (17) admit a stable limit cycle solution, they are crucially different

[8]The general condition which must be fulfilled if this is to happen (Le Corbeiller 1960, p. 390) is that, in the equation (9) – written in terms of the 'velocity-controlled damping', $\ddot{x} + R(\dot{x})\dot{x} + x = 0$ – $R(\dot{x})$ is negative at $\dot{x} = 0$ and there exists a value $\dot{x}_0 > 0$ (< 0), such that $R(\dot{x})$ is negative for $\dot{x} < \dot{x}_0$ ($\dot{x} > \dot{x}_0$) and positive for $\dot{x} > \dot{x}_0$ ($\dot{x} < \dot{x}_0$).

from a qualitative point of view: whether (17) is qualitatively equivalent to the Goodwin oscillator with only the 'ceiling', (16) is qualitatively equivalent to the Goodwin oscillator with only the 'floor'. It could well be that Le Corbeiller, after having written in 1958 the letter to Goodwin, realised that the characteristic of (16) – rather than that of (17) – is what is qualitatively equivalent to Goodwin's 'blackboard sketch'.

10.4 Conclusions

In this chapter we have used the framework introduced by Le Corbeiller (1960) to discuss and qualify Sasakura's contention that, although Goodwin attached importance to the ceiling, the limit cycle in his (1951) model is generated without it. We have stressed in the introduction that both Duesenberry (1950) and Goodwin (1950) promptly wrote reviews of Hicks' book, in both of which it was clearly stated and explained that either the 'ceiling' or the 'floor' will suffice in order to maintain and perpetuate the cycle. Goodwin, however, not only wrote the review, but, as we have discussed, he actually discovered such a one-sided oscillator! From the analysis we have developed, it follows that such a discovery was the outcome of the attempt by Goodwin to explain the persistence of the cycle with the help of only the 'ceiling', in his opinion the basic, single, given, short-run nonlinearity. It appears amazing that this result was obtained by Goodwin in December 1950 or thereabouts, namely, just a couple of weeks before his 1951 *Econometrica* article – with a final equation qualitatively equivalent to (17), such that the persistence of the cycle is obtained with no role for the 'ceiling' – was published.

Appendix 1

As explained by Le Corbeiller (1960, p. 388) and de Figueiredo (1958, p. xvi), a two-stroke oscillator is an oscillator such that the energy stored in it varies from a minimum to a maximum value only once when a complete period of the variable is traversed, whereas a four-stroke oscillator is the (more usual) oscillator in which the energy varies from a minimum to a maximum twice within each period.

To appreciate this distinction and its interpretation in terms of exchanges of energy, it is useful to consider, equation (9) with the following cubic characteristic (see Le Corbeiller 1960, pp. 392-395 and de Figueiredo 1958, pp. 7.1-7.16):

$$F(\dot{x}) = -\varepsilon \left[\left(1 - a^2\right) \dot{x} - a\dot{x}^2 - \frac{\dot{x}^3}{3} \right] \quad \varepsilon > 0,\ 0 < a < 1 \qquad (18)$$

where x is any given variable. As clearly appears from Fig.10, the parameter a is a measure of the asymmetry of the characteristic function $F(\dot{x})$.

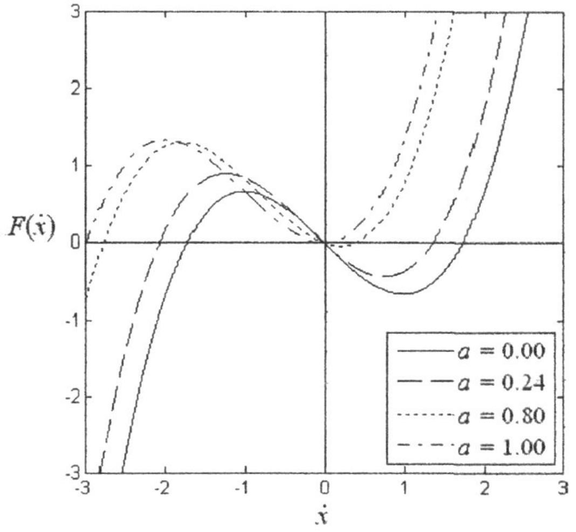

Figure 10: *The characteristic function (18) for different values of the parameter a.*

For $a = 0$, equation (9) reduces to the original Lord Rayleigh equation. This is a (symmetric) four-stroke oscillator such that, as shown in Fig.11(*i*), over the limit cycle, the total energy stored in the system,

$$\frac{x^2}{2} + \frac{\dot{x}^2}{2}$$

increases along the arcs 2-3 and 4-1 and decreases along the arcs 3-4 and 1-2.

As a increases but remains below a certain critical value, equation (9) with the cubic characteristic (18) is still a four-stroke oscillator, although asymmetric, as in Fig.11(*ii*), where $a = 0.10$.

The critical case is then shown in Fig.11(*iii*), where $a = 0.24$ and where the points 3 and 4 of the previous two figures merge.

Finally, the case in Fig.11(*iv*), where $a = 0.80$, illustrates what happens when the parameter is further increased: the total energy stored in the system now increases only once over the cycle (along the arc 2-1) and decreases in the remaining part (along the arc 1-2). It goes without saying that, in all four cases considered, these positive and negative energy exchanges are such that they perfectly compensate over the limit cycle.

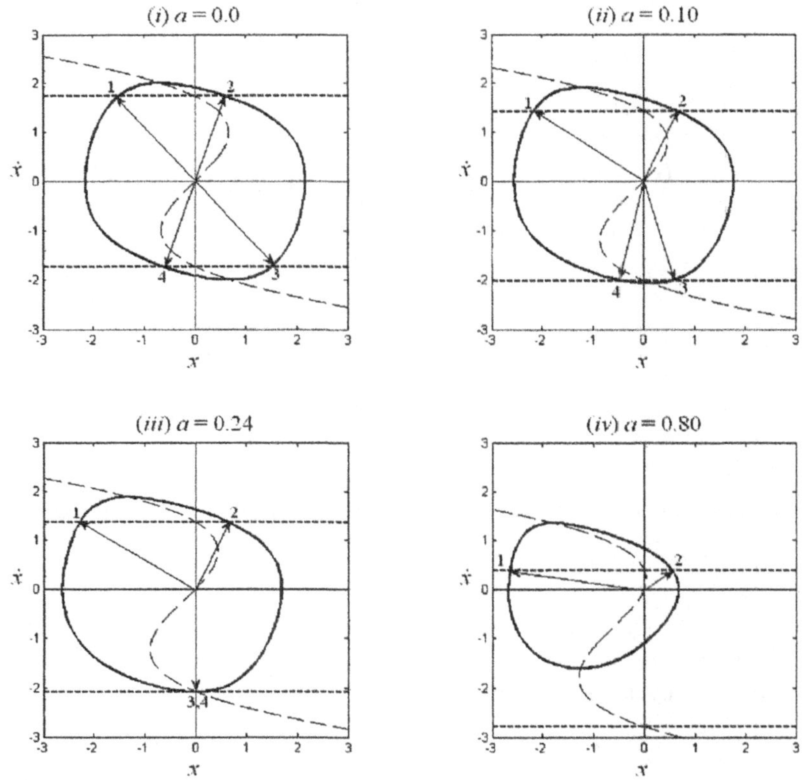

Figure 11: *The limit cycle of the LRT equation (9) with the cubic characteristic (18) for different values of the parameter a.*

To conclude, it is useful to underline two important aspects of the limit cycles of Fig.11 (see Le Corbeiller 1960, p. 302). First, it clearly appears that the distinction between four and two stroke-oscillators does not depend upon the number of points of intersection between the characteristic and the $0y$-axis. Rather, it depends on whether, apart from the origin, there are one or two such points inside the limit cycle. Second, the existence of a limit cycle is not due to the fact that the characteristic is sigmoid. It appears indeed that the parts of the characteristic outside the limit cycle do not play any role.

This is what opens the way to the possibility of having a limit cycle with a so-called Goodwin characteristic as discussed in the next Appendix and in Section 10.3 above.

Appendix 2

Strictly speaking, the 'Goodwin characteristic', as defined by Le Corbeiller (1958, 1960) and analysed at length in Figueiredo's (1958) Ph.D. thesis, is any characteristic made up of two straight lines, *with or without rounded-off corners*, such that equation (9) is a two-stroke oscillator.

One possibility, analysed in detail by de Figueiredo (1958, Ch. 6), is to assume that in equation (9) we have (see Fig. 12(*i*)):[9]

$$F(\dot{x}) = \begin{cases} -\rho_1 \dot{x} \text{ for } \dot{x} \leq \dot{x}_0 \\ \rho_2 \dot{x} - (\rho_1 + \rho_2)\, \dot{x}_0 \text{ for } \dot{x} > \dot{x}_0 \end{cases} \tag{19}$$

where $0 < \rho_1 < 2$, $\rho_2 > \rho_1 > 0$ and $\dot{x}_0 > 0$.

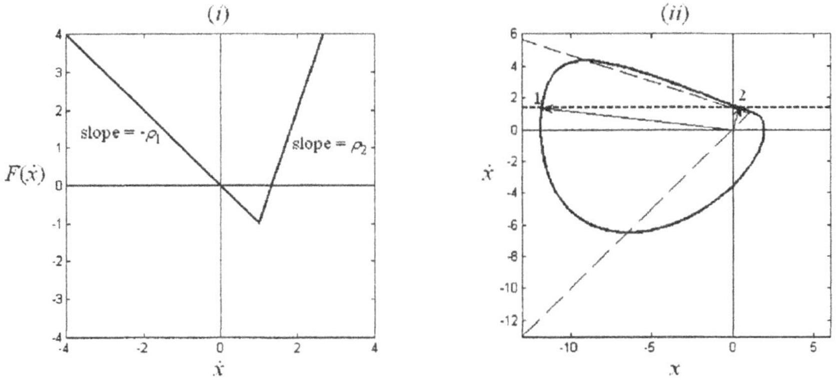

Figure 12: *The two-stroke oscillator with the piecewise linear characteristic (19)* $(\rho_1 = 1, \rho_2 = 3, \dot{x}_0 = 1)$.

[9]In de Figueiredo's contribution this is defined as the 'two-straight-line oscillator'. In a footnote, it is then stressed that this oscillator was first observed by R. Goodwin in economics.

With this characteristic (9) is an oscillator with negative damping for $\dot{x} < \dot{x}_0$ and positive damping for $\dot{x} > \dot{x}_0$. Given that it is a piecewise linear equation, we must study its dynamics in the two regimes separately.

In the first regime, such that $\dot{x} \leq \dot{x}_0$, equation (9) becomes:

$$\ddot{x} - \rho_1 \dot{x} + x = 0 \tag{20}$$

with $x = 0$ as singular point.

From the characteristic equation:

$$\lambda^2 - \rho_1 \lambda + 1 = 0$$

we then find that the eigenvalues:

$$\lambda_{1,2} = \frac{1}{2} \left\{ \rho_1 \pm \sqrt{\rho_1^2 - 4} \right\}$$

are always complex with positive real parts. Thus, we can conclude that the equilibrium point is an *unstable focus*.

In the other regime, such that $\dot{x} > \dot{x}_0$, the LRT equation becomes:

$$\ddot{x} + \rho_2 \dot{x} + x = (\rho_1 + \rho_2)\, \dot{x}_0 \tag{21}$$

From the characteristic equation:

$$\lambda^2 + \rho_2 \lambda + 1 = 0$$

we then find:

$$\lambda_{1,2} = \frac{1}{2} \left\{ -\rho_2 \pm \sqrt{\rho_2^2 - 4} \right\}$$

Thus, the unique equilibrium point of (21) – $x = (\rho_1 + \rho_2)\, \dot{x}_0$ – is either a stable focus, when $0 < \rho_2 < 2$, or a stable node when $\rho_2 > 2$.

Both for $0 < \rho_2 < 2$ and $\rho_2 > 2$, it is possible to prove that equation (9) with (19) fulfills the conditions for a unique stable limit cycle given by de Figueiredo in two theorems (see de Figueiredo 1958, Theorem 4.1 and 5.1 respectively). A case with $\rho_2 > 2$ is illustrated in Fig.12.

References

Duesenberry, J.J., 1950, "Hicks on the trade cycle", *Quarterly Journal of Economics* 64, pp. 464-476.

Figueiredo, R.J.P., de, 1958, *Existence and Uniqueness of Periodic Solutions in Autonomous Oscillators*, Unpublished Ph. Thesis, Harvard University, Cambridge, Mass., December.

Gabisch, G., Lorenz, H.-W., 1989, *Business Cycle Theory. A Survey of Methods and Concepts*, 2nd ed., Springer-Verlag, Berlin.

Gallegati, M., Gardini, L., Puu, T., Sushko, I., 2003, "Hicks' trade cycle theory revisited: cycles and bifurcations", *Mathematics and Computers in Simulation* 63, pp. 505-527.

Gandolfo, G., 1997, *Economic Dynamics*, Study ed., Springer-Verlag, Berlin.

Goodwin, R.M., 1948, "Secular and cyclical aspects of the multiplier and the accelerator", in: *Income, Employment and Public Policy. Essays in Honor of Alvin H. Hansen*, W.W. Norton & Company, Inc., New York, pp. 108-132.

Goodwin, R.M., 1949, "The business cycles as a self-sustaining oscillation", *Econometrica* 17, pp. 184-185.

Goodwin, R.M., 1950, "A non-linear theory of the cycle", *Review of Economics and Statistics* 32, pp. 316-320.

Goodwin, R.M., 1951, "The nonlinear accelerator and the persistence of business cycles", *Econometrica* 19, pp. 1-17.

Goodwin, R.M., 1982, *Essays in Economic Dynamics*, Macmillan, London.

Goodwin, R.M., Punzo, L.F., 1987, *The Dynamics of a Capitalist Economy. A Multi-Sectoral Approach*, Polity Press, Cambridge.

Hicks, J.R., 1950, *A Contribution to the Theory of the Trade Cycle*, Clarendon Press, Oxford.

Le Corbeiller, Ph., 1936, "The nonlinear theory of the maintenance of oscillations", *Journal of the Institution of Electrical Engineers* 79, pp. 361-378.

Le Corbeiller, Ph., 1958, "Letter to Goodwin (March 29)". Reproduced in Velupillai, 1990, pp. 20-23.

Le Corbeiller, Ph., 1960, "Two-stroke oscillators", *IRE Transactions on Circuit Theory* CT-7(4), pp. 387-398.

Sasakura, K., 1996, "The business cycle model with a unique stable limit cycle", *Journal of Economic Dynamics and Control* 20, pp. 1763-1773.

Velupillai, Vela K., 1990. "The (nonlinear) life and (economic) times of Richard M. Goodwin", in: Velupillai, K. (Ed.), *Nonlinear and Multisectoral Macrodynamics*, Macmillan, London, pp. 7-27.

Velupillai, Vela K., 1991. "Theories of the trade cycle: analytical and conceptual perspectives and perplexities", in: Thygesen, N., Velupillai, K., Zambelli, S. (Eds.), *Business Cycles: Theories, Evidence and Analysis*, Macmillan, London, pp. 3-38.

Velupillai, Vela K., 1998, "The vintage economist", *Journal of Economic Behavior and Organization* 37, pp. 1-31.

Velupillai, Vela K., 2004, "Hicksian visions and vignettes on (non-linear) trade cycle theories", *Discussion Paper* n. 7, Università degli Studi di Trento, Dipartimento di Economia.

11 A Goodwin-Type Model with Cubic Investment Function

Iryna Sushko, Tönu Puu and Laura Gardini

11.1 Introduction

The present chapter is in the Goodwin (1951) tradition, with all bounds incorporated in the investment function, even the ceiling, which means that it is the investors who abstain from investing more once available resources put a limit on further expansion (in real terms). Goodwin modelled a continuous-time process, as described in Chapter 10, whereas the present model is cast in discrete time.

Goodwin further advocated a smooth investment function with asymptotes, such as a hyperbolic tangent shape. One of the present authors, Puu (1989) suggested a combination of linear-cubic terms in the investment function. The back-bending, caused by the cubic, needed to be given a factual explanation in terms of economics. Even if the complete model could be tuned so as to limit motion so that the cubic never hit the axes, which would be absurd, the existence of a maximum and a minimum were still responsible for some of the more exotic phenomena, and so needed an explanation.

This was not difficult. If one considers the hyperbolic tangent shape of the investment function as relevant for private investments, one could in addition consider public investments. In particular long-term budgets for infrastructure investments tend to be countercyclically distributed. This is partly due to an active wish to fight excessive changes in the cycle causing unemployment or inflation, and partly due to the advantage of using idle resources and low costs in the slump rather than in the boom.

A slightly different model was studied in Puu and Sushko (2004). The setup was as follows: Consumption was defined as $C_t = (1 - s)Y_{t-1} + \varepsilon s Y_{t-2}$, where $0 < s < 1$ was the complementary proportion saved (or, in terms of other chapters of this book, $1 - s = c$), and a fraction $0 < \varepsilon < 1$ of savings was assumed to be spent after being saved for one period. Investment was defined as $I_t = v((Y_{t-1} - Y_{t-2}) - (Y_{t-1} - Y_{t-2})^3)$. To this we add the income identity $Y_t = C_t + I_t$. As we see, the consumption and investment variables can be eliminated, and the model cast as a second order recurrence equation in income alone, though containing a cubic nonlinearity.

The setup of the model just described obviously is non-generic, as the investment function is symmetric with respect to the origin. The aim of the present study is to also include an even order quadratic term to the investment function: $I_t = a((Y_{t-1} - Y_{t-2}) + b(Y_{t-1} - Y_{t-2})^2 - (Y_{t-1} - Y_{t-2})^3)$, so as to break the symmetry, and produce a more generic model. The consumption function is defined as $C_t = cY_{t-1}$, thus skipping the two-period lagged setup of Puu and Sushko (2004). As before, substituting to the income identity, we get a second order difference equation in income variable:

$$Y_t = cY_{t-1} + a((Y_{t-1} - Y_{t-2}) + b(Y_{t-1} - Y_{t-2})^2 - (Y_{t-1} - Y_{t-2})^3). \quad (1)$$

11.2 Description of the Map

Let $x_t := Y_t$, $y_t := Y_{t-1}$. Then to describe the dynamics of the model introduced above we have to study the behavior of trajectories of a two-dimensional map $F : \mathbb{R}^2 \to \mathbb{R}^2$ given by

$$F : \begin{pmatrix} x \\ y \end{pmatrix} \mapsto \begin{pmatrix} cx + a(x-y) + ab(x-y)^2 - a(x-y)^3 \\ x \end{pmatrix}, \quad (2)$$

where a, b and c are real parameters such that

$$a > 0, \ 0 < c < 1. \quad (3)$$

The parameter b is responsible for the symmetry of the investment function, namely, for $b = 0$ the 'floor' and 'ceiling' are located at equal distance from the origin, while the case $b \neq 0$ is more general.

In this chapter we shall illustrate some local and global bifurcation mechanisms related to the Neimark-Sacker bifurcation in a smooth map (already introduced in Chapter 1). We shall see how the stability loss of the fixed point with a pair of complex-conjugate eigenvalues on the unit circle results in the appearance (in the neighborhood of the fixed point) of an attracting closed invariant curve homeomorphic to a circle[1], and how this curve can be destroyed leading to complex dynamics.

[1] In invertible maps it is also called a two-dimensional torus, being associated with the Poincaré section of a three dimensional flow.

To begin, let us derive some simple properties of the map F. First note that F is a *noninvertible* map: In the phase space there exist two straight lines denoted LC_{-1} and LC'_{-1}, which are related to the vanishing determinant of the Jacobian matrix of F:

$$\begin{aligned} LC_{-1} &= \{(x,y) : y = x - k_1\}\,, \\ LC'_{-1} &= \{(x,y) : y = x - k_2\}\,, \end{aligned}$$

where $k_1 = (b - \sqrt{b^2+3})/3$, $k_2 = (b + \sqrt{b^2+3})/3$. Images of these lines by F are also straight lines, called *critical lines* and denoted LC and LC', respectively:

$$\begin{aligned} LC &= \left\{(x,y) : y = x/c - ak_1(k_1^2 - bk_1 - 1)\right\}, \\ LC' &= \left\{(x,y) : y = x/c - ak_2(k_2^2 - bk_2 - 1)\right\}. \end{aligned}$$

The role of the critical curves LC and LC' is related to the foliation of the Riemann phase plane: Any point between these two lines has three different preimages, while any point outside this strip has only one preimage. Thus, the map F has a noninvertibility of so-called $(Z_1 - Z_3 - Z_1)$ type. Other examples of maps with such a kind of noninvertibility can be seen in Mira *et al.* (1996), Dieci *et al.* (2001), Chiarella *et al.* (2002), Puu and Sushko (2004), Bischi *et al.* (2005).

It is known that the critical lines and their images play an important role for the dynamics of a noninvertible map (for a survey see Mira *et al.* (1996)). As we shall see, these images may define the boundary of an absorbing area to which the attractors of the map, as well as other invariant sets, necessarily belong. A contact of the boundary of some basin of attraction with the critical lines usually results in a global bifurcation causing the appearance of new isolated islands of the basin (Mira *et al.* (1994)). Regarding to an invariant attracting closed curve, which is the main interest of the present chapter, we shall see that the intersection of this curve with LC_{-1} or LC'_{-1} can give rise to the appearance of infinitely many loops, which are impossible in invertible maps (as already emphasized in Mira *et al.* (1996), Frouzakis *et al.* (1997)). We shall also see other features of closed invariant curves, related, in particular, to the homoclinic bifurcation, described in Chapter 1 and Chapter 8 for a fixed point, while here it will be related to a cycle of period 7.

Let us first describe the simplest kind of attractor of the map F, that is, its fixed point. It can be easily seen that F has a unique fixed point

$(x^*, y^*) = (0, 0)$. The eigenvalues of the Jacobian matrix of F at (x^*, y^*) depend on the parameters a and c:

$$\lambda_{1,2} = (a + c \pm \sqrt{(a+c)^2 - 4a})/2, \tag{4}$$

from which we deduce that for the parameter range given in (3) the fixed point (x^*, y^*) is a node if $(c+a)^2 > 4a$, and a focus if $(c+a)^2 < 4a$, being attracting for $a < 1$ and repelling for $a > 1$.

So, for $a < 1$ the fixed point of F is attracting, but it obviously cannot be a global attractor: Due to the cubic shape of the function defining our map, there are initial points whose trajectories are divergent. Indeed, the basin of attraction of the fixed point is bounded by the closure of the stable manifold of a saddle cycle of period 2, denoted $\{p_1, p_2\}$, where $p_1(x_0, y_0) = (bk/(1-c) + \sqrt{k/a}/2, bk/(1-c) - \sqrt{k/a}/2)$, $k = (c + 2a + 1)/2$ and $p_2 = F(p_1)$.

It can be verified that for the parameter range here considered the saddle cycle $\{p_1, p_2\}$ always exists (as an example, see Fig.2), and its stable manifold separates the basin of divergent trajectories from the set of points of the phase plane having bounded trajectories (which may include several disjoint basins and invariant sets). Running ahead we can say that the contact of an attractor with the stable manifold of this saddle results in a *boundary crises* which causes an explosion of the basin of divergent trajectories. Often, after such a contact, almost all the trajectories of F go to infinity and the surviving set is a *chaotic repellor* with a Cantor like structure (although a surviving attractor may also exist, with a basin of attraction so small that it is numerically unobservable).

11.3 Neimark-Sacker Bifurcation and Arnol'd Tongues

At $a = 1$ the fixed point (x^*, y^*) has complex-conjugate eigenvalues on the unit circle. It is known that if there is no so-called *strong resonance,* that is $\mathrm{Re}\,\lambda_{1,2} \neq \cos 2\pi m/n$, where $n \leq 4$, and m/n is an irreducible fraction, then a Neimark-Sacker bifurcation occurs resulting, when supercritical, in an attracting invariant closed curve $\mathcal{C}$ homeomorphic to a circle, which appears in the neighborhood of the fixed point. Note that other generic transversality conditions have to be also fulfilled, see Guckenheimer and Holmes (1985), Kuznetsov (1998). It can be verified that these conditions are satisfied for the parameter range here considered.

The dynamics of the map F on the curve $\mathcal{C}$ are either periodic or quasiperiodic, depending on the parameters. Namely, if at $a = 1$ also the condition

$$c = c_{m/n} \stackrel{def}{=} 2\cos(2\pi m/n) - 1, \tag{5}$$

holds, then after the bifurcation, that is for $a = 1 + \varepsilon$ for a sufficiently small $\varepsilon > 0$, a pair of cycles of period n, an attracting node and a saddle, with rotation number m/n exist on the curve $\mathcal{C}$ (also called a phase-locked torus), so that this curve is made up by the closure of the unstable manifold of the saddle cycle. Note that for $c > 0$ we have $m/n < 1/6$. While if

$$c = c_{\rho} \stackrel{def}{=} 2\cos(2\pi\rho) - 1, \tag{6}$$

where ρ is an irrational number, then after the bifurcation there are quasiperiodic trajectories on the curve $\mathcal{C}$ (also called quasiperiodic torus).

The dynamics of F locally, in the neighborhood of the fixed point, depend only on the parameters a and c, while the parameter b influences, obviously, the global dynamics. Due to the symmetry with respect to the origin of the map F for negative and positive values of b, we can restrict our analysis only to the case $b > 0$ (the case $b < 0$ is analogous, with trajectories symmetric with respect to the origin in the phase space, and symmetric structure of the parameter space). We don't consider in this chapter the particular value $b = 0$, however in such a case F has dynamics qualitatively similar to those described in Puu and Sushko (2004).

Fig.1 presents a two-dimensional bifurcation diagram of the map F in the (a, c)-parameter plane at $b = 0.2$, where the parameter regions corresponding to the attracting cycles of different periods $n \leq 32$, are shown by different gray tonalities. The periodicity regions starting from the bifurcation line $a = 1$ are called *Arnol'd tongues*. It is known that the boundaries of the Arnol'd tongue are two curves corresponding to saddle-node bifurcation of the related cycles (the lower and upper boundaries of the periodicity tongues in Fig.1), while other boundaries (to the right) are related to either period-doubling or Neimark-Sacker bifurcation of the related attracting cycle. The periodicity tongue associated with the rotation number m/n starts from the parameter point $(a, c) = (1, c_{m/n})$, while the parameter point $(a, c) = (1, c_{\rho})$ is the starting point for the curve corresponding to a closed curve with quasiperiodic trajectories, related to the irrational rotation number ρ. Such a structure of the parameter plane reflects the Neimark-Sacker bifurcation theorem mentioned above, according to which for the parameter values taken near the bifurcation line $a = 1$, that is for $a = 1 + \varepsilon$ for some sufficiently small $\varepsilon > 0$, in the neighborhood of the fixed point there exists an attracting invariant closed curve $\mathcal{C}$ on which the map F is reduced to a rotation with rational or irrational rotation number. Examples of the curve $\mathcal{C}$ in case of rotation numbers $1/6$ and $1/7$ can be seen in Fig.2 and Fig.8, respectively.

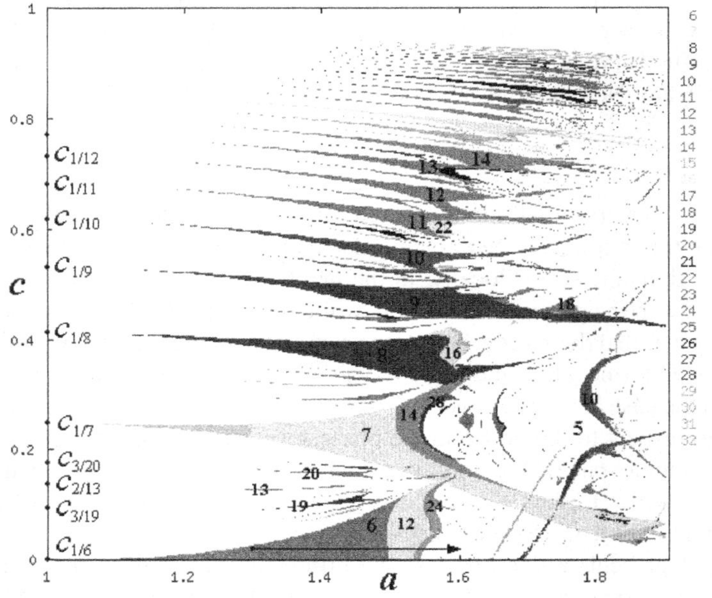

Figure 1: *Two-dimensional bifurcation diagram of the map F in the (a, c)-parameter plane for $b = 0.2$. Parameter regions related to attracting cycles of different periods $n \leq 32$ are shown by different gray tonalities.*

At fixed value of c, on increasing the value of a the curve $\mathcal{C}$ is destroyed and the dynamics of F become more complicated. Let us first recall in short possible scenarios leading to the destruction of a closed invariant attracting curve:

(1) The related attracting cycle, being a node at its birth, becomes a focus. We can say that the closed invariant curve still exists but it is no longer homeomorphic to a circle (an example can be seen in Fig.8). In such a case it is quite common that when the parameter point leaves the periodicity tongue

then the attracting focus undergoes a Neimark-Sacker bifurcation, and cyclical closed invariant curves appear;

(2) The related attracting cycle can undergo period-doubling bifurcation;

(3) The curve C can lose its smoothness and becomes nondifferentiable (due to infinitely many oscillations of one branch of the unstable manifold of the saddle, approaching the node);

(4) The related saddle cycle undergoes homoclinic bifurcation;

(5) Intersection of the curve C with a critical line can lead to the creation of infinitely many loops, that is, to the selfintersections of the unstable manifold of the saddle (see Fig.3).

If the parameter point leaves the periodicity tongue crossing the saddle-node bifurcation curve when C is still smooth, then we have transition from the phase-locked torus to the quasiperiodic one. In the two cases (3) and (4), if the parameter point leaves the periodicity tongue crossing the saddle-node bifurcation curve, then the curve C is transformed into a set with fractal structure.

The destruction of a two-dimensional torus in the case of diffeomorphisms was first described in Afraimovich and Shil'nikov (1983). In Aronson *et. al.* (1982) it was in particular shown that torus can be destroyed also due to the contact with its basin boundary. See also Anishchenko *et al.* (1994), Arnol'd *et al.* (1991) for further details and examples. The first four scenarios can occur both in invertible and noninvertible maps (for the examples related to noninvertible maps see Gumowski and Mira, (1980a,b)), while the case (5) obviously can occur only for a noninvertible map (several examples are given in Mira *et al.* (1996), Frouzakis *et al.* (1997), Maistrenko *et al.* (2003)), and one example will be given also in the next section.

In the last section we shall describe a sequence of transformations occurring at fixed c and increasing a, associated with a 7-node, which becomes at first a 7-focus (i.e. case (1) above), then it becomes a 7-node again (with one negative eigenvalue), which undergoes the flip bifurcation. Futher increase of a leads to appearance of two 7-cyclical closed invariant curves, attracting and repelling, via global bifurcations as described in Chapters 1 and 8.

To close this section we mention an important feature of nonlinear maps for parameter values taken far from the Neimark-Sacker bifurcation curve, which is that the periodicity regions can be overlapped (as it can be seen in Fig.1 or Fig.7). This means that coexistence of attracting cycles of different periods is not a rare phenomenon, and usually this situation leads to several kinds of global bifurcations in the invariant sets and/or in the basins of attraction of the coexisting attracting sets.

11.4 First Example of Bifurcation Sequence: Creation of Loops and Period-Doubling Cascade

In this section we present a bifurcation scenario of transition to complex dynamics, related to the destruction of the closed invariant curve C via creation of infinitely many loops (an effect of the noninvertibility, leading to the self-intersections of the unstable set of the saddle cycle), and the period-doubling cascade of the attracting cycle existing on C.

Let γ_n denote an attracting cycle of period n, and γ_n^+, γ_n^-, denote saddle cycles of period n with, respectively, positive and negative eigenvalue related to the unstable eigendirection.

For the first example we fix $b = 0.2$ and $c = 0.02$ and will increase a starting from $a = 1.3$, as shown in Fig.1 by the straight line with an arrow. The phase portrait of the map F at $a = 1.3$ is presented in Fig.2: There exists an attracting invariant closed curve C made up the unstable manifold of the saddle cycle γ_6^+ approaching points of the attracting cycle γ_6. The

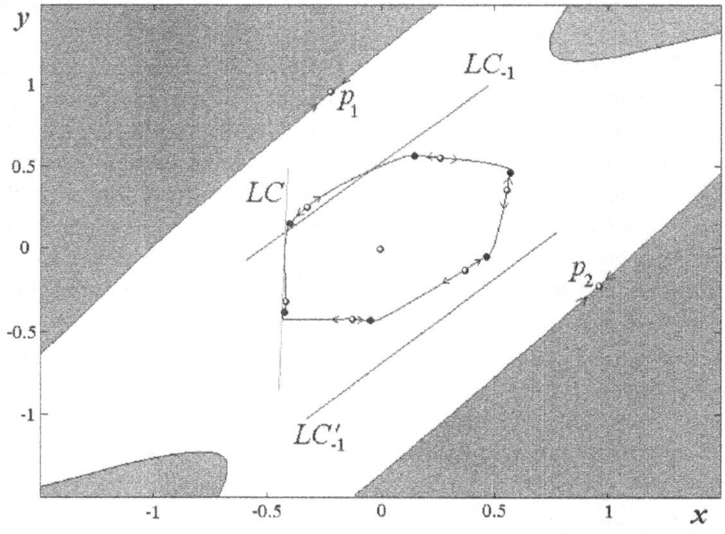

Figure 2: *Phase portrait of the map F at $a = 1.3$, $b = 0.2$, $c = 0.02$. The attracting closed invariant curve is formed by the closure of the unstable manifold of the saddle 6-cycle (shown by white circles), approaching the points of the attracting 6-cycle (the black circles).*

basins of attraction of $\mathcal{C}$ and that of infinity (i.e., of divergent trajectories) are separated by the stable manifold of the saddle cycle $\{p_1, p_2\}$. It can be seen that the curve $\mathcal{C}$ intersects the critical line LC_{-1} and is folded on LC (i.e., tangent to LC and bent to the right) without creation of loops, which in particular means that the map F is invertible on $\mathcal{C}$, and $\mathcal{C}$ is homeomorphic to a circle. However, it is worth noticing that the area bounded by $\mathcal{C}$ is not invariant under application of F: In fact it is invariant only as long as the closed curve $\mathcal{C}$ has no intersections with the lines LC_{-1} and LC'_{-1}, and this is no longer true in the case shown in Fig.2. According to the results stated in Frouzakis *et al.* (1997) (see also Maistrenko *et al.* (2003)), the cusp points and then the loops are created on $\mathcal{C}$ if the slope of the tangent of the curve $\mathcal{C}$ at the point of intersection with LC_{-1} (or LC'_{-1}) at first is the same and then becomes larger then the slope of the eigenvector associated with the zero eigenvalue of the Jacobian matrix of the map F at that point. Fig.3 shows the curve $\mathcal{C}$ at $a = 1.45$ when the loops are already created, thus the map F is noninvertible on the curve $\mathcal{C}$, which obviously is no longer homeomorphic to a circle.

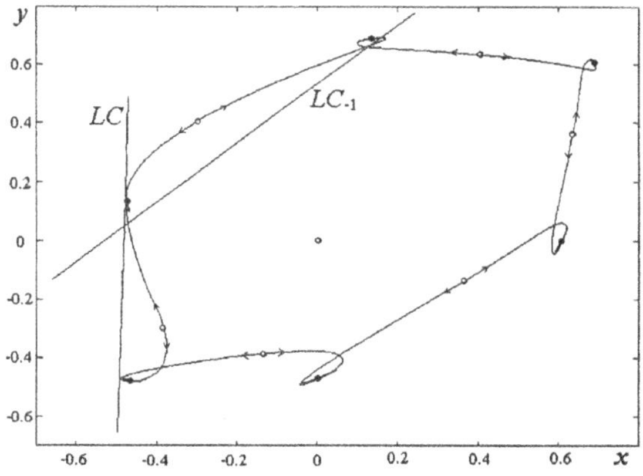

Figure 3: *The attracting closed invariant curve $\mathcal{C}$ with infinitely many loops at* $a = 1.45$, $b = 0.2$, $c = 0.02$.

If we continue to increase the values of a, the cycle γ_6 undergoes a cascade of the period-doubling bifurcations: At $a \approx 1.4952$ the first period-doubling bifurcation occurs resulting in a saddle γ_6^- and attracting cycle γ_{12}. Fig.4 presents the phase portrait of the map F at $a = 1.5$, where the attracting cycle γ_{12} and two saddle cycles γ_6^+ and γ_6^- are shown, together with the unstable manifold of γ_6^+, which has infinitely many loops. The value $a = a^* \approx 1.548481$ is a limit for the values related to the period-doubling cascade of the cycle γ_6. Approaching the value a^* from the opposite side we have a cascade of homoclinic bifurcations for the saddle cycles γ_{6k}^-, $k = 1, ...$, born during the period-doubling cascade of γ_6. Each of these homoclinic bifurcations gives rise to the pairwise merging of pieces of cyclic chaotic attractors. As an example, Fig.5 shows the 12-piece chaotic attractor at $a = 1.56$, near the first homoclinic bifurcation of the cycle γ_6^- (shown by the gray circles). The result of this homoclinic bifurcation is a 6-piece chaotic attractor.

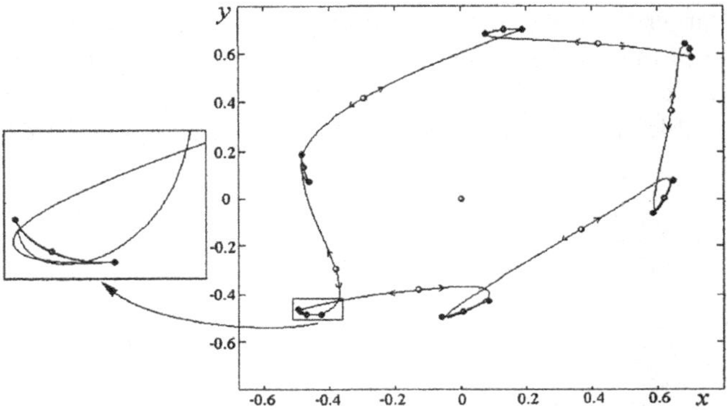

Figure 4: *The phase portrait of the map* F *and its enlarged part at* $a = 1.5$, $b = 0.2$, $c = 0.02$: *The points of the saddle cycles* γ_6^+ *and* γ_6^-, *are shown by white and gray circles, respectively; Black circles indicate points of the attracting cycle* γ_{12}.

The basin of attraction of each of the 6 pieces of the chaotic attractor is separated by the stable manifold of the saddle cycle of period 6, while the unstable branches tend to the attractor (indeed, the closure of the unstable set of the saddle includes the chaotic pieces). Thus, if we consider the map F^6, a contact of the chaotic pieces with the boundary of their immediate basins results in the first homoclinic bifurcation of the 6-saddle. Such a bifurcation gives rise to the merging of these 6 pieces into a one piece chaotic attractor. Fig.6(a) presents a one-piece chaotic attractor soon after this contact bifurcation. In general such a transition is accompanied by a so-called "rare points" phenomenon, reflecting the difference in density of the points along the attractor, as explained in detail in Mira *et al.* (1996), Gardini *et al.* (1996), Maistrenko *et al.* (1998).

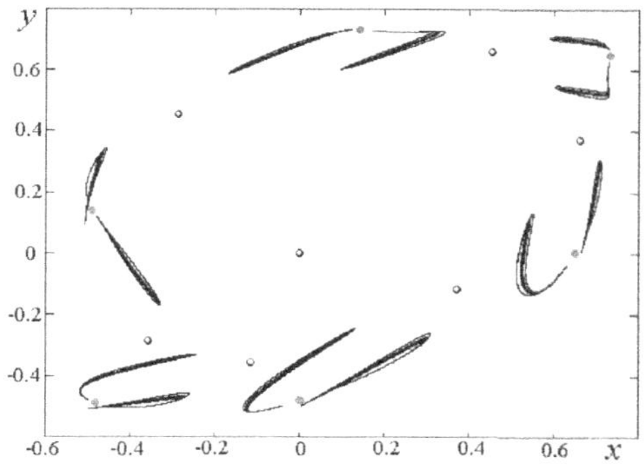

Figure 5: *The 12-piece cyclic chaotic attractor of the map F at $a = 1.56$, $b = 0.2$, $c = 0.02$.*

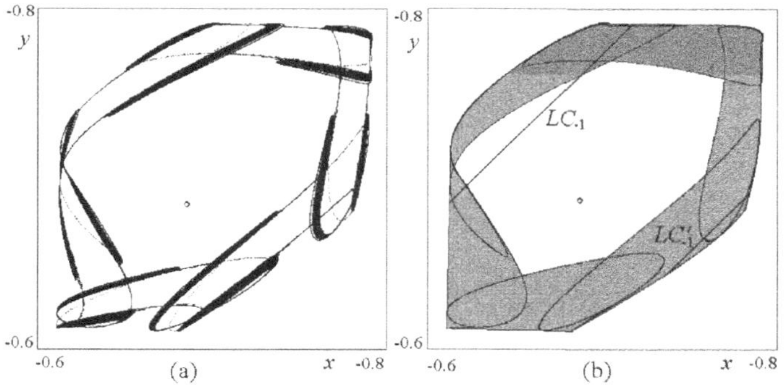

Figure 6: *(a) One-piece chaotic attractor of the map F at $a = 1.5802$, $b = 0.2$, $c = 0.02$; (b) Its absorbing area.*

All the attracting sets of the map F existing in the considered parameter range, after the bifurcation of the fixed point (see Fig.2 up to Fig.6(a)) belong to an absorbing area which is obtained by taking the images of a few segments of LC_{-1} and LC'_{-1}, which are exactly those pieces inside the area. An example is shown in Fig.6(b): The area is bounded by six images of the indicated segments of LC_{-1} and LC'_{-1}. The simply connected area is invariant, while the annular area, shown in gray in Fig.6(b), which more strictly includes all the existing invariant sets (except for the repelling fixed point), is absorbing but not invariant: A thinner annular invariant area can be obtained by using further images of the critical segments.

11.5 Second Example: Focus, Bistability and Global Bifurcations of Closed Invariant Curves

In this section we present one more example of bifurcation sequence which includes the destruction of the closed invariant curve C followed by a particular type of global bifurcation. This transition to complex dynamics is more complicated with respect to the one described in the previous section, as it includes bistability and one more Neimark-Sacker bifurcation. A global bifurcation related to this "secondary" Neimark-Sacker bifurcation will be emphasized, which gives rise to a pair of cyclical closed invariant curves, one attracting and one repelling.

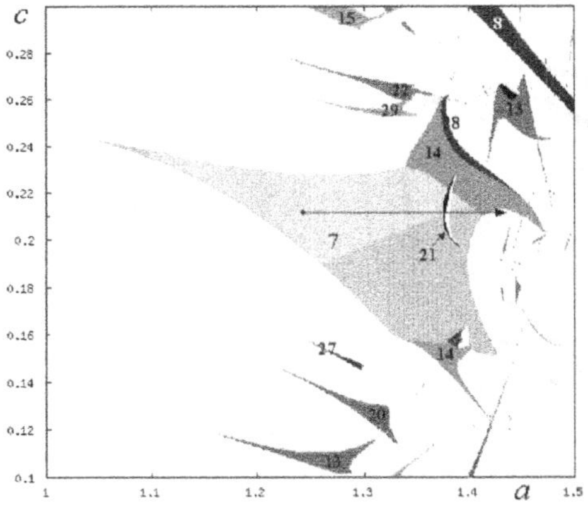

Figure 7: *Two-dimensional bifurcation diagram of the map F in the (a, c)-parameter plane at $b = 0.5$.*

We present a sequence of bifurcations related to the attracting cycle γ_7, fixing the parameters $b = 0.5$, $c = 0.21$ and increasing the value a starting from $a = 1.24$. The corresponding parameter path is shown in Fig.7 by the straight line with an arrow. The phase portrait of the map F at $a = 1.24$ is qualitatively similar to the one shown in Fig.2: Namely, there exists a closed attracting invariant curve $\mathcal{C}$, homeomorphic to a circle, made up by the unstable manifold of the saddle cycle γ_7^+, approaching the points of the attracting node γ_7. Increasing a the cycle γ_7 becomes a focus (see Fig.8 where $a = 1.31$), so that the curve $\mathcal{C}$ is no longer homeomorphic to a circle. The basins of attraction of each point of the attracting cycle γ_7 (considering

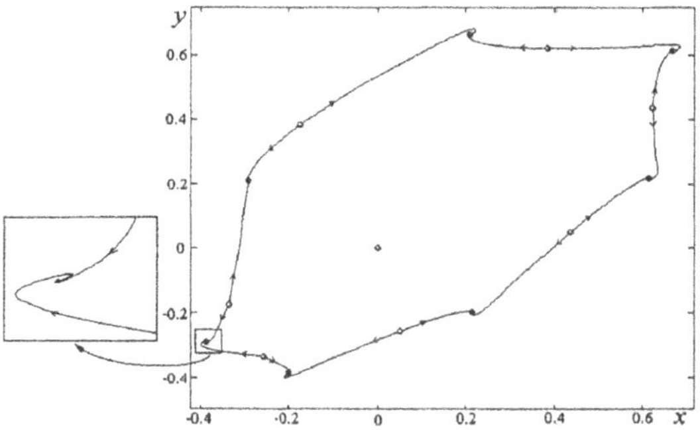

Figure 8: *The phase portrait and its enlarged part of the map F at $a = 1.31$, $b = 0.5$, $c = 0.21$.*

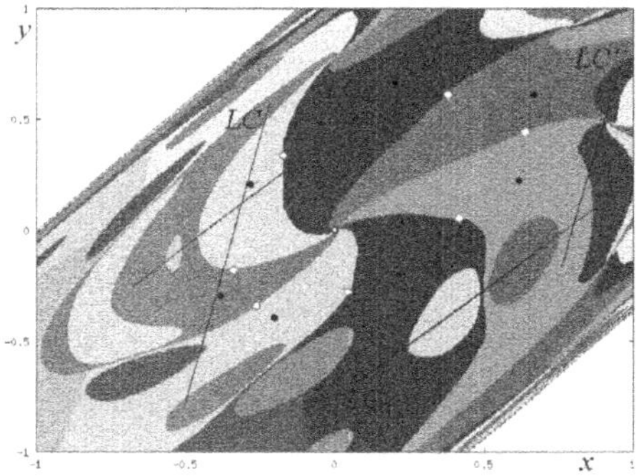

Figure 9: *Individual basins of attraction of points of the attracting cycle γ_7 (the black circles), bounded by the stable manifold of the saddle cycle γ_7^+ (the white circles).*

the map F^7) is presented in Fig.9: The boundary, formed by the stable manifold of the saddle cycle γ_7^+ has a regular structure. The intersection of the basin with the critical lines LC and LC' creates disconnected components of the basins, located on LC_{-1} and LC'_{-1}.

Increasing a a saddle-node bifurcation occurs giving rise to an attracting and a saddle cycle of period 21, and, thus, to bistability: Fig.10 presents the phase portrait of the map F at $a = 1.378$, with the attracting cycles γ_7 and γ_{21} (shown by big and small black circles, respectively), the saddle cycle γ_{21}^+ (the black squares) and the repelling cycle of period 7 (the white circles), which is the former saddle cycle γ_7^+ after the period-doubling bifurcation resulted in the saddle cycle γ_{14}^+ (white squares). The basin of attraction of the cycle γ_{21} is shown in white, while the basin of attraction of γ_7 is shown in dark gray. These two basins are separated by the stable set of γ_{21}^+. The light gray region corresponds to divergent trajectories. Further development of

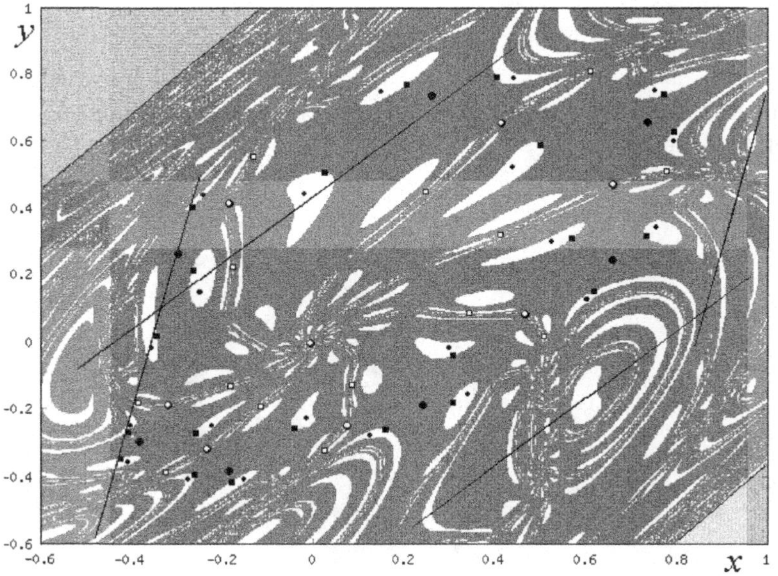

Figure 10: *The phase portrait of the map F at $a = 1.378$, $b = 0.5$, $c = 0.21$ with coexisting attracting cycles γ_{21} and γ_7 whose basins of attraction are shown in white and gray, respectively.*

the scenarios, increasing a, is related to the cascade of the period-doubling bifurcations of the cycle γ_{21}. Fig.11 shows an enlarged part of the phase space with several pieces of a 21-piece cyclic chaotic attractor coexisting with the attracting cycle γ_7 at $a = 1.381$. This chaotic attractor disappears due to a boundary crises, i.e., a contact with its basin boundary, which at the same time is the first homoclinic bifurcation of the saddle cycle γ_{21}^{+}. Soon after this contact there is only one attractor, the cycle γ_7, surrounded by a chaotic repellor created at the mentioned homoclinic bifurcation.

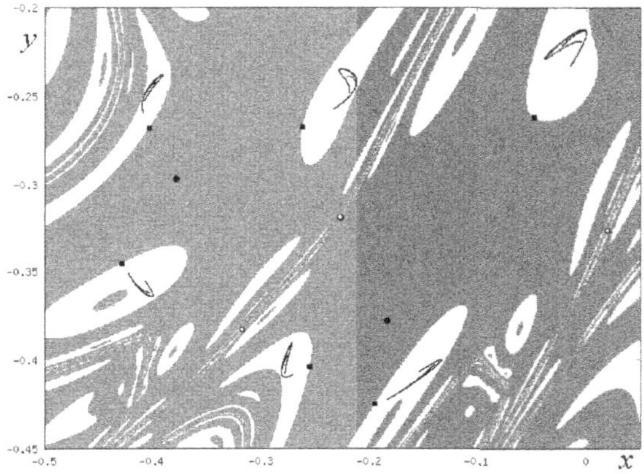

Figure 11: *An enlarged part of the phase space of the map* F *at* $a = 1.381$, $b = 0.5$, $c = 0.21$.

The parameter path shown in Fig.7 is chosen in such a way that at the exit of the 7-periodicity tongue the cycle γ_7 undergoes a period-doubling bifurcation resulting in a saddle cycle γ_7^- and an attracting cycle γ_{14}. For example, at $a = 1.41335$ the parameter point is inside the periodicity region corresponding to an attracting cycle γ_{14}. However, as a increases, the parameter point moves towards a region which is also close to the Neimark-Sacker bifurcation of the 7-cycle, and the global bifurcation may occur, already described in Chapters 1 and 8 (related there with a fixed point of the map). Indeed, such a global bifurcation has been detected, which gives rise to the appearance of a pair of disjoint 7-cyclical closed invariant curves, one attracting, denoted Γ_7, and one repelling, denoted Γ'_7, surrounding the points of the saddle cycle γ_7^- and the attracting cycle γ_{14}. After the first homoclinic bifurcation of the cycle γ_7^- the curve Γ'_7 undergoes pairwise splitting and becomes a 14-cyclical repelling closed invariant curve Γ'_{14}: The phase portrait of the map F at $a = 1.4134$ is shown in Fig.12 (a) and an enlargement is given in Fig.12 (b), where it can be seen one curve of Γ_7 and two curves of Γ'_{14}, which surround the points of the cycles γ_{14} and γ_7^-, shown by black and white circles, respectively. The 14-cyclical repelling closed invariant curve Γ'_{14} bounds the basin of attraction of γ_{14}, while the wider basin (among the points having bounded trajectories) is that of points attracting to Γ_7. As expected, on further increasing of a the cycle γ_{14} becomes unstable via a subcritical Neimark-Sacker bifurcation, leaving the 7-cyclical closed curve Γ_7 as unique attracting set.

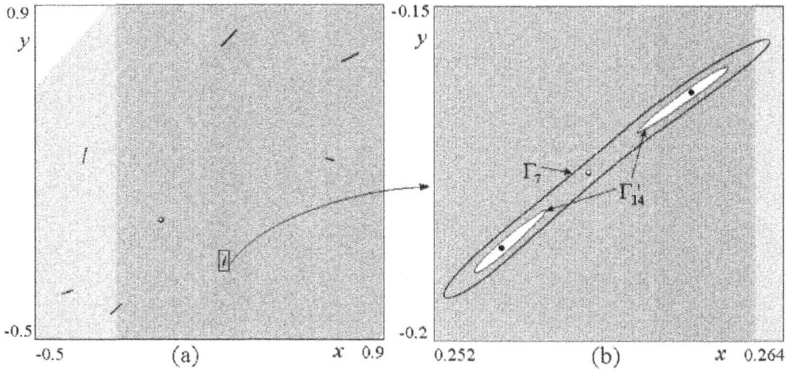

Figure 12: *In (a) the 7-cyclical attracting closed invariant curve* Γ_7 *is visible, while in the enlargement (b), besides one curve of* Γ_7, *it can be also seen two curves of the* 14*-cyclical repelling closed invariant curve* Γ'_{14}, *which bound the basin of attraction of the cycle* γ_{14}.

References

Afraimovich, V.S., Shil'nikov, L.P., 1983, "Invariant two-dimensional tori, their destruction and stochasticity", *Gorkii University*, Gorkii, Russia, pp. 3-26.

Anishchenko, V.S, Safonova, M.A., Feudel, U., Kurths, J., 1994, "Bifurcations and transition to chaos through three-dimensional tori", *Int. J. Bif. and Chaos*, Vol. 4., 3, pp. 595-607.

Arnol'd, V.I., Afraimovich, V.S., Il'iashenko, Yu.S., Shil'nikov, L.P., 1991, *Dynamical Systems*, Vol. 5, Springer, Berlin.

Aronson, D.G., Chory, M.A., Hall, G.R., McGehee, R.P., 1982, "Bifurcations from an invariant circle for two-parameter families of maps of the plane: A computer-assisted study", Commun. Math. Phys. 83, pp. 303-354.

Bischi, G.I., Gardini, L., Mira, C., 2005, "Basin fractalization generated by a two-dimensional family of Z1-Z3-Z1 maps", *Int. J. Bif. and Chaos* (to appear).

Chiarella, C., Dieci, R., Gardini, L., 2002, "Speculative Behaviour and Complex Asset Price Dynamics: A Global Analysis", *Journal of Economic Behavior and Organization*, 49(1), pp. 173-197.

Dieci, R., Bischi, G.-I., Gardini L., 2001, "Multistability and role of noninvertibility in a discrete-time business cycle model", *Central European Journal of Operation Research*, 9, pp. 71-96.

Frouzakis, C.E., Gardini, L., Kevrekidis, I.G., Millerioux, G., Mira, C., 1997, "On some properties of invariant sets of two-dimensional noninvertible maps", *Int. J. Bif. and Chaos*, Vol. 7, 6, pp. 1167-1194.

Gandolfo, G., 1985, *Economic dynamics: methods and models*, Second edition, North Holland, Amsterdam.

Gardini, L., Abraham, R., Record, R.J., Fournier-Prunaret, D., 1994, "A double logistic map", *Int. J. Bif. and Chaos*, 4, pp. 145-176.

Gardini, L., Mira, C., Fournier-Prunaret, D., 1996, "Properties of invariant areas in two-dimensional endomorphisms", In book: *Iteration Theory*, W. Forg-Rob et al. ed.s, World Scientific, pp. 112-125.

Goodwin, R.M., 1951, "The nonlinear accelerator and the persistence of business cycles", *Econometrica,* 19, pp. 1-17.

Guckenheimer, J. and Holmes P., 1985, *Nonlinear Oscillations, Dynamical Systems, and Bifurcations of Vector Fields*, Springer-Verlag.

Gumowski, I. and Mira, C., 1980a, *Dynamique chaotique*, Ed. Cépadues, Toulouse.

Gumowski, I. and Mira, C., 1980b, *Recurrences and discrete dynamic systems*, Lecture notes in Mathematics, Springer.

Herman, M., 1979, "Sur la cojugaison différentiable de difféomorphismes du cercle à des rotations", *Publ. Math.I.H.E.S.* 49, pp. 5-233.

Hicks, J.R., 1950, *A contribution to the theory of the trade cycle*, Clarendon Press, Oxford.

Kuznetsov, Yu., 1998, *Elements of Applied Bifurcation Theory*, Springer-Verlag, New York.

Maistrenko, Y., Sushko, I., Gardini, L., 1998, "About two mechanisms of reunion of chaotic attractors", *Chaos, Solitons and Fractals,* Vol. 9, 8, pp. 1373-1390.

Maistrenko, V., Maistrenko, Yu., Mosekilde, E., 2003, "Torus breakdown in noninvertible maps", *Physical Review E* 67, 046215.

Mira, C., Fournier-Prunaret, D., Gardini, L., Kawakami, H., Cathala, J.C., 1994, "Basin bifurcations of two-dimensional noninvertible maps. Fractalization of basins", *Int. J. Bif. and Chaos*, 4(2), pp. 343-381.

Mira, C., Gardini, L., Barugola, A., Cathala, J.C., 1996, *Chaotic Dynamics in Two-Dimensional Noninvertible Maps*, World Scientific, Singapore.

Neimark, Y., 1959, "On some cases of periodic motions depending on parameters", *Dokl. Acad. Nauk SSSR,* 129, pp. 736-739.

Nitecki, Z., 1971, *Differentiable dynamics*, M.I.T. Press, Cambridge.

Puu, T., 1989, *Nonlinear economic dynamics*, Lecture Notes in Economics and Mathematical Systems 336, Springer-Verlag, Berlin.

Puu, T., Sushko, I., 2004, "A business cycle model with cubic nonlinearity", *Chaos, Solitons and Fractals*, 19, pp. 597-612.

Sacker, R., 1965, "A new approach to the perturbation theory of invariant surfaces", *Comm. Pure Appl. Math.* 18, pp. 717-732.

12 A Goodwin-Type Model with a Piecewise Linear Investment Function

Laura Gardini, Tönu Puu and Iryna Sushko

12.1 Introduction

The model studied in the present chapter is a variation of the one presented in Chapter 11, so for a background we refer to the introduction of that chapter. The difference is that we now replace the cubic investment function by a five-piece linear one (see Fig.1). We shall see that the dynamic behavior of the model is different. In terms of economics we have the advantage that the constant pieces automatically prevent the investment function from cutting the horizontal axis more than once.

12.2 Center Bifurcation of the Fixed Point ($a = 1$)

In Chapter 6 we have described the simplest version of the Hicksian business cycle model defined by a two-dimensional piecewise linear map, showing that the main bifurcation scenarios in the model is the center bifurcation of the fixed point resulting in periodic or quasiperiodic dynamics (see also Hommes (1991), Gallegati *et al.* (2003)). In the present chapter we shall see the emergence of more complex dynamics, such as multistability and chaos, in a different version of the business cycle model also defined by a two-dimensional piecewise linear map.

We consider the dynamical system generated by a family of two - dimensional piecewise linear maps $F : \mathbb{R}^2 \to \mathbb{R}^2$ given by

$$F : \begin{pmatrix} x \\ y \end{pmatrix} \mapsto \begin{pmatrix} cx + I(x - y) \\ x \end{pmatrix}, \qquad (1)$$

where $I(z)$ is the piecewise linear investment function defined as

$$I(z) = \begin{cases} -h, & z \leq -\tau; \\ lz - a + l, & -\tau < z < -1; \\ az, & -1 \leq z \leq 1; \\ lz + a - l, & 1 < z \leq \tau; \\ h, & z \geq \tau; \end{cases} \tag{2}$$

where $\tau = (h - a + l)/l$ (see Fig.1). The map F depends on four real parameters a, c, l and h, such that

$$a > 0, 0 < c < 1, l < 0, 0 < h \leq a. \tag{3}$$

The investment function given in (2) is symmetric with respect to the origin (for an analogous business cycle model with symmetric cubic investment function see Puu and Sushko (2004)). It is not a generic case, and breaking of the symmetry can be introduced in several ways, but in this chapter, for simplicity, we limit our consideration to the symmetric case. It can be easily seen that the map F is also symmetric with respect to the origin, which immediately implies the following

Property. *Any invariant set A of the map F (i.e., such that $F(A) = A$) is either symmetric itself with respect to the origin, or there exists one more invariant set A' symmetric to A with respect to the origin.*

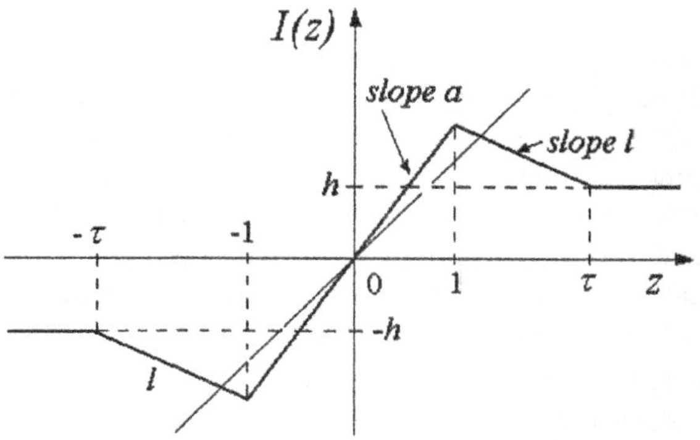

Figure 1: *The investment function.*

One of the aims of the present consideration is to illustrate the *center bifurcation* described in detail in Chapter 2, which occurs for piecewise linear maps when the fixed point loses stability with a pair of complex-conjugate eigenvalues on the unit circle (see also Sushko *et al.* (2003)). In a similarity to the Neimark-Sacker bifurcation (see Chapter 1, or Kuznetsov (1995)) it results in an attracting closed invariant curve C homeomorphic to a circle, and dynamics of F on C is reduced to a rotation with rational or irrational rotation number. We will present some examples of the bifurcation sequences leading through the breakdown of the curve C to complex dynamics.

The map F is given by five linear maps F_i, $i = 1, ..., 5$, defined, respectively, in five regions R_i of the phase plane:

$$\begin{aligned} F_1 &: \begin{pmatrix} x \\ y \end{pmatrix} \mapsto \begin{pmatrix} (c+a)x - ay \\ x \end{pmatrix}, \\ R_1 &= \{(x,y) : x - 1 \leq y \leq x + 1\}; \end{aligned} \tag{4}$$

$$\begin{aligned} F_{2,3} &: \begin{pmatrix} x \\ y \end{pmatrix} \mapsto \begin{pmatrix} (c+l)x - ly \pm (l-a) \\ x \end{pmatrix}, \\ R_2 &= \{(x,y) : x + 1 < y < x + \tau\}, \\ R_3 &= \{(x,y) : x - \tau < y < x - 1\}; \end{aligned} \tag{5}$$

$$\begin{aligned} F_{4,5} &: \begin{pmatrix} x \\ y \end{pmatrix} \mapsto \begin{pmatrix} cx \mp h \\ x \end{pmatrix} \\ R_4 &= \{(x,y) : y \geq x + \tau\}, \\ R_5 &= \{(x,y) : y \leq x - \tau\}. \end{aligned} \tag{6}$$

So, in the phase space of the map F there are four straight lines on which F changes its definition:

$$\begin{aligned} LC_{-1},\ LC_{-1}^{s} &: \ y = x \pm 1, \\ LC'_{-1},\ LC'^{s}_{-1} &: \ y = x \pm \tau. \end{aligned}$$

Their images by F are called *critical lines*:

$$\begin{aligned} LC,\ LC^{s} &: \ y = (x \pm a)/c, \\ LC',\ LC'^{s} &: \ y = (x \pm h)/c. \end{aligned}$$

The i-th iteration by F of the critical line is a broken line, called critical line of rank i.

It can be easily verified that the map F is noninvertible. Fig.2 shows schematically the folding action of F : Any point of the phase plane on the right of LC or on the left of LC^s has zero preimages, any point between LC and LC', or between LC^s and LC'^s has two preimages, any point between LC' and LC'^s has one preimage and, finally, any point of the straight lines LC' and LC'^s has infinitely many preimages (given that the whole regions R_4 and R_5 are mapped, respectively, into the straight lines LC' and LC'^s). So, the map F has noninvertibility of $(Z_0 - Z_2 - Z_\infty - Z_1 - Z_\infty - Z_2 - Z_0)$ kind (as a reference to noninvertibility and theory of critical lines see Mira *et al.* (1996)).

An obvious result can be immediately reached: For the parameter range considered the dynamics of F are always bounded, namely, in the phase plane there exists an absorbing area bounded by the critical lines LC'_{-1}, LC'^s_{-1}, LC and LC^s.

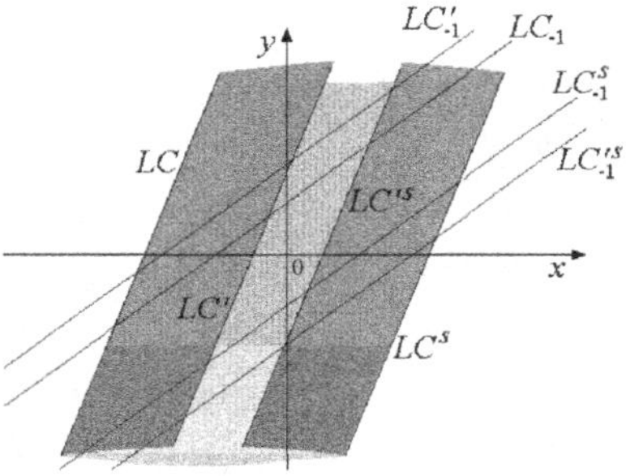

Figure 2: *The folding action of the map F.*

The unique fixed point of F is the fixed point of the map F_1 which is $(x^*, y^*) = (0, 0)$, given that the fixed points of other linear maps F_i, $i = 2, ..., 5$, are on the main diagonal belonging to R_1, and thus they are not fixed points of F. The eigenvalues of the Jacobian matrix of F_1 are

$$\lambda_{1,2} = (a + c \pm \sqrt{(a+c)^2 - 4a})/2, \tag{7}$$

so that for $a > 0$, $0 < c < 1$ the fixed point (x^*, y^*) is a node if $(c + a)^2 > 4a$, and a focus if $(c+a)^2 < 4a$, being attracting for $a < 1$ and repelling for $a > 1$. At $a = 1$ the fixed point undergoes the center bifurcation. Before the description of its results let us first derive some other properties of F.

The eigenvalues of the Jacobian matrix of the maps F_2 and F_3 (which differ only by a shift constant) are

$$\mu_{1,2} = (l + c \pm \sqrt{(l+c)^2 - 4l})/2. \tag{8}$$

Given that $l < 0$, we have that $\mu_{1,2}$ are always real and $0 < \mu_1 < 1$, while $-1 < \mu_2 < 0$ if $c > -2l - 1$, and $\mu_2 < -1$ if $c < -2l - 1$. The eigenvalues of the Jacobian matrix of the maps F_4 and F_5 (which also differ only by a shift constant) are $\nu_1 = c$ and $\nu_2 = 0$. We can state

Proposition 1. *If $a < 1$ and the ranges of c, l and h are as given in* (3), *then the fixed point (x^*, y^*) is the global attractor of the map F.*

Obviously, the map F cannot have divergent trajectories. To see that the proposition is true, we have to show that it cannot have other attractors. For $c > -2l-1$, when all the maps F_i, $i = 1, ..., 5$ are contractions, the statement is obvious. While in case $c < -2l - 1$, when $\mu_{1,2}$ are such that $0 < \mu_1 < 1$ and $\mu_2 < -1$, the statement can be proved by contradiction: Suppose, there exist another attractor. It necessarily must belong to an absorbing area, made up by images of the critical lines, but a simple geometrical reasoning shows that such an area shrinks by F to the origin.

Consider now the map F given in (1) exactly at the bifurcation value $a = 1$, when the fixed point (x^*, y^*) undergoes the center bifurcation. Using the results presented in Section 2.2 of Chapter 2, we can state that at $a = 1$ there exists an invariant region in the phase plane, and its structure depends only on the map F_1 and the critical lines LC_{-1}, LC_{-1}^s (and, thus, it depends only on the parameters a and c). Let us repeat that if at $a = 1$ the map F_1 is defined by the rotation matrix with some rational rotation number m/n, which holds for

$$c = c_{m/n} \stackrel{def}{=} 2\cos(2\pi m/n) - 1, \tag{9}$$

then any point from some neighborhood of the fixed point is periodic with rotation number m/n, and all points of the same periodic orbit are located on an invariant ellipse. The following proposition describes the dynamics of F in such a case:

Proposition 2. *Let $a = 1$, $c = c_{m/n}$, then in the phase plane of the map F there exists an invariant polygon P such that*

- *If n is even then P has n edges which are two generating segments $S_1 \subset LC_{-1}$, $S_1^s \subset LC_{-1}^s$ and their images $S_{i+1} = F_1(S_i) \subset LC_{i-1}$, $S_{i+1}^s = F_1(S_i^s) \subset LC_{i-1}^s$, $i = 1, ..., n/2 - 1$;*

- *If n is odd then P has $2n$ edges which are two generating segment $S_1 \subset LC_{-1}$, $S_1^s \subset LC_{-1}^s$ and their images $S_{i+1} = F_1(S_i) \subset LC_{i-1}$, $S_{i+1}^s = F_1(S_i^s) \subset LC_{i-1}^s$, $i = 1, ..., n-1$.*

Any initial point $(x_0, y_0) \in P$ is periodic with rotation number m/n, while any $(x_0, y_0) \notin P$ is mapped inside P in a finite number of iterations.

See Fig.3 with an example of the polygon P with 14 edges at $a = 1$, $c = c_{1/7}$.

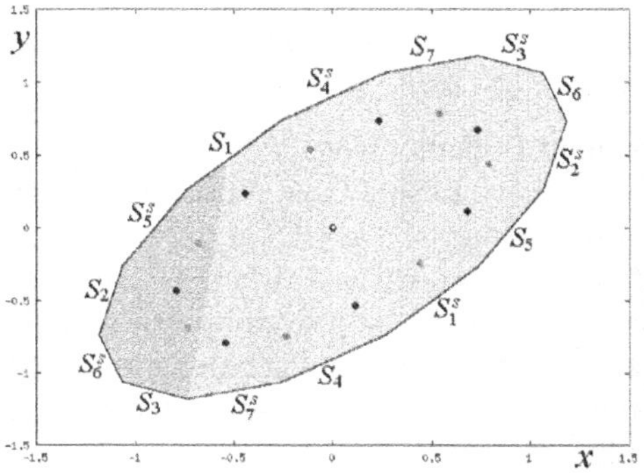

Figure 3: *The invariant polygon P of the map F at $a = 1$, $c = c_{1/7} = 2\cos(2\pi/7) - 1$. Any point of P is periodic with rotation number $1/7$; As an example, two such cycles are shown by black and gray circles.*

If at $a = 1$ the map F_1 is defined by the rotation matrix with an irrational rotation number ρ, which holds for

$$c = c_\rho \stackrel{def}{=} 2\cos(2\pi\rho) - 1, \tag{10}$$

then any point from some neighborhood of the fixed point is quasiperiodic, and all points of the same quasiperiodic orbit are dense on the corresponding invariant ellipse. In such a case the following proposition holds:

Proposition 3. *Let $a = 1$, $c = c_\rho$. Then in the phase space of the map F there exists an invariant region Q, bounded by an invariant ellipse $\mathcal{E}$ of the map F_1 tangent to both critical lines LC_{-1}, LC_{-1}^s (and to all their images). Any initial point $(x_0, y_0) \in Q$ belongs to a quasiperiodic orbit dense in the corresponding ellipse of F_1, while any $(x_0, y_0) \notin Q$ is mapped inside Q in a finite number of iterations.*

Note that Propositions 2 and 3 hold for any values of l and h. We already know that generally, increasing a, i.e., for $a = 1 + \varepsilon$, $\varepsilon > 0$, only the boundary of the region P or Q remains invariant for some sufficiently small ε, being an attracting closed invariant curve $\mathcal{C}$ on which the dynamics of F are periodic or quasiperiodic, respectively. Further increase of a leads to destruction of this curve and then to more complex dynamics.

12.3 Destruction of the Curve $\mathcal{C}$ and Routes to Chaos ($a > 1$)

Before presenting some general description of the dynamics of F for $a > 1$, let us first consider a particular parameter value $a = h$. In such a case we have $\tau = 1$, $LC_{-1} = LC'_{-1}$ (and $LC^s_{-1} = LC'^s_{-1}$) so that the map F is given by three linear maps F_1, F_2 (which is equal to F_4) and F_3 (equals F_5), being noninvertible of $(Z_0 - Z_\infty - Z_1 - Z_\infty - Z_0)$ kind. This case corresponds to the version of the piecewise linear Hicksian business cycle model with both 'floor' and 'ceiling' (which are on the same distance from the origin in our case) incorporated in the investment function. Using the results obtained for piecewise linear maps of such a kind of noninvertibility (see Section 2.3 of Chapter 2), we can state

Proposition 4. *For $a = h > 1$, $0 < c < 1$, in the phase plane of the map F there exists an invariant closed attracting curve $\mathcal{C}$, homeomorphic to a circle, made up by a finite number of images of two generating segments, belonging, respectively, to LC_{-1} and LC^s_{-1}. The map F on $\mathcal{C}$ is reduced to a rotation with rational or irrational rotation number, and has, respectively, either periodic or quasiperiodic dynamics.*

We emphasize that $a = h$ is a particular case in which the curve $\mathcal{C}$ exists for any $a > 1$ and cannot be destroyed. Without going into details we just present an example of the curve $\mathcal{C}$ in a case of rotation number $1/7$, so that the map F has an attracting and a saddle cycle of period 7. Given that such cycles are not symmetric with respect to the origin, then, according to Property stated in the previous section, there must exist two more cycles of period 7, symmetric to the first two cycles, respectively: Fig.4 shows the phase portrait of the map F at $a = h = 2$, $c = 0.21$, with two coexisting attracting cycles of period 7 and their basins of attraction, bounded by the stable sets of two saddle cycles of period 7; The curve $\mathcal{C}$ is made up by 6 segments which are 3 images of the generating segments of LC_{-1} and LC^s_{-1}. The curve $\mathcal{C}$ is also formed by the closure of unstable sets of the saddle cycles of period 7.

Fig.5 presents a two-dimensional bifurcation diagram for the map F at $a = h$, where the regions corresponding to the attracting cycles of period

n, $n \leq 32$, are shown by different gray tonalities. We don't describe here the structure of this bifurcation diagram referring to Chapter 2 where a detailed description of a similar diagram is presented (we only remind that an

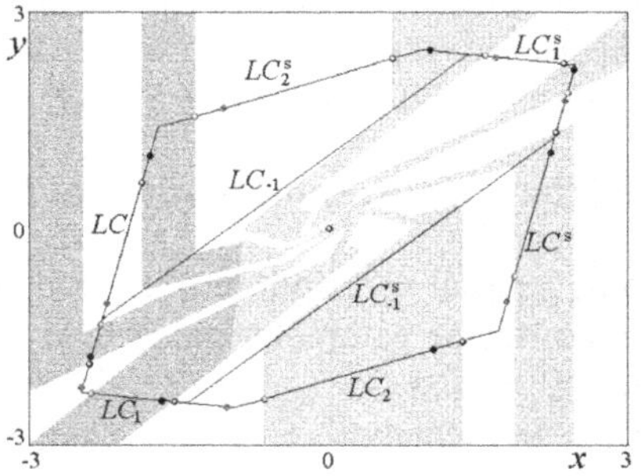

Figure 4: *The phase portrait of the map F at $a = h = 2$, $c = 0.21$: Two coexisting attracting 7-cycles (the black and gray circles) are shown together with their basins of attraction, bounded by the stable sets of two saddle 7-cycles.*

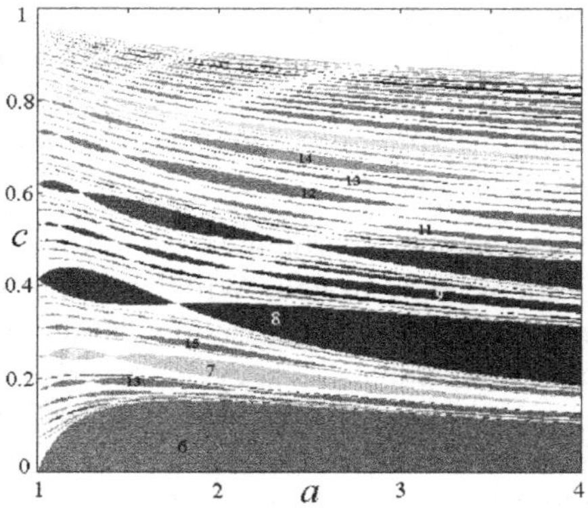

Figure 5: *The two-dimensional bifurcation diagram of the map F in the (a, c)-parameter plane in case $a = h$.*

odd periodicity region is related to two coexisting attracting cycles of the same period and, respectively, two saddle cycles). We would like to compare this diagram with two analogous bifurcation diagrams: One is related to the Hicksian business cycle model with the ‘floor’ in the investment function and the ‘ceiling’ in the income function (see Fig.3 of Chapter 6), and the other one is related to the Hicksian business cycle model with only one limit which is the ‘floor’ in the investment function (see Fig.4 of Chapter 2). All the three versions of the nonlinear Hicksian model possess either periodic or quasiperiodic dynamics and more complex dynamics cannot occur. The first two models never produce divergent trajectories. In the second model for sufficiently large a the main periodicity tongues mainly survive related to a particular trajectory which touches both upper and lower limits, while in the first model all periodicity tongues, born at $a = 1$, exist for any $a > 1$.

Consider now the case $a > h$. Given that the main interest of the present consideration is related to the bifurcation scenarios developing while a increases starting from $a = 1$, we consider $h < 1$. For example, let us fix $h = 0.5$. Regarding the value of the parameter l, note that for $l \to 0_-$ we have $\tau \to \infty$. Obviously, in such a case after the center bifurcation, that is for $a = 1 + \varepsilon$, $\varepsilon > 0$, an attractor of the map F belongs to the regions R_1, R_2, R_3 and has no points in the regions R_4 and R_5. Thus, only the maps F_1, F_2 and F_3 are involved in the asymptotic dynamics. In such a case we can apply the results presented in Section 2.6 of Chapter 2 and state that for sufficiently small $\varepsilon > 0$ in the phase space of the map F there exists an invariant closed attracting curve $\mathcal{C}$ homeomorphic to a circle, and dynamics of F on $\mathcal{C}$ are either periodic or quasiperiodic. The main difference of this case with respect to the case $a = h$ is that the curve $\mathcal{C}$ is not formed exactly by a finite number of proper segments of images the critical lines, but it is just a limit set for such images, and, as a consequence, the curve $\mathcal{C}$ has not finite but infinite number of segments and, thus, infinitely many corner points, which in case of a rational rotation are accumulating to the points of the related attracting cycle. The curve $\mathcal{C}$ can be destroyed by one of the mechanisms recalled in Section 2.6 of Chapter 2. In the example which we describe here this mechanism is related to transformation of the attracting cycle (which is born as a node) to a focus (see Fig.7a).

Fig.6 presents two-dimensional bifurcation diagrams of the map F in the (a, c)-parameter plane at fixed $h = 0.5$ and $l = -0.1$ (a), $l = -0.3$ (b). For the parameter ranges presented in these diagrams only the maps F_i, $i = 1, 2, 3$, are involved in the asymptotic dynamics (i.e., the attractor, or attractors, in case of multistability, are located in the regions R_i). It can be seen that the structure of both diagrams near the bifurcation value $a = 1$ is similar to the case $a = h$, namely, the parameter point $(a, c) = (1, c_{m/n})$ is the starting point for the periodicity tongue related to the attracting cycle with the rotation number m/n (or to the two attracting cycles when n is odd), but increasing the value of a such a periodicity tongue is destroyed. Comparing Fig.6a and Fig.6b, it can be seen that decreasing l such a destruction occurs for smaller values of a.

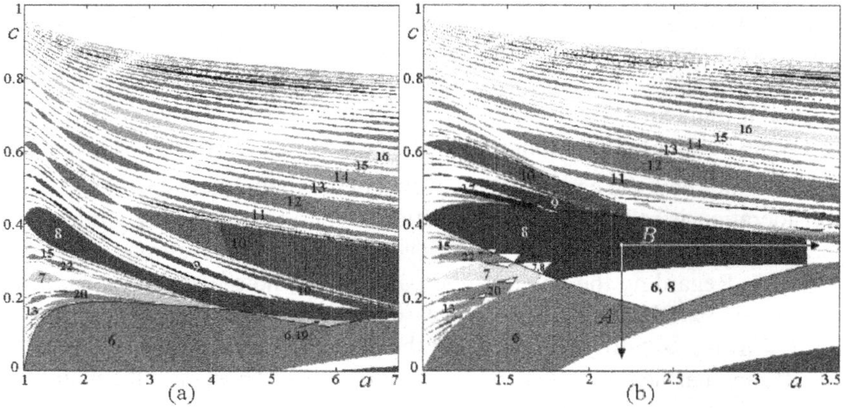

Figure 6: *Two-dimensional bifurcation diagrams of the map F in the (a, c)-parameter plane at $h = 0.5$, $l = -0.1$ (a) and $l = -0.3$ (b).*

Let us give some examples of bifurcation scenarios which can be realized if the (a, c)-parameter point moves inside a periodicity tongue. For this purpose we choose the 8-periodicity tongue and move the parameter point in the directions indicated in Fig.6b by the straight lines A and B. The starting point of the 8-periodicity tongue is $(a, c_{1/8}) = (1, \sqrt{2}-1)$. Increasing a, for example at $a = 1.005$, in the phase plane there exists the closed attracting invariant curve C, made up by the closure of the unstable set of the saddle cycle of period 8, but already for $a = 1.01$ the attracting 8-cycle is a focus, so the curve C is no longer homeomorphic to a circle. Fig.7a presents an example of the saddle-focus connection at $a = 2.2$ and $c = 0.35$.

Starting from this parameter point we decrease the value of c following the parameter path A. Fig.7b presents the phase portrait of the map F at $a = 2.2$, $c = 0.33$: It can be seen that the unstable set of the saddle 8-cycle has selfintersections (which is impossible for invertible maps). At $c \approx 0.3085$ the saddle 8-cycle undergoes a homoclinic bifurcation (see Fig.7c with an enlarged part of the phase plane), after which the saddle-focus connection no longer exists. At $c \approx 0.28$ a border-collision bifurcation (Nusse and Yorke (1995)) occurs giving rise to an attracting and a saddle cycle of period 6 (an analog of the saddle-node bifurcation), so that the parameter point enters the bistability region. The enlarged part of the phase space related to this bifurcation is shown in Fig.7d. We emphasize that at the bifurcation the merging points of the attracting and saddle cycles are critical points. After

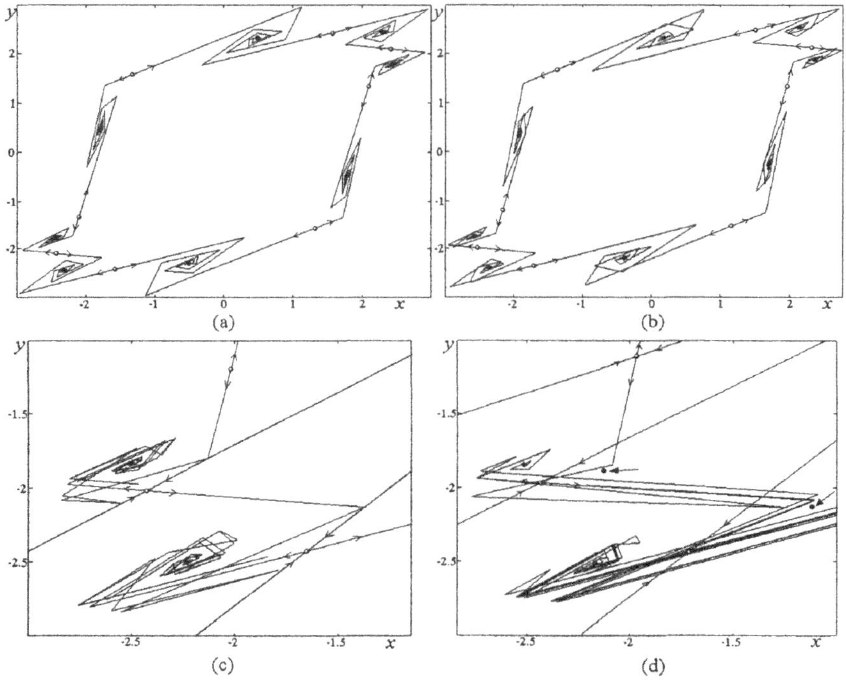

Figure 7: *The saddle-focus connection at* $a = 2.2$, $l = -0.3$, $h = 0.5$, $c = 0.35$ *(a) and* $c = 0.33$ *(b). The enlarged part of the phase plane at* $c = 0.3085$ *(c) (the homoclinic bifurcation of the saddle* 8*-cycle), and at* $c = 0.28$ *(d) (the 'saddle-node' border-collision bifurcation for an attracting and a saddle* 6*-cycle, two couples of merging points of which are shown by gray circles and indicated by the arrows).*

the bifurcation the basin of attraction of the attracting 6-cycle is bounded by the stable set of the saddle 6-cycle, while the basin of attraction of the attracting 8-cycle is bounded by the stable set of the saddle 8-cycle (see Fig.8). If we continue to decrease the value of c the basin of the attracting

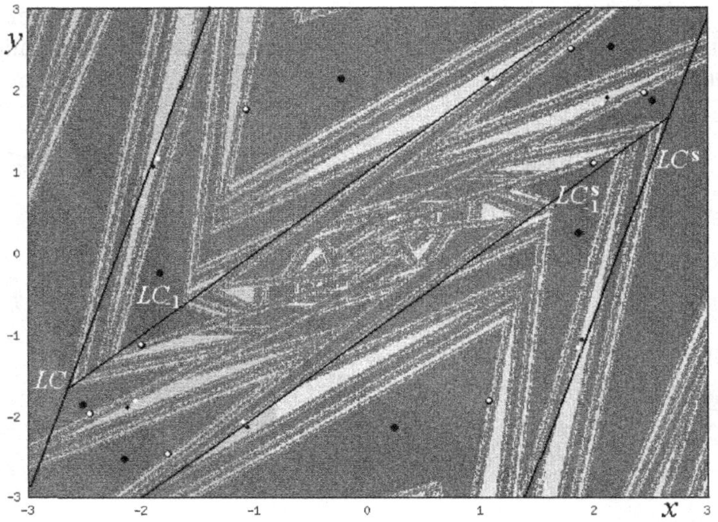

Figure 8: *Basins of attraction of coexisting attracting* 6*-cycle and* 8*-cycle.*

8 cycle decreases. At $c \approx 0.174$ the border-collision bifurcation occurs for the attracting and saddle cycles of period 8, when a pair of points of the attracting and the saddle cycles merges on LC_{-1} and another pair merges on LC^s_{-1}. On further decreasing of c the parameter point leaves the bistability region.

At $c \approx 0.085$ the attracting 6-cycle becomes a regular saddle: One of its eigenvalue passes through 1. Due to the piecewise linear definition of the map F, it is a particular kind of a pitchfork-like border-collision bifurcation: A k-cycle becomes a saddle and two coexisting k-cyclic chaotic attractors appear. Fig.9 shows schematically the phase portrait of the map F at the bifurcation value, where $[l_i, r_i]$, $i = 1, ..., 6$, denotes a segment of the eigenvector related to the eigenvalue 1, passing through the point p_i of the 6-cycle, and l_i, r_i are intersection points of the eigendirection with the related critical lines. Any point of the segment $[p_i, r_i]$ or $[l_i, p_i]$ is periodic of period 6. This bifurcation gives rise to two cyclic chaotic attractors of period 6 (see Fig.10 which shows such attractors at $a = 2.46$, $c = 0.081$). If we increase the value of a then at $a \approx 2.48$ the first homoclinic bifurcation of the saddle 6 cycle gives rise to the pairwise merging of the pieces of the attractors into a 6-pieces cyclic chaotic attractor, which then becomes a one-piece attractor due to the first homoclinic bifurcation of another saddle cycle of period 6, born due to the 'saddle-node' border-collision bifurcation. (For the de-

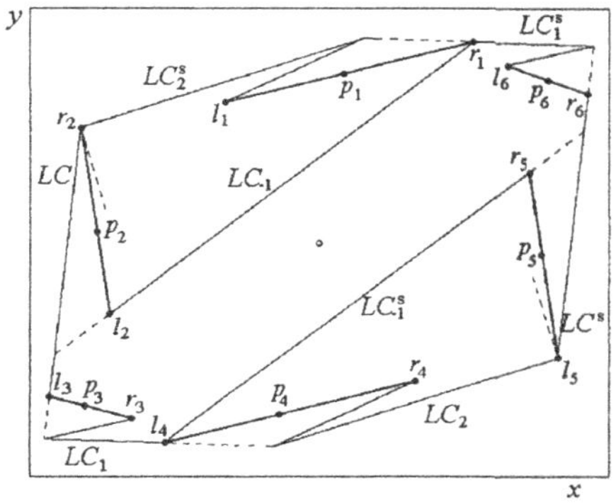

Figure 9: *The schematic view of the phase portrait of the map* F *at the bifurcation value related to the pichfolk bifurcation of the attracting* 6*-cycle.*

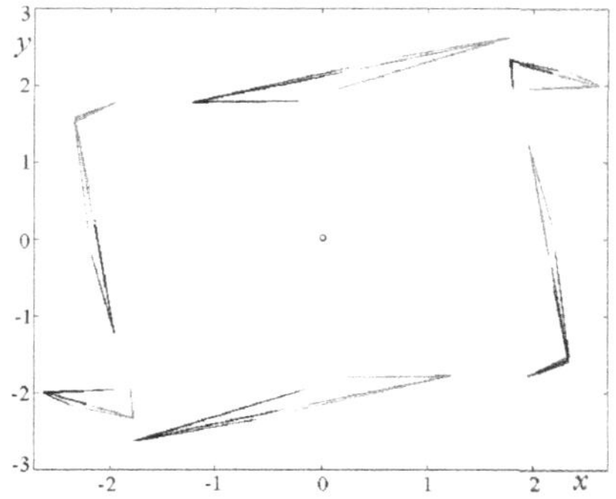

Figure 10: *Two cyclic chaotic attractors of period* 6 *are shown by different gray tonalities. Here* $a = 2.46$, $c = 0.081$, $l = -0.3$, $h = 0.5$.

scription of different mechanisms of reunion of pieces of a cyclical chaotic attractor in piecewise linear maps see Maistrenko *et al* (1998)).

Let us consider now the parameter path indicated in Fig.6b by B, increasing a from $a = 2.2$ at fixed $c = 0.35$. At $a \approx 3.33333$ the attracting 8-cycle undergoes the center bifurcation: At the bifurcation value there exist in the phase space 8 invariant regions (because of numerical precision, we cannot say precisely if the invariant region is bounded by an ellipse, or it is a polygon with a high number of edges). After the bifurcation the map F has 8-cyclic attracting rings (see Fig.11a which shows the attractor at $a = 3.33334$). Further increasing of the value a leads to the merging of 8 pieces of the attractor into one-piece attractor due to the homoclinic bifurcation of the saddle 8 cycle (see Fig.11b which shows the attractor soon after the merging, at $a = 3.335$).

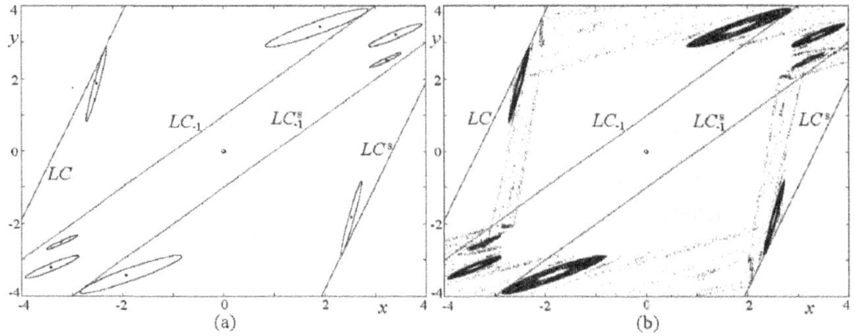

Figure 11: *The attractor of the map* F *at* $c = 0.35$, $l = -0.3$, $h = 0.5$, $a = 3.33334$ *(a) and* $a = 3.335$ *(b).*

All the examples presented above are related to the case in which only the maps F_1, F_2 and F_3 are involved in asymptotic dynamics, that is the constant branches of the investment function $I(z)$ (see Fig.1) play a role only for transient, but not asymptotic dynamics, which seems to be more reasonable from the economic point of view. To give an example of the case in which all five linear maps F_i, $i = 1, ..., 5$ are involved in asymptotic dynamics, we show two bifurcation diagrams in the (l, c)-parameter plane in Fig.12, where $h = 0.5$, $a = 1.1$ (a) and $a = 3$ (b). We have numerically checked whether the trajectory (after some transient) has points in the regions R_4 and R_5. The related parameter values are indicated by black points in Fig.12b (the corresponding attracting set is a one-piece chaotic attractor), while in

Fig.12a for the whole range of l the limit trajectory has no points in these regions.

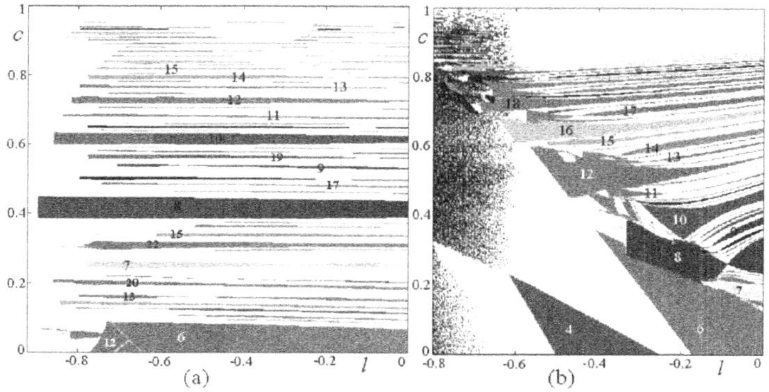

Figure 12: *Two-dimensional bifurcation diagram of the map F in the (l, c)-parameter plane at $h = 0.5$, $a = 1.1$ (a) and $a = 3$ (b).*

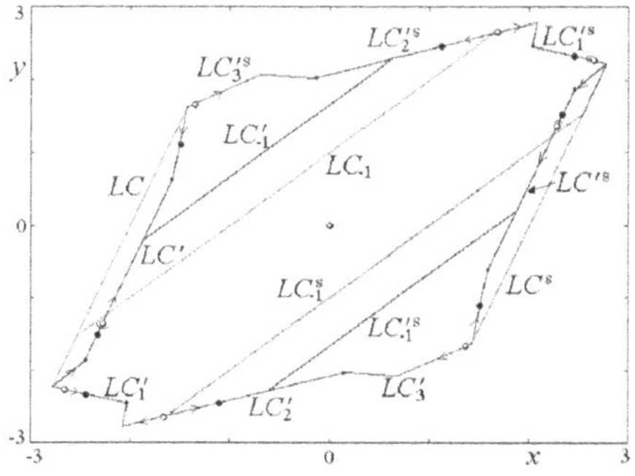

Figure 13: *The attracting closed invariant curve C at $a = 2$, $c = 0.35$, $l = -0.3$ and $h = 1.8$.*

To get a closed invariant attracting curve located in all five regions of the phase space we take $h > 1$: Fig.13 shows an example of such a curve at $a = 2$, $c = 0.35$, $l = -0.3$ and $h = 1.8$. Peculiarity of such a case is related to the fact that now we have a composition of the linear maps with zero and nonzero eigenvalues, and it influences the bifurcation scenarios, which can be realized varying the parameters. The curve C, presented in Fig.13, is made up by 4 images of the generating segment of LC'_{-1} and 4 images of the generating segment of LC'^{s}_{-1}, while the images of the critical lines LC_{-1} and LC^{s}_{-1} bound an absorbing area (or, more precisely, and absorbing ring) including the curve C. The map F is reduced on C to a rotation with the rotation number $1/8$ and has two cycles of period 8, one attracting and one saddle. Increasing a the number of segments of the curve C increases (see Fig.14a), and then coinciding segments of the unstable set of the saddle 8-cycle appear (see Fig.14b). It would be interesting to give a detailed analysis of possible scenarios of the destruction of a closed invariant curve in such a case, but we leave it as a subject for a future study.

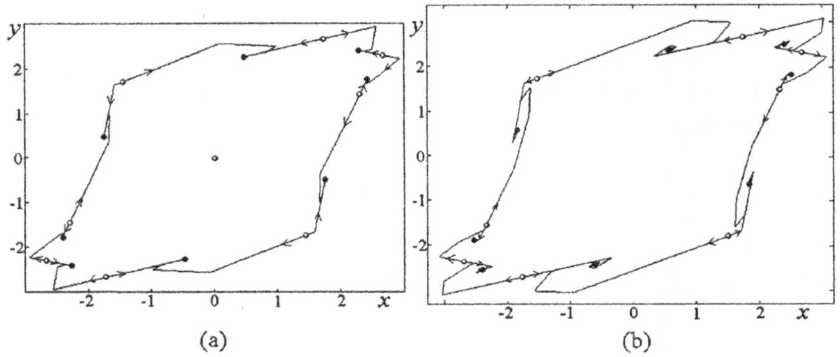

Figure 14: *The attracting closed invariant curve* C *at* $c = 0.35$, $l = -0.3$, $h = 1.8$, $a = 2.16$ *(a) and* $a = 2.3$ *(b).*

References

Gallegati, M., Gardini, L., Puu, T., and Sushko, I., 2003, "Hicks's trade cycle revisited: cycles and bifurcations", *Mathematics and Computers in Simulations,* 63, pp. 505-527.

Kuznetsov, Yu., 1995, *Elements of Applied Bifurcation Theory*, Springer-Verlag, New York.

Maistrenko, Y., Sushko, I., Gardini, L., 1998, "About two mechanisms of reunion of chaotic attractors", *Chaos, Solitons and Fractals* Vol. 9, 8, pp. 1373-1390.

Mira, C., Gardini, L., Barugola, A., Cathala, J.C., 1996, *Chaotic dynamics in two-dimensional noninvertible maps*. Singapore, World Scientific.

Hommes, C.H., 1991, *Chaotic Dynamics in Economic Models: Some Simple Case Studies*, Thesis University of Groningen, Wolters-Noordhoff Groningen.

Nusse, H. E. and Yorke, J. A., 1995, "Border-collision bifurcation for piecewise smooth one-dimensional maps", *International Journal Bifurcation and Chaos 5,* 1, pp. 189-207.

Puu, T., Sushko, I., 2004, "A business cycle model with cubic nonlinearity", *Chaos, Solitons and Fractals*, 19, pp. 597-612.

Sushko, I., Puu, T., Gardini, L., 2003, "The Hicksian floor-roof model for two regions linked by interregional trade", *Chaos Solitons and Fractals*, 18, pp. 593-612.

List of Contributors

Anna Agliari
Faculty of Economics
Catholic University
Via Emilia Parmense 84
29100 Piacenza
Italy
anna.agliari@unicatt.it

Gian-Italo Bischi
Università di Urbino
Istituto di Scienze Economiche
via Saffi, 42
61029 Urbino
Italy
bischi@econ.uniurb.it

Volker Böhm
Bielefeld University
Department of Business
Administration and Economics
P.O. Box 10 01 31
33501 Bielefeld
Germany
vboehm@wiwi.uni-bielefeld.de

José S. Cánovas Peña
Departamento de Matemática
Aplicada y Estadística
Universidad Politécnica de
Cartagena
Paseo Alfonso XIII, 52
30203 Cartagena
Spain
Jose.Canovas@upct.es

Roberto Dieci
Università degli Studi di Bologna
Facoltà di Economia del Polo
di Rimini
Via D. Angherà 22
47900 Rimini
Italy
rdieci@rimini.unibo.it

Laura Gardini
Università di Urbino
Istituto di Scienze Economiche
via Saffi, 42
61029 Urbino
Italy
gardini@econ.uniurb.it

Marji Lines
Department of Statistics
University of Udine
via Treppo, 18
33100 Udine
Italy
lines@dss.uniud.it

Tönu Puu
Centre for Regional Science
Umeå University
SE-90187 Umeå
Sweden
tonu.puu@econ.umu.se

Manuel Ruiz Marín
Departamento de Métodos
Cuantitativos e Informáticos
Universidad Politécnica
de Cartagena
Paseo Alfonso XIII, 50
30203 Cartagena
Spain
Manuel.Ruiz@upct.es

Serena Sordi
University of Siena
Dipartimento di Economia Politica
Piazza San Francesco, 7
53100 Siena
Italy
sordi@unisi.it

Iryna Sushko
Institute of Mathematics
National Academy of Sciences
of Ukraine
3 Tereshchenkivska st.
01601 Kiev-4
Ukraine
sushko@imath.kiev.ua

Frank Westerhoff
University of Osnabrueck
Department of Economics
Rolandstrasse 8
49069 Osnabrueck
Germany
frank.westerhoff@uos.de